First World War
and Army of Occupation
War Diary
France, Belgium and Germany

46 DIVISION
139 Infantry Brigade
Sherwood Foresters
(Nottinghamshire and Derbyshire Regiment)
1/8th Battalion
31 October 1914 - 30 April 1919

WO95/2695/2

The Naval & Military Press Ltd
www.nmarchive.com
Published in association with The National Archives

Published by

The Naval & Military Press Ltd

Unit 10 Ridgewood Industrial Park,

Uckfield, East Sussex,

TN22 5QE England

Tel: +44 (0) 1825 749494

www.naval-military-press.com

www.nmarchive.com

This diary has been reprinted in facsimile from the original. Any imperfections are inevitably reproduced and the quality may fall short of modern type and cartographic standards.

© **Crown Copyright**
Images reproduced by permission of The National Archives, London, England, 2015.

Contents

Document type	Place/Title	Date From	Date To
Heading	WO95/2695 (2)		
Heading	46th Division 139th Infy Bde 8th Bn (Notts & Derby) Sherwood Foresters Regt 1917 Oct-May 1919		
Miscellaneous	46th Division Notts & Derby Infantry Brigade		
War Diary	8th. Battn. Sherwood Foresters.		
War Diary	Notts & Derby Brigade.		
War Diary	North Midland Division.		
War Diary	Mobilisation Station-Newark.		
War Diary	Temporary War Station-Derby.		
War Diary	Stations since occupied subsequent to concentration Luton-Harpenden.		
War Diary	8th Battn. The Sherwood Foresters.		
War Diary	Notts & Derby Brigade.		
War Diary	North Midland Division.		
War Diary	Mobilization Centre-Newark.		
War Diary	Temporary War Station-Derby.		
War Diary	Since occupied-Luton-Harpenden.	31/10/1914	31/10/1914
War Diary	8th Battn. The Sherwood Foresters.		
War Diary	Notts & Derby Brigade.		
War Diary	North Midland Division.		
War Diary	Mobilization Station-Newark.		
War Diary	Temporary War Station-Derby.		
War Diary	Since occupied-Luton-Harpenden-Harlow-Dunmow-Bocking.	30/11/1914	30/11/1914
Miscellaneous	5th Battalion, Notts. & Derbyshire Regt.	05/12/1914	05/12/1914
Heading	139th Inf. Bde. 46th Div. Battn. disembarked Havre from England 3.3.15 8th Battn. The Sherwood Foresters (Nottinghamshire And Derbyshire Regiment). March 1915		
War Diary	Edward Southampton	01/03/1915	03/03/1915
War Diary	Train in N France	04/03/1915	04/03/1915
War Diary	Oudezeele	05/03/1915	08/03/1915
War Diary	Merris	09/03/1915	11/03/1915
War Diary	Bac St Maur	13/03/1915	14/03/1915
War Diary	Neuf Berquin	15/03/1915	24/03/1915
War Diary	Vieux Berquin	24/03/1915	28/03/1915
War Diary	Romarin	28/03/1915	31/03/1915
Heading	139th Inf. Bde. 46th Div. 8th Battn. The Sherwood Foresters (Nottinghamshire And Derbyshire Regiment) April 1915		
War Diary	Vieux Berquin	01/04/1915	01/04/1915
War Diary	Locre	02/04/1915	03/04/1915
War Diary	Kemmel	03/04/1915	07/04/1915
War Diary	Locre	08/04/1915	10/04/1915
War Diary	Kemmel	11/04/1915	15/04/1915
War Diary	Locre	16/04/1915	19/04/1915
War Diary	Kemmel	19/04/1915	25/04/1915
War Diary	Locre	25/04/1915	28/04/1915
War Diary	Kemmel	29/04/1915	30/04/1915
Heading	Appendix I. (Missing)		

Heading	139th Inf. Bde. 46th Div. 8th Battn. The Sherwood Foresters (Nottinghamshire And Derbyshire Regiment). May 1915		
War Diary	Kemmel	01/05/1915	02/05/1915
War Diary	Locre	03/05/1915	06/05/1915
War Diary	Kemmel	07/05/1915	10/05/1915
War Diary	Locre	11/05/1915	15/05/1915
War Diary	Kemmel	16/05/1915	19/05/1915
War Diary	Locre	20/05/1915	23/05/1915
War Diary	Kemmel	24/05/1915	24/05/1915
War Diary	Locre	24/05/1915	24/05/1915
War Diary	Kemmel	25/05/1915	31/05/1915
Heading	139th Inf. Bde. 46th Div. 8th Battn. The Sherwood Foresters (Nottinghamshire And Derbyshire Regiment). June 1915		
War Diary	Locre	01/06/1915	02/06/1915
War Diary	Kemmel	03/06/1915	07/06/1915
War Diary	Locre	08/06/1915	11/06/1915
War Diary	Kemmel	12/06/1915	15/06/1915
War Diary	Locre	16/06/1915	23/06/1915
War Diary	Ypres	24/06/1915	27/06/1915
War Diary	Ypres (Salient)	28/06/1915	30/06/1915
Miscellaneous	War Diary to A.Q.		
Heading	139th Inf. Bde. 46th Div. 8th Battn. The Sherwood Foresters (Nottinghamshire And Derbyshire Regiment). July 1915		
War Diary	Square H. 19. B	01/07/1915	05/07/1915
War Diary	H. 19. D.	06/07/1915	31/07/1915
Heading	Report on Operations 30th/31st July.		
Miscellaneous	Major Becher's Report		
Heading	139th Inf. Bde. 46th Div. 8th Battn. The Sherwood Foresters (Nottinghamshire And Derbyshire Regiment). August 1915		
War Diary		01/08/1915	31/08/1915
Miscellaneous	8th Sherwood Forester Appendix I August 1915		
Miscellaneous	Copy of Telegram received 29/8/15		
Miscellaneous	Appendix III August 1915		
Heading	Report On Operations 2nd/12th August.		
Miscellaneous	Colonel forester Report		
Heading	139th Inf. Bde. 46th Div. 8th Battn. The Sherwood Foresters (Nottinghamshire And Derbyshire Regiment). September 1915		
War Diary		01/09/1915	30/09/1915
Heading	139th Inf. Bde. 46th Div. 8th Battn. The Sherwood Foresters (Nottinghamshire And Derbyshire Regiment). October 1915		
War Diary	Ouderdom	01/10/1915	01/10/1915
War Diary	Bethune	02/10/1915	03/10/1915
War Diary	Mt Bernanchon	04/10/1915	06/10/1915
War Diary	Fouquieres	07/10/1915	14/10/1915
War Diary	Nr "C" Company	14/10/1915	16/10/1915
War Diary	Vaudricourt	16/10/1915	18/10/1915
War Diary	Lapugnoy	20/10/1915	31/10/1915
Map	Map showing New Trenches to Superintendence on 36c N W 3 and Part of 1.		
Map			

Heading	139th Inf. Bde. 46th Div. 8th Battn. The Sherwood Foresters (Nottinghamshire And Derbyshire Regiment). November 1915		
War Diary	Bethune	01/11/1915	03/11/1915
War Diary	Epinette	04/11/1915	05/11/1915
War Diary	Vieille Chapelle	05/11/1915	30/11/1915
Heading	139th Inf. Bde. 46th Div. 8th Battn. The Sherwood Foresters (Nottinghamshire And Derbyshire Regiment). December 1915		
War Diary		01/12/1915	31/12/1915
Heading	1/8 North & Derby Regt. Jan Vol XI		
War Diary	Molinghem	01/01/1916	09/01/1916
War Diary	Marseilles	10/01/1916	26/01/1916
War Diary	In Train	27/01/1916	27/01/1916
War Diary	Pont-Remy	28/01/1916	28/01/1916
War Diary	Ergnies	29/01/1916	09/02/1916
War Diary	Ribeaucourt	10/02/1916	19/02/1916
War Diary	Candas	20/02/1916	05/03/1916
War Diary	Iverny	06/03/1916	07/03/1916
War Diary	Maizieres	08/03/1916	08/03/1916
War Diary	ACQ	09/03/1916	09/03/1916
War Diary	Mont St. Eloy	10/03/1916	31/03/1916
War Diary	Trenches East of Berthonval Farm near Mt. St. Eloy.	01/04/1916	06/04/1916
War Diary	Mt. St. Eloy.	07/04/1916	12/04/1916
War Diary	Trenches East of Berthonval Farm near Mt. St. Eloy.	13/04/1916	20/04/1916
War Diary	Tincques	21/04/1916	28/04/1916
War Diary	Averdoingt	29/04/1916	30/04/1916
Miscellaneous			
Miscellaneous	Operation Order by Lieut Col. G E B Blackwall Comdg. Left Sector	16/04/1916	16/04/1916
War Diary	Averdoingt	01/05/1916	05/05/1916
War Diary	Rebreuviette	06/05/1916	07/05/1916
War Diary	Gaudiempre	08/05/1916	08/05/1916
War Diary	Bienvillers	10/05/1916	18/05/1916
War Diary	Foncquevillers	19/05/1916	05/06/1916
War Diary	Humbercamp	05/06/1916	06/06/1916
War Diary	Le Souich	07/06/1916	14/06/1916
War Diary	Humbercamp	15/06/1916	17/06/1916
War Diary	Foncquevillers	18/06/1916	28/06/1916
War Diary	Pommier	28/06/1916	30/06/1916
Miscellaneous	Operation Orders By Lieutenant Colonel J.E. Blackwall, Commanding 8th Sherwood Foresters	30/06/1916	30/06/1916
War Diary	Foncquevillers	01/07/1916	02/07/1916
War Diary	Gaudiempre	02/07/1916	02/07/1916
War Diary	Bavincourt	03/07/1916	03/07/1916
War Diary	Pommier	04/07/1916	06/07/1916
War Diary	Bienvillers	07/07/1916	09/07/1916
War Diary	Bellacourt	10/07/1916	10/07/1916
War Diary	Trenches	11/07/1916	15/07/1916
War Diary	Trenches	12/07/1916	17/07/1916
War Diary	Bailleulval	18/07/1916	23/07/1916
War Diary	Trenches	23/07/1916	29/07/1916
War Diary	Bellacourt	29/07/1916	31/07/1916
Miscellaneous	Operation Orders By Lieutenant Colonel J.E. Blackwall, Commanding 8th Sherwood Foresters.	06/07/1916	06/07/1916

Miscellaneous	Operation Orders By Lieutenant Colonel J.E. Blackwall, Commanding 8th Sherwood Foresters.	10/07/1916	10/07/1916
Miscellaneous	Operation Orders By Lieut Colonel J.E. Blackwall Commanding 8th Sherwood Foresters.	11/07/1916	11/07/1916
Miscellaneous	Operation Orders By Lieutenant Colonel J.E. Blackwall, Commanding 8th Sherwood Forester.	15/07/1916	15/07/1916
Miscellaneous	Operation Orders By Lieutenant Colonel J.E. Blackwall, Commanding 8th Sherwood Foresters.	17/07/1916	17/07/1916
Miscellaneous	Operation Orders By Lieutenant Colonel J.E. Blackwall, Commanding 8th Sherwood Forester.	23/07/1916	23/07/1916
Miscellaneous	Operation Orders By Lieutenant Colonel J.E. Blackwall, Commanding 8th Sherwood Foresters	29/07/1916	29/07/1916
War Diary	Bellacourt	01/08/1916	03/08/1916
War Diary	Trenches	04/08/1916	10/08/1916
War Diary	Bailleulval	10/08/1916	13/08/1916
War Diary	Bailleulval	11/08/1916	15/08/1916
War Diary	Trenches	16/08/1916	21/08/1916
War Diary	Midnight	22/08/1916	23/08/1916
War Diary	Bellacourt	23/08/1916	27/08/1916
War Diary	Bailleulmont	25/08/1916	25/08/1916
War Diary	Trenches	28/08/1916	31/08/1916
War Diary	Trenches (E. of Bretencourt)	01/09/1916	03/09/1916
War Diary	Bailleulval	03/09/1916	09/09/1916
War Diary	Trenches E. of Bretencourt	09/09/1916	09/09/1916
War Diary	Trenches	10/09/1916	14/09/1916
War Diary	Bellacourt	15/09/1916	19/09/1916
War Diary	Bellacourt	17/09/1916	17/09/1916
War Diary	Trenches	20/09/1916	24/09/1916
War Diary	Bailleulval	25/09/1916	30/09/1916
Miscellaneous	Operation Orders By Lieutenant Colonel J.E. Blackwall, Commanding 8th Sherwood Foresters.	20/09/1916	20/09/1916
Miscellaneous	8th Sherwood Foresters. Detail of Raiding Party.	20/09/1916	20/09/1916
Miscellaneous	Report on Raid Carried out By The 8th Battalion Sherwood Foresters, on The Night 21st/22nd September, Against The German Trenches in X.3.b. Appendix II		
Miscellaneous	To Hqrs Bn Inf. Bde.	02/11/1916	02/11/1916
War Diary	Trenches East of Bretencourt.	01/10/1916	01/10/1916
War Diary	Trenches	01/10/1916	07/10/1916
War Diary	Bellacourt	07/10/1916	07/10/1916
War Diary	Basseux	12/10/1916	12/10/1916
War Diary	Bellacourt	08/10/1916	13/10/1916
War Diary	Trenches East of Bretencourt	13/10/1916	15/10/1916
War Diary	Trenches	13/10/1916	19/10/1916
War Diary	Bailleulval	19/10/1916	25/10/1916
War Diary	Trenches East of Bretencourt	25/10/1916	30/10/1916
War Diary	Le Souich	31/10/1916	31/10/1916
Miscellaneous	Operation Orders By Lieutenant Colonel J.E. Blackwall, Commanding 8th Sherwood Foresters.	28/10/1916	28/10/1916
Miscellaneous	Operation Orders By Lieutenant Colonel J.E. Blackwall, Commanding 8th Sherwood Foresters.	31/10/1916	31/10/1916
War Diary	Neuvillette	01/11/1916	03/11/1916
War Diary	Maison-Ponthieu	04/11/1916	23/11/1916
War Diary	Neuvillette	24/11/1916	25/11/1916
War Diary	Humbercourt	26/11/1916	30/11/1916

Miscellaneous	Operation Orders By Lieutenant Colonel J.E. Blackwall, Commanding 8th Sherwood Foresters	02/11/1916	02/11/1916
Miscellaneous	Operation Orders By Lieutenant Colonel J.E. Blackwall, Commanding 8th Sherwood Foresters.	21/11/1916	21/11/1916
Miscellaneous	Operation Orders By Lieutenant Colonel J.E. Blackwall, Commanding 8th Sherwood Foresters.	22/11/1916	22/11/1916
Miscellaneous	Operation Orders By Lieutenant Colonel J.E. Blackwall, Commanding 8th Sherwood Foresters.	24/11/1916	24/11/1916
War Diary	Humbercourt	01/12/1916	06/12/1916
War Diary	Souastre & Fonquevillers	06/12/1916	11/12/1916
War Diary	Souastre	12/12/1916	12/12/1916
War Diary	Fonquevillers	12/12/1916	18/12/1916
War Diary	Souastre	18/12/1916	22/12/1916
War Diary	Fonquevillers	22/12/1916	26/12/1916
War Diary	Souastre & Fonquevillers	26/12/1916	30/12/1916
War Diary	Fonquevillers	30/12/1916	31/12/1916
Miscellaneous	Operation Orders By Lieutenant Colonel J.E. Blackwall, Commanding 8th Sherwood Foresters	05/12/1916	05/12/1916
Miscellaneous	Operation Orders By Lieut Colonel J.E. Blackwall, Commanding 8th Sherwood Foresters. Appendix II	11/12/1916	11/12/1916
Miscellaneous	Operation Orders By Lieutenant Colonel J.E. Blackwall, Commanding 8th Sherwood Foresters Appendix III	17/12/1916	17/12/1916
Miscellaneous	Operation Orders By Lieut Colonel J.E. Blackwall, Commanding 8th Sherwood Foresters Appendix IV	21/12/1916	21/12/1916
Miscellaneous	Operation Orders By Lieutenant Colonel J.E. Blackwall, Commanding 8th Sherwood Foresters Appendix V	25/12/1916	25/12/1916
Miscellaneous			
Miscellaneous	Operation Orders By Lieut Colonel J.E. Blackwall, Commanding 8th Sherwood Foresters. Appendix VI	29/12/1916	29/12/1916
War Diary	Trenches Foncquevillers	01/01/1917	03/01/1917
War Diary	Souastre	03/01/1917	07/01/1917
War Diary	Foncquevillers Trenches	07/01/1917	07/01/1917
War Diary	Trenches	07/01/1917	11/01/1917
War Diary	Souastre	11/01/1917	15/01/1917
War Diary	Trenches	11/01/1917	19/01/1917
War Diary	Souastre	19/01/1917	23/01/1917
War Diary	Trenches Foncquevillers	23/01/1917	27/01/1917
War Diary	Souastre	27/01/1917	31/01/1917
War Diary	Trenches Foncquevillers	31/01/1917	31/01/1917
Miscellaneous	Operation Orders By Lieut Colonel J.E. Blackwall, D.S.O., Commanding 8th Sherwood Foresters. Appendix I	02/01/1917	02/01/1917
Miscellaneous	Operation Orders By Lieut Colonel J.E. Blackwall, D.S.O., Commanding 8th Sherwood Foresters. Appendix II	06/01/1917	06/01/1917
Miscellaneous	Operation Orders By Major J.K. Lane Commanding 8th Sherwood Foresters Appendix III	10/01/1917	10/01/1917
Miscellaneous	Operation Orders By Major J.K. Lane, Commanding 8th Sherwood Foresters. Appendix IV	14/01/1917	14/01/1917
Miscellaneous	Operation Orders By Major J.K. Lane, Commanding 8th Sherwood Foresters. Appendix V	18/01/1917	18/01/1917
Miscellaneous	Operation Orders By Major J.K. Lane, Commanding 8th Sherwood Foresters. Appendix VI	22/01/1917	22/01/1917

Type	Description	Start	End
Miscellaneous	Operation Orders By Major J.K. Lane, Commanding 8th Sherwood Foresters. Appendix VII	26/01/1917	26/01/1917
Miscellaneous	Operation Orders By Major J.K. Lane, Commanding 8th Sherwood Foresters. Appendix VIII	31/01/1917	31/01/1917
War Diary	Trenches Foncquevillers	01/02/1917	03/02/1917
War Diary	Souastre	04/02/1917	07/02/1917
War Diary	Foncquevillers Trenches	08/02/1917	11/02/1917
War Diary	Souastre	12/02/1917	15/02/1917
War Diary	Trenches Foncquevillers	16/02/1917	18/02/1917
War Diary	St. Amand	19/02/1917	19/02/1917
War Diary	Ivergny	20/02/1917	27/02/1917
War Diary	Grenas	28/02/1917	28/02/1917
Miscellaneous	Operation Orders By Major J.K. Lane, Commanding 8th Sherwood Foresters.	01/02/1917	01/02/1917
Miscellaneous	Operation Orders By Major J.K. Lane, Commanding 8th Sherwood Foresters.	03/02/1917	03/02/1917
Miscellaneous	Operation Orders By Lieut Colonel J.E. Blackwall Commanding 8th Sherwood Foresters.	07/02/1917	07/02/1917
Miscellaneous	Operation Orders By Lieut Colonel J.E. Blackwall D.S.O., Commanding 8th Sherwood Foresters.	11/02/1917	11/02/1917
Miscellaneous	Operation Orders By Lieut. Colonel J.E. Blackwall D.S.O., Commanding 8th Sherwood Foresters.	15/02/1917	15/02/1917
Miscellaneous	Operation Orders By Lieutenant Colonel J.E. Blackwall, D.S.O., Commanding 8th Sherwood Foresters.	18/02/1917	18/02/1917
Miscellaneous	Operation Orders By Lieut. Colonel J.E. Blackwall, Commanding 8th Sherwood Foresters.	19/02/1917	19/02/1917
War Diary	Grenas	01/03/1917	01/03/1917
War Diary	St. Amand	02/03/1917	03/03/1917
War Diary	Gommecourt	03/03/1917	17/03/1917
War Diary	Souastre	18/03/1917	20/03/1917
War Diary	Near Bayencourt	21/03/1917	24/03/1917
War Diary	Bertangles	25/03/1917	25/03/1917
War Diary	Revelles	26/03/1917	28/03/1917
War Diary	Westrehem	29/03/1917	31/03/1917
Miscellaneous	Operation Orders By Lieut Colonel J.E. Blackwall, D.S.O., Commanding 8th Sherwood Foresters. Appendix I	12/03/1917	12/03/1917
Map	Fonquevillers & Hebuterne Sheets 1/10,000		
War Diary	Westrehem	01/04/1917	12/04/1917
War Diary	Westrehem	09/04/1917	09/04/1917
War Diary	Vendin Les Bethune	13/04/1917	13/04/1917
War Diary	Houchin	14/04/1917	17/04/1917
War Diary	Lievin	18/04/1917	30/04/1917
Miscellaneous	Detailed Report of Operations from 12 noon 20th to 12 noon 21st April 1917 by Lieut Colonel J.E. Blackwall, D.S.O. Appendix I	21/04/1917	21/04/1917
Miscellaneous	Daily Situation Report by Lieut. Colonel J.E. Blackwall, D.S.O. from 12 noon April 21st to 12 noon 22nd April 1917. Appendix II (a)	22/04/1917	22/04/1917
Miscellaneous	Operation Orders By Lieut Colonel J.E. Blackwall, D.S.O., Commanding 8th Sherwood Foresters. Appendix II	22/04/1917	22/04/1917
Miscellaneous	Report of Operations	23/04/1917	23/04/1917
Miscellaneous	Report On Mopping Up Platoon. Appendix III (b)	23/04/1917	23/04/1917

Miscellaneous	Operation Orders By Lieut Colonel J.E. Blackwall, D.S.O., Commanding 8th Sherwood Foresters. Appendix II	27/03/1917	27/03/1917
War Diary	Marqueffles Farm	01/05/1917	05/05/1917
War Diary	Loos	06/05/1917	19/05/1917
War Diary	Loos	18/05/1917	01/06/1917
Miscellaneous	Operation Orders By Lieut Colonel J.E. Blackwall, D.S.O., Commanding 8th Sherwood Foresters. Appendix I	05/05/1917	05/05/1917
Miscellaneous	Operation Orders by Lieut. Col. J.E. Blackwall D.S.O. Commanding 8th Bn. Sherwood Foresters. Appendix II	09/05/1917	09/05/1917
Miscellaneous	Operation Orders by Lieut Colonel J.E. Blackwall D.S.O. Commanding 8th Bn. Sherwood Foresters Appendix III	11/05/1917	11/05/1917
Miscellaneous	Operation Orders by Lieut Colonel J.E. Blackwall D.S.O. Commanding 8th Battn Sherwood Foresters Appendix IV	17/05/1917	17/05/1917
Miscellaneous	Operation Orders by Lt. Col. J.E. Blackwall Commanding 8th Sherwood Foresters D.S.O. Appendix V	25/05/1917	25/05/1917
Miscellaneous	Operation Orders by Lieut Col. J.E. Blackwall D.S.O. Commanding 8th Bn. Sherwood Fouster Appendix VI	30/05/1917	30/05/1917
War Diary	Lievin	30/05/1917	09/06/1917
War Diary	Marqueffles Farm	10/06/1917	11/06/1917
War Diary	Loos	15/06/1917	15/06/1917
War Diary	Calonne	18/06/1917	18/06/1917
War Diary	Lievin	21/06/1917	22/06/1917
War Diary	Calonne	23/06/1917	23/06/1917
War Diary	Lievin	25/06/1917	25/06/1917
War Diary	Maroc	27/06/1917	29/06/1917
War Diary	Cite St Pierre	30/06/1917	30/06/1917
Miscellaneous	Operation Orders by Lieut Colonel J.E. Blackwall D.S.O. Commanding 8th Bn. Sherwood Foresters Appendix I	06/06/1917	06/06/1917
Miscellaneous	Operation Orders by Lieut Colonel J.E. Blackwall D.S.O. Commanding 8th Bn. Sherwood Foresters. Appendix 2	09/06/1917	09/06/1917
Miscellaneous	Operations Orders by Lieut Colonel J.E. Blackwall D.S.O. Commanding 8th Bn. Sherwood Foresters Appendix 3	10/06/1917	10/06/1917
Miscellaneous	Operation Orders by Lieut Colonel J.E. Blackwall D.S.O. Commanding 8th Sherwood Foresters Appendix 4	14/06/1917	14/06/1917
Miscellaneous	Operation Orders by Lieut. Colonel J.E. Blackwall, D.S.O., Comdg. 8th Bn. The Sherwood Foresters, Appendix 5	18/06/1917	18/06/1917
Miscellaneous	Operation Orders by Lieut. Colonel J.E. Blackwall, D.S.O., Comdg. 8th Bn. The Sherwood Foresters, Appendix 6	21/06/1917	21/06/1917
Miscellaneous	Operation Orders by Lieut. Colonel J.E. Blackwall, D.S.O., Comdg. 8th Bn. The Sherwood Foresters, Appendix 7	23/06/1917	23/06/1917
War Diary	Cite St Pierre	30/06/1917	23/07/1917
War Diary	Chelers	04/07/1917	23/07/1917
War Diary		17/07/1917	25/07/1917
War Diary		24/07/1917	30/07/1917

War Diary	Philosophe	30/07/1917	31/07/1917
Miscellaneous	Operation Orders by Major J.K. Lane Commanding 8th. Battn. Sherwood Foresters Appendix I	03/07/1917	03/07/1917
Miscellaneous	Operation Orders By Lieut Colonel J.E. Blackwall, D.S.O., Commanding 8th Sherwood Foresters. Appendix II	23/07/1917	23/07/1917
Miscellaneous	Operation Orders by Lieut Col J.E. Blackwall D.S.O. Comdy 8th Sherwood Foresters Appendix III	29/07/1917	29/07/1917
War Diary	Philosophe	01/08/1917	05/08/1917
War Diary	Philosophe	04/08/1917	05/08/1917
War Diary	St. Elie Left Sub-Sector	05/08/1917	10/08/1917
War Diary	Noyelles	10/08/1917	11/08/1917
War Diary	Fouquieres	14/08/1917	14/08/1917
War Diary	Verquin	16/08/1917	26/08/1917
War Diary	Cambrin Left Sub Sector	26/08/1917	30/08/1917
Miscellaneous	Operation Orders by Lieut Colonel J.E. Blackwall D.S.O. Commanding 8th Bn Sherwood Foresters. Appendix I	03/08/1917	03/08/1917
War Diary	Annequin	01/09/1917	07/09/1917
War Diary	Cambrin Sector	07/09/1917	12/09/1917
War Diary	Fouquieres	13/09/1917	20/09/1917
War Diary	Mazingarbe Hill 70	20/09/1917	30/09/1917
Miscellaneous	Operation Orders by Lieut Colonel J.E. Blackwall. DSO Commanding 8th Sherwood Foresters Appendix II	25/08/1917	25/08/1917
War Diary	Hill 70 Left	01/10/1917	04/10/1917
War Diary	Mazingarbe	10/10/1917	10/10/1917
War Diary	Hill 70 Left	16/10/1917	31/10/1917
Miscellaneous	Operation Orders by Lieut Colonel J.E. Blackwall D.S.O. Commanding 8th Battn. Sherwood Foresters Appendix I	10/09/1917	10/09/1917
War Diary	Hill 70 Left	01/11/1917	03/11/1917
War Diary	Mazingarbe	03/11/1917	09/11/1917
War Diary	Hill 70 Left	09/11/1917	15/11/1917
War Diary	Philosophe	15/11/1917	18/11/1917
War Diary	St Elie Left	22/11/1917	28/11/1917
War Diary	St Elie Left	22/11/1917	22/11/1917
War Diary	Verquin	28/11/1917	30/11/1917
Miscellaneous	Operation Order by Lieut Col. J.E. Blackwall Commanding 1/8th Bn Sherwood Foresters Appendix I	14/11/1917	14/11/1917
Miscellaneous	Operation Orders by Major E.M. Ginger Commanding 1/8th Bn Sherwood Foresters. Appendix II	21/11/1917	21/11/1917
War Diary	Verquin	01/12/1917	04/12/1917
War Diary	St Elie (Left)	04/12/1917	10/12/1917
War Diary	Philosophe	10/12/1917	16/12/1917
War Diary	Philosophe	11/12/1917	11/12/1917
War Diary	St Elie (Left)	16/12/1917	22/12/1917
War Diary	Verquin	22/12/1917	28/12/1917
War Diary	St Elie (Left)	28/12/1917	31/12/1917
War Diary	Trenches St Elie Left	01/01/1918	17/01/1918
War Diary	Verquin	17/01/1918	21/01/1918
War Diary	Burbure	21/01/1918	31/01/1918
Miscellaneous	To, Headquarters, 139 Brigade. Appendix I	02/01/1918	02/01/1918
Miscellaneous	Operation Orders By Major E.M.G. Ingell, Commanding 8th Sherwood Foresters. Appendix II	20/01/1918	20/01/1918

Miscellaneous	Operation Orders by Lieut. Colonel J.E. Blackwall, D.S.O. Commanding 8th Bn. The Sherwood Foresters. Appendix III	30/01/1918	30/01/1918
War Diary	Mazingarbe & Burbure	01/02/1918	07/02/1918
War Diary	Laires	09/02/1918	09/02/1918
War Diary	Enquin	13/02/1918	05/03/1918
War Diary	Westrehem	05/03/1918	05/03/1918
War Diary	Bethune	06/03/1918	14/03/1918
War Diary	Annequin	14/03/1918	16/03/1918
War Diary	Cambrin	20/03/1918	22/03/1918
War Diary	Beuvry	24/03/1918	25/03/1918
War Diary	Calonne	27/03/1918	27/03/1918
War Diary	St Emile	28/03/1918	31/03/1918
War Diary	St. Pierre	31/03/1918	31/03/1918
Miscellaneous	8th Sherwood Foresters, Report on Raid carried out by the enemy on Night 21/22nd. March, 1918	21/03/1918	21/03/1918
Heading	139th Brigade. 46th Division. 1/8th Battalion Sherwood Foresters April 1918.		
War Diary	Cite St Pierre	01/04/1918	01/04/1918
War Diary	Trenches St Emile Left Sub Sector	03/04/1918	05/04/1918
War Diary	Cite St Pierre	09/04/1918	09/04/1918
War Diary	Noeux Les Mines	11/04/1918	11/04/1918
War Diary	Vaudricourt	11/04/1918	17/04/1918
War Diary	Sailly La Bourse	18/04/1918	19/04/1918
War Diary	Vaudricourt	20/04/1918	23/04/1918
War Diary	Bethune	23/04/1918	24/04/1918
War Diary	Essar Sector Right Sub Sector	24/04/1918	24/04/1918
War Diary	Fouquieres	28/04/1918	30/04/1918
Map			
War Diary	Fouquieres	01/05/1918	01/05/1918
War Diary	Le Quesnoy	02/05/1918	02/05/1918
War Diary	Gorre Right	04/05/1918	04/05/1918
War Diary	Le Quesnoy	08/05/1918	08/05/1918
War Diary	Vaudricourt	10/05/1918	10/05/1918
War Diary	Essars	10/05/1918	20/05/1918
War Diary	Verquin	25/05/1918	28/05/1918
War Diary	Gorre	30/05/1918	30/05/1918
War Diary	Line Gorre Right Sub Section	01/06/1918	03/06/1918
War Diary	Lequesnoy	04/06/1918	07/06/1918
War Diary	Vaudricourt	08/06/1918	12/06/1918
War Diary	Line Essars Left Subsector	12/06/1918	12/06/1918
War Diary	Essars	19/06/1918	19/06/1918
War Diary	Vaudricourt	20/06/1918	23/06/1918
War Diary	Forre Left Sub-Sector	24/06/1918	30/06/1918
War Diary	Line. Gorre Left Sector.	01/07/1918	01/07/1918
War Diary	Gorre	01/07/1918	01/07/1918
War Diary	Verquin	02/07/1918	05/07/1918
War Diary	Essars	05/07/1918	09/07/1918
War Diary	Right Sub. Sector	10/07/1918	15/07/1918
War Diary	Vaudricourt Wood	16/07/1918	16/07/1918
War Diary	Hesdigneul	18/07/1918	18/07/1918
War Diary	Vaudricourt	20/07/1918	21/07/1918
War Diary	Essars Right.	22/07/1918	29/07/1918
War Diary	Essars Bde Support	29/07/1918	02/08/1918
War Diary	Essars	02/08/1918	02/08/1918
War Diary	Vaudricourt	03/08/1918	03/08/1918

War Diary	Gorre	08/08/1918	08/08/1918
War Diary	Gorre Right Sub Sector (Front)	12/08/1918	12/08/1918
War Diary	Essars	14/08/1918	19/08/1918
War Diary	Verquin	20/08/1918	20/08/1918
War Diary	Fouqueries	22/08/1918	22/08/1918
War Diary	Essars	22/08/1918	22/08/1918
War Diary	Fouqueries	22/08/1918	22/08/1918
War Diary	Gorre	25/08/1918	31/08/1918
War Diary	Trenches Richebourg St Vaast	01/09/1918	05/09/1918
War Diary	Richebourg St Vaast	05/09/1918	06/09/1918
War Diary	Auchel	07/09/1918	12/09/1918
War Diary	Corbie	12/09/1918	12/09/1918
War Diary	Lahoussoye	13/09/1918	18/09/1918
War Diary	Poeilly	19/09/1918	19/09/1918
War Diary	Bellenglise	20/09/1918	30/09/1918
Miscellaneous	Ref. Map. Richebourg 1/10,000. Appendix I	04/09/1918	04/09/1918
Miscellaneous	8th. Bn. Sherwood Foresters Order No. 42. Appendix 2	10/09/1918	10/09/1918
Miscellaneous	8th. Battn. Sherwood Foresters. Train Orders. Appendix II		
Operation(al) Order(s)	Warning Order. No. 1 Appendix 3	23/09/1918	23/09/1918
Miscellaneous	Belenglise Operation. 1/8th Bn. Sherwood Foresters. Instruction No. 1. Appendix 4	27/09/1918	27/09/1918
Operation(al) Order(s)	8th Battn. Sherwood Foresters. Operation Orders. No. 1 Appendix 5	28/09/1918	28/09/1918
Miscellaneous	8th Sherwood Foresters. Belenglise Operation Instruction No. 2 Appendix 6	28/09/1918	28/09/1918
Miscellaneous	Report on the Bellenglise Operation. Appendix 7	30/09/1918	30/09/1918
War Diary		01/10/1918	30/10/1918
Miscellaneous	8th Sherwood Foresters	09/10/1918	09/10/1918
Miscellaneous	8th Bn. Sherwood Foresters. Instructions No. 2. Appendix I	02/10/1918	02/10/1918
Miscellaneous	Report on attack on Montbrehain Appendix No 1	03/10/1918	03/10/1918
Operation(al) Order(s)	8th Bn. The Sherwood Foresters. Movement Order No. 1	16/10/1918	16/10/1918
Miscellaneous	Report on Attack on Regnicourt. Appendix 2	17/10/1918	17/10/1918
War Diary	Bohain	01/11/1918	02/11/1918
War Diary	Escaufourt	03/11/1918	03/11/1918
War Diary	St Souplet & Catillon	04/11/1918	04/11/1918
War Diary	Mezieres	05/11/1918	05/11/1918
War Diary	Priches & Cartigny	06/11/1918	06/11/1918
War Diary	Cartigny	07/11/1918	09/11/1918
War Diary	Boulogne Sur Helpe	10/11/1918	13/11/1918
War Diary	Landrecies	14/11/1918	30/11/1918
Miscellaneous	8th Battn Sherwood Foresters for the month of November 1918		
War Diary	Landrecies	01/12/1918	31/12/1918
Miscellaneous	D.A.A.G. (1) War Diaries.	05/02/1919	05/02/1919
War Diary	Landrecies	01/01/1919	03/01/1919
War Diary	Prisches	04/01/1919	31/01/1919
War Diary	Priches Ref. Sheet 57th 1/40,000	01/02/1919	19/02/1919
War Diary	Bethencourt Ref. Valebuciennes No. 12 1/100,000		
War Diary	Stray		
War Diary	Bethencourt Sheet 57 B. 1/40000		
War Diary	Bethencourt Ref Sheet 57 B 1/40000	01/04/1919	30/04/1919
War Diary	Bethencourt (Nord)		

worn 29/9/95 (1)

worn 2/9/95 (2)

46TH DIVISION
139TH INFY BDE

8TH BN (NOTTS & DERBY) SHERWOOD FORESTERS

19 OCT ~~MAR 1915~~ - MAY 1919

46<u>TH</u> DIVISION

<u>NOTTS & DERBY</u>
<u>INFANTRY BRIGADE</u>

<u>5TH BN. SHERWOOD FORESTERS</u>
<u>6TH BN.   "   "   "   "</u>
<u>7TH BN.   "   "   "   "</u>
✓ <u>8TH BN.   "   "   "   "</u>

<u>UNIT STATEMENTS</u>
<u>UNITED KINGDOM</u>

(8 N & D
  Mar 15
  May 19
)

WAR DIARY
or
INTELLIGENCE SUMMARY.

(Erase heading not required.)

Army Form C. 2118.

Yours truly
[signature] p.p.
J. Notts & Derby [?]

Instructions regarding War Diaries and Intelligence Summaries are contained in F. S. Regs., Part II. and the Staff Manual respectively. Title pages will be prepared in manuscript.

Hour, Date, Place	Summary of Events and Information	Remarks and references to Appendices
8th. BATTN. SHERWOOD FORESTERS. NOTTS & DERBY BRIGADE. NORTH MIDLAND DIVISION. Mobilisation Station – NEWARK. Temporary War Station – DERBY. Stations since occupied subsequent to concentration LUTON – HARPENDEN.	**1. MOBILISATION.** The Mobilisation of the Unit was satisfactorily accomplished and the details of the Scheme of Mobilisation were systematically carried out. The fact that the Battalion was in Camp at HUMBANBY immediately previous to receipt of orders to mobilise no doubt helped matters, but as it dispersed to the various Company Peace Headquarters from Camp, the whole details of the preliminary stages of mobilisation had to be carried out. The postal and telephone services at each Company's Headquarters and at NEWARK were excellent and rendered the greatest assistance to all concerned, throughout the night on which mobilisation was ordered, and subsequently. Considerable difficulties were experienced by Coy. Officers in obtaining necessaries on mobilisation for their men – the system of local contractors broke down in the small country towns, and time was lost in procuring articles such as boots from large towns. Had a system of procuring all necessaries in bulk at Battn. Head Qrs.	

Army Form C. 2118.

WAR DIARY
or
INTELLIGENCE SUMMARY.

(Erase heading not required.)

Instructions regarding War Diaries and Intelligence Summaries are contained in F. S. Regs., Part II. and the Staff Manual respectively. Title pages will be prepared in manuscript.

Hour, Date, Place	Summary of Events and Information	Remarks and references to Appendices
	or at the County Associations Stores been in Force Companies would have been able to assemble at their Mobilisation Station on the morning of the second day of mobilisation, at latest.	
	The spare clothing was not sufficient, only 10% being allowed on the Battalion ledgers - at least 25% spares are necessary in a scattered County Battalion.	
	The medical examination at Company Headquarters was carried out by civilian practitioners but it was found that these were not sufficiently acquainted with the requirements of military service. For example the SHEEHEN eye test was not invariably used. On arrival at mobilisation centre a certain number of men were there rejected by the Battalion M.O. Examination was made for Home Service only on this occasion.	
	The Orderly Room staff was quite insufficient for the work and but for the kindness of the G.O. in providing two Clerks the office work would have got much in arrears. Additional strength also had to be loaned when the Battalion left for War Station and the Depot was formed.	

(9 29 6) W 3332—1107 100,000 10/13 H W V Forms/C. 2118/10.

Army Form C. 2118.

WAR DIARY
or
INTELLIGENCE SUMMARY.

(Erase heading not required.)

Instructions regarding War Diaries and Intelligence Summaries are contained in F. S. Regs., Part II. and the Staff Manual respectively. Title pages will be prepared in manuscript.

Hour, Date, Place	Summary of Events and Information	Remarks and references to Appendices
	II. CONCENTRATION AT WAR STATION.	
	This concentration was made by road. The first day's march was only 12 miles, but the second day's march of 23 miles was a considerable tax on the mens feet, which were not sufficiently hardened and in many cases were wearing new boots. A move by rail would have been preferable.	
	III. TRAINING.	
	The Training throughout has been under the orders of the Brigade Commander. All Recruits on joining the Battalion are put into separate squads under the Permanent Staff or specially selected Territorial N.C.O's., and are trained according to instructions laid down in the Manuals. Special classes for Officers and N.C.O's have been held continuously with the greatest benefit to all, including instruction in Squad, Section, Company and Battalion Drill, Physical Training, Bayonet Fighting, Musketry.	
	IV. DISCIPLINE.	
	The discipline of the Battalion has been good and the military police detailed to look after the conduct of the men when off parade have fulfilled their duties in a satisfactory and capable manner.	
	V. ADMINISTRATION.	
	(1) <u>Medical Services.</u> The Medical Field Panniers issued are of the 1898 pattern and no more can be obtained. They do not contain a sufficient variety of drugs e.g., there is nothing in them suitable for rheumatic complaints. A standard type of medical cart would be advantageous although the one purchased on	

(9 29 6) W 3352-1197 100,000 10/13 H W V Forms/C. 2118/10.

Army Form C. 2118.

WAR DIARY
or
INTELLIGENCE SUMMARY.
(Erase heading not required.)

Instructions regarding War Diaries and Intelligence Summaries are contained in F. S. Regs., Part II. and the Staff Manual respectively. Title pages will be prepared in manuscript.

Hour, Date, Place	Summary of Events and Information	Remarks and references to Appendices
	mobilisation (a Baker's cart) low hung, two wheel, with back entrance) has proved quite satisfactory.	
	(2) Billeting. Considerable variety of billets have been occupied by the Battalion at its various stations. The large Council Schools at Derby were no doubt, the most convenient and sanitary, being easy to control and with ample means of ventilation. At other stations, LUTON and HARPENDEN, in most cases houses of the artisan type have been used, the front room only being occupied by a small number of men. This type of billet is very popular with the men as it necessitates in many cases their own homes, but the difficulties of control for the Company Officer are very great. In most cases where the women of the house have agreed to cook for the men they live in great comfort. Mess tents have not been used by the Battalion since mobilisation.	
	The sanitary conditions of this type of billet are not always good and require constant supervision and an efficient squad of sanitary police. The civil authorities have rendered great help in these matters.	
	VI. REORGANISATION OF T.F. INTO HOME & IMPERIAL SERVICE.	
	Previous to mobilisation an "Imperial Service" Section had been started in the Battalion, but it was of no great strength. After the outbreak of war a considerable number of men gave in their names to this Section, and later when the serious nature of the struggle before the country was realised 80% of the Battalion volunteered for Foreign Service. Those who cannot only undertake Home Service have been drafted into a Home Battalion and their places filled with recruits. An additional number of men were rejected as Medically Unfit for Foreign Service. No doubt more Imperial Service men might have been obtained in Peace time had the question been pressed, but it	

WAR DIARY
OR
INTELLIGENCE SUMMARY.
(Erase heading not required.)

Army Form C. 2118.

Hour, Date, Place	Summary of Events and Information	Remarks and references to Appendices
	would appear to be invidious to make distinction between the two conditions of service in Peace time. As a voluntarily enlisted Force there must necessarily be men in it who cannot undertake service abroad so easily as some others may, and if distinction is made between the two types of services, these men would in Peace time undoubtedly hold back. If, however, no distinction is made and all classes feel that, they are equal, with the knowledge perhaps that those with less interests at home can volunteer for Foreign Service at once, and that the others lose no status by their doing so, the T.F. may continue to exist. With a system of universal service, there would on the other hand be no objection to Home and Imperial Service Battalions being organised for the T.F. and separately trained. Charles Hunter Lieut. Colonel, Comdg. 8| Sherwood Foresters.	

Instructions regarding War Diaries and Intelligence Summaries are contained in F. S. Regs., Part II. and the Staff Manual respectively. Title pages will be prepared in manuscript.

Army Form C. 2118.

WAR DIARY
or
INTELLIGENCE SUMMARY.
(Erase heading not required.)

Instructions regarding War Diaries and Intelligence Summaries are contained in F.S. Regs., Part II. and the Staff Manual respectively. Title pages will be prepared in manuscript.

Hour, Date, Place	Summary of Events and Information	Remarks and references to Appendices
8th Battn. THE SHERWOOD FORESTERS, Notts & Derby Brigade, North Midland Division, Mobilization Centre - NEWARK. Temporary War Station - DERBY. Since occupied - LUTON - HARPENDEN. October, 31st. 1914.	(d) TRAINING. (1) Officers and N.C.O's. Junior Officers and all N.C.O's have been trained together at early morning parades constantly during the month under the Permanent Staff and considerable improvement in their work can be seen. Commencing with elementary work, gradual progress has been made to that of a more advanced nature. If more time were available greater progress would no doubt be evident. Two points are especially notable. First, the zeal with which all the Permanent Staff apply themselves to the giving of instruction to these Classes and secondly the improvement in confidence and power of command shewn by those Territorial N.C.O's who have been selected to assist in the Recruits Training. When these N.C.O's go back to their Companies they shew vastly more ability to handle and instruct their men in comparison with those N.C.O's who have not been detailed to assist at Recruit Training. (2) Trained Men. Company Training has been carried on according to Brigade Programmes. A considerable amount of entrenching has been done, and by the collier companies particularly has been most, successfully carried out. Provided a sufficient number of tools are available and the work required to be done has been set out quickly and accurately these Companies would stand comparison with any of other Battalions. More Practice in making Head Cover and in finishing off trenches in all kinds of soil would be useful. Material for the former and time for the latter has not often been available. (3) Recruit Training. has been carried on as already described and gradually these have been drafted into the Companies. The progress made by Recruits under Permanent Staff was phenomenal, but it is evident that when the Recruits join their	

Army Form C. 2118.

WAR DIARY
or
INTELLIGENCE SUMMARY.
(Erase heading not required.)

Instructions regarding War Diaries and Intelligence Summaries are contained in F.S. Regs., Part II. and the Staff Manual respectively. Title pages will be prepared in manuscript.

Hour, Date, Place	Summary of Events and Information	Remarks and references to Appendices
	Companies considerable time is still required to make them fitted for work in the field.	
	(e) DISCIPLINE.	
	A gradual stiffening of the discipline of the Battalion has been made and though still there is much to be done, undoubtedly men now realize the reasons for dealing severely with even the more minor crimes. The work of the Provost Sergeant has been excellently carried on throughout the month.	
	(f) ADMINISTRATION.	
	(4) Transport Services. There still is apparent the necessity of having men who are thoroughly used to horses in civil life to look after the Transport horses, otherwise the loss by deterioration will be very great. Even after 2 or 3 months experience men not used to horses before do not show that ability to care for and "turn out" their horses and vehicles as do men whose constant occupation it is.	
	(5) The Billeting of the Battalion in small houses continues to be satisfactory and except for some loss of control owing to dispersion of billets the system is highly satisfactory.	
	(g) REORGANISATION of Territorial Force into Imperial and Home Service Units. During this month the Home Service Battalion has been definitely constituted. Under the conditions of the present war it is evident that frequent transfer of Officers and Men from one Battalion to another will have to be made. The present method of application to the G.O.C. of the Command involves considerable delay. It is suggested that if the same relations between	

Army Form C. 2118.

WAR DIARY
or
INTELLIGENCE SUMMARY.
(Erase heading not required.)

Instructions regarding War Diaries and Intelligence Summaries are contained in F.S. Regs., Part II. and the Staff Manual respectively. Title pages will be prepared in manuscript.

Hour, Date, Place	Summary of Events and Information	Remarks and references to Appendices
	the two Battalions could exist as do now between the 1st and 2nd. Line Battalions of a Regular Regiment considerable delays at what may be critical times, might be saved. M/Hinson Lieut. Colonel, Comdg. 8/ Sherwood Foresters.	

Army Form C. 2118.

WAR DIARY
or
INTELLIGENCE SUMMARY.
(Erase heading not required.)

Instructions regarding War Diaries and Intelligence Summaries are contained in F.S. Regs., Part II. and the Staff Manual respectively. Title pages will be prepared in manuscript.

Hour, Date, Place	Summary of Events and Information	Remarks and references to Appendices
8th Battn. THE SHERWOOD FORESTERS.		
NOTTS & DERBY BRIGADE.	1. MOBILIZATION. Discussed in previous notes (September 30th.).	
NORTH MIDLAND DIVISION.	2. CONCENTRATION AT WAR STATION. "	
Mobilization Station - NEWARK.	3. TRAINING. The training of the first week of the month consisted of Brigade or Divisional days, which proved of great value to Senior Officers of Battalions as they were confronted with problems similar to those which they would have to meet, on service, and of which they had previously had but little experience. The Divisional days at KENSWORTH, when Cavalry, Artillery and Infantry were combined must be especially noteworthy. During the second week of the month Company training was reverted to and small schemes of Companies acting against each other were drawn up. These proved of the greatest interest to Company Officers, N.C.O's and Men as, in these schemes, every one gets into action and the necessity of co-operation between small Units was particularly demonstrated.	
Temporary War Station - DERBY.		
Since occupied - LUTON - HARPENDEN - HARLOW - DUNMOW - BOCKING.	The sudden move of the Division into Essex stopped these schemes. The training at BOCKING has consisted entirely of digging, and it is to be hoped has hardened mens hands for the work ahead of them. March Discipline. The long march to HARLOW on 16th instant proved the necessity of constant practice in marching. Men must be used to carrying their full loads in packs and ammunition. Many men that day wore their new boots as they thought they were going by train, and the results were disastrous. The short march, 12 miles, to DUNMOW, the next day produced large numbers of casualties. If the length of the march had had to be more than 20 miles the result would have been very bad. Keeping step, opening the ranks out for air, and halting at the stated time without fatiguing men by closing up distances lost, are the points which Company Officers should constantly bear in mind.	
NOVEMBER, 30th., 1914.	1.	

WAR DIARY
or
INTELLIGENCE SUMMARY.
(Erase heading not required.)

Army Form C. 2118.

Hour, Date, Place	Summary of Events and Information	Remarks and references to Appendices
	4. DISCIPLINE. The necessity of dealing severely with cases of insubordination has been constantly emphasized and must always be borne in mind. Non Commissioned Officers of all ranks must be made to realize the responsibilities of their positions as regards discipline. 5. ADMINISTRATION. (1) Medical Services. These have been satisfactory. The new Maltes Cart, a plain open cart, does not appear to be as suitable a vehicle as the covered cart bought on mobilization. (2) Billeting. Considerable experience of this has been had during the month. The Billeting parties must arrive at the destination for the night, well ahead of the Main Body, as unless a complete survey of the place can be made faulty allotment of areas is sure to arise. For a Brigade 5 hours margin would not be excessive. This could easily be done by motor. Billeting Officers and parties should be the same, or have constant practice at the work. It must be noted that the men generally fare better in small houses, of the 5/6 room cottage type, where only about six men can billet, together than in larger houses of the middle class where 10/15 are often put. In the smaller house the woman of the house cooks for them, but this does not happen in the larger ones. Schools are convenient for one night halts, but uncomfortable for longer ones. Rates for billeting having been definitely fixed at either 3d. or 9d. (3) Transport. During the moves to HARLOW and onwards considerable delay was caused by the late arrival for loading of the 4 G.S. Wagons sent by the A.S.C. It is possible that the loading, transit and unloading at destinations of these wagons would be very much quicker if they were always under Battalion control and simply Brigaded for the march. Under the	

WAR DIARY
or
INTELLIGENCE SUMMARY.
(Erase heading not required.)

Army Form C. 2118.

Hour, Date, Place	Summary of Events and Information	Remarks and references to Appendices

control of the A.S.C. the wagons of a particular Battalion lose their identity and the drivers have no particular interest in the owners of the stores they carry — hence delays and disappointment.

The shortage of 3 Cooks Wagons, due under Establishment, caused the overloading of the Transport, and consequent fatigue to horses.

(as the Mills Cookers of the 7th Battalion did) should not march as 1st. Line Transport, as their delays hang up and unduly tire Battalions in rear.

(4) Equipment. The new leather equipment, with web pack, arrived during this month and was issued with most unsatisfactory results. The design of attachment of the pack to the brace was bad, as was also the stitching, and worst of all the leather braces were absolutely frail. After only a few days wear the packs began to break away and the leather to split. If the Battalion had been compelled to go abroad with this equipment, the result could only have been deplorable. It was admitted by the makers to be the first slot of equipment of this type issued to a Battalion. Luckily the older pattern W^b Equipment has been promised for delivery early in December, so this leather equipment will be done away with. Compare. The Mark VII Rifles has been issued, but the ammunition for it has not yet been received. *This equipment was bought by the T. F. Association when the web equipment could not be procured. The latter has now been received from the O. Dep^t. E.S.*

Field Travelling Kitchens, if they are likely to break down

(5) Rifles.

6. REORGANISATION OF T.F. This has been discussed in notes of September and October. It is becoming increasingly evident that the old voluntary system of recruiting for the Territorial Force is absolutely unsuitable for the Country's need. National Service must come into force. If we had had National Service for two years before the outbreak of war

3.

Army Form C. 2118.

WAR DIARY
or
INTELLIGENCE SUMMARY.
(Erase heading not required.)

Instructions regarding War Diaries and Intelligence Summaries are contained in F.S. Regs., Part II. and the Staff Manual respectively. Title pages will be prepared in manuscript.

Hour, Date, Place	Summary of Events and Information	Remarks and references to Appendices
	We should now have had 1,000,000 men available to re-inforce the Regular Army immediately - armed, trained and equipped. Under the present system, only now, after four months of war, is the Territorial Force becoming fit for its best Battalions to be sent to the scene of active operations.	

Charles I Hudson
O.C. S. Batt S.F.

8th Batty
Notts & Derbys

Statement in connection with WAR DIARY,
NOVEMBER, 1914.

5th Battalion, Notts. & Derbyshire Regt.
Notts. & Derbyshire Infantry Brigade.
North Midland Division.
Mobilisation Centre - DERBY.
Temporary War Station - DERBY.
Stations since occupied subsequent to concentration:
    LUTON.
    HARPENDEN.
    HARLOW (one day only-marching through).
    BISHOP (do. do.).
    BRAINTREE.
    DUNMOW.

TRAINING.

All ranks are apparently becoming much better fitted physically to undertake their duties in the field.

Musketry. The classification practices were interrupted by the change of stations and were unfinished, although some Companies got further than others. The weather conditions on the 11th November were extremely bad. A gale of wind blew all day from the W. with constant rain increasing in violence at frequent intervals, so that sometimes it was almost impossible to distinguish the targets. The latter constantly blew away. In some instances, men who are good shots were unable to find the target at all. It is submitted that it would be inequitable to base proficiency pay on the results of shooting under such conditions.

The field practices at DUNSTABLE were intelligently carried out by O.C. Companies and should prove of value to all concerned.

ADMINISTRATION.

Medical Services. The diseases from which the men have suffered during the past month have been chiefly those affecting the respiratory system and are caused by inclement weather, inferior boots, and the difficulty of carrying a change of clothes. Probably these complaints will be prevalent during the winter and it is suggested that it should be the rule to treat the men in local hospitals, however small, as transfers to central hospitals must involve the risk of aggravating the complaint.

Supply Services. The failure of the train to keep pace with the Brigade on the march to HARLOW, while the 1st Line Transport succeeded in doing so may be noted. Possibly on such marches, it might be advantageous for part of the train to accompany the 1st line transport.

DISCIPLINE.

Considerable improvement is required from the non-commissioned officers, who do not yet quite realise
                                                       their

(2)

their responsibilities and powers in maintaining
and upholding discipline.   Special steps have been
taken to remedy this state of things and it is trusted
that in consequence progress will be made.

                                                                        Lieut. Col.
                        Commanding,
                                5th Bn. Notts. & Derbyshire Regt.

Dunmow,
    9th December, 1914.

139th Inf.Bde.
46th Div.

Battn. disembarked
Havre from England
3.3.15.

8th BATTN. THE SHERWOOD FORESTERS (NOTTINGHAMSHIRE
AND DERBYSHIRE REGIMENT).

M A R C H

1 9 1 5

WAR DIARY OR INTELLIGENCE SUMMARY

Army Form C. 2118.

18th Hussars Field [?]

March 1915

Hour, Date, Place	Summary of Events and Information	Remarks and references to Appendices
March 1st 1915 S.S. KING EDWARD	Received orders to disembark. This was completed in 2 hours - marched to "Rest Camp" and had dinner.	
SOUTHAMPTON 3.0 PM	Received orders to march to NATL. MEMORIAL HALL. This was done and Batln. quickly settled down with Cookhouse & Quarters - Officers billeted at ye CENTRAL HOTEL.	
March 2nd " 7.15 AM	Running / Physical Training	
10.0 AM	Company Drill	
11.15	Received orders to re-embark at 4.30 PM	
2.0 PM	Musketry	
4.0 [?]	Hands off and re-embark in KING EDWARD.	
9.15	Sailed - clear night and sea - began rough - storm afterwards [?] lasting but "Shining" did which had us spined[?] by Admiralty. Very few men bad ill. - A gentleman to control us arose and no incident known to us happened	
3rd 4.50 AM	Reached HAVRE & th- unhypekateQ[?]	
8.0	Disembarked and sent to camp in Shed 7 - drawn for carts and other equipment. YMCA did very much appreciated by all ranks. Major Clerke, Capt Hayhurst & Down [?] reported.	
1.30 PM	Batln reached N[?] entraining port - Entrained Transport and	
5.15	... - 23 trucks for men - 11 horses, 10 [?] Waggons. 1 Officers waggon 36 in a truck - board & very clean [?] Left for N France - with 2 days Rations with it.	

11th Advanced Trenches Folio 2

WAR DIARY
or
INTELLIGENCE SUMMARY.
(Erase heading not required.)

Army Form C. 2118.

1915

Hour, Date, Place	Summary of Events and Information	Remarks and references to Appendices
March 4. 5. Train 5:30 AM in FRANCE	Met Refno at ABBEVILLE but only 35 minutes allowed, which was scarcely enough for hurried lunch which were received.	
11.30 AM	Took the Operation in CALAIS to STOMER where inspection was made as to travel to CASSELL. The Relief was reached at 12:45. Capt. ASHWELL met up at station. Detraining & Transport commenced. Staff men and were completed in 1hr 5 mins - Men detrained, their Iron Ration marched via WAEMER CAPPEL to OUDEZEELE, which was reached at 5:30 Men rations that night Iron for Coy's and new boots. Billets were already allotted and after Tea Four Companies were taken to the - all in Barns and within bivouac - The next afternoon Brigade handing over it to the Trenches, their Billets when previously allotted to the 7th NELC Brigade.	
March 5. OUDEZEELE 2:30	Inspection by CO of new Rations all in Billets	
9:0 PM	GOC came to decline Officers and Senior NCOs on the instructions which their Battn is then.	
10 PM	Capt. Beckn arrived, having been sent to be CALED PMA for day before.	

Forms/C. 2118/10

WAR DIARY
INTELLIGENCE SUMMARY

Army Form C. 2118.

15th Middlesex Regt.
March
M15
Folio 3

Hour, Date, Place	Summary of Events and Information	Remarks and references to Appendices
March 6 OOEZEELE 7.0 - 7.30 9.0 3.0	Running, Physical Training. Batt. staffs for Route March and Go under O.C. Classes/Instruction to NCOs, Sent / NCO's/Bath & Pres. Range Finders etc, Conferences under O.C. for Marching Very heavy rain all [day?] in afternoon. Wet & warm.	
" 7 2.45 P.M.	CO lectures N.C.O.s & Disciplin under ROUTINE ORDERS to him. Orders received that the Bn. gave will move on Tuesday. Billeting Officer gone to make arrangements in [area].	
" 7 *		
" 8 7.0 - 7.30 10.0 AM	Running Physical Training Batt. Route March to WORMHOUDT, where a lot of French soldiers gave the Batt. a fine welcome. They all look very fit and are back from the Trenches for a rest.	
1.0 P.M.	Orders received that the march with the brickies Regt. to STRAZEELE tomorrow - The march [?] has to go a long way round S. of CASSEL but allowed the Bn Route mainly by STEENVORDE are packed up by 5 P.M. night - Cookers not allowed to [?] with Batt. Wheels heavy [?]. NY	

Army Form C. 2118.

1/8 Thanet Tanks

WAR DIARY
or
INTELLIGENCE SUMMARY.

(Erase heading not required.)

Instructions regarding War Diaries and Intelligence Summaries are contained in F.S. Regs., Part II. and the Staff Manual respectively. Title pages will be prepared in manuscript.

4

Hour, Date, Place	Summary of Events and Information	Remarks and references to Appendices
morning — 9 AM	Left OUDEZEELE, 10am. with LINC-LEICS Bgde at CASSEL and march via CAESTRE, where Gen Sir H. Smith Dorrien begs two Bgdes, to STRAZEELE. The L-L Bgde halted and the Both	Motor Bus Transport for Skin Coats & gum-boots.
MERRIS 3.0 PM	go on to MERRIS, where good billets have been obtained - The rest of the Brigade are here, back from their centre in the Trenches - Perree is very difficult for march on. Inspection of billets and Co's mess & C.	
" 10⁵⁰ " 9.0		
" 11⁰⁰ 9.15.	Bn HQ Pte to bivouac; but at 10.40 received orders to move in an hour. - By 12.0, all was packed ready to move, and men are received that Bgde will march to SAILLY. Starting at 12.30. This was managed easily by 8⁰ B.M.R. The 5th were late. (very fine march, no halt. Bgde train not allowed to go into SAILLY which was sent round by ROUGE CROIX, only reaching area allotted to Rifles = BAC ST MAUR of 8.0PM. Great confusion as Canadian Troops had not cleared out of billets - After some delay, men gone up in diff. after all their road cut by 9.30 PM, but Batt⁰ men billeted – in rather dirty places & very close to the trenches it seemed. Mr guns been quite near.	Transport Brigaded.

WAR DIARY
INTELLIGENCE SUMMARY

HQ Second Troops (Regt)

Army Form C. 2118.

5

Hour, Date, Place	Summary of Events and Information	Remarks and references to Appendices
March 12 - BAC ST MAUR	Cleaning up in his morning. Heard at mid-day that we might be attached to his 2nd Cavalry Division for a offensive purpose.	
7.0 PM	Orders to be ready to move any minute, but no further orders came. As troop arrived	
" 13" 12.50 AM	Heard that "move" was put off - Waited all morning, and at last got orders for Bgde to move at 1.15 PM - The route he to be via necessity to travel light. To do his there we much overloaded, a lot of Superfluous clothing is left at an inn here	
4.0 PM	March via ESTAIRES, where a lot of troops are seen - to NEUF BERQUIN. It very crowded billets - Some horses were not available owing to being Containing teams in trenches which ate through (her of German occupation (last October). Made a great difficulty - Weather little better, and even into his car. Many men are down with diarrhoea. Capt Beecher is specially for this. - Rayham Commande at night was heard	
" 14"	Billets in Neuf Berquin stat. Aprica Commande was heard at night	M.T.

Pl. Hampshire Cyclists

WAR DIARY
or
INTELLIGENCE SUMMARY.
(Erase heading not required.)

Army Form C. 2118.

Hour, Date, Place		Summary of Events and Information	Remarks and references to Appendices
NEUF BERQUIN. March 15.	7.0 9-0 3.0	Running Brigade Route March, about 7 miles only. Officers & NCO's practise Bout Thierry, a very much talked of station just at present	
" 16	6.45. 9.0 3.0	Running – many sick – feet (wolfskin) & diarrhoea. Brigade Route March about 12 miles, to MERVILLE A & B Co. Bout Thierry – Steenie Cleman helpless. Mass de	
" 17	6.45 9.0	Running – Again many sick. Feet and skin all Route march to DOULIEU, about 12 miles Major Parker with 2½ officers to Lille (truck) – to Headquarter for Certain & his five strong day.	
" 18	6.45 9.0	Running Battle with 1st RHA. Arm. Scheme was AG attacking Armée fort. hill M.G.s – General Group has heard we criticised work Some this conception at the start. We Co. and a too large detachment to flank was made – but the main died hopeless and the General was pleased	
" 19	9.0	Run in early morning – Bgde marches to BOIS D'AVAL for West Tipperar, but heavy snow storms stopped this and We Bgde marched back to billets.	

[9-29-6] W 3552-1107 100,000 10/13 HWV Forms/C. 2118/10

WAR DIARY or INTELLIGENCE SUMMARY.

Army Form C. 2118.

(Erase heading not required.)

Place	Hour, Date	Summary of Events and Information	Remarks and references to Appendices
NEUF BERQUIN	March 20th 7.7.30 / 9.15-1's	Running. Companies digging and further organisation of trenches, who Front Systems as marked in Pamphlet sent round.	
	" 21st	Standing to at Stand	
	" 22nd 9.0.	March to Bois DEVAL & thence marching through woods - Attiled by snipers.	
	3.30	Nais't Macoin Claus - Huerele - Admirel Gre - Great hunting of communicator trenches - Van and the gunners shown.	
	" 23rd 7.7.30	Company at disposal of A.S.C. A+B do attacks in open country	
	9.0	C.D. in two lines thus and again organised attacks pleasit.	
	7.7.30	17 Brig. Great improvement shown.	
	3.0	Clean'd parade & Sipelos - tents - Ships - Benz/Primers - transport all farage with Major CLARKE	
	" 24th 6.30	Packing transport.	
	9.0.	Leave for Klebs with report for VIEUX BERQUIN	
VIEUX BERQUIN		Anticipated damages received from MAIRE and arranged by Capt. HODGKINSON.	
		New Billets are now Committees who men will hold quarters for Officers.	

WAR DIARY
Edward Ink
INTELLIGENCE SUMMARY.

Army Form C. 2118.

(Erase heading not required.)

Hour, Date, Place	Summary of Events and Information	Remarks and references to Appendices

VIEUX BERQUIN – March 25

9.0 AM — Bn formed. C. Co. go digging — followed by D-A-B in 2 hour relays — a light northern breeze.

12.30 — Packing up to move. Have rec'd from LINC LANCS Bde to march to ROMARIN. Join up at STEINWERKE, and arrive ROMARIN at 3.30 pm, being met by General HULL at RA BOI — Guilford Wals, lot rather (excellent). A very instructive programme has been arranged here.

27 **7.0** — Rum Issue stopped, much to everyone's regret. Running in morning — been relieved by SEAFORTH Officer in his stead left of Kincarine trench which does not adhere as to orders "Jam – Rf"

5.15 — A.C. Co. go into the Trenches – A & the Royal Irish Fusiliers C to the DUBLINS – 2nd Platoon to ARGYLL & SUTHERLAND HRS. C. Co. has a lot of casualties and we look but unlucky very much rather expect.

28 **5.0** — 2nd Platn goes to Argylls. 6.7.8. to Royal Irish D. Co. to Dublins — Co. adjt to Royal Irish. We move independently. The excellent Trench discipline of the Royal Irish and but TW

WAR DIARY or INTELLIGENCE SUMMARY

Army Form C. 2118.

[Thaval Trenches ?]

Hour, Date, Place	Summary of Events and Information	Remarks and references to Appendices
ARMARIN March 28th	(contd.) Excellent line j[unction?] trenches which they kept - They go in to V Loopholes. Am pleased our [Bn?] rets short Sanitation and much [wiring?] - Sniping is in our corner till he looks an sharp. D.Co. into the Dubleins have heavy shelling, and got 2 men wounded - The [trenches] here are not so good and much more isolated.	
" 29	B.D. spent the day in the trenches - relieved at 7.0 by A.C. - The Royal Irish & Dublins are relieved by the Seaforths and Warwicks - The Argylls have been here ever since. On arrival here in our Coy work by platoons, each kept responsible for a definite [trench] -	
" 30	They are not much shelled - Lt-Col [Arthgir?] Hutchinson got hit by a bullet in right wrist and through. A Co. does not suffer at all	
6.0 PM	B.D. goes again at 6.0 PM, and have uneventful evening, no lives have to be out in to early morning for the time next day	[MO?]

WAR DIARY or INTELLIGENCE SUMMARY

Army Form C. 2118.

Allenward Staff 10

(Erase heading not required.)

Hour, Date, Place	Summary of Events and Information	Remarks and references to Appendices
ROMARIN March 31st	B.O. Came at at 5.0 AM. Wife and Mrs Crowell to Parkers up and sparring Whiff's	
9.30	March off and join up with two Leica Bgde – March through STEIN WERKE – Lot of Bulr Bank at DOULIEU and arrived old billets at BERQUIN at 2.30 PM. All ranks very much appreciated the 4 days of trench training clean, and but for knowing that men under fire was altogether excellent. The difficulty really was to make them keep him knees dry — The men with Smith and McMichael horse discipline is quite different and no one is too great to move this.	
4 – 6 PM	Preparing for fresh move — as we hear we are back into N.M.D. and entrest trent a Friday	

M

Arthur Ille.

139th Inf.Bde.
46th Div.

8th BATTN. THE SHERWOOD FORESTERS (NOTTINGHAMSHIRE AND DERBYSHIRE REGIMENT).

A P R I L

1 9 1 5

WAR DIARY or INTELLIGENCE SUMMARY

Army Form C. 2118.

1/8 Devon T. 7

April 1917

Hour, Date, Place	Summary of Events and Information	Remarks and references to Appendices
April 1st VIEUX BERQUIN 10.30 A.M.	Bn HQ Parade - Parade dispersed from tactical exercise owing to a very successful scheme broken out, but want of commanders.	
2.30 - 5	Schemes - Discussive live in steam	
	Company in under B & C ½ Batt	
"2nd 11.15 AM	Leave in Rdls, and march into 7 RWK (Leaders) Hr BAILLEUL to LOCRE - 10 mile - Emptying baggage & Wave and the march in (fairly) well carried out.	
LOCRE 4.0 PM	Major LOCRE and Major Reardon billets	
9.0	CO and AJ OC Co of 7 KEMMEL and went to Co. DEVONS we are to relieve, also went to Bomb of 7 Inntes. CO & recovered Rev DEVON Co. OC C Co Attn/Lie 24 Trunk in log Trenches	
"3rd AM	Bn HQ pass to service taken by Bishop of LONDON.	
7.30 PM	handed to artillery via N KEMMEL - half of Bandstand b/guide 7 DEVON Regt and each Trench guide taken in - This has been successfully carried out in spite of a bright moon and much sniping.	
	Disposition - O. Co - Bn Hq / G1 G2 G6. B Co. S4 - G4A A Co G3 G4 H. G4A D Co H2 H3 H4 H5 Rett of "B" in Reserve	

HWV

WAR DIARY
or
INTELLIGENCE SUMMARY.
(Erase heading not required.)

Army Form C. 2118.

Hour, Date, Place	Summary of Events and Information	Remarks and references to Appendices
KEMMEL April 3rd	Transient calm there and West too. Weather apparent the Staff — except Curtess which stay at KEMMEL	
" 4th 9 am	"C" Co Ambrym and the Enemy make overtures for a truce — listening to whistle play — and about 11/50 of them appear after O.C asked for instructions — and noted that no truce can be allowed — that the enemy were left warned that we should fire on them if they don't withdraw. They do have before his message reaches O.C. The interpreter has from Capt Headley a few shouted to warn. the Germans here and an —	Report in Trenches — and took Over the Appendix I.
" 11 P.M	Enemy bombs not very badly on his known — and Mewbombs are born at 62 without damage	
" 5th 11 am	Rain sets in and very men-like conditions therein. Things fairly quiet, except for an Artillery bombardment near SHA which does very little damage.	
	At 6 "Batt." and Company officers conveyed to evening to 24 hours. Little else in Trenches as they are taking over the line — Much less sniping when gas masks in our line —	

MW

WAR DIARY
INTELLIGENCE SUMMARY

Army Form C. 2118.

B/Norrist Fusiliers
April 1915

Hour, Date, Place	Summary of Events and Information	Remarks and references to Appendices
KEMMEL April 6th	Very wet day, but much firing by day. but got more active by night - kind work in between on shelter.	
noon	Gotham MAR & Officer came over and discuss site of New Communication Trench. When this is done, relief will be much easier; Captain Crees not well.	
" 7th	Pte Hyde (A Co) shot in the head by sniper, on post	
9.0 PM	Fatality. Again heavy intermittent fire. Relieving Batt arrives and relief commences - This proceeds very slowly and is not complete till 2.30 AM. New tanks no change to the note - Everybody	
"C" 2-4.30 AM	unceasingly carried out. Platoons reach rest billets and all ranks settle down to a welcome rest.	
LOCRE		
6.0 PM	Conference of Coy Officers and B.H.Q. introducing the Bn to his Trenches - A scheme taken in hand by the Bdr and published in Divis Order.	

2nd Monmouthshire

WAR DIARY
or
INTELLIGENCE SUMMARY.

(Erase heading not required.)

April 1915

Army Form C. 2118.

Hour, Date, Place	Summary of Events and Information	Remarks and references to Appendices
April 9th LOCRE 10 AM	Go to billets of MC.	
2.30	Conference of Officers in room burnt during stay in trenches.	
7.30	Walking parties found by A and C Company	
" 10th " 11-1	Companies inspected by Cos.	
7.30 PM	Working carrying parties from A, B, C Companies found. Pte Richardson 7 A. Co. shot through his head and another man wounded.	
" 11th 9.0 PM	Gen. Sir Charles Fergusson called at Battn Hdqrs.	
	The Commences relief of 6th Batt. which is successfully accomplished	
	by 1.1 AM. — Same distribution as before — except that "B" Co. got H2-H3-H4-H5 and "D" Co. got in Reserve — A great deal of work has been done by the 6th. officials in G2, but there is	
KEMMEL	Also much to do. Headquarters of firing lotus 2 + 3 AM.	
" 12 6 AM	Pte Finney (C) Co shot through head. Pte 7 Pitts A Co shot through his head in afternoon. Except his and some trench mortar in afternoon it has been quiet one — Arrange his own also a lot of truth — The ground is drying up very keen killed and is a both above is quite good.	

WAR DIARY or INTELLIGENCE SUMMARY

Army Form C. 2118.

8th Seaforth Highlanders

April 1915

Hour, Date, Place	Summary of Events and Information	Remarks and references to Appendices
April 13th KEMMEL	A quiet morning. Gen Stuart Wortley called at HQrs. Our guns commence firing in the afternoon, and this acts as an H.E. Shrapnel being sited by enemy. Serious effect. Lt Muirhead wounded – Bombs on trenches to B and A & "G" trenches in his trench. A quiet night. Lt Col Torrance goes sick.	
11 AM		
2–4 PM	Again a quiet morning. Traffic now on it. Trenches are again shelled. This time the enemy for two attacks by a battery from another sector firing into the German trenches. Monto his H.Q.S. replied manner.	
5–6.	Heavily developed bombarded by heavy guns – searching from artillery.	
7. PM	Line of Intrenched Communication briefly haphazard and CO.	
11.0.	A Furious Cannonade heard to the North – but except to please our lines take my little notice, and again – quiet. In fact. Capt Hutchinson took over "D" Co from Mr James.	

Capt HWV Forms/C. 2118/10.

WAR DIARY or INTELLIGENCE SUMMARY

Army Form C. 2118.

2nd Mounted Infantry (?)

April 1915

Hour, Date, Place	Summary of Events and Information	Remarks and references to Appendices
April 15 - KEMMEL to Midday	Enemy attack at 2 here while flags of truce Hs, but he shot fire on them. Think they were intended to artillery purposes. A 3rd flag was hoisted to be a demonstration opposite our lines — and that relief minute.	
9.0 PM	After minutely later — very quiet afternoon. Relief by 6th Batt. commences — we hear & know that time many accomplished as quickly as possible — Patrols sent out to enemy's line report that this is latest — Some delay in finishing relief as A'Co has to wait to complete garrison of GHQ. As Canadians counter hits are mounted to a field SE of village where he himself accomplished.	Pte Atkinson B.G. shot in the back and died in a few hours.
4.16 2.32 AM 3.25 " LOCRE 5.0	Mme M and air clear of KEMMEL by 4.0 AM - Reach rest billets and very welcome tea and bisc. Very little done that day as everyone is very tired.	
"17 7.0 9.0 10–12.30	Running Pistol/Rifle Companies under M.C. for Musketry, Rifle + Bayonet exs. Fit & drill. After own washing — many men are Vermin on now. Issue G. istroke tin baths. Are very much appreciated. New Rifles (70) are fund defective — but hands firm to Shot. Why show shank in the NNR — he are hand little ready.	
7.0 PM		

Army Form C. 2118.

WAR DIARY
or
INTELLIGENCE SUMMARY

2nd Batt/ Sherwood
April 1915

(Erase heading not required.)

Hour, Date, Place	Summary of Events and Information	Remarks and references to Appendices
April 18th LOCRE – Sunday 7.0 A.M.	Very Little done except mine watching	Dispositions in Trenches.
" 19th " 10–12.30	Running of machine and Gas drill	G1 D.Co – Capt Hodgkinson
" " 6.0 P.M.	Companies march off to relieve 6th Bn.	G6
	at ½ km intervals – Thos make regts in order D-B-A-C to relieve 6th Bn.	G2 I.P.C.Co. under "D"
KEMMEL 9.0.	in Congelin in KEMMEL avoided. Relief starts at 9 P.M. and is complete by 12.20	G3 "A"Co Capt Ashmore
	2 Full Cookers (knownrolling 74pts) 1 Carton Size arrive for hot Baths.	G4 A " "
	Thos had had hayous returned	H1 " "
" 20th "	A very unlucky day for Lt Batt – he lose 6 men into Trenches.	G4 1 Platoon "C" Co "
5–7 A.M.	Capt Wiersma (B.Co) is the greatest loss – he was shot through the throat whilst out of his trench – he was a very gallant section and all	H2 "B" Co Capt
	ranks mourn his loss. The others killed were 2243 Pte J Winfield "C Co"	H3 " Major Becher
	2712 Trickett "D.Co" 2791 Beresford "B.Co" 1418 Adams "A.Co" Hayman "A.Co" in 3 cases have been shot thro' the parapet – they must be	H4 " " "
	wastefull and trophies for any work	H5 " " "
3–5 P.M.	G.2. was thanked very handsomely and on R.E. leapt in here. Asn killed, hurt / Pte Tyrott Olstsnyiel – Oct D.Co draw attention	S4 I.P.C.Co. ParkBatt S4A 2P " Mr. Fisher
	to this excellent behaviour of all ranks under very trying circumstance – this gallant behaviour has never been the German	½ P.C. Co KEMMEL
	Orders received trust Loskers be sent to 6th & 5th Batts Sowthon gone to LAGACHE F.M. 6th Batt R HWT Communication Trench

Army Form C. 2118.

WAR DIARY
or
INTELLIGENCE SUMMARY

8th Bn East Surrey Regt

April 1915

(Erase heading not required.)

Hour, Date, Place	Summary of Events and Information	Remarks and references to Appendices
April 21st / KEMMEL	B. Co. have been moving in & Trenches, but neglected them. Ha. the Trenches has done very numerous tasks — thank little good reconstruction by Verrier. Quiet in the afternoon. Lt Col met the C.O. about that they hunt get on with living in (not) of their trenches — Major thought R.E. have ordered several about them — Lt. Fallon attempted a hutting and does regularly after their hut but has drift to the — Artrois Service. A quiet night — attempt by the Xths about top ... most of the aeroplane attack. All trenches shelled during afternoon — Hand Grenade Shell — Killed and wounded in H2 — Antrype Bulb. 17 here Hand — have photo taken.	2nd Ed Edition Munder & Casualties Below. Stansbury B.
7:30 PM	Got quieter in the afternoon — Report — Gas of shooting eyes and open knee like them — all men trenches whether shed in some time — the wet made fire but making everyone rather smelting in his nur — Precaution ? — but Clothe handy taken — and Trenches are well kept. Fired it necessary 100 to in a very stiff wind. Capt Holzhausen hit in head (slightly) about 6 PM. Capt Murdoch taken in to his car. Walker Baulks with them and helped reserve to Kemmel.	

Army Form C. 2118.

E Thewnt WAR DIARY
April 1915
or
INTELLIGENCE SUMMARY
(Erase heading not required.)

Instructions regarding War Diaries and Intelligence Summaries are contained in F.S. Regs., Part II. and the Staff Manual respectively. Title pages will be prepared in manuscript.

Hour, Date, Place	Summary of Events and Information	Remarks and references to Appendices
KEMMEL. April 23rd	Quiet early morning — at 8.45 AM Col G.2 Lab was heavily bombarded with h/e explosive — and [?] one man killed a good deal of damage is done. The howitzers stand in G.1 and G.6 — Also AM after visiting and his rest of the day &	Pte Stevenson H. C Coy killed 2237 Yproes G.2
"	quite quiet — Major Howard visits G.I.A & H.S. — He is delighted with the line also but not so [?] the line; the [?] restrained the [?] on —	Pte Taylor — Died of wounds 2696. [?] hospital
"	The Eny communication [?] during in G.6 — But it will but not [?] [?] time line, and except in a few cases in effects of last nights atmospheric conditions [?]	
" 6·0 PM	5 pm quietly — but at 6.0 PM a bombardment by a French howitzer opens. [?] [?] against C and H.3 trenches. Col. Parket am Pten Ann and Gray, Allis [?] [?] to F.S Trench — 8 men wounded and 8 [?] here — Capt [?] [?] an [?] to be made but it was but — A machine gun was however turned in the trench and this was [?] under its fire, with great gallantry by Capt Manley, assisted by Mr Hocking, Mr Malone, Sergt Philips, who showed the greatest keenness [?]	

By 2nd Lieut. Trevitt

WAR DIARY
INTELLIGENCE SUMMARY
(Erase heading not required.)

Army Form C. 2118.

Hour, Date, Place	Summary of Events and Information	Remarks and references to Appendices
KEMMEL April 24th 6.0 PM P.30	By P.30 the hamlet was retained and the 2 features which had withdrawn here took Reinforcements from KEMMEL under Capt. Wright but also arrived and the Retirement under Br. Butcher the party rendered the greatest assistance — Altogether here all! Lt. Col. H.A. Alison lived highly and highly & made — Mr. Vann. Since started it out at the hunt men who another took came killing and when 6 men killed Thunderer — Mr. Vann was thrown 5 yards in the air and severely shaken, his position was up from the with a section of Mitchell's Platoon, and his Captain had occupied — Assistance also arrived for his Royal Scots and reinforcements for the Village under Capt. Philipson, as — the hamlet was retained and the dead shoulded fit set — luckily the enemy did not fire in the party who were getting out his losses only in the initial harder of Official mention his name of Sergt. Becher, Lt. Mann & Mellis. LaCpl. Henderson must be recorded but also Mr. Vanne section as well as Artillery behaved Absolutely under very trying circumstances At 12-midnight Relief by 6 Bar Churchill at – Both WULLOT & KEMMEL ??	Killed. B.Co. 1346 Pte W Hunt " 864 " C Renwile " 879 " W Butcher " 2260 " C Philips " 2133 " R East " 1093 " J Bonner D.Co 2434 " H Grant " 2002 " H Husband " 1067 " W Johnson " 76 " W Patten " 2174 L.Sgt W Ashby " 1213 Pte Hicks " 1039 " H Randle " 1849 " E Wethington Number wounded were 2 Officers — 14 rank & file

WAR DIARY

April 1915

Hour, Date, Place		Summary of Events and Information	Remarks and references to Appendices
April 25th KEMMEL		Remained in Billets. KEMMEL till 6.0 AM when Bn marched	
		have by Festina. Full Orders refused time.	
LOCRE	6.0 AM	All in at rest billets - Quiet day	
		Brigadier General spoke to the Batt'n a parade thanking	
		them for the good work done ; largely retaking KEMMEL	
26th "	5.0 P.M.	Go at Bn head qtrs G. to nominate	
		GOC N.MID DIV spoke of the men and	
		Congratulated Bn on good behaviour under fire	
		All ranks stayed in billets	
27th "	10 to 12.30	Go inspects OC - Officers NCOs Runners	Cpt Adams - Ranks Runner
	1-4.	Batters and Special Classes.	Lt Hollies - Three German Raiders
		Trench tactics 125 men	
28th "	10-12.30	Co inspects O.C.	
		There rearranges his amt / Arrange to be taken at 1 Plng GI Sec	"B" C. in reserve in KEMMEL
		At this Battn (V, VI)	(Major Barker)
		Battalions meet - No 62 Propter Hooker	Lut Mitchaway allotted
		OC Capt Hooker Co3 { 63 Rhubarb } G.4 A 1 Peloton S 4 A - 1 Peloton	to B. Co Twenty...
			(Holley)
		S4 1 Peloton	
		A Co G1A - G2A H1 - Capt Hookerscott (Adams)	
		D Co H2 H3 H4 H5 - Under Capt Lane	
		Major Clarke H1 of Bn - Resup Commenced at 9. Finished 11.55	
		Battns tourhpit except for reserved units & oppte Pon Proper-house	

Army Form C. 2118.

2nd Batt'n Royal Irish Fusiliers WAR DIARY
or
INTELLIGENCE SUMMARY.
(Erase heading not required.)

April 1915

Hour, Date, Place	Summary of Events and Information	Remarks and references to Appendices
April 24th KEMMEL	Against many but in afternoon shells a greater noise the by enemy — There is some difficulty in getting in — no intention for which pills is asked without any results — Possibly shells are fired in reply for heart	Pte Brindley "D" Co killed & Francis Flanner wounded (Whelan)
	Re the Enemy. The snake bite of the trenches is very much felt. RF are pipe in retaliation of off own and lower to harass — Pte said to the dish beyond head — he gripped it tightly as he gave in which he tumbles about & is just but it is attempted to ease him. A shot hurt at a time before any step is taken — H.Q A Coy. —	
"30"	A very quick morning and afternoon — On our hunter gets to work at which kind of manner — two Germans who have of grand to hunt, get badly knocked about, & then is killed in B.G. The rear end of MAGELIA is taken — held by B Co and 7th Barr. working parties and Carpenter excellent — true flooring as far as Observation Pan — this is very fine piece of work — well done	Pte Powell RIFle

APPENDIX I.

(Missing)

139th Inf.Bde.
46th Div.

8th BATTN. THE SHERWOOD FORESTERS (NOTTINGHAMSHIRE AND DERBYSHIRE REGIMENT).

M A Y

1 9 1 5

8th The Queens Regt.

WAR DIARY or INTELLIGENCE SUMMARY

(Erase heading not required.)

Army Form C. 2118.

Hour, Date, Place	Summary of Events and Information	Remarks and references to Appendices
May 1st KEMMEL	Gen. shelled in morning - Brown wounded by one burst of shrapnel. A quiet afternoon but at 6.0 pm the enemy fired a couple salvos of trees guns behind "F" trench. Luckily no damage was done but it was a revelation of what artillery they have yet supplied. Some bombing but this was ineffective. Good work done by patrols at night in examining German wire. The importance of more lof. B/kos. knows and a lower parapet explained to O.C. & hectares - also a more aggressive attitude.	
2nd	A quiet day until evening when a snipe cannonade is heard to the North. The Germans are observed in PETIT BOIS working at a probable lof. - also from G3 coming up into the firing line from to far. Fires at but with no result.	22.49 2nd Lt C. Laws died of wounds. G.2. 10.30 Capt E. Parker shot in the trench by sniper.
9.0 pm "	Relieved by 6th Batln. Very slow in taking over but complete until nearly 1.0 a.m. Traces of gas are noticed in KEMMEL during return drifts from NORTH.	

WAR DIARY
INTELLIGENCE SUMMARY.
(Erase heading not required.)

Army Form C. 2118.

1st Cheshire Regt.

Instructions regarding War Diaries and Intelligence Summaries are contained in F.S. Regs., Part II. and the Staff Manual respectively. Title pages will be prepared in manuscript.

Hour, Date, Place	Summary of Events and Information	Remarks and references to Appendices
May 3. LOCRE. Noon	Return to cantilevers & got to get there. Bathing at BAILLEUL under Company arrangements. Bathing equipment elected. Heavy difference rode up from line. Nothing reported to their dolls concerning situation.	
4. " afternoon	Company parades to that dolls concerning situation. At a meeting of Officers the position of fresh approaching action was discussed, but actually was very sanguine.	
5. "	Company parades - instructions in night extensions, changing bayonet fighting. Instructions in use of respirators as issued by Asst Director, Brewlario Dept. Short route marches by Cos.	
6. " 7.30 pm	Parade for march to KEMMEL to relieve 1st Battn.	A woodman shot this month while going to workes. 753 L/cpl Ridgard died from wounds rec'd. 1594 Pte Sean A.V. shot in front of G.4.A. (head)
7. KEMMEL	Relief completed by 12.50 am. Dispositions in our hand. French light thrower over Petit bois on completion of relief. Artillery offices drawing copies were withdrawing to their lines before daylight. A very quiet day. C.R.	

(9 29 6) W 3332-1107 100,000 10/13 H W V   Forms/C. 2118/10

9th Chemin Couture

WAR DIARY
or
INTELLIGENCE SUMMARY.
(Erase heading not required.)

Army Form C. 2118.

Hour, Date, Place	Summary of Events and Information	Remarks and references to Appendices
May 8 ROMER	Quiet day until about 3.30 pm when enemy trench mortar artillery fire on to the trenches of 'B' and 'C' area behind Gn. Pusticelli. No damage was done. Orientation of the enemy's hostility to they will have kept Sea to try knocked out to be useless for a garrison. This bombardment lasted nearly 3 hours. 11.30pm 'C' Co wanted gas on further investigation. Gas was found to come from a dead horse.	
9	Another quiet day. W/ngt Lt/Oate started with a patrol of 6 men & landed who spurs. Wrak now was got to within about 30 yds Germans were too strong, but afternoon officer with two men - the officer was Lt/Ath Lt/Oate & his man [bayonetted] a German. Lw the German was wounded but made off. Lt/Oate then shot also wet a German fatal - one of the German was wounded & also no. 1 man went on. However bombed & also no. 1 man went on however flesh wound was decided it were not to follow.	13.5.9 Lt/Oate Pristly was wounded thro' bursting of ryle grenade

8th Sherwood Foresters

WAR DIARY
or
INTELLIGENCE SUMMARY.
(Erase heading not required.)

Army Form C. 2118.

Hour, Date, Place	Summary of Events and Information	Remarks and references to Appendices

May 10. KEMMEL. Heard early that we were to be relieved by 7th Batt. and with a billets. A quiet day with billey completed by 11.45 pm.

May 11. LOCRE. 1.30am All were in huts and got to be all to best.
Afternoon spent in baths, washing clothing meanwhile.

12 " Early morning run to river & trench stiffness.
Later came a flag rual & new respirators.
Afternoon route marches by companies. Officers meeting to talk hints of interest in last 10 days spell.
Several Canadian reg.ts marches through about 1pm returning from fighting around YPRES and we to.
Many of our men turned out, cheered them and the Brigade Band played them through.

13 " Church Parade (Ascension Day). of course class
for recruits, bomb throwers, machine gunners do

8th Sherwood Foresters

WAR DIARY
or
INTELLIGENCE SUMMARY
(Erase heading not required.)

Army Form C. 2118.

Hour, Date, Place		Summary of Events and Information	Remarks and references to Appendices
May 14. LOCRE		Parade by Coy for ½ hours steady drill. Orders received	
	4.70 a.m.	that we were not to relieve 9th Bn in trenches. Digging parties have been with the new front line. Bivos have proceeded by motor 'bus to the vicinity of Mill to to dig for 5th Divn. The work was not heavy - two days for 13 hrs, remaining 10½ for 3½ hours. The ground bore traces of the very heavy fighting. Troops were conveyed back to LOCRE in the motor 'buses which took them out.	
	5 am	Arrived back in LOCRE. Relieved 7th Bn in trenches - taking over to the front tour T1, T2, T3a, T3 right and J10	
16. KEMMEL	12.50 a.m.	Relief completed. Situation unchanged. A very quiet day and no casualties reported. This was the first day we should free from casualties since we took over our own portion of the line.	CD

8th Cheshire Regiment

WAR DIARY
or
INTELLIGENCE SUMMARY.
(Erase heading not required.)

Army Form C. 2118.

Hour, Date, Place	Summary of Events and Information	Remarks and references to Appendices
May 16 ROMMEL 8pm	Our trench mortar was brought up & used with effect from behind G2. This caused the enemy to put a good deal of shrapnel to which we replied in a similar way.	
10pm	The fire behind G4 was noticed like on fire, probably a result of shelling.	
17 4.41am	Zeppelin was observed travelling E over YPRES. Another great day ensued only by the arrival of headquarters of Brigade Rescue Apparatus. Wrighad intends training the apparatus and in its use. Brigade Staff then themselves from have from promptly ordered to themselves wore have put (a bare average) in their apparatus & made to his horrible appearance alone. A good chance of trying any model.	3am L Vickers hit by Vickers right knee
18	A remarkably quiet night — the air which has been continuous all the evening continued steadily all night. Hardly a shot was fired. Rain later all day. Towards evening when the weather cleared a little our trench mortar was fired with good Battn with good effect. Enemy flooded all the trenches machine-gunned.	Lt. Whirly M.C. and 2nd/Lt.G.L. operation duty never taken strength of battn.

Army Form C. 2118.

8th Sherwood Foresters

WAR DIARY
OR
INTELLIGENCE SUMMARY.
(Erase heading not required.)

Hour, Date, Place	Summary of Events and Information	Remarks and references to Appendices
19. 3.30	took up posn leaving great difficulty. A little desultory shelling by own carried on by Bose. One of our troopers in No 5 spotted killing 9 German who were in 9 tanks carrying turks behind their lines. During great day — our own are so got be trenches cleared of water to a great extent and have them in a fairly good state for 7th Bn. who took over at 12 a.m. During the 4 days we started collecting empty cartridge cases + winding them on with ration parties also as damaged rifles etc. which were found turned in. (late) taken NIEDERDALL BECK 4th Foster is to the front working in certain area. Though right hung the commencing to fire from union near Inchinton 8/cm.	
2.0 LOCRE.	The Bn. returned to billets by 1.0 a.m. — The day was spent in bathing fitting up all were with clothing equipment etc.	

8th Sherwood Foresters

WAR DIARY
or
INTELLIGENCE SUMMARY.
(Erase heading not required.)

Army Form C. 2118.

Hour, Date, Place	Summary of Events and Information	Remarks and references to Appendices
21	Rifles were inspected by Armourer. 1/2 Brigade Armourer lang on MOUNT ROUGE was hindered by to-day's first wad for better sniper practice. All Company watched by C.O. Classes for senior machine gunners & transport personnel etc in afternoon.	
22	Inspection full kits. Owing to the fact that fewer troops are now quartered in local many of the billets has been changed greatly to the men's advantage. Morning spent under Coy officers to steady drill in the afternoon men had a well-earned rest.	
23	Church Service Parade was held at 11am. It is intending to invite the 10 men were a parade who attended the Voluntary Watchable Camp in 1914. Relieved 7th Rn in trenches. Information received that in order to garrison the T Trenches for one Batt. completed at 11.30 pm OC	

8th Sherwood Foresters

WAR DIARY
or
INTELLIGENCE SUMMARY.
(Erase heading not required.)

Army Form C. 2118.

Hour, Date, Place	Summary of Events and Information	Remarks and references to Appendices
May 24. KEMMEL 3am	Soon after dawn the enemy were noticed close in the village but a big rumour reached Pte. & infantry Hd. Qtrs. that his dead all see in the trenches. In the evening troops were again noticed in T.T. & to prevent being sent out their eyes smarted badly. All were in. We were then reinforced from Spur where large was first noticed.	Pte Horrocks W. 2096 Gas dead Handy F. 2268 T. killed Killed by sniper
LOCRE 3am	Batt. paraded at LOCRE and the hostile Table Major threw traces of gas, not enough to cause much eye smart but it made tears of the mouth.	
25. KEMMEL	A very quiet day until Platoon intermittent shrapnel shelling in vicinity of Batn Headquarters. In afternoon a working party was. Thieves from Pl. believed the German lines the means of telescope as we were able	Pte Spademan 2530 Killed instantly by an unused bullet km T3 sight.

CD

WAR DIARY or INTELLIGENCE SUMMARY

Army Form C. 2118.

8 Staffords Winter

(Erase heading not required.)

Hour, Date, Place	Summary of Events and Information	Remarks and references to Appendices
	to Bttn Headqtrs + RC. It is noted that aeroplanes has been used a lot lately and that RE's trench are being dug in. This trench is 300 yds from sniping was going on. the enemies — Bethleem housed "A" Company during the day. our guns cannonaded this place and it is so near our own lines the enemy Sp. was forced to night to the first time — a frienda post urged with marked wire and a road improvement on to OA St. Some farms are being used or the during the afternoon — All situated on the distances Rd — a large farm near Dranoutre Reamed Dranoutre the origin of the firing at N. Bynn	

Forms/C. 2118/19

Army Form C. 2118.

9th Sherwood Foresters

WAR DIARY
or
INTELLIGENCE SUMMARY.
(Erase heading not required.)

Hour, Date, Place		Summary of Events and Information	Remarks and references to Appendices
May 26		Could not be traced, believed held J trenches	
	3 a.m.	Capt Hare wounded when wiring	
		A quiet day, nothing to report beyond sniper fire from behind the J trenches	
27		We continued to hold the J trenches. A quiet day	
	3 p.m.	9th & 9/1 Edge made a very valuable reconnaissance in front of our Gaa. His aim was to find whether it was possible for the enemy to attack our line by creeping up through the vegetation – He brought back much valuable information + went within 50 yds of enemy trenches.	
		Relieved by 7th Mx. Relief was completed by 11.20 p.m.	
		Returned to little athome, all being safely in shortly after 12.30 am. So far no	
28		earliest return from the trenches.	

8th Sherwood Foresters

WAR DIARY
or
INTELLIGENCE SUMMARY

Army Form C. 2118.

Hour, Date, Place	Summary of Events and Information	Remarks and references to Appendices
29	Company inspection - baths - since getting reserves 8th Bn K.R.R.C. arrived in LOCRE being attached to this Bde for instruction. They were to first unit of the new army we had seen. Running drill - Steady company drill - bayonet fighting. Classes for Grenadiers - reserve machine gunners signallers. Officers of K.R.R.C. went about with many of our officers seeking all the information they could obtain.	
30. 19 noon	Joint Church Parade with 8th K.R.R.C. Our host officers (relieved) to their NCOs on bomb throwing.	
31.	Running drill. Company drills. Classes for reserve Machine Gunners etc. Musketry for one Co. on the miniature range. The A.O.C. is wonderful - during the month we have had a plentiful supply of clothing etc + everything demanded has been supplied in a wonderful way.	[signature] Lieut. Colonel Comdg. 8/ Sherwood F.

139th Inf.Bde.
46th Div.

8th BATTN. THE SHERWOOD FORESTERS (NOTTINGHAMSHIRE AND DERBYSHIRE REGIMENT).

J U N E

1 9 1 5

9th Cheshire Regt

Army Form C. 2118.

WAR DIARY
or
INTELLIGENCE SUMMARY.
(Erase heading not required.)

Hour, Date, Place		Summary of Events and Information	Remarks and references to Appendices
June 1	LOCRE	Early morning running and bayonet fighting. Inspection of Coys by C.O. followed by 2 hours musketry — one Coy on range.	
2	do	Early morning running, physical exercises. Two hours steady Company drill. Billet inspection. Evening parade to relieve 7th Bn in trenches.	
3	KEMMEL	Relief completed by 1.30 a.m. Trenches taken over H3, H4, H5, J1, J10 by "B" Coy. J2, J3 & right J3 nose J11 by "C" Coy. J3 left K1, K1a SP12. S6 by "A" Coy. "D" Coy in reserve at Siege Farm. Two companies of 8th K.R.R. attached to the Battn. for instruction. Difficulty experienced by Battn. Transport in reaching KEMMEL as road was blocked by digging parties of Canadians + Generals. During night green lights were seen in front of J3. We put up no lights for a test as artillery signals. At dawn a board appeared opposite J3 with the word "PREMYSYL". This led to a brisk exchange of opinion between to Enemy + our men. S6 shelled in afternoon. MC

Army Form C. 2118.

8th Sherwood Foresters

WAR DIARY
or
INTELLIGENCE SUMMARY.
(Erase heading not required.)

Instructions regarding War Diaries and Intelligence Summaries are contained in F.S. Regs., Part II. and the Staff Manual respectively. Title pages will be prepared in manuscript.

Hour, Date, Place	Summary of Events and Information	Remarks and references to Appendices
June 4 KEMMEL	German artillery active KEMMEL SHELLED Col Jessop killed + others wounded in the village. About 4.30 shell dropped in garden of dressing station. Several shots also at S.B. but the aim was not good. During the night the Boche tried his luck with rifle grenades but his arrangement for discharging them was not very successful. The German put up a flag about 80 yds from #3 trench were [sic] caves not got. It in	2nd Oates g.s.w. shoulder outside dug-out #3
June 5 do	Batn HQ moved to Rossignol farm — not so luxurious. During night #4 had been heavily shelled. At 11 p.m. 3 a.m. and 7 a.m. In throwing Gee went round the trenches. About mid-day half a dozen shells dropped near the Lauspert line near here and fortunately ended in inspection of horses by A.D.V.S.	Pte Wells killed. V2 shell shaving 2 K.R.Rs wound
June 6 do	During night much signalling observed from Spanbroek. Early intimation received that we were not to be shelled during relief or an [word] A quiet day until a shell from a battery of guns unknown went to ground	Capt H.G. Wright killed V3. Pte T. Munsen killed.

8th Sherwood Foresters

WAR DIARY
or
INTELLIGENCE SUMMARY.
(Erase heading not required.)

Army Form C. 2118.

Hour, Date, Place	Summary of Events and Information	Remarks and references to Appendices
June 7. KEMMEL	Within 10 y'ds of the C.O's bivouac at Headquarters. A quiet day. Several men were hit when on the way out of the trenches on the road near Ridgewood as there was particularly heavy fire on our right and a large number of spent bullets ricochet shots were flying about. Officer Patrol also from K.i.A.	
June 8. LOCRE	Relief not completed until 2 a.m. Men returned to billets and except for inspection of rifles by Coy. Armourers and inspection tracing of boots & clothing. Orders received from Bde that there on the trenches nothing in the nature of a parade to take place between 10 a.m and 4 p.m owing to the excessively hot weather. 5.30 a.m fire to sick parade. 6-8 Coy parades. 9.15 Church parade. In the evening classes of Bomb throwers Signallers etc held. Bomb instruction given to K.S.L.I. officers.	

8/5/6) W 3332–1107 100,000 10/15 H W V Forms/C. 2118/10

8th Sherwood Foresters.

WAR DIARY
or
INTELLIGENCE SUMMARY.
(Erase heading not required.)

Army Form C. 2118.

Hour, Date, Place	Summary of Events and Information	Remarks and references to Appendices
June 10. LOCRE	Working parties supplied in shifts all day for the new S.P. Remainder Platoon shows drill 6-8 and C.O.'s inspection 9.0 am.	20 reinforcements arrived from England.
June 11. LOCRE	A complete holiday except for Sick Parade & orderly Room. Parade in evening by Coy. (to relieve 7th Battn.) Leave trenches as before.	
June 12. KEMMEL	Relief completed by 12.40. SIEGE FARM. 3 men were wounded and one killed just after taking over. Enemy very active with rifle grenades but little damage done. The new gunners heavily bombarded the white Château and made a good display. Two men of the Hussars were drawn from T3 batteries (no more information came) dressed in khaki. In obtained about them.	2334 Pte F. Pring Killed.
June 13. KEMMEL	A quiet day followed a very quiet night. S.b. shelled towards evening. One man only being wounded.	Afternoon came in attack. Capt Ashwells took over temporary command of 401 Coy.

Army Form C. 2118.

8th Devonshires

WAR DIARY
or
INTELLIGENCE SUMMARY.
(Erase heading not required.)

Hour, Date, Place	Summary of Events and Information	Remarks and references to Appendices
June 13 KEMMEL	A quiet uneventful day with nothing of importance to report	2/Lt J. Wilson killed в wig.
June 14 do.		
June 15 do.	Another quiet day until 9 pm just before relief due to commence. At 9 trenches heavily shelled by minnies + trench mortars + trench mortars. Same warning + harsh mortar. The enemy got into the crater and were driven out at point of bayonet by "C" Coy. Shrapnel burst over SIEGE FARM (Reserve Coys billet) + Batt. dump. Wires were all broken + there was no communication between HQ + remainder of trenches. The rifle fire was extraordinary for about 20 mins. heavy rifle became res lost + relieve. The 5th Batn (W Ride Reserve) were called up to KEMMEL and 7th stood by before relieving. About 11 pm relief started + was carried out as usual. Confirmation quiet the night becoming Confirmation quiet	KILLED. Lt A. J. O Dobson with M.G. 3/c W. H. Watkins with burying party. 167 Cpl J. West 2585 Pte S. Armitage — 2422 Pte B. Cott 2533 Pte P. May 932 — R. W. Morton 2460 — L. Richardson 2400 J. Kill Missing 199 Pte C. Bryan 950 A. Cork. 1/2 K.O.Y.L.I. attached to us several casualties

8th Sherwood Foresters

WAR DIARY
or
INTELLIGENCE SUMMARY.

(Erase heading not required.)

Army Form C. 2118.

Hour, Date, Place	Summary of Events and Information	Remarks and references to Appendices
June 16. LOCRE.	Reach billets which all reached by 3.30 a.m. C.O. inspected Companies in afternoon.	
June 17. do	Running drill before breakfast. Coy parades for 2 hours and inspection of rifles by Bttn armourer.	
June 18. do	Working parties by day on new S.B. Brigadier inspected Battn + also Regt Transport in evening.	
June 19. do	Company roll call. All employed men present and part took its checked. 4.O Battn Route march about 6 miles. The first full marching order about 6 miles. The first march for many weeks and quite well done. Church parade held in morning.	
June 20. do	C.O. inspected all billets companies. Operation orders received from Brigade. Battn. vacated billets by 4pm and bivouaced until 9 pm when the Brigade marched to huts on the YPRES-OUDERDOM road arriving about midnight. Square H.14.c.	

8th Sherwood Foresters
WAR DIARY
or
INTELLIGENCE SUMMARY.
(Erase heading not required.)

Army Form C. 2118.

Hour, Date, Place	Summary of Events and Information	Remarks and references to Appendices
June 21.	Battn rested in huts. No orders received about proceeding to trenches. About 2 pm Germans shelled huts. Head - Apparently 6" minenwerfer. Direct hit forced to move back. No casualties. Sand deep narrow trenches all round the huts afforded excellent protection. C.O. & officers visited trenches in morning. Battn received orders to proceed to trenches following night. No shell.	
June 22.	Shelling again about 4 pm. No casualties except driver of motor ambulance in road hit by splinter.	
June 23. 7.30 PM	Marched to KRUISSTRAAT where guides were picked up and marched to ZILLE BEKE to SANCTUARY WOOD and relieve 5 Batt° Yorks Regt. - no casualties marching to Distribution. A Co: Trenches 7 and 8 . B. Co. 9. 10. 11 ... C. Co. 12. D in Reserve. Trenches in fair condition — narrow and deep.	

MC

6th Monmouth Regt
WAR DIARY
or
INTELLIGENCE SUMMARY.

Army Form C. 2118.

Hour, Date, Place	Summary of Events and Information	Remarks and references to Appendices
June 24th YPRES	Everything quiet during night. Artillery came under his own artillery fire no casualties. Headquarters kept up in the wood. Quiet day comparatively in trenches. Relieved under difficulties. Enemy artillery constantly bombarded the trenches on our left between 1½ and 3 A.M. and were active sniping against the dugouts – but heavy quiets today. Aferquiet day and the chance given to get into main trenches and Captain Heathcote went on leave.	
" 25th		
" 26th	Trenches 7 & 8 are heavily shelled and M.Gy all day and in the afternoon they turn in to Sanctuary wood and kill 5 of the Y Batt. with one shot – the rest of us a pleasant place to be in – shells we constant for hours.	
" 27.	Very heavy trench mortar fire later trenches and his own artillery opened at 5.30 am but cannot say quite what much. Two hundred rifles fire from enemy and 3 M.Gun. Three men were killed in 8th trench. Shelling starts in afternoon and we expect an attack in his evening but it then does not come on.	Casualties 2003 LCpl T. Chinn 1579 Pte T. Edwards 1095 " Cpl Alston

WAR DIARY or INTELLIGENCE SUMMARY

5th Mount [Rifles?]

Hour, Date, Place	Summary of Events and Information	Remarks and references to Appendices
June 28th YPRES (Salient)	A quiet night but some rifle fire on our right. Enemy seem to be working hard opposite our trenches. Working party of the 7th Batt. commence to trench but communication trenches, where a lot is needed.	
" 29 "	A quiet day — but our guns open fire at 11.30 and further we heard result. No heavy effective reply. Things quieter after that & it is thought that Enemy observed to be resting camp timber in our left pastures to a mine/wire & mechanical defence. The 5th Inniss. Engineers continued — attack on enemy slowly and we did not get away till after midnight. Our [lorries] came not independently and concentrated 2 mile SW of VLAMERTINGHE, where coffee were [offered?] then another [trudge?] to our next bivouac, a charming camp — where we have a welcome rest. The new draft of 9th [men] — [Officers?] into 11 rejoined me. Then are without Officers but a L/Sgt — not a very good looking [lot?]	2" heavy [Howitzers?] [struck?] 1st Battr. Maher gone [leave?] M. Pringle Lt.

139th Inf.Bde.
46th Div.

8th BATTN. THE SHERWOOD FORESTERS (NOTTINGHAMSHIRE AND DERBYSHIRE REGIMENT).

J U L Y

1 9 1 5

Attached:

Report on Operations 30th/31st July.

6th Howard Faulton

WAR DIARY
or
INTELLIGENCE SUMMARY.
(Erase heading not required.)

Army Form C. 2118.

Hour, Date, Place	Summary of Events and Information	Remarks and references to Appendices
July 1st Sapone H.Q.B.	A welcome rest day – Companies filled out their own with deficiencies – Clothing ration sheets. Camp inspected by C.O. in afternoon.	
" 2nd	7–7.30	Trip Rivers Cuthbert returns from leave; Capt Ashmore Coll Collin [?] took Vann Litt [?] go on leave	
	9.30–12	New draft – man recruits [?] has posted to Companies	
		Running – Draft Indian [?] Company	
	2.30–4	Company Drill	
" 3rd		Draft only Sh. G.O.C. inspected Camp which was [?] posted. Pioneers – Sanitary [?] [?] re-organised.	
	6.30–7	Physical training – Kreacant [?] in the stores department.	
	9–11.30	Route march & Mind [?] chicken and fresh heads.	
		In future – Inclement weather weekly informed upon	
		by C.O. Hitchcock.	
" 4th		Very quiet wet day – Im myk [?] done; inoculated	
		Running – Maj–Gen Clarke [?] made leave	
" 5th	6–6.30	C.O. Nicoll: held senior inspection hand,	
	9–10.30	Billets again: both & trade found at defeat	

Folio 2.

Army Form C. 2118.

2nd Mount Field
WAR DIARY
or
INTELLIGENCE SUMMARY.
(Erase heading not required.)

July 1915

Hour, Date, Place		Summary of Events and Information	Remarks and references to Appendices
July 6th H.Q.D.	6-6.30	Physical training	
	8-12	Route march to ABEELE. Guerlest, Intragne nie —	
"7" "	6.6.30	Felint. Zeppelin reported. Wires cut to Hd.qrs. of the Batt. — Concert in evening given by the Batt.	
	8-10.30	Running — Bomb throwers classes begin	
		Company Drill — Battn formations — Estimen went up for Musketry	
		Capt Collin Ashwell admn from Base	
"8" "	6-3°	Capt Ashwell goes to St OMER to take on the Reinforcements who have have been there for training	
	7-6.31	Physical Training	
	8-11.30	Route march. Bgnt Thomson discoursing on Musketry Ranges	
	11-5	Rifts march to Hd. the CATS. — Rifts that are for going that training together — Butt to have trade	
"9" "	6-6.30	Running — trenches from KM2 the CATS Range	
	8-10.30	Co. Drill — Battn formations — between for Assault "Attack"	
	4-5	Batt. Bomt. Thrower at work	

Forms/C. 2118/10

WAR DIARY or INTELLIGENCE SUMMARY

2nd Mounted Brigade

July 1915

Army Form C. 2118.

Hour, Date, Place	Summary of Events and Information	Remarks and references to Appendices
July 10. 6–6.30	Physical Training	
7–10.30	Company Drill. Capt M.R.L.G. Yhaym Rechi Co. Visits are tactics the Lieut-tna General Cricket match between Officers and NCOs won by Officers Capt Dimenhal returned from CHQ	
July 11. 6.	Camp cleaned up. Entrances filled down. Material saved by R.M.	
2.	Marched off to Jerusalem. A halfmade before ALRUWEITRAT for tea. Men's feet cannot stand Transport	
4.50	Relief completed with no fight casualty. No sports of sniping received to German trenches were very close. It appears admissible to begin. Considerable number to trench mortars rifle grenades used by enemy between whops.	2nd Lt A R Robinson killed
July 12.	And 5 am. No damage done. The enemy very accurate during the day carrying heavy trench mortars Pdr. Sawing	CJ

9th Sherwood Foresters

WAR DIARY
or
INTELLIGENCE SUMMARY.
(Erase heading not required.)

Army Form C. 2118.

Hour, Date, Place	Summary of Events and Information	Remarks and references to Appendices
July 13	was also hard and ripe was asked to sanction a protective arrangement in Bn. Commanders request. Front line Bn trench struck troops wanted. Remainder B & making parapet bullet proof. Reserve Coy – straightened her trenches were wiring done in Bn 137 a new loophole built in C parapet. A patrol went out & seen if the enemy had a listening post advanced trench but although they found that a small leaf of firing was done here how they took they could not ascertain whether it was intended as a post.	X
11.30.	Three fresh earth Mounds were seen early am ¾ between listening post trenches have been heard. Considerable amount of wiring done in Bn & Bg. Bays were trenches were started. Coys in teams of 13 n. 13.7. B.8. A good deal of grenade work by both sides during the 24 hrs. The enemy did little damage to us. A patrol reported nothing on enemy's parapet in fronts 187. CP.	

9th Sherwood Foresters

WAR DIARY
or
INTELLIGENCE SUMMARY.
(Erase heading not required.)

Hour, Date, Place	Summary of Events and Information	Remarks and references to Appendices
July 14.	Enemy abnormally quiet all day. A few rifle grenades were sent over at us but practically no damage was done. A considerable amount of work was done improving both the trenches & the supporting dugouts. Enemy aeroplane was actively busy in making a plan of Stirling Castle afterwards with good results. Our trenches were very active.	
July 15.	A quiet night and so during the day. Our OP in Bn. Sap on well-butting heard something an enemy sap. A considerable amount of wiring done. Enemy round northward getting uneasy because of our trenches. Towards evening enemy became more offensive & many HE shells fell between SOUVE and SANCTUARY WOOD. Our artillery replied freely but many of them shells were blind. Patrols reported enemy quiet except to not in their trenches. Towards stand-to enemy fired many afternoon heavy but – some fell in support trench & half CP.	
July 16.		

WAR DIARY
or
INTELLIGENCE SUMMARY.

(Erase heading not required.)

Army Form C. 2118.

Hour, Date, Place	Summary of Events and Information	Remarks and references to Appendices
July 17.	Augt men were numbered & looking wet day — trenches very bad. A serious amount of repairing done to parapets B7 and B8. Situation remains unchanged and but little used rifle grenades fired. Marked advantage in enemy notices us SHELLING CASTLE. Looks like a gun position. No artillery action. Our wire netting on the parapet saved grenades to burst in the air instead of in the bottom of the trench then not jarred a surface. It was noticed early that no work was being done to STIRLING CASTLE. Enemy were aggressive with more rifle fire in our front. We think he was men to rifle grenades and suffered some casualties from German reports. We state that the trenches became very badly made on think & minute great number of bombs had needed. Communication trenches badly used starring they will be practically useless. CP/	4/2 Pte G. Tinker Killed 983 Cpl P. Lockey accidently killed in dug-out.

9th Sherwood Foresters

WAR DIARY
or
INTELLIGENCE SUMMARY.

Army Form C. 2118.

(Erase heading not required.)

Hour, Date, Place	Summary of Events and Information	Remarks and references to Appendices
July 18.	Very little went done - everybody busy taking. Considerable activity on both sides with rifle grenades during the night. Our wave patrols had nothing to report. No change in situation at dawn. No artillery action on our front.	636 Cpl J. Denshop. Killed
July 19.	More activity again towards evening - continuous rifle fire during the night and machine gun fire on our flanks. Enemy again used many grenades, but no artillery fire on our sector. We harassed enemy snipers and rifles. A considerable amount of work done during the day. 2 Rifles fires in every trench on definite objects and fired according to a time table afterwards. A comparatively quiet day followed by trouble at night. We lost 80 bombs of all sorts to 9th Bde as their supply failed (their wagon of bombs blown up on way to dump)	Now B.3 taken over from 7th Bn S.F. CB/

Army Form C. 2118.

9th Stafford Kieghts

WAR DIARY
or
INTELLIGENCE SUMMARY.
(Erase heading not required.)

Hour, Date, Place	Summary of Events and Information	Remarks and references to Appendices
July 20.	The Midleans Regt reported unable to hold the trench they had taken owing to shortage of bombs. It was suggested to us that a store of bombs should be kept midway between H.2 and trenches occupied on trenches enemy were fairly quiet. A Rifle grenade was early in the morning. A considerable amount of sniping + firing from fixed rifles done by us. On left in B7 + was finished but nothing done in B7. This was originally intended to be merely a defensive mine but the plan was changed the matter taken out of our hands by V Corps & orders had been heard Westfront mining for 2 days but lots of wires without which he made no arrival as this happens before 72 mine was known of. Considerable amount of digging and draining work was done. At night there was a trifle bombardment	2557 Pte G. Richardson Killed

9th Sherwood Foresters

WAR DIARY
or
INTELLIGENCE SUMMARY.
(Erase heading not required.)

Army Form C. 2118.

Hour, Date, Place	Summary of Events and Information	Remarks and references to Appendices
July 21	In trenches near HOOGE. No damage was done to our trenches by fire.	
	A comparatively quiet day after last night's bombardment. A great many wire balls made by day and put out at night to form 3 rounds from 3.7" trench mortar + one got home - the other failed to explode. The enemy were busy repairing damage.	1973 Pte C Taylor Killed.
July 22	Quiet night - enemy's artillery doing very little. No more rounds of 4" heavy anything were heard in B3, but very suspicious sounds in B2 caused Capt Heathcote to withdraw men with outpost trench Boyce near right.	2703. Pte J Horsehill killed.
1700 Pte G Hilton died from wounds in No 10 C.C.S. Gun. abdomen.
	Heavy enemy fire in SANCTUARY WOOD during the day. Apparently stores have been left in the dump by another B.O.C. + these and OP been noticed by enemy aeroplanes.	

(9 29 6) W 4141—463 100,000 9/14 HWV Forms/C. 2118/10

Army Form C. 2118.

2/7 Sherwood Foresters

WAR DIARY
or
INTELLIGENCE SUMMARY.
(Erase heading not required.)

Hour, Date, Place	Summary of Events and Information	Remarks and references to Appendices
July 23.	A test communication with 139th Battery by O.P. B3 proved satisfactory. Communication cd. not be established through F.O.O. whose whereabouts were not known. Message finally got through F.O.O 109th Batt; and the last shell was fired 4 minutes after asked for. A comparatively quiet day. Trenches continue improvement. Relieved by 7th Bn.	
July 24.	The Bn. went into bivouac near OUDERDOM, last company arrived about 7.30 a.m. Everybody moved by shelling - 7 or 8 fell in the field where the bivouacs were situated. About 20 minutes later another salvo + then one or two every ten minutes or so for an hour + a half. Very good hunting CR. for pcs of enemy. No casualties. No ill.	
1.15 pm		

Army Form C. 2118.

Strength Returns

WAR DIARY
or
INTELLIGENCE SUMMARY.
(Erase heading not required.)

Hour, Date, Place	Summary of Events and Information	Remarks and references to Appendices
July 25.	had been known here before. Later Mr Drummond inspected rifles of party sent out to his brother. files to Bwana.	
July 26.	He took over a half from III Bon. men BUSSEROMA 2474 Pte J Watson in evening voluntary services were held. did himself accidentally injured. No 10 C.C.S.	
July 27.	Our parties engaged on trail fatigue. One were at disposal of Supply Officers for filling, scrubbing etc. Two parties were again required for bat fatigue in all 45 Officers and 296 men. Remainder used RWF baths at POPERINGHE.	
July 28.	7.7.5 a.m. Physical drill. Inspection by C.O. of each company ; Inshren PR. Specialino Transport. also Camp.	CO

WAR DIARY or INTELLIGENCE SUMMARY

Army Form C. 2118.

Hour, Date, Place	Summary of Events and Information	Remarks and references to Appendices
July 29. 2 pm	Camp struck stores loaded in	
	Parade to Kruisstraat Huts in B3, B4, B7, B8	
11.25	Relief complete without casualties.	
July 30. 3.30am	Enemy commenced heavy bombardment on HOOGE. Grenade	2664 Pte Coy A. Ruskin
	Welby reported went on fire in front [?]then subsequent	1616 [Ruskin]
	attack by by a party of Germans. Prio was a heartrending	1717 Hope C
	but they left in strewn dead & wounded	2737 Dorman R
	Enquiring position from Lt [?] 7 K.R.R. Bn	2756 Morris S
	stated that enemy had attacked with liquid fire	1859 Haskell R
	that his Brigade had lost to trenches 63,69,64 and	2507 [?]
	he could not say whether his Battn was in touch	5442 Parker F
	with the Battn on left or support line or not.	2628 Ennis C
	Reported situation to Brigade who stated that we	1421 [?] J.S.
	were to hold the line at all costs and that	2256 [?]
	[?] we feared the enemy came through 20 on NO	2599 Jackson H
	Note. He wanted counter attack with his reserve	973 Waters R
		1519 Rayner [?]
		2186 Walstar L
		all killed in early hours [?] morning

WAR DIARY or INTELLIGENCE SUMMARY

Army Form C. 2118

(Erase heading not required.)

Place	Date	Hour	Summary of Events and Information	Remarks and references to Appendices
		2 pm	MC BG took steps to strengthen the flank of his trench in case our line was evacuated by troops on our left. Bombard. went of the trenches taken by enemy.	
		8.15	Counter attack - failed. Attack owing to exhaustion of men - (the bbs on our left) orders S.F. were subsequently issued at refusal of 10th Bn. on our urgent representation to line serving from B.O STOAHE WOOD on an urgent representation. The BDe Commander to sacrifice allowed them to dig themselves in in order to protect our flanks	
	31st	2.30	Very heavy bombardment by both sides on our left though no infantry attack started. Bombing Pats. kennery again attacked B & tus. were driven in. only bombs and rifle fire. Remainder of day quiet except for cemetery shelling. 41st BDe on our left relieved by 43rd BDe during night. Heavy shelling of ZOUAVE WOOD	14.29 Cpl S Kurluter 97 Cpl J Welch 2130 Cp(?) R/ Hutson were killed

C. Crawsford Capt
O.S.T

REPORT ON OPERATIONS 30TH/31ST JULY.

Major Becher's report

I have the honour to report:

30.7.15 At about 3.30 a.m a heavy bombardment by the enemy of the trenches on our left started and almost simultaneously it was reported to me by the O.C. B4 that the wood in front of his trench was on fire.

From subsequent enquiries it appears that what took place in front of my part of the line was as follows:

B4 & B7 trenches

Flames suddenly sprang up about 10 yards in front of the left of B4 trench which after a minute or two turned into dense black smoke. Almost immediately the fire started parties of the enemy were observed coming round the flanks of the fire. The estimates being 20 or 30 on the left and 40 or 50 on the right. They advanced towards the right 3 bays of B7 and the left 6 bays of B4 and this part of the line was heavily bombed. As soon as observed rapid fire was opened from B7 and the machine gun behind B4 which however was put out of action after firing 100 rounds by one of the enemy trench mortars.

On the fire it appears that the men in the left 6 bays of B4 retired to B7 support trench which was where they had been ordered to rally in case of emergency but

2

four men Ptes Grantham, Finn, Blake & Morris remained at their posts and Sergt Foster arrived at the right end of the face attacked from B7 support where he was stationed and threw some 30 bombs which were met with the enemy bombs falling at & round and I think did a good deal to check the enemy at this spot.

Pte Grantham behaved with very great coolness and presence of mind remaining himself in the trench while he sent Pte Finn for assistance. Pte Grantham killed one of the German officers leading the attacking party on the parapet and probably others.

Meanwhile 2nd Lt Hindley ~~finding that the~~ who was in command of the platoon occupying the right of B7 having discovered that the ~~Coy~~ left of B4 was empty sent a bombing party under the command of Sergt Shepherd to regain touch with the Company on the right. This he did notwithstanding that his own trench was at the time being heavily bombed and he deprived himself of his men of supts.

Sergt Shepherd's bombing party proceeded from bay to bay and discovered 3 Germans in the 3rd bay they entered. These quickly fled for their own trench but did not reach it. They left behind a rifle, cap, and bundle of sandbags which makes me believe they intended to occupy the trench. Sergt Shepherd ordered

3

his party to man the empty bays as he went along leaving one man in each of the six bays until he got in touch with the next Company. 2nd Lt Hindley had meanwhile sent to Lt Thorne who was commanding B7 trench for reinforcement and 21 men were sent at once. Sergt Smith had also rich engagement with the M.G. in B7 ordered to fire on the parapet of B7 which they did in short bursts until things had quieted down. ~~I sent the~~ He then superintended the redistribution of the men to cover the left of B4.

I consider the promptitude and ability with which these ~~measures~~ measures were taken ~~largely contributed~~ prevented the enemy getting any real footing in the trench.

Sergt Shepherd and Private Tyne continued to reply to the enemy bombs and finding that the double cylinder bombs they were throwing did not explode properly they threw back 3 of the enemy own bombs all of which they made explode.

Very few of the enemy seem to have got up to our parapet but they left several dead bodies about 15 yards away. When they withdrew they opened fire with a machine gun but a bomb thrown by either Sergt Dodd or 2nd Lt A Hackey who had come up afterwards put it out of action. This bomb set fire to something in the enemy trench

4

and is a flame spring up followed by thick clouds of smoke, and two or three of the enemy were seen to spring on their fascines and collapse. This was observed not only by Mr. Hacking but also by Serjt Smith of B7.

Two further attempts to attack were made by the enemy during the course of the day but on both occasions the enemy was prevented by our fire from getting more than a yard or two from their own parapet.

B 8.

From this trench flames were thrown both opposite B4 and on the left up on the Hooge ridge, and the enemy opened heavy rifle and machine gun fire on this trench, bombs bursting dropped both behind & on it. Very soon wounded from the battalion on the left began to pour through the trench, also men asking for ammunition, bombs, & reinforcements as the trenches on the left had been lost. Lt Jarvis immediately sent them all the ammunition and bombs he could spare, telephoning to H.2. for a further supply. Lt Webster one of his men was killed at G. when helping to carry ammunition. He also telephoned to the O.C. B7 for reinforcements and to H. Q. and he was sent from B7 a platoon of the 16ᵗʰ L.F. and from H.Q. a platoon on the for the Rennes.

5

Having regard to the effect of the loss of the trenches on the Hill on his left flank 2nd Lt. James commanding B Coy

Lt. James at once redistributed his men manning the between and any other breastworks facing N trenches constructing fresh ones and taking all steps to meet a possible attack from his left and left rear. Throughout the day a constant stream of more or less disorganised troops were forcing into their trench from the left and I am informed from all sides that these officers assisted by Capt. Phillipson who commanded the Platoon occupying the left of B8 dealt with the situation with very great coolness and ability.

General

As soon as I had ascertained that my front was all right and could hold its own I went to see the O.C. the Battalion on my left to ascertain the exact position. He informed me that the enemy had attacked with liquid fire and that we had lost the trenches from C3 to C10 but he believed he still held C1 and part of C2 but was not sure.

At 2 p.m. our artillery commenced a heavy bombardment of the trenches taken by the enemy and at 2.45 the Brigade on our left launched its counter attack.

6

At about 3.15 p.m. I was informed by the O.C. B8 that he had been told by the O.C. the 7 K.R.R. that the counter attack had completely failed and that the situation was rather worse than before.
On this I at once saw the Col. of the S.K.R.R. with senior officer of the two Battalions on my left and pointed out to him the position in which my battalion was left unless some steps were taken to connect B8 with Zouave Wood which through again without promising to put before his General.
On instructions from Gen. Shipley I subsequently saw the O.C. the 4th Brigade at his H.Q. and put the position before him when he eventually agreed that the 7th S.F. who had been placed at his disposal should not only occupy the edge of the wood but dig themselves in.

31st July.

At about 2.30 a.m. a heavy bombardment by both sides of the left commenced and at the same time a party of the enemy left their trench opposite B4 but were driven back by our M.G. and rifle fire. The enemy also heavily bombed the left of B4 and right of B7 to which Sergt Shepherd and Pte Tyn replied.

7

The casualties of the Battalion during these two days amounted to 20 killed and 51 wounded and in addition the Company of the 16th S.F. who were attached for instruction had 10 wounded.

I should like to put on record my appreciation of the behaviour of the Company, the men of whom were under fire for the first time and the assistance which was rendered by Capt Goodale who was in command of the Company and his officers.

I should like to draw special attention to the work performed during these two days by the following:

B. Coy. Lt. J.L. Turner
2nd Lt. Hindley
Serjt. Smith
L.Serjt. Shepherd
Cpl. Cox
Pte. Tyne

C. Coy. { Serjt. Porter
{ Pte. Grantham

D. Coy. Lt. James
2nd Lt. Vann
Serjt. A. Phillips (since killed)

8.

At midnight on the 31st the Batt[n] took over from the 7th Batt[n] the position of G1 which was still held.

Aug 1st & 2nd Nothing of special importance occurred on these days.

Col. Fowler returned to duty on the night of the 2nd.

139th Inf.Bde.
46th Div.

8th BATTN. THE SHERWOOD FORESTERS (NOTTINGHAMSHIRE AND DERBYSHIRE REGIMENT).

A U G U S T

1 9 1 5

Attached:

Report on Operations
2nd/12th August.

Army Form C. 2118

8th Yorkshire Regiment

WAR DIARY
or
INTELLIGENCE SUMMARY

(Erase heading not required.)

Instructions regarding War Diaries and Intelligence Summaries are contained in F.S. Regs., Part II. and the Staff Manual respectively. Title Pages will be prepared in manuscript.

Place	Date	Hour	Summary of Events and Information	Remarks and references to Appendices
	1/9/15		A comparatively quiet day after two very heavy days. We were able to continue forward the Sap in B3 and to a considerable amount of repairing but the work suffered considerably from the shortage of men. Three heavy trench mortars were fired at C1 and the Sap but did not damage the trench although we caused several casualties. About the same time the enemy bombed B4 but all the bombs fell short. At midnight Nos 12171 and 2396 Pte Nicholson went out about 100 yds alongside 91 and 92 and were then forced to retire owing to our own artillery fire.	741 Pte Stephenson killed
	2/9/15	4 am	Between 4 and 6 am several H.S. shrapnel were fired from the direction of GE. One shell burst close to the parados and caused several casualties. Difficulty was experienced during the day as regards work owing to the fact that when our heavy artillery were firing on the enemy's trenches there was so much danger of flowbacks. During the early hours a man was killed by a piece of one of our own shells which burst near the enemy's lines. B3 was continued forward and the parapet in B4 considerably repaired.	
		10.5	Heavy artillery bombardment on our left which however did not affect us at all.	

8th Sherwood Foresters.

WAR DIARY
or
INTELLIGENCE SUMMARY
(Erase heading not required.)

Army Form C. 2118

Place	Date	Hour	Summary of Events and Information	Remarks and references to Appendices
	3/8/15		A good deal of wiring was done during the night in front of B4 and a number of wire balls were thrown out in front of B3. A quiet day, no great activity of the enemy noted except that they were carrying straw and timber along trench opposite night of B3. Fresh earth and sandbags also observed. The About 8p.m. our trench mortar fired 5 shells to registering on the redoubt opposite B8 and obtained good results. The enemy sent two large mortars into B8 half an hour later. No firing was reported. A patrol consisting of 2/Lt Oldham + 2 men went out along G2 to the junction of G1 and back along G1. Barricade but no signs of enemy's movements or occupation were observed.	
	4/8/15		About 2.45 a.m. a light artillery duel commenced. The enemy chiefly shelled ZOUAVE WOOD. This duel died down about 3.30. During the night the Company of 10th Sherwood Foresters who has been attached for instruction was withdrawn. The garrison of our trenches much depleted. The 7th Sherwoods helped to man B8 but B3, B4 and B7 were not adequately manned. A certain amount of work in draining and deepening was carried out. No report of the enemy's use of bombs or rifle grenades. Reports had been given that spy's digging has been observed by sentries in a communication trench in front of B4 + that a tracking and + pt (??) had went out from our night listening post to explore the trench which leaves our line at this point. This patrol was able to explore a trench	2318 Pte 7? Fox killed

Army Form C. 2118

8th Sherwood Foresters

WAR DIARY
or
INTELLIGENCE SUMMARY
(Erase heading not required.)

Instructions regarding War Diaries and Intelligence Summaries are contained in F.S. Regs., Part II. and the Staff Manual respectively. Title Pages will be prepared in manuscript.

Place	Date	Hour	Summary of Events and Information	Remarks and references to Appendices
	5/8/15		running at right angles and which showed signs of recent work. It was at once decided to treat as open sap from the bay nearest to the trench between R&R. The Major, where signs of work were most serious, in order to keep this work under close observation and if necessary to break men working in it. 2/Lieut Wilson and two men went out at midnight along G.2 and reported that men could be seen down this trench. Bombers were collected at the barrier in Chee ? attack and although Battery were asked to fire no reply came. No reply. This battery also failed to fire on redoubt opposite B.8 to B.9 notwithstanding requests to do so. Towards morning were heard in No 2 Sap B.3 and a howitzer shaft was commenced by the Brigade Miners. A considerable amount of work done especially in B.8 where a new barrier his trench was made. Completed. Overhead traverses were built in the last bay. The Machine Gun Section started work on 2 more gun emplacements. During the day the enemy's aeroplanes were very active and SANCTUARY WOOD, TOURVE WOOD and MAPLE COPSE were all frequently shrapnelled. Towards evening we had a number of rifle grenades in reply to enemy's Grenat M attack. L/Sergt went out from right 7/3 & brought written report. C/Sergt the Widdowson went out recovered a dead German rifle which was forwarded to Bde HQ. A listening patrol found a look which was forwarded to G.1 and G.2 but nothing to report C.D.	3000 P.o. C. Champion Killed

1875 Wt. W593/826 1,000,000 4/15 J.B.C. & A. A.D.S.S./Forms/C. 2118.

8th Sherwood Foresters

WAR DIARY
or
INTELLIGENCE SUMMARY
(Erase heading not required.)

Army Form C. 2118

Place	Date	Hour	Summary of Events and Information	Remarks and references to Appendices
	19/9/15		Our trenches were held by 6.00 12th Bde + 6.8. 2nd Sherwood Foresters A good deal of work in erection of head cover for protection against splinters has been done. The Sap in B4 was carried forward towards the unoccupied new enemy trench. The 2nd Sherwood Frs took over garrison of B8 beyond the barrios and also B.11. At 6 attacking again went out in front of By one up the old German catwin trench on which we had previously worked. About 30 yds up it he found 2 sandbag barricade about 15 yds in front of the advanced All was quiet. He then went out on patrol with a patrol of the 2nd S.F. The enemy infantry were quiet except for sniping during the 24 hours but at 6.15 pm a heavy bombardment of ZOUAVE WOOD took place. Lasted about 7 minutes.	2nd Lt P'te R. Moore wtd —1759 P'te a Scott wd'd
	20/9/15	2.30pm	A heavy bombardment by the enemy on ZOUAVE and SANCTUARY WOODS.	
			About 2.55 one 8 in gun fired between 3.15 and 3.30 a.m. we were unable to fire to man guns fired again between 3.15 and 3.30 a.m. we were unable to trace the battery concerned work in connection with head cover carried on between periods. Nothing of importance happened during the day beyond the usual violent artillery bombardment.	
	21/9/15		This was a very lovely day. The artillery on both sides were very active in view of the coming attack received supplies of bombs	8 Sgt A.Willis wd'd-Harry 16066 P. Scott 3415 P. J Fell 1016 P. R Jacob 2679 P. T. Spencer 12466 P. F Kemp

8th Sherwood Foresters

WAR DIARY
or
INTELLIGENCE SUMMARY
(Erase heading not required.)

Army Form C. 2118

Place	Date	Hour	Summary of Events and Information	Remarks and references to Appendices
	9/8/15	2.45am	ammunition and rations & water were brought up to trenches and & day. The 138th Brigade attacked the German trenches from their position on our left and the Batt'n stood to in readiness to assist if necessary. Meanwhile guns had been placed in B4 to sweep the German trenches opposite B7 and B8 but no sign of the enemy were seen in those trenches. All day two Maxim guns had been also placed in the left of B9 to cover the advance of the attacking party.	
		2.55	The enemy began using trench mortars and a few minutes later 7.5 Shrapnel burst over Head Quarters. Later about 3.30 B4 suffered rather badly from grenades and Capt. Heathcote reported that he did not want any further artillery assistance as enemy's artillery was clearer and he had grenades only to deal with. At 4.5 a report reached Batt'n HQ that B8 attack had been successful. This report was unofficial two minutes later some reported of the 2nd Bt'n ? said that Maurice front trench was taken. This was quite wrong. At 4.15 the enemy were heard afforded B7, B8 intently blowing whistles. A minute after Capt Heathcote rang up that & numerous 7./S.K.1 reported but 3 lines of trenches taken. At 4.30 the 7.08 Batty ? .... at this time sent up bunches of white light	

Army Form C. 2118

2nd Sherwood Foresters

WAR DIARY
or
INTELLIGENCE SUMMARY
(Erase heading not required.)

Place	Date	Hour	Summary of Events and Information	Remarks and references to Appendices

in front of B8. At the same time B1 Coy of 2nd Sherwood Foresters went up to
the left to reinforce. Bn reported nothing unusual. Or so on learning
our position in B8 was knocked down and B1 were apprised that the
Coy's but the condition of Post 13 became I doubt. At 4:55 a message
came through that 2nd Dfs were digging in on approximate final position.
Later verbal reports confirmed this message. About the same time 2nd
Coy sent up a platoon to the barrier as reinforcement. Report received
that 2nd Bn I were digging in just beyond Crater and were in touch
with 2/5 Sherwood Foresters who had left heavily and C₁, at 5.25
18th 95 reported "Have got 9.3 but do not know if they are across the road
yet". At the same time O.C. "B" Coy in 9.3 reported our artillery
shelling on our men. At 5.45 more ammunition was sent
up to B9. Our 2" Trench Mortar was put out of action at 5.55,
and about 10 minutes later a shell dropped close up to
H.Q. of B2. Major Beeler went out to see the situation and returned
at 6.20 reporting "C" Coy occupying B8. 2 men to a bay
and "B" Coy extending out. "A" Coy forked excellent work by our
artillery. At 7.15 O.C. "B" Coy reported that the Germans were

C.A.

WAR DIARY or INTELLIGENCE SUMMARY

withdrawing from front trenches to second line to Coy reported having been
Lt Adams asked permission to take Machine Gun pack parties which was
granted. At 7.20 T.D.S.C. reported that 2/O Reynard Parties were not
sending patrols out. At same time he reported that there were no signs of the
enemy strongly holding the trenches opposite him and that they had been
seen going into a dugout. At 7.40 the following message was received
from 7th Bn R.F. by 2nd Bn S.F. Wainor "Capt Chatterton B Coy 2nd S.F.
only 3 Officers & 500 men on right of crater, have 9 men on with 2nd
Small Jelly or refuse from, and bags urgently wanted. Lt Taylor Clark,
afterwards the artillery died down considerably. At 7.30 the B.o.c.
Major reported that he thought the attack had been very successful as
the situation had been taken. At 10.30 am a report was received
that one of our aeroplanes had seen 5 Coys of enemy at 8.15 am
at Ghuluveldt marching west and 2 more Coys further east also
marching west along MENIN ROAD At midday an urgent message
was received from OC for reinforcements and machine guns and a
Lewis gun was taken up by Lt Adams to this trench. The
whole line at that time was being very heavily shelled and the enemy
were evidently developing the trenches the of our naval guns

Lt Sherwood Foster

WAR DIARY
or
INTELLIGENCE SUMMARY
(Erase heading not required.)

Army Form C. 2118

Instructions regarding War Diaries and Intelligence Summaries are contained in F. S. Regs., Part II. and the Staff Manual respectively. Title Pages will be prepared in manuscript.

Place	Date	Hour	Summary of Events and Information	Remarks and references to Appendices
	10/8/15		Biggest harm by dropping 6" shells into B3, B4, B9 with very disastrous results – This did more harm in demolishing the new trench than anything else and the gun could not be traced all day. A heavy artillery bombardment was continued all day along the line Aldsights. The enemy were fairly quiet except for occasional shelling of ZOUAVE WOOD. In the early morning the enemy had a few minor air and trench to which we replied but could not tell with what effect. The enemy kept up an intermittent bombardment, but the day was comparatively quiet and the men benefited by it. They were still very apprehensive of damage from our own shells. One naval gun did not as our own shore firing the night, some of the heavier firing in Zw/13 were dangerous of those firing the night to enemy used a great variety of coloured lightspatriculaly in the HOOGE section. A new kind of light was observed to North of ZOUAVE WOOD like a steam stacks being freed through a narrow tube. These were especially noticeable between 10 pm and midnight. CA	

1875 Wt. W593/826 1,000,000 4/15 J.B.C. & A. A.D.S.S./Forms/C. 2118.

WAR DIARY or INTELLIGENCE SUMMARY

8th Sherwood Foresters

Place	Date	Hour	Summary of Events and Information	Remarks and references to Appendices
	1/8/15		The enemy were only reported carrying long timber – according to one sentry wiring timber – upholds B & left. Striving to lay a considerable amount from in clearing up the trenches and there and a certain amount of parapet repaired. Arnold, 3 officers patrols were out in accordance with instructions received from Bde. Commander. Lt Venn and Lt S.M. Harding went out from the Sap head in A.K. The former went 100x towards Q5 so far as the edge of the wood and to forking "W" and South so far as the fruit bushes above which run into B8. Venn & Lt Dean reported going through 2 lines of trench wire in front of Q1, found trench practically intact. About 250yds in front of Q1, found trench an old Communication trench was crossed – evidently English from the number of bully beef tins lying about. They was hitting of the enemy was heard nothing at all until they came to within 10 yards of the Sap corner made by the hedge & the enemy's trench in the avenue from that corner a sentry sent up a flare down the avenue. The patrol turned left and went due North to head of the enemy's advanced trench in	

WAR DIARY
or Intelligence
INTELLIGENCE SUMMARY

(Erase heading not required.)

Army Form C. 2118

8th ~~Grenadier Brigade~~

Place	Date	Hour	Summary of Events and Information	Remarks and references to Appendices

Three flares went up nearly from a point about 20 yds north of the avenue and three shots were fired from the corner of the trench and avenue. The patrol obtained a little and went to the edge of the wood without seeing or hearing anything further. The patrol returned to G.1. at 7.45 a.m.

Lt Hacking and Lieut Walker went out with the object of finding out exactly the enemy's front line was held between the 2 avenues. About 40 yds from the enemy's trenches the patrol crossed a communication trench which had the appearance of being recently used. Nothing was heard, they then retired and followed the German lines on side of the communication trench towards the German lines at point. It was deep enough to shelter a man upright but in open places it was in a very tumble down state. The patrol continued along the trench to within 25 yds of enemy's line, stopping to listening every few yards. There was no sound at all from front trench. On very little wire was encountered. On the way back this patrol encountered 2 men working on what seemed to be the German wire and withdrew on encounter.

CD

WAR DIARY or INTELLIGENCE SUMMARY

Army Form C. 2118

Place	Date	Hour	Summary of Events and Information	Remarks and references to Appendices
	9/9/16		as close to the enemy's trenches as possible, whilst another patrol the enemy's trenches hoping to be taken for a German patrol. Inner right and got out of sight and returned to their own trench. 1) Lieuten. Of ?rner went out toward 11.30 and got up to the enemy's front line, whilst they walked its trench in front of the enemy's front line, whilst they walked there several shots were fired from the trench and it was thought that the trench was used for a few sentries but the patrol got to within 80 yds of enemy's trench and listened for nearly an hour but heard nothing. 2) Lieuten. ?Old ?anner went out again and reported it was no signs of life a few ?res in the enemy's trenches. ?hereon how ?Mann made a careful study of the ground with telescope as far as No.9 W.N. and came to the conclusion that the enemy's line was not very thoroughly held. During the day a great deal of cleaning up etc was done in the trenches. Bay 7 in F9 which has been destroyed by shell fire was built up again. Altogether a good deal of	(D)

WAR DIARY
INTELLIGENCE SUMMARY

Army Form C. 2118

Place	Date	Hour	Summary of Events and Information	Remarks and references to Appendices
	13/8/15		[Handwritten entry, largely illegible due to faded writing] hose was the thrown out in front of B7. At 7 p.m. the enemy threw several bombs which did not reach our parapet and we replied with... a Stoker... in front of B9 reported... a listening patrol in front of B9 reported large German patrol coming from R3 towards corner of B9 near B3. As the situation was asked we... but to fire we did not. No confirmation of the report was made and nothing unusual occurred. We stood to during most of night. During the evening the 5th Sherwoods Foresters took over B3 & 20 for no May 14. A good deal of work down, repairing sandbags, rebuilding traverses etc. Floorboards were raised and floors drained. The enemy were fairly active with bombs but we answered vigorously. Continuous observation of enemy's trenches was kept up yesterday and after dawn a party of 50 men were observed near Junction of R1 and again about 6:30 am a party of 200 men observed at some place. Rain was fired on. They wore dresses and in grey/ brown in blue and all wore helmets. CA	

WAR DIARY or INTELLIGENCE SUMMARY

Army Form C. 2118

Place	Date	Hour	Summary of Events and Information	Remarks and references to Appendices
	14/8/15		During the day several smaller working parties were observed and fired on from the trenches. The Kanaka practically relieved by the normal artillery. No reply. Sapping were heard. Gas was half informing was done and a few snipers kept trenches in. B.1. The enemy were very quiet. A few trailing parties were observed and treated in the same way as yesterday. Enemy considerable bursting of rear the later hr. gun burst quiet. The Road from his S.E. badly shelled today. We coming up and returning.	19/8/15 20.20 PM to Febr 25.29 PM to Wralgen
	15/8/15		A quiet day. not fully spent in informing trenches. Sniping at working parties again. Three parties were very active rifle near MENIN ROAD and at a place known as trench near ZONNEBEKE. O great artillery bombardment on our left. Enemy had very heavy trench bursting with dense yellow & black smoke. Enemy very quiet in trenches opposite Ba. Sounds from work had opposite Ba.	

WAR DIARY or INTELLIGENCE SUMMARY

Army Form C. 2118

8th Sherwood Foresters

Place	Date	Hour	Summary of Events and Information	Remarks and references to Appendices
	16/7/16		Trees were damaged in many places in enemy lines after heavy shell fire. Very unusual sight to see a relief. The trenches were in a very bad state again owing to heavy rain for 12 hours previous and not much work could be done. Great trouble caused by a small stream running under parapet in Bay 18. Efforts on line the enemy were quiet. Towards evening he started to attack both sides were fairly active. Much bombing near the Crater.	
	17/7/16	2 am	The enemy searches the Bamford Rd with shrapnel and about 5a but we several very heavy shells - destination unknown. The enemy were again quiet. Our men were very much cleared at midnight. Hopes of relief. 7th Bn Sherwood Foresters arrived at midnight. Returned to conference 2 miles to rest Camp. Very dark night and pouring rain. Packs were carried half way by bearers and all ranks were in by 6 am and had breakfast and after roll call slept for remainder of day.	232nd Pt 9 Remainders
	18/7/16		10 officers 25 other ranks reinforcements arrived from C It D.	

Army Form C. 2118

9th Sherwood Foresters

WAR DIARY
or
INTELLIGENCE SUMMARY

(Erase heading not required.)

Instructions regarding War Diaries and Intelligence Summaries are contained in F.S. Regs., Part II. and the Staff Manual respectively. Title Pages will be prepared in manuscript.

Place	Date	Hour	Summary of Events and Information	Remarks and references to Appendices
	19/8/15		Companies spent the day in digging shelter trenches making rifle pits etc. Rifles were inspected by the Armourer R.M.S. the Battn. returned in having a very nice clean field for parade and fell sheltered from view by a natural wood.	
	20/8/15		Early morning running and physical drill. Improvement shewn. Neatly pitted officers, lance corporals and privates under the Adjutant morning and afternoon. Machine gun teachers etc is organised and incentive filled up in trenches. In afternoon an excellent entertainment manoeuvres as yesterday.	
	21/8/15		Given by Div Concert Party. 30 reinforcements arrived from the Battn. S.R.	
	22/8/15		A quiet Sunday. Church parade 10 am with Bde Commander.	
	23/8/15		7-7.30 Physical drill. 10-10.30 Inspection. It all seems by Bde Commander had nearly all been fitted up with new clothing etc and were good and steady. Working party of 100 at RUISSEAUT all day.	

1875 Wt. W593/826 1,000,000 4/15 J.B.C.&A. A.D.S.S./Forms/C. 2118.

WAR DIARY or INTELLIGENCE SUMMARY

Army Form C. 2118

8th Nov[ ] Bn.

Place	Date	Hour	Summary of Events and Information	Remarks and references to Appendices
	24/8/15	7-7.30	Running & Physical Drill. Bn. Baths at POPERINGHE used by all Coys in morning. Afternoon classes for Reserve Signallers and Machine Gunners. 150 men on working party near RENINGHELST.	
	25/8/15		Early morning running 7 to 10 am. Short route march in shirt sleeves. The Corps Commander inspected Baths in afternoon and congratulated Keau on their work in the recent fighting and also was astonished — I think — impressed by the very neat and clean turn-out. Working parties about 250 men. Newly joined Officers & nco's afforded and privates for instruction under the Adjutant. Complimentary letter received from Lt. Col. 4th Bde. containing message of congratulation from Commander in Chief.	
	26-8-15			
	27-8-15	7-7.30	Running and Saluting. Warm short route march in shirt sleeves. Afternoon classes for machine Gunners etc.	
	28-8-15		Companies used Bn. Baths at POPERINGHE. Covered by Bn. Concert Party & 6 pm very much appreciated. Practical Club Baths present. CR	

Army Form C. 2118

8th Cheshire Regt &c.

WAR DIARY
or
INTELLIGENCE SUMMARY
(Erase heading not required.)

Instructions regarding War Diaries and Intelligence Summaries are contained in F.S. Regs., Part II. and the Staff Manual respectively. Title Pages will be prepared in manuscript.

Place	Date	Hour	Summary of Events and Information	Remarks and references to Appendices
	2/8/15	9.0 am	Church Parade 9.0 am. Both parties for trenches at 2.30 pm. Conference marched off independently. KRUISSTRAAT were they halted. Both relieved 7th Bn in trenches. Relief completed by midnight.	2999 P.C. 9th Cheshires kia.
	3/8/15		A considerable amount of work done in reping trench 30. Many mines were there to parapet and ammunition recesses made. French howitzer German trench registered with 2 rounds of which burst in German trench. Rifle Battery fired 750 rounds. A quiet day only actively being sniping on both sides.	
	4/8/15		A fairly quiet day. The enemy was rather lively but were quickly silenced by the Belgian force. Communication trenches were deepened and widened.	Lieut. S. Phillips apptd from 9th Cheshires. Reinforcements arrived 1346 No 5 Refers.

Chinapin Cpl 9th S.L.

Appendix I
August 1915

Army Form C. 2118

WAR DIARY
or
INTELLIGENCE SUMMARY
(Erase heading not required.)

Place	Date	Hour	Summary of Events and Information	Remarks and references to Appendices
			Awards.	
			His Imperial Majesty the Emperor of Russia has been graciously pleased to confer with the approval of His Majesty the King, the undermentioned rewards for Gallantry and Distinguished Service in the field.	
			"Medal of St. George 4th Class."	
			No 2228. Dmr J. W. Newton. "B" Bty.	
			" 1245. Pte J. Sharman "B" Bty.	
			" 1265. Dmr W. Rott. "B" Bty.	

9th Sherwood Foresters

Appendix V
August 1915

Army Form C. 2118

WAR DIARY
or
INTELLIGENCE SUMMARY
(Erase heading not required.)

Place	Date	Hour	Summary of Events and Information	Remarks and references to Appendices
			Copy of Telegram received 29/8/15	
			"Allow me as High Sheriff of this County, to express to you as Commanding Officer and through you to the Officers, Non-commissioned Officers & Men of your Battalion my sincere congratulations and deep admiration at the gallant part taken by the 8th Sherwood Foresters in the fighting near HOOGE when your regiment in conjunction with the Robin Hoods so worthily upheld and added to the high reputation already attained by both the City & County Battalions.	
			(signed) G. Hanley Birkin. CD	

Army Form C. 2118

Appendix III August 1915

WAR DIARY
or
INTELLIGENCE SUMMARY
(Erase heading not required.)

Instructions regarding War Diaries and Intelligence Summaries are contained in F. S. Regs., Part II. and the Staff Manual respectively. Title Pages will be prepared in manuscript.

Place	Date	Hour	Summary of Events and Information	Remarks and references to Appendices
V Corps			Headquarters. 46th Division. Y/Branch	
			The Army Commander has read the report forwarded under your No. Y.X.2220 of 21st instant in the part played by the 8th Bn Sherwood Foresters during the recent fighting in the vicinity of HOOGE. From this report and previous ones the Army Commander recognises the excellent work done by the Battalion and wishes you to convey to the C.O. and all ranks of the 8th Sherwood Foresters his appreciation of the gallantry and steadiness displayed by them under trying circumstances.	
	24th August '15.		(signed) H. B. Williams. M.G.G.S. 2nd Army.	
46th Division.			5th Corps. G.X. 2220.	
			It gives the Corps Commander great pleasure to pass on to the 8th Battn Sherwood Foresters the well deserved appreciation of the Army Commander.	
	24th August '15.		(signed) H. Prince Maj. for B.G.G.S. 5th Corps.	

REPORT ON OPERATIONS 2ND/12TH AUGUST.

Colonel Fowler's report

I have the honour to report that I returned to duty on 2nd inst and reached the trench headquarters at 6.0 P.M. The situation on our left then was that B8 was held by D Co of this Battn, 2 platoons of the 7th SF and 1 Platoon of the 10th SF - the whole under the Command of Lieut James - The barrier on the left of B8 had been lengthened and loop-holed and a machine gun put in. A portion of C1 and the "Appendix" was also held by this garrison. Two Companies of the 7th (Robin Hood) SF were holding the new trench which had been dug through the wood 2 days before.

Aug 3rd was a quiet day except for artillery bombardments on our left in the early morning and afternoon. In the evening according to orders received and in Conjunction with OC 7th Battn, 2 patrols were sent out led respectively by Lieut Walton of 7th and Lieut Vann of 8th Battn to reconnoitre C1, C2 and C3 and the communication trenches in rear. This reconnaissance was successfully carried out and his report has been rendered.

Aug 4. Fairly quiet day but SANCTUARY WOOD shelled by enemy at 6.0 P.M. close to Battn headquarters. At midnight a patrol reported enemy in C2 but he was only probably a patrol, as no attempt to attack or bomb was made: The enemy were seen making observations opposite B8 and B7.

Aug 5. in the early morning and afterwards shewed great activity in sniping. It was probably a relief night.

Aug 5 (Contd) Enemy's artillery shelled SANCTUARY WOOD and MAPLE COPSE during the day.

Aug 6. The 7th (Robin Hood) Battn S.F. were relieved by the D.L.I. and the part of C.1 held by the 8th Battn as far as the barrier was taken over by the 2nd Battn S.F.
Lieut Vann and Lieut Walsh of the 2nd Battn went on patrol along C.1 and C.2 to report on condition of these trenches and the wire in front of them.
Lieut A Hocking also went out on patrol from B.4 to reconnoitre a communication trench which he had discovered the previous night running across our front towards the enemy's small redoubt opposite and found signs of work having been done in this vicinity.
The 7th Battn took over the garrisoning of B.3 trench thus helping us considerably.

Aug 7th Nothing except the usual artillery bombardments of both sides happened during the day

Aug 8 Was a very noisy day, the artillery on both sides being very active on both sides.

Aug 9 The 10th Brigade attacked the German trenches from their position on our left, and the Battn stood in readiness to assist by fire should occasion arise. Machine guns had been placed in B.4 to sweep the German trenches opposite B.7 & B-8 with fire, but no signs of the enemy were seen in these trenches during the day.

3.

Aug 9th (Cntd) Two machine guns had been placed on the left of B8 to cover the advance of the attacking troops, but no targets presented themselves. At 5 A.M. the 2nd Batt. S.F. sent for reinforcements and M.G. ammunition and 14 boxes were taken up to them by Lieut Adams as far as G2. At midday an urgent message was passed down from G2 for reinforcements and machine guns and a Lewis gun was taken up by Mr Adams to this trench. I consider that the action of this Officer is worthy of notice as all the line was at that time under the heaviest fire and the trenches were being demolished by the German artillery.
The German bombardment after the attack was terrific and B.8 suffered considerably - 5 men (including Sergt A Phillipson who has done such good work so often) being killed and 2 wounded.

Aug 10th Except for a more or less continued bombardment of the position won very little was done.

Aug 11/12 During the night 3 Officers patrols ledby Lieut Turner 2nd Lieuts Vann and F.M. Hacking went out and reported on condition of German trenches opposite B8 and B7 - these have been duly rendered

General. From the day the Batt. into the trenches to midday 11th the total casualties were 4 Officers wounded 30 men killed and 89 wounded.

General. In addition to the names mentioned in my report, I should like to draw attention to the magnificent work done by Surgeon Lieut Johnson CB who treated at our dressing station immense numbers of the wounded of the KRRs and Rifle Brigade on July 30 and July 31st and also a great number of the 2nd Sherwood Foresters on the 9th Aug. He has worked throughout with the greatest devotion and although at times being far from well. He was mostly ably assisted by his Medical Orderly, Corporal Sisson — (now time expired) and his successor Cpl. Martin 2402.

2049. Cpl. Beserly and his stretcher bearers also did a tremendous amount of good work.

There are also his several other NCOs and men who have on many occasions shown their coolness and courage on the various patrols that have been sent out — of these 2169 L/Cpl Wilson. 2396 Pte Nicholson, 1174 Pte Thompson / Consider are worthy of special mention.

J H Fowler Lt Col
5th Sherwood Foresters

139th Inf.Bde.
46th Div.

8th BATTN. THE SHERWOOD FORESTERS (NOTTINGHAMSHIRE
AND DERBYSHIRE REGIMENT).

S E P T E M B E R

1 9 1 5

Army Form C. 2118

WAR DIARY
or
INTELLIGENCE SUMMARY
(Erase heading not required.)

Lt. Sherwood Foster

Instructions regarding War Diaries and Intelligence Summaries are contained in F.S. Regs., Part II. and the Staff Manual respectively. Title Pages will be prepared in manuscript.

Place	Date	Hour	Summary of Events and Information	Remarks and references to Appendices
	September 1914		Much work was done in widening and deepening and repairing existing parapet in 30. 4 More periscopic rifles were fixed up in 30. The situation remained unchanged - no bombardment by enemy artillery and comparatively little sniping. The new Batn. Headquarters which was hit yesterday repaired.	
	2nd		A good deal of work again possible. Brigade Mining Section reported sounds of mining Sap in 30 crumps fired towards 29. Several opposite 32 carrying notched timber. The enemy snipers were again inactive owing possibly to an extensive use of snipersscope rifles. Heavy rainfall in the evening	
	3rd		The rain continued steadily and prevented much work. About 5am enemy fired high explosive over us but many were blind. The trenches were flooded and the dug-outs half full of water and the conditions generally were very bad. Parapets collapsed in several places and as much repairing as weather allowed was done. Enemy were quiet during the 24 hrs - both artillery & infantry.	

CD

WAR DIARY or INTELLIGENCE SUMMARY

8th Staffords

Army Form C. 2118

Place	Date	Hour	Summary of Events and Information	Remarks and references to Appendices
	Sept 4		Another comparatively quiet day. Repairing damage caused by the heavy rain again occupied much attention. The battalion was relieved by 7th S.F. and went into support in the dug-outs on the CANAL BANK.	
	5		The Battn found much work to do in repairing and improving left sector Comm. trenches. One Company went to work on Strainer Trench whilst a company was at work on Pen Avenue and Main C.T. One Coy garrisoned strong post.	
	6		The Coy garrisoned strong post. Yesterday's work continued. The conditions still very bad - the men working in water and mud well over the boot tops. One Coy provided wiring fatigue. Strained the work was allotted as yesterday. Our portion of the Bde H.Q. line trailed formed a fair state of affairs	
	7		During the night much wiring was done in front of Strained Trench. Men worked continuously in shifts during the 24 hrs. on this trench. One Company employed in making a new H.Q. (?)	

WAR DIARY or INTELLIGENCE SUMMARY

8th Sherwood Foresters

Army Form C. 2118

(Erase heading not required.)

Place	Date	Hour	Summary of Events and Information	Remarks and references to Appendices
to Battn in Left Sector	8		Work continued on Extension trench, Main C.T. and Pear Tree Work. 45 yds wiring done in front and and floorboards laid. Work hampered greatly by lack of material and tools.	
	9		More work done on the three C.Ts mentioned yesterday. 300 men found working party to deepen & wearify trenches west of Canal Lock. Battn relieved 7th S.F. in Reft Sectn at 8 p.m.	
	10		A quiet day in the trenches. A good deal of improvement made in raising parapets etc. Heavy shelling of area behind the trenches — it was necessary to move a reserve platoon. A report of sounds of enemy mining was received from 30. Bde Mining Section were notified. Opposite 31 enemy wire observed jumping water through a hole in the parapet.	
	11		A Sap was commenced in 30 in view of the noises heard yesterday. A good deal of work done in all the trenches in building up parapets & renewing sandbags. CTs also deepened.	CO

Army Form C. 2118

9th Stewart Foster

WAR DIARY
or
INTELLIGENCE SUMMARY

(Erase heading not required.)

Instructions regarding War Diaries and Intelligence Summaries are contained in F.S. Regs., Part II. and the Staff Manual respectively. Title Pages will be prepared in manuscript.

Place	Date	Hour	Summary of Events and Information	Remarks and references to Appendices
	12.		and drained. O stent was kept with the building of a new bomb store. Considerable movement of enemy transport was heard throughout the night. At 5 am sounds were heard which seemed to be dumping of girders. Work was carried mainly in repairing parapets and wire in places. Snipers had clipped. The enemy showed several times during the day opposite 32. Opposite 31 at 9 am several looked over the parapet. They were grey caps with red bands. Enemy appeared to be working briskly all day - sounds of hammering and hauling frequently heard. Several Germans periscopes were observed opposite 31 & 32. Enemy snipers were observed firing that have M.G. fire when no target was visible.	
	13.		More repairing done in the fire & communication trenches. The enemy were very quiet during the night and also quieter than usual during the day. Their firing seemed less systematic & there was no artillery action. No sounds of work heard to-day. It was noticed that enemy was using many	

CA

Army Form C. 2118

WAR DIARY
or
INTELLIGENCE SUMMARY
(Erase heading not required.)

Place	Date	Hour	Summary of Events and Information	Remarks and references to Appendices
	14		dark coloured sand-bags on top of the other sand bags. Work done consisted in repairing + deepening trenches. A telephone dug-out + ammunition dug-out completed in 32. The enemy were searchy [searching] more active than yesterday. A party was observed digging a CT between pt + 2nd line in front of 30. Our patrols went out from 30 to examine wire + reported it to be better than it looked from the trench. Our Snipers were very active. Trenches still very wet + much difficulty experienced in draining.	
	15		Quieter quiet day. Much work done in repairing etc. Dirt wire laid along the whole front of 32 S. Our Snipercifs [Snipers'] rifles were again busy + one rifle battery fired 500 rounds. No artillery action.	
	16		More wiring done in support trenches. Enemy still quiet except for one burst of machine gun + rifle fire during the night. No artillery action. Our snipers continued firing. Battn relieved in trenches by 7th S.?	

CD

WAR DIARY
or
INTELLIGENCE SUMMARY

(Erase heading not required.)

Army Form C. 2118

Place	Date	Hour	Summary of Events and Information	Remarks and references to Appendices
	17.		Battn. returned to the new Bde Rest Camp near OUDERDOM. The last Coy arriving about 3.30 a.m.	
	18.		Rifles inspected by Battn. Armourer Sgt. in afternoon. Battn. was Billet Baths at POPERINGHE. Coys fitted out with clothing etc.	
	19.		7 – 7.30 am Physical drill. 200 men dug shelter trenches during the morning. In the afternoon classes for Reserve Signallers, Machine Gunners Bombers were held. A large working party furnished for KRUISSTRAAT.	
	20.		Range working parties again furnished for digging near KRUISSTRAAT. The Battn. was inspected at the camp by G.O.C. 2nd Army who expressed his satisfaction at the smart turn-out.	
	21.		In the morning classes for Bombers Signallers Machine Gunners were held and Capt Colwell lectured all newly-joined Officers on "Trench Orders". Battn. cheered	C.D.

Army Form C. 2118

8th Staffordshire

WAR DIARY
or
INTELLIGENCE SUMMARY
(Erase heading not required.)

Instructions regarding War Diaries and Intelligence Summaries are contained in F.S. Regs., Part II. and the Staff Manual respectively. Title Pages will be prepared in manuscript.

Place	Date	Hour	Summary of Events and Information	Remarks and references to Appendices
	22.		7th S.? in left sector. Relief was completed by 10.1 pm. A quiet night with no artillery action. Work concentrated on making splinter proof shelters behind 32.S. Our snipers were active during the day.	
	23.		The enemy were again very quiet. The enemy artillery bombarded from 4.10 to 4.50 am. Our artillery bombarded from 4.10 to 4.50 am. The enemy were still remarkably quiet. We were constantly throughout the night as we believe they were at work repairing damaged parapets. All companies concentrated on completing the splinter proof shelters.	
	24.		More work done in constructing splinter proof shelters. Our snipers were very active. In 32.8 wagon loads of straw laid ready to put on parapet to his receive a cloud of smoke. The wind was not favourable for such a scheme and the straw was left. He started a heavy bombardment at	
	25.		3.50 and continued to 4.30 am. Enemy relied	

Army Form C. 2118

8th Sherwood Foresters.

WAR DIARY
or
INTELLIGENCE SUMMARY
(Erase heading not required.)

Place	Date	Hour	Summary of Events and Information	Remarks and references to Appendices
			Shelling 31 R and MAUD C.T. from 5–5.30 a.m. they fired several trench mortars at left 30. One dug out was destroyed. One of Humphrey's trench mortars at left believed to have silenced one of their mortars and a considerable number of Uncles stores in enemy trench from 31. At 5.56 a.m. an demonstration of smoke bombs and machine gun fire started. This lasted about an hour and by 7.15 a.m. everything was practically quiet & the men stood down. Much of the debris caused by yesterday's shelling was cleared up. No reports of sapping were received. Enemy was very quiet during the day apparently busy repairing damages trenches.	31.30 L/Cpl Humphrey killed.
	26		Our patrols went out during the night. Nos Left NoP.O & P.I.S. and S men went from Bayburbo along the old trench leading to the Russian trench. No sign of patches or listening posts. Across this patrol went to within 30 yds of german knife rests which they estimated at 60 yds from German trenches.	C.A.

WAR DIARY
or
INTELLIGENCE SUMMARY

9th Sherwood Foresters

Army Form C. 2118

Place	Date	Hour	Summary of Events and Information	Remarks and references to Appendices
	27.		Hd R.S. NEMMING WAY + a patrol searched an old trench which runs into Bn Bay 10. This had aroused suspicion as the German trenches. A considerable amount of repairing done to both fire + C trenches. Our sniperscope rifles were busy all day. The enemy were very lively towards evening. Several small ammunition dug-outs were built and a large number of floor-boards put down. The enemy's snipers were very active. The enemy threw a lot of wire over large deers and a steel girder in the fire trench. A great deal of trapping + talking was heard in the early morning. No artillery action.	
	28		The enemy again were more aggressive and shelled Communication trenches heavily. Very little work was possible. The Pn was relieved by 7th S.F and went into support in CANAL BANK dug-outs. CO	

Army Form C. 2118

8th Sherwood Foresters

WAR DIARY
or
INTELLIGENCE SUMMARY

(Erase heading not required.)

Instructions regarding War Diaries and Intelligence Summaries are contained in F.S. Regs., Part II. and the Staff Manual respectively. Title Pages will be prepared in manuscript.

Place	Date	Hour	Summary of Events and Information	Remarks and references to Appendices
	29.		The day was occupied in work on communication trenches. A few specially selected men were instructed by Signalling Officer.	
	30.		Work on CTs. In the afternoon heavy shelling by the enemy stopped all work. Enemy shells 'gonorrhr' until 10pm - many HE went over towards Bridge 18 + KRUISS TRAAT and both dumps were heavily shelled. The Bn. left the trenches about 11pm except 'C' Coy who were helping 6th S.F. in trench which had been blown up. Bns. marched to a field near Transport Lines and bivouaced the	

C Davenport Capt.

1875 Wt. W593/826 1,000,000 4/15 J.B.C. & A. A.D.S.S./Forms/C. 2118.

139th Inf.Bde.
46th Div.

8th BATTN. THE SHERWOOD FORESTERS (NOTTINGHAMSHIRE AND DERBYSHIRE REGIMENT).

OCTOBER

1915

9th Sherwood Foresters

WAR DIARY
or
INTELLIGENCE SUMMARY
(Erase heading not required.)

Army Form C. 2118

Place	Date	Hour	Summary of Events and Information	Remarks and references to Appendices
OUDERDOM	1st Oct		The morning was spent cleaning up ground and wagons and packing wagons. Companies drew clothing etc from Q.M. Stores.	
		3pm	Transport and Machine Gun wagons moved off by road.	
		4pm	Batt. with M.G. wagons marched to ABEELE station and entrained with little delay.	
		7pm	S.A.A. Cart moved by road with Armt Claxon.	
		10pm	Batt. detrained at POPERINGHE and marched to BETHUNE. Billets were then found.	
BETHUNE	2nd		Early in the morning orders were received to move into another area and a billeting party left. At 2pm the Transport arrived and went to new area with Batt. Orders received to leave that area in following morning.	
BETHUNE	3rd		Batt. marched out from BETHUNE and went into billets at BERGUANCTION arriving about noon. Remainder of day was spent in settling down.	
Nr BERNAMCOURT			Bombing Practice in morning. Reserve machine Gunners with M.G.O. had to Batt. was falling in for afternoon	
		4pm	Parade orders received to entrain at 8.30 to proceed to	

CR

8th Seaforth Highlanders

WAR DIARY
or
INTELLIGENCE SUMMARY
(Erase heading not required.)

Army Form C. 2118

Place	Date	Hour	Summary of Events and Information	Remarks and references to Appendices
	5th/6th cont.		a point near VERMELLES. The Battn went into bivouac near Vermelles and were occupied on night of 3/4th in clearing up trenches. Several casualties from enemy shell fire occurred. Battn knew nothing of return arrangements and there was great difficulty in obtaining any water. Orders were received about 3pm to leave trenches and march to MAZINGARBE where billets had been arranged by Staff Capt Cookers. Were brought to new billets and thereinafter for the men on arrival about 7am.	
	6th 7th cont.		Battn marched out of MAZINGARBE at 9 am and went to FOUQUIÈRES-LES-BÉTHUNE. Some difficulty experienced with billets but Battn was all settled in by 2pm.	
FOUQUIÈRES	8th		Battn had an easy day. Classes held for Buglers, Machine Gunners Signallers etc. Companies paraded in morning for drill under Coy arrangements. Parties were drawn from Bethune in afternoon and evening 7-15-7-45 Physical Exercises. Route march at 10 am until dinner. Afternoon classes were held for buglers, signallers etc.	CD

9th Sherwood Foresters

WAR DIARY
or
INTELLIGENCE SUMMARY

Army Form C. 2118

Place	Date	Hour	Summary of Events and Information	Remarks and references to Appendices
POUVIERES	9th	7.15-7.45	Physical Drill Running. All men received instruction in bombing. In the intervals of bombing rapid loading & bayonet exercises were practised – 2pm Battn Route March. The Battn received notice to be ready to move at an hour's notice owing to attack on XI Corps front	
	10th		Battn Church Parade at 10 am. After Church Parade O.C. Coys took their NCO's to see the model of Hohenzollern Redoubt near Bn. HQ. An officers meeting was at 2pm at which C.O. explained the aim of the coming attack.	
	11th	7.15-7.45	Physical Drill. The morning was spent in Bombing, Bayonet fighting, Aiming Drill and Rapid Loading. At 2pm Battn went for a route march.	
	12th		Early morning inspection of identity discs, iron rations etc. Baggage packed and men's valises blankets etc. Paty of Ns Paradians under 2/Lt R.E. Hemingway left at 3pm. Remainder of Battn left at 4.15pm. A halfway made near NOVELLES for tea and Bn then moved into SUSSEX TRENCH and was in position by 11pm. CD	

8th Sherwood Foresters

WAR DIARY
or
INTELLIGENCE SUMMARY

Army Form C. 2118

Place	Date	Hour	Summary of Events and Information	Remarks and references to Appendices
	13th	7 am	At 7 am every available man was employed in carrying water and rations from VERMELLES to 137 and 138 Brigades. This work was not completed until 11.30 pm. The British Bombardment began at noon but the enemy's reply did not damage the trench occupied by the Batt'n.	
		2.45 pm	Order received from 139 Bde "Move your Batt'n into Reserve Trench and report when you have arrived there". The Batt'n moved immediately but the trenches were very congested and at 4.45 pm the Batt'n was reported in position in RESERVE TRENCH with Right in BART'S ALLEY and Left on RAILWAY ALLEY. A very few casualties occurred here from enemy's shell fire. At 4.10 pm a message from 139 Bde ordered "Move your Batt'n down RESERVE TRENCH to join right so far as BOYAU.V.K.". This was done at once. At 5 pm 138 Bde sent following message "The 8th Bn Sherwood Foresters is now under Command of 137 Brigade."	
		6 pm	Message received stating that 7th Sherwood Foresters had been forced to retire. All available bombers and scouts were sent up at request 2nd I/C 7th Batt'n S.F. Capt Innes with "B" Coy went up and received orders from Capt Bradwell 7th Bn. to take his company up to support trench behind the old British fire Trench. All the bombers	

Army Form C. 2118

9th Sherwood Foresters

WAR DIARY
or
INTELLIGENCE SUMMARY
(Erase heading not required.)

Instructions regarding War Diaries and Intelligence Summaries are contained in F. S. Regs., Part II. and the Staff Manual respectively. Title Pages will be prepared in manuscript.

Place	Date	Hour	Summary of Events and Information	Remarks and references to Appendices
				Map attached
	14th		of this Co. were sent up to the Hohenzollern REDOUBT. About 9 p.m. the rest of this Co. were ordered to dig in the C.T between our first line and the HOHENZOLLERN REDOUBT. The men worked under heavy rifle fire on this for 8 hours and before they stopped at dawn had made a traversable trench between the REDOUBT and our line. This Company was then withdrawn to support trenches where it remained until 14th. During the evening G.O.C 139 Bde visited our trenches and said that this Batt. would probably have to make an attack on Hohenzollern line near POINT 60 in order to ease matters on WEST FACE. Major BECHER endeavoured to get information as to the junction of the British troops in BIG WILLIE whilst Col FOWLER and the Adjutant reconnoitred the ground between the old British front line and the HOHENZOLLERN REDOUBT.	
	14th	1.45am	Orders were received from G.O 139 Bde. to attack WEST FACE and trench out the evening up to POINT 60 as soon as possible and block the SOUTH FACE at its junction with BIG WILLIE and consolidate the end of the HOHENZOLLERN REDOUBT.	

9th Sherwood Foresters

WAR DIARY
INTELLIGENCE SUMMARY
(Erase heading not required.)

Army Form C.2118.

Hour, Date, Place	Summary of Events and Information	Remarks and references to Appendices
	At the same time we were informed that the 15th Bde would be bombing at the same time along B/G WILLIE towards POINT 60. Owing to the difficulty in communicating orders the preparation for the attack took considerable time and it was not until 4.0 am that "A" and "D" Companies had taken up a position in front of the old British line to advance to the attack. These 2 Companies were commanded by Major ASHWELL and CAPT VANN respectively, and "C" Coy under CAPT HANDFORD remained in support in HAYWARD'S HEATH.	
4.15 am	2nd Lt FOWLER led the attack, trying to keep direction whilst it was very difficult to keep direction but by the aid of a flashlight worked by MAJOR BECHER the troops reached their objective and advanced along WESTFACE towards POINT 60 with bombing parties and drove back the enemy for some little distance. The attack	C/O

WAR DIARY
or
INTELLIGENCE SUMMARY

Army Form C. 2118.

Jn Sherwood Forests.

were subjected to heavy rifle fire throughout the latter part of the advance both from SOUTH FACE and BIG WILLIE. In the latter the enemy were holding a great length of trench than we had anticipated. There did not appear to be any support from 137 Bde on the right. Our casualties in these 2 companies were very heavy and it was found quite impossible to attempt the blocking of SOUTH FACE. Lt Col FOWLER accordingly issued orders to consolidate the gains in WEST FACE. This was done and work was carried on throughout the day. The block thus made in WEST FACE was about 30 yards from POINT 60. A heavy artillery bombardment was carried on by both sides during the time we occupied WEST FACE and hostile casualties rented snipers were also very active, and we suffered considerably and our right flank from the enemy's bombs. CD

9th Sherwood Foresters

WAR DIARY
or
INTELLIGENCE SUMMARY.

Army Form C. 2118.

Hour, Date, Place	Summary of Events and Information	Remarks and references to Appendices
Pr "C" Company 5 am	Shortly after 5 am a platoon was detailed to carry bombs to the REDOUBT to "A" Company and remain with the garrison.	
7.30	Remainder of Coy received orders from Lt Col JONES to move across the open to the REDOUBT to carry bombs and water. Very heavy rifle machine gun fire was opened on this party as soon as it was over the parapet and orders were given to withdraw. The casualties were very heavy. The men who were left then received orders to proceed via the sap to take stores to the REDOUBT. This party stayed in the sap until relieved about 6 am on 15th inst.	
9 pm.	The Battn received orders that they would be relieved forthwith but it was not until about 6 am that the relief commenced. The relief was not completed until 7.30 am. Details about 7 am 2nd Lt FOWLER was killed by a sniper. CD.	

84 Steward Trafs.

WAR DIARY
or
INTELLIGENCE SUMMARY.
(Erase heading not required.)

Army Form C. 2118.

Instructions regarding War Diaries and Intelligence Summaries are contained in F.S. Regs., Part II. and the Staff Manual respectively. Title pages will be prepared in manuscript.

Hour, Date, Place	Summary of Events and Information	Remarks and references to Appendices
15th Oct.	On relief being completed Battn concentrated in RESERVE TRENCH. Battn remained here for the day, and was relieved by 2 Coys of the IRISH GUARDS at about 7pm.	
16th Oct. 1am VAUDRICOURT	Battn marched by easy stages (including a halt for tea) to VAUDRICOURT where billets had been allotted. Lt Col FOWLER was buried at 2.30pm at POUQUIERES Churchyard. Ratt'n of Pioneers arrived. Battn Church Parade at 10am. 12 noon.	
17th Oct.	Draft of 24 men arrived. Battn was visited in morning by G.O.C. Division. Bath was completed all ranks in their work in the attack. In the afternoon classes were held for Lewis machine gunners etc.	
18th Oct.	The morning was spent in cleaning up billets etc. At 7.30 pm Battn moved out from	

WAR DIARY
INTELLIGENCE SUMMARY

Army Form C. 2118.

8th Sherwood Foresters

(Erase heading not required.)

Instructions regarding War Diaries and Intelligence Summaries are contained in F.S. Regs., Part II. and the Staff Manual respectively. Title pages will be prepared in manuscript.

Hour, Date, Place	Summary of Events and Information	Remarks and references to Appendices
LAPUGNOY 20th Oct	VAVRICOURT and went to LAPUGNOY where comfortable billets were obtained.	
21st Oct	In the morning Companies went to C.O. practised buting physical exercises. Afternoon was spent in classes for stretcher bearers etc.	
	Running Physical exercises before breakfast. Every Company practised buting in the morning. All Companies also had baths at the Brewery during the day and the men enjoyed these were flies up in physical exercises during rapid loading. Machine gun section used Range near the Headquarters.	
28th Oct	All Bombers practised with live bombs at Bee trenches. Employed men all used baths.	CD

8th Sherwood Foresters

WAR DIARY
or
INTELLIGENCE SUMMARY.
(Erase heading not required.)

Army Form C. 2118.

Hour, Date, Place	Summary of Events and Information	Remarks and references to Appendices
6/1/23.	An intervals of bombing companies under the O.C. are engaged in division, rapid loading and physical drill. Arrangement was made for washing of clothing so that all men had underclothing washed during rest. Machine Gunners on Range. Bombers at the head. 9am - 12 noon. Remainder of battalion went for a short route march. Demonstration on blowing up trenches by different kinds of explosives was attended by 2 officers and the officers commanding practice bombing & classes were held for Lewis machine gunners, signallers etc.	
6/1/24.	No work done. Church Parade at 10.15am with 6th Batt. S.F.	
6/1/25.	Running before breakfast. Dino companies spent morning bombing and bayonet fighting etc.	

WAR DIARY or INTELLIGENCE SUMMARY

8th Sherwood Foresters

Hour, Date, Place	Summary of Events and Information	Remarks and references to Appendices
	Whilst the other 2 Companies practised rapid loading, aiming, muscle exercises etc. In the afternoon the companies which did bayonet fighting & bombing in the morning did musketry and the other companies bombing etc.	
26 Oct	The morning was spent in cleaning up billets and loading wagons etc. At 3 pm Batty. moved to BETHUNE when they were billeted in ST. NICHOLAS' ORPHANAGE. In the morning camp leaders ranges billows etc & drew equipment from store. One Company (250) and a platoon (50) were selected to proceed to BETHUN at a moments notice. At 6 pm the C.o. handed off to a practice inspection.	
27 Oct		

8th Seaforth Highlanders.

WAR DIARY
or
INTELLIGENCE SUMMARY
(Erase heading not required.)

Army Form C. 2118.

Hour, Date, Place	Summary of Events and Information	Remarks and references to Appendices
Oct 28	The Coy of platoon for inspection marched off at 8 am to HEDAUVILLE. Remainder of Battn. was employed in the morning on various fatigues. All others behind in trenches in afternoon.	
Oct 29	Continued practice bombing, bayonet fighting, aircraft flooding in the morning. In the afternoon B Coy. bathed in Louge & took specialists, fatigue & parties of sentries. All coys practised smoke helmet drill.	
Oct 30	Battn. went march in morning, working party of 150 under R.E.s at work on horse standings all day. C.O. inspected last 3 coys at 2 pm. Remainder of Battn. bayonet fitting.	
Oct 31	Specially observed as a day of rest by order of G.O.C. Church Parade with 6th Battn. at 10 am.	Cheerful Capt.

9.9.15.

SECRET.
No 155
MAP SHOWING NEW TRENCHES
TO SUPERIMPOSE ON 36C NW 3
AND PART OF 1.

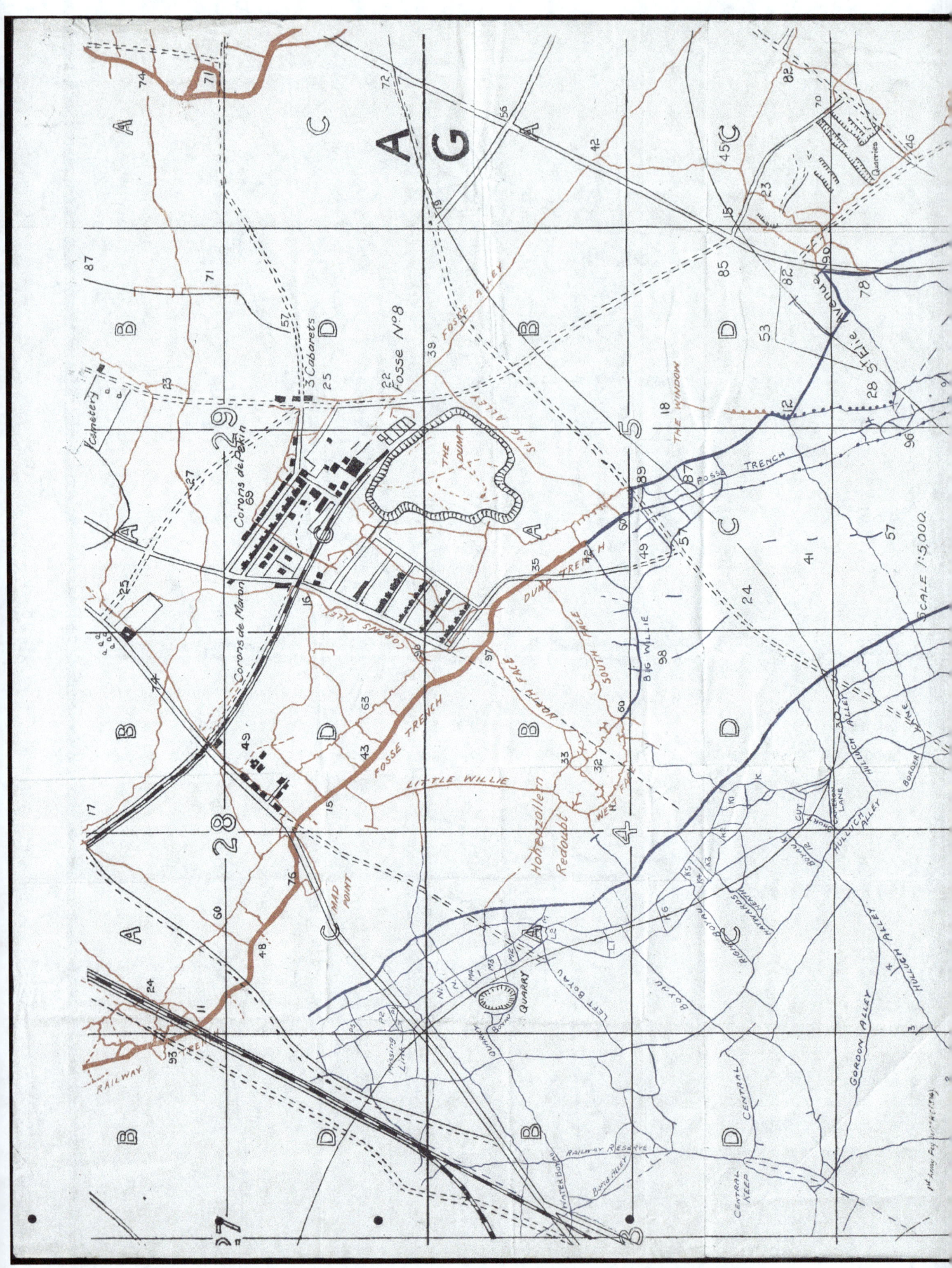

139th Inf.Bde.
46th Div.

8th BATTN. THE SHERWOOD FORESTERS (NOTTINGHAMSHIRE AND DERBYSHIRE REGIMENT).

N O V E M B E R

1 9 1 5

Army Form C. 2118

WAR DIARY
8th Staffords Regiment
INTELLIGENCE SUMMARY
(Erase heading not required.)

Instructions regarding War Diaries and Intelligence Summaries are contained in F. S. Regs., Part II. and the Staff Manual respectively. Title Pages will be prepared in manuscript.

Place	Date	Hour	Summary of Events and Information	Remarks and references to Appendices
BETHUNE	1/11/15		Companies engaged in bombing practice, bayonet fighting and smoke helmet drill in morning. Classes for reserve machine gunners etc. Lecture by C.O. to all officers on trench warfare. Companies drew clothing etc. from stores.	
	2/11/15	10 am	Brigade Grenade Throwing Competition, attended by all bombers. All Coys. did an hour's bombing. M.O. lectured all Coys on use of first field Dressing. Classes for Reserve machine gunners etc. Baths at disposal of Bn. in afternoon.	
	3/11/15		Yesterday's work repeated. Orders to move received about midday. Evening spent in packing up. Draft of 30 arrived.	
EPINETTE	4/11/15	8 am	Left BETHUNE and marched to EPINETTE arriving here about noon. Took over billets from Lincolns.	
	5/11/15		Marched from EPINETTE to VIEILLE CHAPELLE Coys. got settled in by noon and. Arrangements made for trench relief.	
VIEILLE CHAPELLE	6/11/15		Coys busy in the morning cleaning up. Batt. took over trenches between CINDER TRACK and COPSE ST near AUB DU BOIS. Batt H.Q. near Windy Corner - we relieved 58th Rifles, Meerut Divn.	
	7/11/15		A quiet day. Two M.G. reinforcements arrived. German showed across a fond during the day. It was of note seen that	

WAR DIARY

8th Shewood Foresters

INTELLIGENCE SUMMARY

Army Form C. 2118

(Erase heading not required.)

Instructions regarding War Diaries and Intelligence Summaries are contained in F.S. Regs., Part II. and the Staff Manual respectively. Title Pages will be prepared in manuscript.

Place	Date	Hour	Summary of Events and Information	Remarks and references to Appendices
	8/11/15		A great deal of repairs to parapet trenches have to be taken in hand at once. The enemy were very quiet all day and very little artillery fire was heard. About 7.30 two shells fell 30 yds behind Grenadier Guards Trench. A good many folks of sandbags were reported. The Reserve Coys. busy all day cleaning up strong points & rest houses.	
	9/11/15		The firing trenches right of BOND ST were all cleaned up - 16 bays cleared in GUARDS TRENCH. Enemy more active especially with machine guns. Very heavy rain in early hours did much damage to the trenches.	
	10/11/15		Very quiet day. A certain amount of rebuilding parapet of GUARDS TRENCH was done. CORPSE ST. C.T. was also repaired where fallen in.	
	11/11/15		A very wet day. More traverses fell in. Trenches waterlogged in many places. Lt C.W. Hughes killed by sniper. Enemy snipers were very active in the early morning. Evening was very quiet. The Rifles joined and in a very bad state.	
	12/11/15		A quiet day again. Very little sniping. About 11.10 pm HE dropped over RUE du BOIS between 2 & 3 pm. Signalling was seen from hit beams lying between to a farm in rear of enemies line which we were firing. Enemy appeared to be building	C.D

WAR DIARY
8th Shermore Graders
INTELLIGENCE SUMMARY
(Erase heading not required.)

Army Form C. 2118

Place	Date	Hour	Summary of Events and Information	Remarks and references to Appendices
	13/11/15		A machine gun emplacement in front line opposite COPSE STREET. Continued heavy rains have made trenches very bad.	
	14/11/15		A wet and cold day. A good deal of baling done and most urgent repairs. A very quiet day. A good deal of accurate sniping by enemy at night. Enemy appear to be busier and not so apathetic prior to a relief having taken place.	
	15/11/15		A very cold day. Nothing of note occurred. Frost improves condition of trenches a little. We were relieved by 5th & 9th R.S. Sherwoods. Took over 1st line to billets in VIEILLE CHAPELLE at 9 p.m. Breakfasts 10 a.m. Companies spent the morning in cleaning up as the men and their clothing was in a very bad state. A good supply of clothing necessaries available for issue from QMs stores.	
	16/11/15		Coys were at disposal of Coy officers for inspection of feet, rifles etc. Specimen trench works + communication trenches	CD

WAR DIARY
8th Sherwood Foresters
INTELLIGENCE SUMMARY

(Erase heading not required.)

Army Form C. 2118

Instructions regarding War Diaries and Intelligence Summaries are contained in F. S. Regs, Part II. and the Staff Manual respectively. Title Pages will be prepared in manuscript.

Place	Date	Hour	Summary of Events and Information	Remarks and references to Appendices
	17/11/15		Burial by R. E's. The baths at NEUVE CHAPELLE were used and inspected in the morning by Lt. HR.H The Prince of Wales. A very wet and rough day. Remaining coys used baths. All coys practiced bombing.	
	18/11/15		Batt" had to furnish a large working party at 6pm to work on new line of breastworks in rear of present line. This party was not back in billets until about 1am. No work was done during the preceding day.	
	19/11/15		Brigade Snipers section formed. Batt" relieved 5th Sherwood Foresters in same trenches. Relief completed early - 7pm. Batt" extended to COPSE ST on the left & relieved part of No S.T. A good deal of repairs done to parapet.	
	20/11/15		Sand bags filled & placed in position. Many flare bombs laid. Region of ROE DU BOIS shelled several times with H.E. Shrapnel. The enemy appeared to be working hard all night. A good deal of machine gun rifle fire in the night.	CD/

Army Form C. 2118

WAR DIARY
8th Sherwood Foresters
INTELLIGENCE SUMMARY
(Erase heading not required.)

Place	Date	Hour	Summary of Events and Information	Remarks and references to Appendices
	27/11/15		Much work done towards repairing and improving Trench near BOARS HEAD were flooded. A gap was left in sandbags in BOARS HEAD re laid. Enemy artillery active especially between 1pm and 3pm. Shrapnel burst over GUARDS TRENCH and also in BOND ST which was badly damaged in two or three places. Our guns made several direct hits on front line parapets BOARS HEAD. About 8pm a working party of enemy opposite BOARS HEAD was dispersed by our machine gun fire.	
	28/11/15		More repairs done to parapet opposite. Enemy shelled Festing Corner + RUE DU BOIS between 1pm + 4pm but did little damage. Snipers rather active by day + night. A patrol under 2nd Lt. S. Hopkinson went out to investigate a place between the lines where it was believed that the enemy was working on an old trench. The patrol reported that no work was going on there. A heavy fog came over about 5pm + stopped nearly all work owing to necessity for larger numbers on sentry.	

Army Form C. 2118

WAR DIARY
8th Sherwood Foresters
INTELLIGENCE SUMMARY

(Erase heading not required.)

Instructions regarding War Diaries and Intelligence Summaries are contained in F.S. Regs., Part II. and the Staff Manual respectively. Title Pages will be prepared in manuscript.

Place	Date	Hour	Summary of Events and Information	Remarks and references to Appendices
	23/11/15		Enemy put a good deal of shrapnel over BOIS DU BOIS, otherwise it was a fairly quiet day. Men were busy cleaning up trenches & improving their condition. Bn relieved by 6th Sherwood Foresters and 'A' & 'D' Coys billeted in RICHEBOURG ST VAAST, leaving farriers for RICHEBOURG and ST VAAST hats. 'B'd' Coys Headquarters were at LACOUTURE.	
	24/11/15		Companies drew clothing etc. Baths at VIEILLE CHAPELLE at disposal of Coys. Working party of 250 provided for work on the new breast work behind present line.	
	25/11/15		Companies resting & improving billets. Working party as last night.	
	26/11/15		Yesterday's work repeated.	
	27/11/15		Ditto	
	28/11/15		Relieved 5th Sherwood Foresters in left sector - between COPSE ST and CRESCENT TRENCH. Relief completed early. J.4.5/-	

CD J.4.5/-

Army Form C. 2118

WAR DIARY
8th Sherwood Foresters
INTELLIGENCE SUMMARY
(Erase heading not required.)

Instructions regarding War Diaries and Intelligence Summaries are contained in F. S. Regs., Part II. and the Staff Manual respectively. Title Pages will be prepared in manuscript.

Place	Date	Hour	Summary of Events and Information	Remarks and references to Appendices
	29/11/15		Parapet repaired in several places. Not much work possible owing to hard frost which however turned to rain later. This made the trenches very bad - worse than ever. Enemy sent over several whizzbangs & shrapnel along RUE DU BOIS between 11 + 12 a.m and 2 + 3 pm but no damage done. Machine Gun bursts fired regularly during the night sweeping parapets of front-line, GUARDS TRENCH & houses along RUE DU BOIS.	
	30/11/15		Our artillery bombarded in the morning on the left, chiefly the German m.g. emplacements. Men also cut wire between 2 + 4 pm. Casualties however were very few. Machine gun fire continually swept across front-line parapets & RUE DU BOIS.	

C. Davenport Capt.

139th Inf.Bde.
46th Div.

8th BATTN. THE SHERWOOD FORESTERS (NOTTINGHAMSHIRE AND DERBYSHIRE REGIMENT).

DECEMBER

1915

WAR DIARY
8th Bn Cheshire Foresters
INTELLIGENCE SUMMARY

Place	Date	Hour	Summary of Events and Information	Remarks and references to Appendices
	Dec 1		Situation remained normal and a quiet day was experienced. During the afternoon the enemy snipers were rather more aggressive. Between 2 + 3 pm the 2nd Staff Batten fired at the enemy M.G emplacement at S10 B0.9. Inwards dusk the enemy elevated a front deal, enquiring what regiment was opposite taken + referring to plum pudding. Regretted a great deal. A good day's work in shaving + moving mud.	
	Dec 2		Another normal day. Enemy's machine guns more active and except across RUE DU BOIS frequently. HAZARA TRENCH thoroughly cleaned by the Cy in Reserve. Relief commenced at 4pm and by 7pm the 7th Bn had taken over. All were back in billets in NEUVE CHAPELLE by 9pm. About 9.30pm the C.O was sent for to go to Bde HQ at once and was warned to expect orders to move back next day.	
	Dec 3	5 am	Orders received to be clear of billets by 11. Battn marched to HAVERSKERQUE, halting for dinners just outside MERVILLE. Billets reached about 7.30pm	
	4		The day was spent in cleaning up billets and settling in.	
	5		Coys were at disposal of Cy officers to drawing clothing etc. Skin Coats withdrawn and packed at Q.M Stores	

CP

WAR DIARY

8th Bn The Cheshire Regt
INTELLIGENCE SUMMARY

(Erase heading not required.)

Army Form C. 2118

Place	Date	Hour	Summary of Events and Information	Remarks and references to Appendices
See 6	7.		Early morning running drill. Batts Route March - about 5 miles. Coys at disposal of Coy commander if day to kit inspection etc.	
	8.		The C.O inspected Coys on their own parade ground in the morning and the G.O.C. Division inspected the Battn at 3.30 p.m. The Battn. was highly complimented by G.O.C. as being the best turned out of the had inspected. All heavy draught horses were withdrawn and mules and F.D. Waggons in exchange. Two small drafts arrived. C.O inspected drafts. Running before breakfast. 11 - 1 Batt Route march. 2-3 Platoon drill under supervision of O.C. Coys.	
	9.		7.45 Running for 20 minutes. 10-12 Subaltern officers with rifle bayonet. Corporals & Lance-Corporals exercises under Regt Sergt Major in duties of Guards, guard-mounting etc. Companies under O.C. Coy Platoon sergeants in Squad, Platoon & Coy drill. Saluting. 2-3 Coy communicating drill. Classes for reserve officers, machine gunners, transport drivers.	
	10.		Morning work as yesterday. At 2.30 p.m the A.D.M.S. inspected the Battn. A few men were selected for special examination as to their Physical fitness.	CP/

Army Form C. 2118

WAR DIARY
8th Bn. Sherwood Foresters
INTELLIGENCE SUMMARY
(Erase heading not required.)

Place	Date	Hour	Summary of Events and Information	Remarks and references to Appendices
	Dec 11		7.45 Running. 9.30 – 10.30 Subaltern Officers newly appointed Corporals. Places & spaces under R.S.M. 10.30 – 12.30 Kit inspection. A present for every Officer man arrives from Cttee. of Nottingham Comforts Fund. Church Parade at A.S.C. Canteen at 11.45 followed by Holy Communion. 2.30 pm C.O. lectures all Officers on interior economy.	
	12			
	13.		7.45 Running. 10 – 11 Coy. Platoon squad drill under Coy Coy. 11–12 Arm drill saluting. Subaltern Officers trainee NCOs under R.S.M. Batt. Route march – about 3½ miles.	
	14.		7.45 Running. 10 – 11 Physical Exercises. 11–12 Bayonet fighting. Coy drill under Coy Commanders. Junior Officers NCOs under R.S.M. Sergts under the Adjutant in Bayonet fighting. Classes to resume Spandau machine gunner.	
	15.		7.45 Running. 10 – 11. Coy. Platoon squad drill under O.C. Coy. Junior NCOs under Adjutant for bayonet fighting. Two Platoons of each Coy for one hour's unit march independently. 2–3. Two Platoons of each Coy route march independently. Junior NCOs under R.S.M. for instruction in Physical exercises.	

Army Form C. 2118

WAR DIARY
8th Sherwood Foresters
INTELLIGENCE SUMMARY
(Erase heading not required.)

Place	Date	Hour	Summary of Events and Information	Remarks and references to Appendices
	16 Dec		7.45 am Running. 10-11 Senior NCO instruction practice of drill movements. Coy in saluting drill. 11-12 Junior Officers in detail of bayonet fighting under Adjt. R.S.C. Coy lectured on entraining duties in Boxcar Ship. 2-3 Junior NCOs under R.S.M. Coy one hour route march under own arrangements. Machine Gunner & grenadiers special instruction.	
	17 Dec		7.45 am Running. 10-11 Coy platoon drill. Junior NCOs class of instruction in detail of rifle exercises under R.S.M. 11-12 Saluting drill. Senior NCOs in physical exercises under R.S.M. 2pm Batt. Route march	
	18 Dec		7.45 am Running. 9-11 Coy bathing, cleaning up billets and laying out kit. 11-12.30 Kit inspection by C.O.	
	19. Dec.		Batt. left HAVERSKERQUE at 9am and reached via THIENNES to LE CORNET near WITTES. Billets were reached about 4pm. Remainder of day spent in settling down	
	20 1960		9 am Batt. on Running Parade with drums and double. Clothing etc drawn from stores. Feet inspected.	
	21 Dec.		8 am Batt Running. 10.30-12.30 Batt. Parade for practice in rifle exercises so as to synchronize the various movements CD	

Army Form C. 2118

WAR DIARY
9th Stationary Hospital [?]
INTELLIGENCE SUMMARY

(Erase heading not required.)

Instructions regarding War Diaries and Intelligence Summaries are contained in F.S. Regs., Part II. and the Staff Manual respectively. Title Pages will be prepared in manuscript.

Place	Date	Hour	Summary of Events and Information	Remarks and references to Appendices
	22.	2.30 – 3.30	Ammunition drill for Junior NCOs under R.S.M. [?]. Lectures for reserve specialists, machine gunners etc. Lectures to 2 Coy on Musketry Discipline & firing of Mistakes and to 2 Coy on Sanitation and the Care of feet.	Cleave
	23.		8 am Running to drum – to one Bath. Route march. 2-3 Coy at Coy. Platoon squad drill under O.C. Coy. Classes for Specialists and for Junior NCOs near R.S.M. Brigadier Route march. 3 & 4 on Parade & R. "C" Coy found the Rear Guard. Bn. returned to billets about 2pm.	
	24.	10–12	Coys under O.C. Coy for physical exercises & lectures and for muscle exercises. M.O. lectured to the remaining 2 Coys on Care of feet and Sanitation. 10-11 Junior NCOs instruction under R.S.M. 2-3 Coys drew clothing equipment. A message was received from the Brigadier General expressing his satisfaction at the manner in which the unit march was carried out yesterday.	

1875 Wt. W593/826 1,000,000 4/15 J.B.C. & A. A.D.S.S./Forms/C. 2118.

WAR DIARY
Shannon or Neale
INTELLIGENCE SUMMARY
(Erase heading not required.)

Army Form C. 2118

Instructions regarding War Diaries and Intelligence Summaries are contained in F.S. Regs., Part II. and the Staff Manual respectively. Title Pages will be prepared in manuscript.

Place	Date	Hour	Summary of Events and Information	Remarks and references to Appendices
	25.		Men were C of E and Wesleyan services in morning. Remainder of day with company football	
	26.	10.30	Bde moved to MOLING HEM via ATRA. The Battn left at 10.30 & were settled down in new billets by 2.30 p.m.	
	27.		Observed as a holiday. Inter Coy football matches	
	28.	9.45	Running under Platoon commanders. 9-10 Lecture by CO. 10's C. Coys on Outposts. Coys at physical drill. 10-11. O.C. Coys lectured Platoon commanders on outposts. Junior N.C.Os were	
		11-12.	Platoon Commanders lectured on outposts	
		R.S.M.		
		4.p.m.	Inter Coy football match. Details beat 4th Coy	
	29.	9.45	Running. 9.30-11. Lebaldein officers under R.S.M. in drill order for instruction in hand duties etc. Lecture to C/b Co's on outposts. Blankets ironed. Junior N.C.Os under R.S.M. from 11. — 12.30	
		2 p.m.	Inter Batt: football — 8th Battn. S.F. I, 5th Battn. S.F. nil	CO

WAR DIARY

8th Sherwood Foresters

INTELLIGENCE SUMMARY

Army Form C. 2118

(Erase heading not required.)

Place	Date	Hour	Summary of Events and Information	Remarks and references to Appendices
	30		7.45 am Running. 9-10 Squad & Platoon drill. 10.45 Battn route march. Reserve machine gunners under M.G.O. for morning. 2pm Trial inter-Battn Football. 8th Battn S.F. 3 7th Battn nil.	
	31		7.45 am Running. 9.45 Bde Route March. "A & B" Coy under Capt. E.H. HEATHCOTE formed Advance Guard. 3-4. Coy cleaning clothes & blankets with hot irons. Reserve machine gunners under M.G.O. all day. 2-3. Riding class for officers. CA	

J.E. Blackwall Lt. Col.
O.C. 8th Sherwood Foresters.

1/8 Notts & Derby Regt.
Jan
Vol XI

1/8th Sherwood Foresters.

WAR DIARY for Month of January 1916.
Army Form C. 2118
INTELLIGENCE SUMMARY
(Erase heading not required.)

Place	Date	Hour	Summary of Events and Information	Remarks and references to Appendices
MOLINGHEM	Jany 1-		Arrived in Brigade bivouac.	
	2-	12 noon	Church parade in conjunction with 5th Batt.	
	3-	10.30 am	1st Line Transport inspected by Major Hall. Battalion Officers class for instruction	
		7.45 am	Running 9.20 to 10.30 am Coy. marched with greatcoats	
		10.30 am	under R.S.M. Kit inspection.	
		2.30 pm	Conf. of Lieut. 6 12.30 pm. Officers Riding class.	
			2.30 pm. Officers Haversacks Relay Action.	
	4-	7.45 am	Running. 9.30 am. Practice in contd. communication & signals	
		10.30 am	Physical exercises. Practice in recognition of Bugle Calls.	
		11.30 am	Salute. 2.30 pm. Officers Riding class.	
		2.30 pm	2 Courts of Inquiry into cases of 5 men missing since Haversacks Relay Action.	R.I.H.
	5-	7.45 am	Running. 9.30 — 10.30 am. Senior NCO's. Physical exercises under R.I.H.	
		11 am	Batt. Route march thro' LAMBRES & MAZING HEM.	
		2.30 pm	6 3.30 pm. Co. Platoon drill. Offrs. class for physical exercises under R.P.M.	
		2.30	Court of Inquiry into case of 3 men missing since Haversacks Relay Action.	

2.

8th Sherwood Foresters.

WAR DIARY for month of January 1916.

Army Form C. 2118

INTELLIGENCE SUMMARY

(Erase heading not required.)

Instructions regarding War Diaries and Intelligence Summaries are contained in F. S. Regs., Part II. and the Staff Manual respectively. Title Pages will be prepared in manuscript.

Place	Date	Hour	Summary of Events and Information	Remarks and references to Appendices
MOLINGHEM	Jany 6th	7·45 am	Running.	
		9–10 am	Supr. Officer & Senr. NCO's Physical exercise under R.S.M.	
		10 am	Physical exercise. 11 am. Practice in recognition of bugle calls.	
	7th		Enlistment 11th Batt. Sherwood Foresters, who marched over from STEENBECQUE.	
		2·15 pm	Football match v. 11th Batt: score 2–1.	
	8th	10·0 am to 11·30 am	B. & D. Coys. Platoon drill & bayonet fighting. 11·30 am. Co. A. & C. Coys. Cleaning billets & clothing.	
		12·30 pm	Cleaning (Coy details) began. St. Heathcote returned at BERGUETTE. Coy under	
		1·21 pm	to MARSEILLES. also half 1st line Transport vehicles. Brigade Ph. & section completed weekly programme of work changed by clothing. R. & D. Coys. details bathing at A.T.R.E & cleaning clothing.	
	9th		Billets all cleared up in morning inspected by C.O.	
		5·10 pm	B. & D. Coys, H.Q.s. & remainder of vehicles entrained at BERGUETTE Stn. for MARSEILLES. Transport Annual effort MOLINGHEN.	
MARSEILLES	10th	3·0 am	A. & C. Coys. obtained at MARSEILLES marched to BOREL Camp. Moved into fresh tents during afternoon. Various fatigues were found for camp duties.	[sig]

3.
8th Hereford Repl[?]

WAR DIARY for Month of January 1916.
or
INTELLIGENCE SUMMARY
(Erase heading not required.)

Army Form C. 2118

Instructions regarding War Diaries and Intelligence Summaries are contained in F.S. Regs., Part II. and the Staff Manual respectively. Title Pages will be prepared in manuscript.

Place	Date	Hour	Summary of Events and Information	Remarks and references to Appendices
MARSEILLES	Jany. 11th	10.0 a.m.	100 men of A.T.C. Co. marched down to baths. Inspection by O.C. Co. Usual camp fatigues. Draft of 39 Other ranks joined from France. Transport Animals under Transport Officer entrained at LILLERS Stn. for MARSEILLES.	
	12th	9.0 a.m.	H.Qrs. B.&D. Co. & details detrained at MARSEILLES and marched to BORELY Camp and settled down in billet. Remainder went for route march.	
		10.0 a.m.	100 men of A.T.C. Co. bathed: remainder went for route march.	
		10.30 a.m.	Inspection of draft by C.O. & M.O.	
	13th	6.12.30 p.m.	A.T.C. Co. route march. B.&D. Co. sea bathing & Physical exercises. Heavy camp fatigues. Fatigues provided.	
		2.30 p.m.	B.&D. Co. & drums moved from billet up to MOUSSOT Camp under Major E.A. Heathcote.	
		11.0 p.m.	Transport animals detrained at MARSEILLES and marched to lines in BORELY Camp.	[sgd?]

4. Sherwood Forests.

Army Form C. 2118

WAR DIARY

of

INTELLIGENCE SUMMARY

for month of January 1916

(Erase heading not required.)

Instructions regarding War Diaries and Intelligence Summaries are contained in F. S. Regs., Part II. and the Staff Manual respectively. Title Pages will be prepared in manuscript.

Place	Date	Hour	Summary of Events and Information	Remarks and references to Appendices
MARSEILLES	Jany 14"	9.30.	A. T. C. Co. sent 25 men back for both.	
		7.45am	All Co. running on sea front.	
			Junior N.C.O.s instructional class under R.S.M.	
		10-0 - 11. am	Platoon drill & Rifle exercise.	
		11.0 am to 12 Noon	Squad Coy. drill. Junior Officers & Senior N.C.O.s under R.S.M.	
	15"	7.45am	Running.	
		9.30 am to 10.30 am	Squad drill saluting. Class fire	
			Junior Officers & Senior N.C.O.s under R.S.M. { 2 Lieut. Sorbinson Holgen for Marshall joined from Ey Land as supernumerary.	
		10.30 am to 12.30 pm	Kit inspection.	
	16"	8.0 am	H.B. Communion at Marque in BORELY Camp.	
		10.0 am	Parade Service (C. of E.) at MOUSSOT Camp. Friends provided for BORELY Camp.	
		2.0 pm	Vaccination parade at BORELY.	
	17"	7.45am	Running.	
		10.0 am to 12.30 pm	Training in drill, marching &c.	
		2.0 pm	Vaccination parade.	
	18"	"	Usual morning programme of training.	New
			H.Qrs and Signal Section moved to MOUSSOT Camp and Bryn. L.H. Headcote 10th per se command at BORELY Camp.	
	19"		Usual training with classes for Scouts & Semaphore practice.	

5. 8th Leicesters.

WAR DIARY for month of January 1916.

INTELLIGENCE SUMMARY

Army Form C. 2118

Place	Date	Hour	Summary of Events and Information	Remarks and references to Appendices
MARSEILLES	Jany 20	2.0 p.m.	Usual Programme of training. Vaccination parade.	
	21st	2.0 p.m.	Usual training including Posting scheme at MOUSSOT. Class began for instruction in use of Hauritzer. Vaccination parade.	
	22nd		Semaphore practice. Kit inspection.	
	23rd	10.30am	Vaccination parade	
		10 am	Church Parade at MOUSSOT CAMP with 7th Sherwood Forsters.	
	24th	7.30 am	Running. Squad drill. 9.30am. Co. route to C. Co. for Semaphore practice. Squad drill. Issue of clothing. Fire Coy. bathing.	
		10.0 am	Squad marching. Use of Hauritzer. Range finder.	
		12.0 Noon	Bde. Major inspected Battalion Officers & N.C.O.s at drill.	
	25th	6-12.30 p.m	Battn. marched to Race Course & carried out Battalion drill	
		7.30 p.m	Paraded & marched through MARSEILLES to GARE D'ARENC to entrain for NORTH — transport included. — Battalion left MARSEILLES.	
	26th	4.10 am	Entraining completed	hw

6. 2/Sherwood Foresters.

WAR DIARY *for month of January 1916.* Army Form C. 2118

INTELLIGENCE SUMMARY

(Erase heading not required.)

Place	Date	Hour	Summary of Events and Information	Remarks and references to Appendices
In train.	Jany 27th		Travelled via LYON, CHALONS & NOGENT-SUR-SEINE.	
PONT-REMY	28th	11.30am	Arrived at PONT-REMY detrained. Marched 7 mls to billets at ERGNIES, port vacated by 14th Royal Irish Rifles. Settled into billets.	
ERGNIES	29th		Kit & other inspections.	
	30th	11.45am	Church Parade with 3rd Sherwood Foresters at Brigade HQrs, the Château, GORENFLOS. Chaplain present.	
	31st	9.30am to 10.30am	Extended order drill. 11.0am to 12 noon Sewaphone practice, M.G. Section & Grenadiers instructional class. Bayonets.	

J.C. Blackwall
Lieut. Colonel,
Comdg. 2/ Sherwood Foresters

3-2-16.

WAR DIARY or INTELLIGENCE SUMMARY

Army Form C. 2118

1/5 North Staffords
In Front of February 1916

(Erase heading not required.)

Instructions regarding War Diaries and Intelligence Summaries are contained in F. S. Regs., Part II. and the Staff Manual respectively. Title Pages will be prepared in manuscript.

Place	Date	Hour	Summary of Events and Information	Remarks and references to Appendices
ERQUIES	Feb 1st		Batt'n Route March in morning. Training in afternoon.	
do	2nd		Ceremonial drill in morning. Usual training in afternoon.	
	3rd		Batt'n left town in Brigade Ceremonial Parade when Brig. Gen. C.T. Shipley, Comd'g took over a work done by Brigade by Brevet time done keeping & France, and read out his Honours and decoration received.	
	4th		Usual Batt'n training.	
	5th			
	6th		Church Parade with 6th Batt'n North Staffords.	
	7th		Training. Small detachment of 5th N. Staffs joined for return.	
	8th			
	9th		Usual Batt'n training.	
RIBEMCOURT	10th		Batt'n moved from ERQUIES to over ten billets at RIBEMCOURT.	
	11th to		Usual training.	

WAR DIARY / INTELLIGENCE SUMMARY

8th Seaforth Highlanders — For the month of February 1916

Army Form C. 2118

Place	Date	Hour	Summary of Events and Information	Remarks and references to Appendices
RIBEAUCOURT	13th	9.30am	Church Parade.	
	14th		Batln training. In Coy front 2 Platoons at 200 yds Range.	
	15th		Grand training. Very not day.	
	16th		Lectures to Bandsmen, Signallers, M.G. Section. Two Officers 35 N.C.Os & men found Pioneers to take the place of the Pioneer Section originally formed to take the place of Interpreters.	
	17th		General training.	
	18th		Selected Officers went to inspect & take trenches at FORCEVILLE. 3 Cos carried out musketry (practices) at 200 yds Range.	
	19th		Kit inspection. General training.	
CANDAS	20th		Battn moved in Motor lorries to CANDAS and took over 10.1 Billets Area.	

8th Sherwood Foresters

WAR DIARY for the month of February 1916.

INTELLIGENCE SUMMARY
(Erase heading not required.)

Army Form C. 2118

Instructions regarding War Diaries and Intelligence Summaries are contained in F. S. Regs., Part II. and the Staff Manual respectively. Title Pages will be prepared in manuscript.

Place	Date	Hour	Summary of Events and Information	Remarks and references to Appendices
CANDAS	Feb 25th to 26th		Batt. engaged in Railway construction work under orders of 112th Coy. R.E.	Kw
	27th 28th 29th		tit infantry Railway work.	

Edgar H Hartwell
Maj. O.C. 8th Sherwood Foresters.

Army Form C. 2118.

WAR DIARY
or
INTELLIGENCE SUMMARY.
(Erase heading not required.)

Instructions regarding War Diaries and Intelligence Summaries are contained in F. S. Regs., Part II. and the Staff Manual respectively. Title pages will be prepared in manuscript.

W.S. Mounted Troops -
H/Q Mounted Troops 1st Army Corps
March 1916

Place	Date	Hour	Summary of Events and Information	Remarks and references to Appendices
	1916			
CANDAS	Mch 1,2,3		Training including Coys Route marches.	
	4		Squadron presented arms for inspection.	
	5		Church Service.	
			Party of Officers went to MONT ST. ELOY, near SOUCHEZ. Billets at Bruch, 6 the latter passed through.	
IVERNY	6		Proceeded from CANDAS and reached 62nd Bde at IVERNY.	
	7		Started training programme carried out	
MAIZIERES	8		Proceeded to new area to MAIZIERES.	
ACR	9		Marched to fresh billets at ACR.	
MONT ST. ELOY	10		Left Area for Area east of MONT ST. ELOY in support of 6th-6th 7th B.C.A. Div., also relieved 296e, 114e & 125e French Regiments.	
	11,12,13,14		Work in support trenches consisted chiefly in stiffing, improving dugouts, saps, parapets, & repairing communication trenches to French positions.	
	15		Relieved by 2 Regts Royal Park Rifles, returned to respective billets at MONT ST. ELOY.	
	16		Cleaning up camp - Ruts taken over from French.	

2. 8 Reserve Jaeger.

Army Form C. 2118.

WAR DIARY
of Mont St.
INTELLIGENCE SUMMARY.
March 1916.

(Erase heading not required.)

Instructions regarding War Diaries and Intelligence Summaries are contained in F.S. Regs., Part II. and the Staff Manual respectively. Title pages will be prepared in manuscript.

Place	Date	Hour	Summary of Events and Information	Remarks and references to Appendices
MONT ST. ELOY.	15th		Battn. to training at Bruj. Genl. comm'd 129 Inf. Bde. inspected new draft of 143.	
	18th-19th		Training for short time Schotten.	
	19th	10pm	Relieved 7th R.W.F. in LEFT SECTOR Trenches EAST of MONT ST. ELOY to 138 Inf. Regt. being on our left.	
	19th/26th	25th	Occupied trenches. Work consisted of construction of good line of defence as far as possible. Several shelling trips carried out by both sides, but nothing serious happened. 1 OR. has been killed.	
	25th		Relieved by 7 R.W.F. and returned to rest billets at MONT ST. ELOY.	
	26th-31st		Training up & drawing reserve camp and white trenches.	
			carried out daily.	
	31st		Relieved 7 R.W.F. in LEFT SECTOR trenches (as above). ALW.	

J.E. Blackwell
8.4.16
Lt. Col.
Ot. 8 Reserve Jaeger.

J. B. Shenard Fowler

WAR DIARY for Month of April 1916.
or
INTELLIGENCE SUMMARY
(Erase heading not required.)

Army Form C. 2118

Instructions regarding War Diaries and Intelligence Summaries are contained in F.S. Regs., Part II. and the Staff Manual respectively. Title Pages will be prepared in manuscript.

Place	Date April	Hour	Summary of Events and Information	Remarks and references to Appendices
Trenches East of BERTHONVAL Farm near Mt. St. ELOY	1st 2nd		In trenches. Interchange of hand grenades with 138th Inf. Bde on left. Nothing of importance. Usual artillery on both sides.	
	3rd		German aeroplane brought down by one of ours, fell just behind our HQrs dugout.	
	4th		Enemy shelled our front line heavily & did some damage to trenches & minenwerfers.	
	5th 6th		Usual trench work. Batt.n was relieved by 7th Kenmore Fowlers & went back to HQrs in rear of Mt. St. ELOY trench.	
Mt. St. ELOY	7th 8th		Cleaning up. Nothing to in report.	
	9th		Church Parade in "bowl" adjoining billets.	14
	10th 11th		2 platoons of D Coy sent to 46th Div Reserve for drill practice for mid-day. Usual drill — training.	
	12th		G.O.C. 46th Div. inspected Batt.n near billets. Batt.n relieved 7th Notts in left sect.n trenches (same as occupied previously).	

2/ 8th Cheshire Soldiers

WAR DIARY for month of April 1916

INTELLIGENCE SUMMARY

Army Form C. 2118

Place	Date	Hour	Summary of Events and Information	Remarks and references to Appendices
Trenches Sect	Apr 13			
of BERTHONVAL	14		Usual trench work; a forced stand had the men every ½ an hour or so.	
	15		Enemy shelled front line heavily – what were enemy trenches. Hostile aeroplane flew over huts about 11.0 p.m.	
Mt. ST. ELOY	16		French mines exploded mine on front of right of our sector. Capt. C.L. Hill's Coy. (D. Coy.) occupied nearest of craters, consolidated position – (Operation Orders attached).	
	17		Afternoon quiet day. Enemy sprang mine opposite our left at midnight 17/18. Bn A. Coy. established post on nearest lip of crater, but was not able to consolidate position.	
	18		Another mine sprang close in consolidating position, or near lip of crater just mentioned.	
	19		Relieved by Lincolns, relieved also by Spahis. Relieved at night by 10 Shrops Cheshire Regt.	
	20			
TINCQUES	21		Taken in lorries to new billet at TINCQUES for rest. Chances of stealing. Party of 50 men sent to 17 C Corps H.Q. as escort for lorries	
	22			

3. 8th Sherwood Foresters.

Army Form C. 2118

WAR DIARY for month of April 1916
or
INTELLIGENCE SUMMARY

(Erase heading not required.)

Instructions regarding War Diaries and Intelligence Summaries are contained in F. S. Regs., Part II. and the Staff Manual respectively. Title Pages will be prepared in manuscript.

Place	Date	Hour	Summary of Events and Information	Remarks and references to Appendices
TINCQUES	23rd Apl		Easter Day. Church Parade.	
	24th		Party of Officers reconnoitred Corps line between MOROEUIL & MONT ST ELOY.	
	25th		Party of 100 men sent to 2nd School for instruction. Hand training etc.	
	26th		Brig. ord. commanding 139th Inf. Bde. inspected Bn3. represented at lecture of Hurst hmost Women.	
	27th 28th		Usual drill obtaining.	
AVERDOIGNT	29th		Battn moved from TINCQUES and took over billets in AVERDOIGNT from 6th Lincolns.	
	30th		Church Parade.	

J.C. Blackwall
Lt. Colonel,
Comdg 8/ Sherwood Foresters
1-5-16

on the right flank of the crater.

6. A Party of 4 Batt. Bombers from the right of P.77 will be stationed at the head of DUFFIELD and will immediately after the explosion move along the observation line to left flank of crater to repel possible German counter attack, and assist in covering withdrawal of raiding party.

7. O.C. "D" Company will find a Digging party of half a platoon to be stationed in GRANGE in rear of covering party provided with sandbags, shovels and picks, who will follow the covering party to crater formed and proceed to clear Outpost trench or, where that is completely destroyed, dig new trench in solid ground as close as possible to the near lip of the crater to connect up with Outpost Line to right and left and with communication trench in rear. One or two forward posts will be constructed to overlook interior of crater.

8. A carrying party will follow above with further supply of sandbags, 2 reels barbed wire, 40 corkscrews, wire palisades, trench ladders and loophole plates.

9. O.C. "D" Company will find flanking party of 2 Lewis Guns and detachments (to be detailed by L.M.G. Officer) 2 Rifle Grenadiers, 4 Bombers and 12 Rifles under an Officer to be posted in Retrenchment South of GRANGE at a point South of party of Bombers mentioned in para. 5 above. They will follow those Bombers into the Outpost Line and cover with fire the right flank of the crater.

10. O.C. "D" Company will find a second flanking party similar to above in Outpost Line NORTH of DUFFIELD.

11. O.C. "D" Company will place a post in GRANGE at junction with P.76 to prevent stragglers from getting to the rear.

12. Battalion Scouts under Scout Officer will keep up communication between forward operations and Battn. Battle Headquarters.

Operation Orders by Lieut-Col J E Blackwell Comdg.
Left Sector.
16th April 1916

1. Mines will be exploded by the French at 12-0 midnight 16th/17th instant :-
   (a) at head of BIRKIN C.T.
   (b) at head of GRANGE C.T.

2. O.C "D" Company, 8th S.F. will clear Outpost Line by 11-45pm, between GRANGE and DUFFIELD, also GRANGE Retrenchment between GRANGE and GRANGE Retrenchment C.T.

3. He will find a raiding party of One Officer (2/Lieut A. BEDFORD) and 12 Other Ranks, namely, 7 Bayonet men and 5 Bombers who will be stationed in GRANGE facing East, with head at GOERIN, bayonet men being in front and will immediately on explosion of the mine(s) rush up GRANGE round left flank of crater formed to new forward German trench and will capture any German found there, or in the German sap in the continuation of GRANGE. A live specimen will be brought back the remainder being killed and the party returning as quickly as possible, the Bombers covering their withdrawal. The party must not, however, become so involved as to be unable to extricate itself quickly.

4. O.C "D" Company will find a covering party of half a platoon in GRANGE behind the raiding party to hold near lip of crater formed.

5. A party of 4 Battn Bombers from the junction of GUERIN & GRANGE will be stationed in Retrenchment South of GRANGE at point 40yds South of TIDSA and will immediately after the explosion move up TIDSA and along the observation line towards the crater to operate against any possible attack

13. The working party found by 7th Batt. S. Fors. will be in Support in GUERIN, P.76.

14. Battalion Grenade Officer will refill forward stores of grenades, and send forward supplies to bombers as required.

15. Lewis Gun Officer and 2 Reserve Lewis Guns, and Teams will be stationed at the right of P.76.

16. The West Thrower in DUFFIELD and Rifle Grenade Stands will be operated by Brigade Grenade Officer, teams being provided by Battn. Grenade Officer.

17. One gun of the Stokes Battery near GRANGE will fire on German front line North of the crater formed.

18. "B" "C" & "A" Companies will cease work and "stand to" at 11-45 p.m., resuming work at discretion of O's C. Companies.

19. Reports to Sergeants Dugout in P.76, 20 yds from GRANGE.

W.C. Wellman
Capt & Adjutant
8/Sherwood Foresters

Issued at 7-45 p.m. to:-

No. 1 Copy   — War Diary.
 " 2 "   — 137th Inf. Bde.
 " 3 "   — C.R.A.
 " 4 "   — O.C "A" Compy.
 " 5 "   —   "   "B"   "
 " 6 "   —   "   "C"   "
 " 7 "   —   "   "D"   "
 " 8 "   — Compy of Support Battn.
 " 9 "   — 6th S.F.
 " 10 "   — 7th S.F.
 " 11 "   — Left Compy. Right Sector.
 " 12 "   — Grenade Officer.
 " 13 "   — Lewis Gun Officer.

1/8th Sherwood Foresters

Army Form C. 2118.

8. Notts 6D

WAR DIARY
INTELLIGENCE SUMMARY.
(Erase heading not required.)

for month of Nov 1915

Instructions regarding War Diaries and Intelligence Summaries are contained in F. S. Regs., Part II. and the Staff Manual respectively. Title pages will be prepared in manuscript.

Place	Date	Hour	Summary of Events and Information	Remarks and references to Appendices
AVERDOINGT	1915 May 1st		Enemy bombed town.	
	2–3rd		Batt'n took part in practice counter attack with 6th & 7th Notts at TINCQUES.	
	4th		30 men & 1 Offr. Sent proceed to T. POC to dig in Rear 3rd Army. Bomb training.	
REBREUVIETTE	5th		Batt'n moved to billets at REBREUVIETTE.	
	6th		Batt'n marched out 6.30–7.0 E. Rally and occupied new billets at GAUDIEMPRÉ.	
GAUDIEMPRÉ	7th			
	8 + 9		Bomb training. Advance body formed for 7th Batt R.E. (except transport).	
BIENVILLERS 10th			Batt'n moved to BIENVILLERS (except transport). Transport moved to HUMBERCAMPS.	
	10 – 18		Large fatigue parties found daily for improving communications between FONCQUEVILLERS and FONCQUEVILLERS & front line.	
FONCQUE-VILLERS	19th		Batt'n moved to FONCQUEVILLERS and took over billets &c. of support batt'n from 5th Nottss batt'n.	

2/1. 8 Sherwood Foresters.

Army Form C. 2118.

WAR DIARY
or
INTELLIGENCE SUMMARY.

(Erase heading not required.)

War diary for month of May 1916.

Place	Date	Hour	Summary of Events and Information	Remarks and references to Appendices
FONCQUEVILLERS	May 20th 19th-26th		Transferred to SOUASTRE. Remained in support to 5th, 6th & 7th Batts Sherwood Foresters who occupied whole of 46th Div. front. 5th Batt being on right. Working parties provided daily to open out communication trenches running from FONCQUEVILLERS village to front line.	
Do.	27th		Relieved 6th Batt Sherwood Foresters in centre sector - right & left Batts remaining in same positions.	
Do.	28th, 29th, 30th, 31st		Very quiet time in trenches. Little activity being displayed by either side. The Batt was busy improving trenches which were not in good order.	

J.W....
O.C. 8 Sherwood Foresters

WAR DIARY
INTELLIGENCE SUMMARY.
(Erase heading not required.)

Army Form C. 2118.

For month of June 1916
1/5 North Staffs Battn
Vol 16

Place	Date	Hour	Summary of Events and Information	Remarks and references to Appendices
FONCQUEVILLERS	June 1916 1st & 2nd		Usual trench work. Rated on Wiring opposite June – CENTRE SECTOR at present held by this Battn.	
	3rd		H.M. the King's Birthday. Bombardment of enemy's trenches in front of GOMMECOURT WOOD which did considerable damage.	
	4th		Usual trench routine.	
	5th		Battn was relieved at night by 4th Batt Leicestershire Regt & marched to HUMBERCAMP & huts.	
HUMBERCAMP	6th	9.30pm	Marched from HUMBERCAMP and proceeded via GAUDIEMPRÉ, LE SOUICH KILLED	
LE SOUICH	7th	3.00am	MONDICOURT and LUCHEUX to LE SOUICH.	
	8th – 14th		Training & signal Training when Nos Attack practice over Sus St. LEGER Bayonet fighting Athletics sprinting & marching parties found daily from work in LUCHEUX FOREST.	
HUMBERCAMP	15th	5.30pm	Battn moved from LE SOUICH & proceeded via Sus St LEGER – WARLUZEL – COUTURELLE & NOUVILLE to HUMBERCAMP	
	16,17,–18		Working parts found for digging & etc evening approach trenches, re. Nyli 1919 – 18th New positions of LEFT SECTOR Trenches air FONCQUEVILLERS	
FONCQUE-VILLERS	18th			

Henry Fowler

WAR DIARY
or
INTELLIGENCE SUMMARY.
(Erase heading not required.)

Army Form C. 2118.

Month of June 1916.

Place	Date	Hour	Summary of Events and Information	Remarks and references to Appendices
FONCQUEVILLERS.	5/6		From 5th Battn Yorkshire Regt., 11th Royal Warwick being on (left of 37th Division).	
	19th–27th		Continued to occupy above trenches. Be latter part of the time were very wet. The knobs [?] of us very bad condition, in most cases being 2ft. 0 ins. deep in mud and water. Pitching hard work in attempting to keep them clear.	
			In the last 4 days on Artillery constantly bombarded Enemy positions doing considerable damage.	
			Few casualties during the 5th Battn. Yorkshire Suffered one [?] wounded.	
	27/28th		Battn. was relieved by 5th Battn. Yorkshire Regt. and marched back to billets at POMMIER.	
POMMIER.	29th 30th		Resting and cleaning up at POMMIER. Battn. marched from POMMIER to FONCQUEVILLERS. Took part in attack by 46th Divn on GOMMECOURT. Copy of Operation Order is attached.	[signature]

J. W. Leatham, Lt
N. W. Cunningham
[Lt?] [?]

1.

OPERATION ORDERS BY LIEUTENANT COLONEL J.R.BLACKWALL, COMMANDING
8th Sherwood Foresters,
June 30th 1916.

MOVE. The Battalion will move up to the trenches tonight to take part in the attack by the 139th Infantry Brigade tomorrow, against German trenches North of GOMMECOURT WOOD.

GENERAL
DISPOSITIONS. General Dispositions in accordance with Brigade operation orders already communicated.

DISTRIBUTION. The battalion will be in Brigade Reserve and will be distributed as follows:-

'D' Company, with 2 Lewis Guns and teams. (BUSH TRENCH - BASTION - and (1st SUPPORT LINE, North of (RAYMOND AVENUE.

'A' Company. NAMELESS ROAD, with right on Battalion Headquarters.

'B' Company (less two platoons) (ditto with left on (RAYMOND AVENUE.

'B' Company (remainder) LISIERE- left on RAYMOND AVENUE.

'C' Company (less two platoons) (ditto. left on ROBERTS (AVENUE.

'C' Company (remainder) ditto. right on ROBERTS AVENUE.

Lewis Gunners - remainder.) Dugouts - SNIPERS SQUARE.
(6 Guns and teams), under)
Lewis Gun Officer)
Bombers (under Grenade Officer))
Signallers & Battn. Runners.) ditto.
Scouts and Snipers.)

'A' Company will act as carrying Company.

ALLOTMENT
OF C.T's. C.T's are alloted as follows:-
RAYMOND AND ROBERTS AVENUES - UP.
ROTTEN ROW & REGENTS STREET - DOWN.
STAFFORD AVENUE - DOWN, for both Brigades for wounded.
The Battalion will move up to Support Lines Nos. 1 & 2 as these become vacant in following order:-
'B' Company via RAYMOND AVENUE to 1st Support Line astride RAYMOND AVENUE.
'C' Company via ROBERTS AVENUE to 1st Support Line left of ROBERTS AVENUE.
'A' Company via ROBERTS AVENUE to 2nd Support Line left of ROBERTS AVENUE.
Details in SNIPERS SQUARE will move up to 1st Support Line on right of ROBERTS AVENUE and take up position from left to right in order - Runners and Signallers, Lewis Gunners, Bombers, Scouts and Snipers - with left on ROBERTS AVENUE.
Battalion Headquarters will move up to Battalion Headquarters in 1st Support Line right of ROBERTS AVENUE.

RUNNERS. 5 Runners per Company will be at Battalion Headquarters for working there and at Brigade Headquarters. They will parade tonight with the Signallers. They will only carry 10 rounds S.A.A. per man.

DUMPS FOR
STORES. All ranks must be acquainted with the positions of S.A.A. stores, Grenades, R.E.Stores, T.M. Ammunition, Water and Rations, particulars of which have already been issued.

RATIONS &c. Every man will carry his Iron Ration, tomorrows ration and a
bacon and bread sandwich.   Water bottles will be taken up
full.   In all probability no further water supply will be
available for 24 hours.
Cookers will be on Western side of FONQUEVILLERS and soup will
be issued before going in to trenches (except to 'B' Company for
which other arrangements will be made.
Rum and tea will be issued early tomorrow morning under arrangements to be notified later.

EQUIPMENT. Every N.C.O. and man will carry :-
 (1) 200 rounds S.A.A.
 (2) 4 sandbags, worn in front under braces.
 (3) 2 Mills grenades.
 (4) 2 Gas helmets.
 (5) Haversack and water proof sheet.
 (6) In addition each Company and H.Q.Details will carry 16 pairs
     wire cutters.   Gloves will be distributed equally, between
     these parties.   These will be drawn before the Battalion
     leaves billets.
S.A.A., Stores, etc., mentioned under (1) (2) & (3) will be
drawn from the dump at FONQUEVILLERS BEFORE PROCEEDING TO THE
trenches.
There are also 70 Trench Grids at entrance to C.T's from MAIN ROAD
which will be drawn and carried by 'A' 'B' & 'C' Companies &
H.Qrs Details in equal numbers.

PACKS,   Packs of all ranks will be stacked in yard at Headquarters by
GREATCOATS, 6-0 pm, greatcoats in rooms at School at same time, properly
etc.   labelled and all arranged in heaps by Companies and Sections.
Officers valises to be at yard at Headquarters by 6-0pm.

BLOCKING   Corporal Cross and 1 N.C.O. per company, already told off, with
POSTS.   15 Light and EX. Duty men to be told off later, will take charge
of 5 Blocking Posts.   These will march with Headquarters in rear
of the Battalion, and receive further instructions tonight at
FONQUEVILLERS.

OFFICERS AND The Officers and N.C.O's not going into action will proceed as a
N.C.O's not   party under the senior Officer immediately behind the Battalion
GOING INTO   to the Headquarters of the 7th Battalion Sherwood Foresters at
ACTION.   BIENVILLERS where they will await further instructions.
Major A.L.Ashwell, D.S.O. and Lieut R.A.Abrams will proceed to
advanced Battalion Headquarters and remain there.

BATTLEFIELD Police for duty on the Battlefield to see that no looting occurs
POLICE.   during the collection of dead and wounded will be detailed later.

TIME.   Watches will be synchronised to-day by Runner from H.Q. who will
carry a watch shewing Brigade time.

DOCUMENTS.   Regimental Officers and O.R. will not carry on their person
any documents, copies of orders or plans shewing any details
of our own disposition or trenches.   Maps will not be sent to
Battalion Headquarters.

HEADQUARTERS. Battalion Headquarters will close at POMMIER at 8-0 pm tonight
and will reopen at Battle H.Qrs. near SNIPERS SQUARE at 3-0 am.
During the interval messages for H.Qrs should be sent to junk
junction of FONQUEVILLERS - BIENVILLERS ROAD, with road west of
WESTERN LISERE.

                                (Signed) W.C.C.Weetman,
                                    Captain & Adjutant.

Army Form C. 2118.

WAR DIARY or INTELLIGENCE SUMMARY.

(Erase heading not required.)

Instructions regarding War Diaries and Intelligence Summaries are contained in F. S. Regs., Part II. and the Staff Manual respectively. Title pages will be prepared in manuscript.

8th Reserve Fusiliers — 118th W & 69 Bridge — for month of July 1916. — Vol 17

Place	Date	Hour	Summary of Events and Information	Remarks and references to Appendices
FONCQUE-VILLERS	1916 July 1st	1.15am	Battalion began move up from FONCQUEVILLERS. Take its place in trenches allotted to Reserve Batt.	Appendix 1.
		3.15am	Batt. was in position, sweep-in company parties taking up headquarters	
			Wire heights B 5ᵃ, 6ᵃ & 7ᵃ Batt.s which reported later	
		6.25am	Intense Bombardment began, lasted until 7.30 am.	
		7.25	Smoke discharged continued for ½ hour.	
		7.30	Battⁿˢ moved off to the assault. Heavy losses on our front.	
			Wire none or no portion.	
		8-10.30 am	Companies began to move forward to support line which however in many cases were blocked by killed & wounded — & little progress was made. The hospital in four instances (no one successful) communication with German front line has not been made hope was had all cleared away.	
		Noon	Little action of any kind — very little information received as to	
		3.0pm	progress made by assaulting Batt.ˢ	
		3.0pm	Fresh bombardment began on right brigade front.	
		3.30	Bombardment continued by 20, with a new fresh attack being launched	[?]
		4.15pm		

17

Army Form C. 2118.

8th Sherwood Foresters.

WAR DIARY
INTELLIGENCE SUMMARY.
(Erase heading not required.)

Instructions regarding War Diaries and Intelligence Summaries are contained in F. S. Regs., Part II. and the Staff Manual respectively. Title pages will be prepared in manuscript.

Place	Date	Hour	Summary of Events and Information	Remarks and references to Appendices
FONCQUE- VILLERS	1916 July 1st		Arty. Bos. & 6th Batt. which however was cancelled.	
		5.55 p.␣	Orders were received to send out daylight patrols to ascertain enemy positions. These were sent out, but could not get far. They brought back some useful information.	
		6.10 p.␣	Orders received to relieve Robins in old front line reformed line. 5th & 7th to pass Batts. whilst our & A. Co., both our line, with D. on left, C. Co. in support line & B. Co. at SNIPER'S SQUARE.	
		9.30 p.␣	Orders received that 5th Lincs would attack from our line at midnight. We were accordingly rearranged & A. Co's area taken over by 5th Lincs	
	1/2	m.n.	5th Lincs attacked towards Gommecourt - but came back without success.	
	2nd		A. Co. sent out after the attack to collect wounded etc. Batt. was completely relieved in trenches by 5th Lincs & Northamptons to billets at GROVIESMPRE.	
GROVIESMPRE				
BAVINCOURT	3rd		Batt. moved to camp at BAVINCOURT.	
POMMIER	4th		Batt. left BAVINCOURT. marched through Halloy-au-POMMIER with A. Co. at BIENVILLERS.	Gws

T2134. Wt. W708 -776. 500000. 4/15. Sir J. C. & S.

8 (S) Seaforth Highlanders

Army Form C. 2118.

WAR DIARY
or
INTELLIGENCE SUMMARY.

(Erase heading not required.)

for month of July 1916

Hour, Date, Place	Summary of Events and Information	Remarks and references to Appendices
July 5th & 6th POMMIER	Working parties provided for schools at PONCQUEVILLERS. A coy. working on trenches in Divisional line at BIENVILLERS.	
7th BIENVILLERS.	Remainder of Batt: left POMMIER and joined BIENVILLERS.	Appendix 2.
8th "	A bye. R.E. carrying parties found for trenches near MONCHY.	
9th "	Special R.E. carrying parties found for trenches near MONCHY. – Special Carrying parties.	
	Intended Church Service by Major Forbes – cancelled	Appendix 3.
10th BELLACOURT.	Batt: left BIENVILLERS & proceeded by route to BELLACOURT & billeted there, halting for dinners at BASSEUX en route.	" 4.
11th Trenches –	Relieved LIVERPOOL SCOTTISH in trenches in front of BRETENCOURT, opposite BEAUVILLE 6th Batt: Seaforth Highlanders being on right & 5th Gordons on left.	
11th to 15th Trenches.	Varied trench work – nothing of importance except a bombardment between 4.0 & 5.0 a.m. on 13th of French Front line trench section, inflicting 10 casualties.	

8th Sherwood Foresters

WAR DIARY of month of July 1916

Army Form C. 2118.

INTELLIGENCE SUMMARY.

Hour, Date, Place	Summary of Events and Information	Remarks and references to Appendices
July 14th Trenches	9th Batt'n took over a little extra line on its left from the 6th LIVERPOOL REGT	
15th "	Slight redistribution - by 8th Batt'n moving left, taking over our own right Coy area	Appendix 5
17th "	Batt'n was relieved at night by 7th Sherwood Foresters & marched back to billets at BAILLEUL VAL & bivouac	" 6
18th - 22nd BAILLEUL-VAL	Reserve. Cleaning up - Lewis training, including Coy commanders, physical exercise, bayonet fighting, route marches, etc. Stokes over drill, bombing return from practice. Inspection by G.O.C. Division on parade ground.	
19th 10.30am "	Church parade addressed by Maj. Genl Commanding 139th Inf. Bde.	
23rd BAILLEUL-VAL	Relieved 7th Sherwood Foresters in LEFT SECTOR trenches at night.	Appendix 7.

Bews

5. 8th Sherwood Foresters.

WAR DIARY
~~or~~
INTELLIGENCE SUMMARY

Army Form C. 2118

for month of July, 1916.

Place	Date 1916	Hour	Summary of Events and Information	Remarks and references to Appendices
Trenches	July 23rd to 29th		Held LEFT SECTOR Trenches with 5th DORSET REGT. on left. 6th SHERWOOD FORESTERS on right. A quiet time and nothing of importance happened.	Appendix 8.
BELLACOURT	29th		Relieved in left sector by 2nd Batt. Sherwood Foresters removed back into Brigade Reserve. 3 Co. in BELLACOURT. one Coy. occupying Strong posts in Brigade Area. Co. bathing cleaning up.	
"	30th		Church Parade - Co. found working parties.	
"	31st		Station carried on instruction training. parties for R.E.	
			Casualties. Officers wounded :- Capt. R.W. VANN, 2/Lt. A.H.G. COX & 2/Lt. H. de C. MARTELLI. Other ranks:- killed 4; wounded 54; died of wounds 6.	

A.J. Ashwell
Major
O.C.
8th Sherwood Foresters

2.

OPERATION ORDERS BY LIEUTENANT COLONEL J.E.BLACKWALL, COMMANDING
8th Sherwood Foresters.
July 6th 1916.

1. ~~Remainder of~~ Battalion (less A Coy) will move to BIENVILLERS tonight at times to be notified later.

2. O's.C. 'B' 'C' & 'D' Companies will arrange to have their Companies packs ready for the Transport to pick up at their H.Qrs billets.

3. Cookers and water carts will go to billets at BIENVILLERS.

4. Transport will move to LA CAUCHIE also Q.M. Stores.

5. Officers valises and other stores of Companies to be carried will be sent to Q.M. Stores by 6-0 pm.

6. Billets must be left thoroughly clean and Company Messes paid for.

7. Exact time to leave will be notified later, but preparations must be made at once as the Battalion has to be clear of POMMIER by 8-0 pm.

(Signed) W.C.C.Weetman,
Captain & Adjutant,
8th Sherwood Foresters.

3.

OPERATION ORDERS BY LIEUTENANT COLONEL J.E.BLACKWALL, COMMANDING
8th Sherwood Foresters,
July 10th 1916.

1. The Battalion will move to-day by route march to BELLACOURT via POMMIER - LA CAUCHIE - V.18.b.central - W.7.d. - BAILLEUMONT - BAILLEULVAL - BASSEUX.

2. Battalion will move off by platoons at 4 minute intervals in the following order:-
   Signallers, Scouts and Snipers, Bombers, 'A' 'B' 'C' 'D' Lewis Gunners, Stretcher Bearers & Headquarter Details.
   Each Section will count as one platoon; the first platoon will leave at 12-0 noon. Watches will be synchronised before that hour.
   Dress - full marching order.
   Company Cookers will march in rear of each company. A halt will be made at BASSEUX for dinners.
   Transport will move independently to BAILLEUMONT.

3. Officers valises and all stores to be carried on Transport will be at Headquarters by 11-0 am. No surplus kit of Officers will be carried on Mess cart.

4. Billets must be left thoroughly clean and certificates to this effect together with marching out states must be rendered to Orderly Room by 11.30 am.

5. A billeting party of one N.C.O. per Company and Section will meet 2nd Lieutenant A.H.G.Cox at Headquarters at 12-0 noon, dress - full marching order. Bicycles will NOT be provided for this party.

6. O.C. 'D' Company will detail a leading party of 1 N.C.O. and 7 men to load baggage wagons at Headquarters at times to be notified later.

7. Battalion Headquarters will close at BIENVILLERS at 1.30 pm and open at BELLACOURT on arrival.

(Signed) W.C.C.Weetman,
Captain & Adjutant.

4

SECRET

OPERATION ORDERS BY LIEUT COLONEL J.E.BLACKWALL, COMMANDING
8th Sherwood Foresters.
July 11th 1916.

RELIEF.   The Battalion will relieve the LIVERPOOL SCOTTISH in the Left
Sector (Trenches 149 to 161 inclusive) to-day. The distribution
will be as follows:-

Trench Area.		Company.
THE WILLOWS (Right)	- 2 Platoons in Front Line and 2 Platoons in support.	'A'
THE OSIERS (Centre)	ditto.	'B'
THE RAVINE (Left)	ditto.	'C'
BRETENCOURT	Reserve Company.	'D'

Bombers, Lewis Gunners, Signallers, Scouts and Snipers will take
over corresponding Posts and Stations of the outgoing Battn.

ORDER OF   Relief will take place in the following order:-
RELIEF.
10-0 am - Signallers, Scouts and Snipers. Guides will be at
Headquarter Mess at that time.
1 Officer and 1 N.C.O per Company will proceed to
Trenches to take over Stores &c. under above mentioned
Guides.
11-0 am - Lewis Gun Officer with 8 Lewis Gun Teams. 8 Guides
will be at Headquarter Mess at that time for the 8
Teams.
2-0 pm - Guides for 7 Bombing Posts will be at Headquarters
Mess. Posts will be provided as follows:-
Battalion Bombers will provide 2 Posts each for 'B'
and 'C' Company.
'A' Company will provide 3 Posts from its Company
Bombers.
'A' 'B' & 'C' Companies will move by platoons this afternoon at
half hour intervals. The first platoon of each Company
leaving at 2.10pm. One Guide per platoon will be provided.
'D' Company will move in small parties to BRETENCOURT, the first
party leaving at 2.10 pm.
O's.C.Cos. will send 1 Runner each to H.Qrs Mess at 2-0 pm to
conduct Guides to their Company Headquarters.
Headquarter Details will be arranged later.

COOKING &c.   No cooking will be done in the trenches. Hot food will be
carried up by a party from the Reserve Company, details of which
will be notified. Company cookers will move to BRETENCOURT
this afternoon, also 1 Water Cart.
Dry rations will be carried up nightly by working parties.

BILLETS,   Billets must be left clean and tidy. Certificates as to this
STORES, &c. to be rendered before Companies move off.
List of stores in present billets to be handed over to incoming
Battalion to be sent to Orderly Room by 12 noon.
List of stores taken over from the LIVERPOOL SCOTTISH will be
forwarded to Orderly Room by 12 noon tomorrow.
Report on Vermorel Sprayers by 10-0 am.
O's.C. 'A' 'B' & 'C' Companies will each draw from the stores
before leaving billets 2 box periscopes, 6 vigilants, 2 1" &
1 1½" Verey Pistols.

TRENCH   O's.C.Cos will forward to Orderly Room by noon tomorrow, garrison
GARRISON. strength return on usual proforma. The Signalling Officer
will report for Headquarters Details.

(OVER.)

OFFICERS VALISES.	Officers valises will be sent to Stores by 2-0 pm.
WATER DUTY MEN.	The R.A.M.C. Details attached will carry out their usual water duties.
SICK PARADE.	Sick parade will be at 2-0 pm daily.
ARTILLERY SUPPORT.	Details of Artillery Support will be forwarded.

                                                                                    Captain & Adjutant.
                                                                                    8th Sherwood Foresters.

SECRET.

OPERATION ORDERS BY LIEUTENANT COLONEL J.H.BLACKWALL, COMMANDING
8th Sherwood Foresters,
July 15th 1916.

RELIEF.
(1) 'A' Company will be relieved in the WILLOWS Section, trenches 149 to 152 inclusive, tonight by a Company of 6th Battalion S.F. 1 Guide per platoon from 'A' Company will be at the Headquarters of the 5th Battalion S.F. in BELLACOURT by 5.30 pm to guide the 4 platoons of the Company of the 6th Battalion to the trenches. The guides will call at Orderly Room on their way down for a cyclist guide. A

(2) On relief 'E' Company will take over the OSIERS Section from 'B' Company. All arrangements for the relief will be made between O's.C.Cos. concerned.

(3) On relief, 'B' Company moving by platoons, will take over billets in BRETENCOURT occupied by the carrying Company of the 5th S.F. They will also take over carrying duties of that Company, beginning with the carrying of breakfasts tomorrow morning, also any road or police duties in BRETENCOURT.
O.C. 'B' Company will take particular care to prevent men entering unoccupied gardens or houses of inhabitants, by a proper system of policing.

LEWIS GUN-NERS.
The two Lewis Guns and teams in 'B' Company area will be relieved and withdrawn to dug-outs in QUARRIES under arrangements to be made by Lewis Gun Officer.

BOMBERS.
'A' Company Bombers will take over the two Bombing Posts in the OSIERS Section at present held by Battalion Bombers. The two Battalion groups thus relieved, will withdraw to billets in BRETENCOURT under arrangements to be made between Grenade Officer and O.C. 'B' Company.

STORES.
Trench Stores taken over on relief will be handed over in each case to the relieving Company and receipts obtained. O.C. 'B' Company on relief, will hand in to Orderly Room all Battalion Stores, i.e., periscopes, Verey Pistols and wire cutters (if any).

July 15th 1916.
Captain & Adjutant.
8th Sherwood Foresters.

SECRET.

OPERATION ORDERS BY LIEUTENANT COLONEL J.E. BLACKWALL, COMMANDING,
8th Sherwood Foresters,
July 17th 1916.

1. RELIEF. The Battalion (less Support Company) will be relieved by 7th Battn. Sherwood Foresters tonight.

2. ORDER OF RELIEF. Relief will take place in following order:-
Signallers, Bombers, Lewis Gunners, during afternoon.
'A' 'C' & 'D' Companies, tonight.
The relieved Bombers and Lewis Gunners will remain at their Posts until Companies begin to relieve to-night. Lewis Gun Officer will arrange for removal of guns this evening.

3. GUIDES, &c. Guides for Signallers, Lewis Gunners & Bombers will leave H.Qrs. at 1.30 pm to be at point R.26.B.3.4. to meet relieving Sections at 2.30 pm.
Guides for Companies will be as follows:-

8th Sherwood Foresters.					7th S.F.
'A' Coy.-	4 (2 front & 2 support),		for	'A' &	'C' Cos.
'C' " -	2 (1 "	1 ")	"	'B' Company.
'D' " -	2 (1 "	1 ")	"	'D' "

These guides will report at Battalion Headquarters at 7.30 pm and be taken by Signallers to point R.26.B.3.4. where relieving Battn. will be met at 8.30 pm.
1 Officer and 1 N.C.O. per Company will take over stores, &c., by daylight.
RIGHT Company will move via ENGINEER STREET, Centre by QUARRY & LAMOTTE, AND Left by BLAMONT & BLAIREVILLE.

4. MOVEMENT. On relief Sections and Companies by Platoons at intervals will move viz cross roads near old Headquarters BELLACOURT to BAILLEUVAL (in Divisional Reserve) and take over billets arranged by Q.M.

5. COOKERS. Cookers (except 'B' Cos.) will move after tea.

6. STORES. Stores &c. to be taken on Transport will be at dump BRETENCOURT by 9-0 pm.
Periscopes, Verey pistols and wire cutters in possession will be taken out by Companies and handed into Orderly Room by noon tomorrow.
List of stores to be handed over to be sent to O.R. & 7. pm today.

7. OFFICERS SERVANTS. Two Officers servants per Company may go out with Officers Stores &c., at 9-0 pm and accompany Transport to billets.

8. SUPPORT COMPANY. 'B' Company will remain in present billets as a supporting Coy. to LEFT SECTOR and will be at disposal of O.C. 7th Battn. tactically and for carrying *and working if required*

9. REPORT ON WORK. O's.C.Cos. will render within 24 hours of relief, brief report of work done during tour. Headings for report will be sent round.

10. INTERIM REPORT. A short report for period noon to 8-0 pm will be sent in by 8.30 pm. *today.*

W.C. Weedman
Captain & Adjutant.
8th Sherwood Foresters.

July 17th 1916.

7.

OPERATION ORDERS BY LIEUTENANT COLONEL J.E.BLACKWALL COMMANDING,
8th Sherwood Foresters,
July 23rd 1916.

RELIEF.
The Battalion will relieve the 7th Battn. S.F. in LEFT SECTOR trenches to-day. The distribution will be as follows:-

Area.			Company.
OSIERS	- -	(2 Platoons in front line)	'A' Company.
		(2 " " Support.)	
RAVINE	- -	ditto.	'B' "
EPSOM	- -	ditto.	'D' "
BRETENCOURT	-	(Reserve Company.)	'C' Company.

Bombers, Lewis Gunners, Signallers & Scouts will take over corresponding posts and stations from outgoing Battalion.
Scouts, Reserve Lewis Gunners & Bombers will be stationed in dugouts in QUARRIES.

ORDER OF RELIEF.
Relief will take place in the following order:-
Signallers, Scouts, Lewis Gunners, D, B & A Cos & Battn. Bombers, and Headquarter Details.
The first three Sections will relieve during the afternoon by arrangements between O's.C. Sections concerned - Lewis Gunners parading at L.G's billet at 2.30 pm in full marching order.
The remainder will move by platoons, at 4 minute intervals, D Coy. leaving at 7.15 pm.
Battalion Runners - 2 each from 'B' & 'D' Companies, 3 from 'C' Company and 1 from 'A' Company - will parade with Signallers at times to be notified by Signalling Officer.
The special party of 'A' Company will remain for the present at BRETENCOURT.
One Officer and 2 N.C.O's per Company will proceed to trenches by 4-0 pm to take over stores &c.

COOKING, &c.
Carrying parties for rations &c., will be furnished by the Company in Reserve.
Company Cookers and 1 water cart will move to BRETENCOURT after tea to-day.

BILLETS.
The usual billet certificates, including payment for Company Messes, to be rendered by 6-0 pm.

BILLET STORES.
Stores in present billets will be handed over to 5th Battn. and must be left tidily arranged.

TRENCH STORES.
Following returns are due at Headquarters on day following relief:-
(1) List of stores taken over - by noon.
(2) Report on Vermorel Sprayers, blankets, &c. for dugouts - by 10-0 am.
(3) Certificates that 1 pick and 1 shovel are in every dugout in trenches by - by 6-0 pm.

BATTALION STORES.
O's.C. 'A' 'B' & 'D' Companies will each draw from Orderly Room before leaving for trenches:-
2 Box Periscopes, 10 Vigilants.
2 1" Verey Pistols (except 'B' Company who will draw one only)
1 1½" ditto.
Centre Company should take over 2 1" and 1 1½" pistols from 7th S.F. Notification of this to be sent to Battalion Headquarters.

(P.T.O.)

TRENCH GARRISON.	O's.C. Trench Sections will forward to Headquarters by noon tomorrow. Garrison strength return on usual proforma. Signalling Officer will report for Headquarters Details.
VALISES.	Officers valises will be sent to Stores by 6-0pm.
WATER DUTY MEN.	The R.A.M.C. Details attached will carry out their usual water duties at Transport Lines and BRETENCOURT.
SICK PARADE.	Sick parade will be at 2-0 pm daily.
ARTILLERY SUPPORT.	Details of Artillery Support will be forwarded. O.C. "OSIERS" will test Battery once nightly.

Captain & Adjutant,
8th Sherwood Foresters.

OPERATION ORDERS BY LIEUTENANT COLONEL J.E.BLACKWALL, COMMANDING
8th Sherwood Foresters,
July 29th 1916.

RELIEF. The Battalion will be relieved tonight by the 7th Battalion S.F.

ORDER OF RELIEF. Relief will take place in the following order:-
    Lewis Gunners beginning at 2.30 pm.
    Bombers   "   " 3.30 pm.
    Signallers   "   " 4-0 pm.
    'A' Company   "   " 6-0 pm.
    'B' 'C' & 'D' Companies and Headquarters Details (including servants) beginning at 8.45 pm.

POSTS. 'A' Company will take over the following Posts when relieved:-
    BURNT FARM,   ORCHARD,
    STARFISH,   BOUNDARY.
One platoon under an Officer will garrison each Post; the Lewis Gun Officer will also arrange for one Lewis Gun and team to be placed at each Post.

MOVEMENT. Other Companies (moving by platoons) and Sections will, on relief, proceed to take over billets from the 7th S.F. at BELLACOURT, in Brigade Reserve.

GUIDES. The 7th Battn.S.F. will provide 4 Guides, one for each platoon of 'A' Company, to conduct platoons to the various Posts.

BILLETS. The Q.M. will arrange for C.Q.M.Sergts. to take over billets during the day and meet their Companies at Divisional Canteen at night.
O's.C. Sections will send on one N.C.O. per Section to take over billets and meet their Sections on arrival.

STORES. Major A.L.Ashwell will arrange to take over stores in the village. One Officer per Company of the relieving Battalion will come up to the trenches during the day to take over trench stores: list of these will be sent to Headquarters by noon.
Officer's stores, etc., to be taken on Transport will be at dump, BRETENCOURT, by 7-0 pm.
Periscopes, Verey pistols, wire cutters, etc., in possession will be taken out by Companies and handed in to Orderly Room by noon tomorrow.

OFFICERS SERVANTS. Two Officer's servants per Company may go out with Officer's stores, etc., at 7-0 pm and accompany Transport to billets.

REPORT ON WORK. O's.C. Cos. will render within 24 hours of relief, brief report on work done during tour. Headings of report have already been notified.

INTERIM REPORT. A short report for period up to 7-0 pm will be sent in to Orderly Room by 7.30 pm.

July 29th 1916.

Lieut Colonel,
O.C., 8th Sherwood Foresters.

1. 1/8th Sherwood Foresters.

Army Form C. 2118.

WAR DIARY
for the Month of August 1916.

INTELLIGENCE SUMMARY.
(Erase heading not required.)

Instructions regarding War Diaries and Intelligence Summaries are contained in F. S. Regs., Part II. and the Staff Manual respectively. Title pages will be prepared in manuscript.

Vol 18

Hour, Date, Place	Summary of Events and Information	Remarks and references to Appendices
1916.		
Aug. 1st BELLACOURT.	2 Officers & 32 Other Ranks joined Brigade Company for special work on dug-outs.	
" 2nd "	Battn was in Brigade Reserve. Large parties were provided daily to work on trenches, & under R.E.	
" 3rd "		
" 4th Trenches.	Relieved 7th Battn Sherwood Foresters in LEFT SECTOR, with Support Coy at BRETENCOURT.	
" 5th "	4 quiet days in trenches: nothing of importance to report.	6
" 6 – 9 "		
" 10th " 11.0pm	Trenches taken over by 7th Battn Sherwood Foresters.	
Nq Lt 10/11th BAILLEULVAL.	Battn marched to Baillelval in Divisional Reserve.	
" 11th "		
" 12th "	2 Officers & 50 Other Ranks proceeded to Divisional School	
" 13 "	for diverse purposes. Church Parade.	18
" 14th-15th "	Large working parties provided daily for work under R.E.; Battn holding & made up deficiencies. A little evening was carried out – & firing practice at range.	W.W.

Forms/C. 2118/10

2. 1/8th Sherwood Forester.

WAR DIARY of

INTELLIGENCE SUMMARY. August 1916.

Army Form C. 2118.

1916. Hour, Date, Place	Summary of Events and Information	Remarks and references to Appendices
Aug. 16th Trenches. 11.0 p.m.	Batt. relieved 7th Batt. Sherwood Foresters in LEFT SECTOR Trenches, Support Coy. being at BRETENCOURT. 1 Officer & 14 Other ranks of 1/1st R.D. Guards with 4 Hotchkiss guns joined garrison of Left Sector.	
" 21st "		
" 17th – 21st "	Very quiet tour in trenches: very little activity shewn by enemy.	
" 22nd/23rd midnight.	7 B Sherwood Foresters took over trenches, both over trenches, relief being very late. Our Batt'n moved out to billets at BELLACOURT, one Coy. being in 4 Stony Posts.	
" 23 – 27th BELLACOURT.	Very working parties furnished daily for R.E. & work on trenches & dugouts. Training shortened & bathing. Church Parade. Lt. General T.D. Snow Commanding 7 Corps. Inspected held address to Officers & OR. Batt. relieved 7th Batt. Sherwood Foresters in LEFT SECTOR.	
" 27th		
" 25th BAILLEULMONT		
" 28th Trenches 10.0 p.m.	Support Coy. being in BRETENCOURT.	
" 29 – 31st Trenches.	Enemy extremely quiet. Relieved have been received voice on our front. Nothing of importance to report. 2/Lt. H.J. Fox wounded (an accident) & other ranks wounded.	W.W. Hibbert Lt Col. O.C. 8th Service Forester 1.9.16

Casualties for month:-

1/8 Sherwood Foresters

WAR DIARY of month of September 1916.
or
INTELLIGENCE SUMMARY.
Army Form C. 2118.

Hour, Date, Place	Summary of Events and Information	Remarks and references to Appendices
Sept. 1st – 2nd TRENCHES (E. of BRETENCOURT)	A quiet tour except for registration of trenches by enemy, who were believed to have carried out a relief.	
3rd – 10th BAILLEULVAL 4th – 5th – 6th	Relieved by 7th Sherwood Foresters and proceeded to BAILLEULVAL to Divisional Reserve. General training. "Ceremonial Drill"	
11.0 a.m. 7th	Inspection by Lt. Gen. T.D'O Snow, commanding 7th Corps + Maj. Gen. N. Thwaits, commanding 46th Div.	
8th 9th	Musketry Course &c. General training Church Parade	
10.30 p.m. 9th	Relieved 7th Sherwood Foresters in Left Sector Trenches.	
10th – 14th TRENCHES (E. of BRETENCOURT) TRENCHES.	Daily practice firing in trenches.	

1/8 [Rover Bgh?]

WAR DIARY
or
INTELLIGENCE SUMMARY. [for month of] September 1916

Army Form C. 2118.

Hour, Date, Place	Summary of Events and Information	Remarks and references to Appendices
15th Noon BELLACOURT 16th – 18th – 19th	Relieved by 7th Monmouths. Proceeded to BELLACOURT in Brigade Reserve. Day working parties provided.	
11.30 am – 19th	General Parade.	
10.0 pm – 20th S. TRENCHES Night 21st/22nd	Relieved 7 Monmouth Regt in left Sector trenches. Carried out successful raid on German trenches near BLAIRVILLE, capturing 5 prisoners.	Appendix I – Operation Order. " II – Account of Raid.
22 – 23 D° S.	Enemy fairly active with heavy Trench Mortars. Southern sector some damage. Shrubs.	
25th 10.30 pm BAILLEULVAL 26th – 29th & 30th B.	Relieved by 7th Monmouth Regt. Proceeded to BAILLEULVAL Bn. in Divisional Reserve. Several training & few working parties. Short offrs to few drawn on the 28th to complete this Battalion.	

Jas. Turner Capt. [Quarter?]
for O.C. 8th [Sherwood] [Foresters]

S E C R E T.

OPERATION ORDERS BY LIEUTENANT-COLONEL J.E.BLACKWALL, COMMANDING
8th Sherwood Foresters,
September 20th 1916.

Reference Map - F I C H E U X. 1/10,000. Edition 3A.

1. GENERAL SCHEME.	A raid will be carried out on the enemy's front line trench at X.3.b.68.78., and on the sap at X.3.b.51.87., on the night of the 21/22nd September 1916, for the purpose of obtaining identification and causing casualties and damage to the enemy.
2. RAIDING PARTY.	The raiding party will be commanded by Captain B.W.Vann, M.C., and will consist of 4 other Officers and 136 Other Ranks, with 2 Machine Guns, 1 Lewis Gun and 2 10lb. ammonal tubes.
3. CUTTING OF OUR WIRE.	During the night 20/21st inst. O.C. RIGHT Company will cut wide gaps in our wire at CAVENDISH SAP, JOHN O'GAUNTS SAP and Trench 155.
4. CUTTING OF ENEMY WIRE.	Gaps will be cut in the enemy's wire at the points to be raided, during the afternoon of the 21st Sept. by 18 pdrs. and 2" Trench Mortars.
5. WIRE PATROL AND TAPE LAYING.	At 8-0 pm a patrol will move out from CAVENDISH SAP to examine and report on gaps in enemy wire. The patrol will lay tapes from the gaps to CAVENDISH SAP.
6. MAINTENANCE OF GAPS IN WIRE.	If complete gaps are cut, O.C. 139th M.G. Coy. will be notified and will arrange for machine gun fire from our support line to be brought to bear on the gaps so as to prevent their being repaired from the time the patrol returns, till 11.30 pm, when fire will be turned on to the enemy front line, West of X.3.b.0.2. and gradually cease.
7. AMMONAL WIRE CUTTING.	If the patrol reports that complete gaps have not been cut by 2" Trench Mortars, scouts will go forward at 11-0 pm to the gaps accompanied by 4 Sappers and 2 - 24' ammonal tubes, to complete the gaps. This party will return to CAVENDISH SAP at 11.30 pm.
8. POSITION OF ASSEMBLY.	The raiding parties will assemble, told off in parties, in the support line between 'B' & 'C' Groups at 9.30 pm on the 21st inst. It will move at 11-0 pm to a position in front of our wire at CAVENDISH SAP.
9. BOMBARDMENT.	Enemy trenches will be bombarded at 12.15 am, 22nd Sept., by 18 pdrs., 4.5 & 6" Howitzers, and 2" Trench Mortars and 2" Stokes Mortars.
10. ADVANCE.	At 12.15 am the raiding party will move forward towards the objectives, getting up as close as possible behind the barrage.
11. ASSAULT.	At 12.28 am the barrage will lift and the parties will at once enter the trench and sap.
12. RETURN TAPE LAYING.	The tape laying patrol will move the tapes so that they lead back from the gaps to JOHN O'GAUNTS SAP.

(Continued).

13. FLANKING M.G's.	The two M.G's will take up positions on either flank in 'No Man's Land' and keep up a fire on the adjoining enemy sap, so as to protect the raiding party from possible flank attack in 'No Man's Land'. Fire will not be opened unless a counter attack develops or enemy M.G's open fire. The latter will at once be engaged.
14. RETURN SIGNAL.	6 RED Rockets fired in quick succession at 12.43 am from Battn. H.Qrs. will be the signal for the return of the party. A bugle will also sound the 'Dinner Call' in our front trench and a second bugle will sound in the German trench.
15. DRESSING STATION.	The forward Dressing Station will be used at the junction of our front trench and the BLAMONT – RANSART Road.
16. BATTALION H.Qrs.	Battalion forward Headquarters will be at the M.G. emplacement at the junction of our trench and the BLAMONT – RANSART road, where reports will be handed in. Battalion Signalling Officer will connect this Headquarters with Right Company Headquarters.
17. SYNCHRONIS- ATION of WATCHES.	Watches will be synchronised at 9-0 pm at forward Battalion H.Qrs.
18. CHECKING ON RETURN.	On its return the raiding party will file along trench 155, through the tunnel (where an officer will check the party) and back to billets in BELLACOURT. None of the party will stop or loiter in the trenches on the way out.
19.	Acknowledge.

Captain & Adjutant,
8th Sherwood Foresters.

20-9-16.

Issued at 6-0 pm, 20-9-16.

No 1 & 2 War diary.
 3 Captain B.W.Vann, M.C.
 4 O.C. 'C' Coy. (Right Coy.).
 5 139th Infantry Brigade.
 6 O.C. 6th Sherwood Foresters.
 7 O.C. Left Battalion. (6th Royal West Surrey.)
 8 O.C. 139th M.G. Company.
 9 O.C. 139th T.M. Battery.
10 O.C. 'Z' T.M. Battery.
11 O.C. 2/1st Field Coy. R.E.
12 O.C. Left Group R.A.

SECRET.

8th Sherwood Foresters.

DETAIL OF RAIDING PARTY.

'A' PARTY.
    2nd Lieut H.de C.Martelli,   7 N.C.O's and 16 men.

'B' PARTY.
    2nd Lieut W.P.Duff,   6 N.C.O's and 20 men.

'C' PARTY.
    C.S.M. Powell,   5 N.C.O's and 18 men.
                        1 N.C.O. and 2 men. (R.E's.)

'C1' PARTY.
    2nd Lieut. J.B.White,   1 N.C.O. and 3 men.

'D' PARTY.
    2nd Lieut B.W.Hall,   2 N.C.O's and 13 men.
                                          4 men. (R.E's.)

'E' PARTY
    O.C. RAID.   4 N.C.O's and 17 men.
        with 1 Lewis Gun, 2 bugles and 2 Stretchers.

'FLANK COVERING PARTIES.
    -    2 N.C.O's and 12 men.
            with Machine Guns.

                29.   107.
                    136

20-9-16.

                                  Captain & Adjutant,
                                8th Sherwood Foresters.

SECRET.
******

Appendix II

REPORT ON RAID CARRIED OUT BY THE 8th BATTALION SHERWOOD
FORESTERS, ON THE NIGHT 21st/22nd SEPTEMBER, AGAINST THE GERMAN
TRENCHES IN X.3.b.

1. OBJECT.   The object of the Raid was to enter the enemy Sap (ITALY) at X.3.b.51.87 and the front line near point X.3.b.68.78, for the purpose of obtaining identification and inflicting Casualties.
The party was ordered not to proceed beyond the front line (except to block Communication Trenches) nor on the flanks further than points X.3.b.58.69 and X.3.b.98.98.

2. STRENGTH OF PARTY.   The Raiding Party ("A" Company, 8th Battalion Sherwood Foresters) under command of Captain B.W.VANN, M.C., consisted of 5 Officers and 136 other ranks, made up as follows:-

   "A" Party - 2/Lieut.H.De.C.MARTELLI and 21 other ranks, to deal with ITALY SAP.
   "B" Party - 2/Lieut.W.P.DUFF and 26 other ranks, to work left, along front line, block C.T's, bomb dugouts and obtain identification.
   "C" Party - Coy.S.M.G.POWELL and 23 other ranks, to work to right along front line with same object as "B" Party.
   "C.1" Party - 2/Lieut.J.B.WHITE and 4 other ranks, to deal with possible Company Headquarters in small dead end trench near Sap.
   "D" Party - 2/Lieut.B.W.HALL and 15 other ranks, wire patrol and escort for ammonal party.
   "E" Party - Sergt.WILSON and 23 other ranks, to ensure exits for main party, deal with wounded and, take charge of prisoners. One Lewis Gun with this party was to deal with possible attack across open from Support Line.
   2 Stretcher Bearers also accompanied this party.
   Flank covering parties - 2 Parties each of 1 N.C.O and 5 men from the 139th Machine Gun Company, with 3 riflemen and 2 Machine Guns - to deal with possible flank attacks or hostile Machine Guns.
   R.E's.   2 R.E's accompanied "C" Party with two short ammonal tubes for blowing up dugouts.
   1 N.C.O and 4 men were held in readiness with two 24' ammonal tubes for completing gaps in wire if wire was not well cut.

3. PREPARATION. Trench Mortar Emplacements were commenced three weeks before the bombardment.
The Training of the Party was begun about 10th September - a facsimile of the enemy Sap and front line being dug to a depth of 6 inches and wired.
Advanced Battalion Headquarters were fixed at the junction of the BLAMONT - RANSART ROAD and our front line, and a Dressing Station was placed close by.

--2--

4. **WIRE CUTTING.** Carried out between 2 p.m. and 7 p.m. by X & Z/46 Trench Mortar Batteries, at the points of entry and at point R.34.c.25.40.
By 7 p.m. approximately 600 rounds had been fired and it was apparent that a good gap existed at X.3.b.51.87 and that the wire at the junction of ITALY SAP and the front line had been very badly knocked about.

5. **BOMBARDMENT.** (a) 12.15 am - 12.20 am
46th Divisional Artillery (1 18 pr: Battery and one 4.5" Howitzer)
Two 2" Trench Mortars and 1 Battery 6" Howitzers bombarded the front line R.34.c.17.27 to R.34.c.38.44 and the Sap at R.34.c.34.57.

12.20 am - 12.28 am. Field Batteries lifted to the Support Line.
6" Howitzers to X.4.a.62.95, and
2" Trench Mortars to Sap R.33.d.95.28.

12.28 am - "All Clear" Field Batteries and 6" Howitzers dropped to their original targets.

(b) At 12.15 am, the Left Group, 46th Divisional Artillery opened fire with two 18 prs: on ITALY SAP.
6-18 prs on the enemy's front line X.3.b.6.7 to R.34.c.20.17., and
1-18 pr: on the Sap at R.33.d.95.28., and 5 2" Trench Mortars.
2 4.5" Howitzers engaged the front line X.3.b.6.7 to X.3.b.75.81., and the trench junction at X.3.b.69.63.
1 Stokes Mortar engaged the Sap X.3.b.03.71.
Three bombarded ITALY SAP and the front line in rear..

12.25 a.m. 4.5" Howitzers lifted to trench junctions in rear of the objectives, and 2" Trench Mortars switched to points in the front line on the flanks.

At 12.28 a.m. 18 prs: lifted to the trench X.3.b.55.35 to X.4.a.03.45, and the Stokes to the Sap R.33.d.95.28.

Throughout the operation 3 Stokes Mortars engaged the front line R.34.b.39.31 - R.34.b.49.64.
661 rounds were fired by the 7 Stokes Mortars with only 4 misfires.

6. **ACCOUNT BY OFFICER COMMANDING RAIDING PARTY.:** Wire cutting was done by 2" Trench Mortars from 2 p.m. to 6.30 p.m. It could be seen that a gap had been made at the Sap head and considerable damage had been done to wire at junction of Sap and Front Line.
At 8 p.m. the wire patrol went out fromt CAVENDISH SAP, to investigate gaps in enemy's wire and at 10 p.m. reported that gaps were good and that ammonal tubes were not required.
Machine Gun Fire was turned on to gaps.
At 11.15 p.m. the wire patrol laid tapes from gaps back to CAVENDISH SAP.
At 11.20 p.m. the Parties began to move forward through CAVENDISH SAP, and by 12 midnight were in position in groups at distances varying from 70 to 125 yards from CAVENDISH SAP, on the tapes leading to their entrances, with two Machine Guns and their covering parties on the flanks.

(Contd)

4. Wire Cutting (Contd)   60 yards of wire were also badly damaged close to R.34.c.25.40.
During this time the enemy retaliated with Trench Mortars and Rifle Grenades on our front line - while the Support Line and the BLAMONT - RANSART ROAD were shelled by a 5.9" Battery.

By 12.15 a.m. parties were up to enemy's wire and when bombardment started it was found that parties were too near and they withdrew about twenty yards. One dud Trench Mortar came within ten yards of "A" Party. We had one casualty - shell splinter in right arm, probably from our own shells.
At 12.25 a.m. warning to get ready was passed down.
At 12.27 a.m. orders were passed down to move forward. The last shells &c, fell into trench and at 12.28 a.m. the whole raiding party went through gaps and were in the enemy's trench almost immediately. Sap party were held up for about two minutes by iron knife rests having been blown back into their gap.
A German who was in the trench was at once bayoneted.
"B" Party went to the left and "C" to the right. "A" and "C" parties met in the Sap and it was found that "B" and "C" instead of entering front line had entered the Sap near its junction with the front line.
"A" Party investigated a dead end on the Southern side of the Sap, and found nothing. Then went right up to the top of the Sap nearest to our lines, and found the trench very much damaged. Portions of a man were also discovered. There was only one dug-out, which was bombed and entered. Nothing was found and it was left in flames.
"B" Party soon came to the front line and a blocking post was established on the right of the junction and bombers and bayonet men pushed along the front line bombing dug-out entrances. By this time "C" party went to front line and bombed dug-outs. One was set on fire by a "P" Grenade and even the woodwork in the trench began to burn, but was extinguished. One dug-out near junction was blown up by the R.E.s with an ammonal tube.
An enemy Machine Gun opened fire on us from Sap to right, but was at once engaged by the Lewis Gun on parapet and by the right flanking Brigade Machine Gun and silenced at once. It did not fire again. I went along parapet with my runner and two buglers to help "B" party along their trench and a German bomb burst quite near, wounding my runner and a bugler. This appeared to come from C.T. about X.3.b.84.85, but the thrower was soon silenced. Bombing along parapet & trench we found another dug-out entrance and someone at once went down and called to the Huns to come out. Two who came up with bayonets fixed were shot, one through the head and another through the thigh. This man was pulled out and four others, including a Stretcher bearer, came out with hands up, shouting "KAMERAD", "KAMERAD" and crying for mercy. They were very frightened. They were sent over the parapet under escort. Some showed fight in their own wire, but were speedily suppressed and brought across to our lines.
During the last Ten minutes the Huns had surrounded the occupied portion of trench with red lights and their Artillery had begun to shell both the front line and ITALY SAP, making it necessary to take all but 5 men out of ITALY SAP. One shell landed in their front line, beyond where we were. Two hit their parados, and two fell in the Southern derlict arm of ITALY SAP.
At 12-49½ I ordered my bugler to sound the Recall. At this moment the rocket signals went up from Battalion Headquarters, and a bugle sounded the "Cook House Door" in our own trenches. The enemy had been firing from his Support Line and from the two Saps near the BLAMONT-RANSART ROAD. Bullets also passed over very high from the N. side of the SUNKEN ROAD.

One man of "B" Party was badly wounded by a Bomb just before withdrawal & was carried back to our lines.

There was

(Contd)

There was fairly strong rifle fire as we withdrew, and plenty of Verey Lights. No one was hit. Tapes were cut just outside enemy wire and were brought in.
All men reported by 12.55 a.m. The enemy was shelling our front line, C.T's and Supports fairly heavy, which gradually died down and ceased about 3.45 am.
Five Germans were killed by the raiding party apart from those in dugouts which were bombed, and five prisoners taken (one wounded).
Our Casualties were very slight - eight men being wounded (only one seriously).

7. NOTES BY OFFICER COMMANDING RAINDING PARTY.

Final Assembly. Everyone was quite close to enemys' trenches during bombardment (about 60 yards).
This was by far the safest place as large fragments fell behind us.

Wire. The wire was well cut and no real difficulty was experienced in getting through. Iron kniferests with thick wire, will, however, always prove a difficult obstacle even though smashed.
Many of the party were tripped up by the fragments.

Trenches. Entrance into the enemy trench was easy.
The Sap was very badly knocked about, the dugout still intact, but was left in flames. A new entrance was being made but had not been joined up.
Some blocking gates had been destroyed and were at the bottom of the trench near front line.
In the Sap and in the front line were several knife rests some of which had evidently been put in by the enemy.
The front line was not knocked about so much. It varied in depth from 8' to 11 or 12'. There was a strong fire-step, revetted with stout timber. The trench itself was revetted with timber very like railway sleepers and iron girders. It was quite wide and ran in curves with scarcely any obdinary traverses.

Enemy Signals. The red lights sent up all round the trench we were occupying did not go up very high. They were white for about 30' high, bursting then into 2 red lights, which hung in the air for several seconds.
Their Artillery replied quickly by shelling their own trenches.

Dugouts. There were six entrances to dugouts in the parapet of the front line as far as we went to the left. A light was seen in one but was speedily extinguished. These entrances may have led to one dugout, but as smoke bombs and M.S.K.Bombs were thrown down five, and yet when I went down the sixth entrance to fetch the prisoners out there was no smoke visible so they may not have been connected.

In my opinion a raid can be materially assisted if provision is made for strong parapet parties to clear the trenches. Officers or determined N.C.Os can push the bombing parties along the trench much more quickly in this way as they are sometimes inclined to hold back.
To do this it is necessary for the enemy wire to be cut all along his parapet. This was done in our case.

"H.Q." 39ᵗʰ Inf. Bde.

Hewitt Tour
Diary for month
of Oct. 1916.

J.E. Blackwell
Lt. 8ᵗʰ Harwood ?

2.11.16

1/8th Sherwood Foresters

Army Form C. 2118.

WAR DIARY
INTELLIGENCE SUMMARY.
(Erase heading not required.)

for Month of Nov & Part Dec
Oct. 1916.

Hour, Date, Place	Summary of Events and Information	Remarks and references to Appendices
Oct. 1916.		
1st 8.40 p.m. TRENCHES EAST OF BRETENCOURT.	Battalion left billets at BAILLEULVAL at 5.30 p.m. relieved 7th Sherwood Foresters in LEFT SECTOR.	
1st - 7th TRENCHES	Fairly quiet time, except considerable shelling front parts of sector on 7th, but little damage done.	
7th - BELLACOURT	Batt. was relieved by 7th Sherwood Foresters about 2 a.m. & heads moved to billets at BELLACOURT in relief; one personnel transport train remained in BRETENCOURT in support to 7th Batt.	
12th 2.0 - 5.0 p.m. BASSEUX	9.0 p.m. to take part in 139 Inf. Bde. Batt. sent lorries to take part in 5 events out of Inter-Company who won Competitions. Bayonet Fighting. Physical Drill Comp?	
R.8. bg.	Physical Drill Race. Obstacle Race. Bombing. Relay Race. Last day for R.Es.	
8th - 13th L. BELLACOURT	Large working parties found each day for R.E.	

2...1/8 "Sherwood Foresters"

Army Form C. 2118.

WAR DIARY of 1/8 Sherwood Foresters
INTELLIGENCE SUMMARY. Dec 5.16.
(Erase heading not required.)

Instructions regarding War Diaries and Intelligence Summaries are contained in F.S. Regs., Part II. and the Staff Manual respectively. Title pages will be prepared in manuscript.

Hour, Date, Place	Summary of Events and Information	Remarks and references to Appendices
Dec 1916		
13 – 9 a.m. TRENCHES EAST OF BRETENCOURT.	Bn. left Boisleux at 6.0/- relieved 7th Sherwood Foresters in LEFT SECTOR Trenches.	
8.30 a.m – 15th	Batt. Hqrs & BRETENCOURT. Heavily shelled by 4.2's throughout, about 300 being fired, but little damage was done.	
13th – 19th TRENCHES.	Enemy sniper was active for shelling front mentioned.	
19th – 25th BAILLEULVAL.	Bn was relieved by 7th Sherwood Foresters. Trenches handed over to Batt. & BAILLEULVAL.	
" 19 – 25 "	Training and refitting in huts.	
7.30 p.m. – 25th R. TRENCHES EAST OF BRETENCOURT.	Batt. relieved 7th Sherwood Foresters & LEFT SECTOR Trenches.	
25 – 29 "	Very quiet time in trenches. Cont. wet.	
12.30 p.m. 29th	Relieved by 16th MANCHESTER Regt. and marched to BAILLEULVAL.	
6.0 p.m. 29th	Left BAILLEULVAL and marched to WARLUZEL.	Appendix I attached

Army Form C. 2118.

3 — H'qs Thurn Park'ns

WAR DIARY for month of
or
INTELLIGENCE SUMMARY. Feb. 1916.

(Erase heading not required.)

Instructions regarding War Diaries and Intelligence Summaries are contained in F. S. Regs., Part II. and the Staff Manual respectively. Title pages will be prepared in manuscript.

Hour, Date, Place	Summary of Events and Information	Remarks and references to Appendices
Feb 1916.		
10.30 a.m. 30th	Left WARLUZEL and marched to new billets at LE SOUICH.	
31st LE SOUICH	Resting in billets.	
	Casualties.	
	Officers – Nil.	
	O.R. – Killed 1 ; Wounded 8 (accidental)	
		F.S. Blackwell
		Lt Col
		H.Q. 8 Thurn Park'ns

Appendix I.

SECRET.

OPERATION ORDERS BY LIEUTENANT COLONEL J. R. BLACKWALL, COMMANDING
8th Sherwood Foresters,
October 28th 1916

RELIEF.	The Battalion will be relieved on Sunday, 29th inst., by the 16th Manchesters.
ORDER OF RELIEF.	Relief will take place in order:- Signallers, Lewis Gunners, Scouts, Bombers, 'D' 'B' 'C' 'A' Cos., Headquarter Details.
GUIDES.	O's.C. Signallers, Lewis Gunners, Scouts and Bombers will arrange for guides to meet relieving Sections at Cross Roads, BRETENCOURT, at 8.30 am. O.C. 'D' Company will detail 2 guides each for 'A' 'B' & 'C' Cos. viz:- 1 for front line and 1 for support line, to meet incoming Companies at Cross Roads at entrance to BELLACOURT from BASSEUX at 9-0 am. Each guide will be given exact instructions as to the point to which he is to conduct his party. Centre and Left Companies will be taken up by QUARRY, and right Company by ENGINEER.
MOVEMENT.	Companies (moving by platoons) and Sections, will, on relief, proceed to take over billets at BAILLEULVAL, where C.Q.M.Sgts. will meet Companies. O's.C. Sections will each send on early, one N.C.O. & their cook. Movement for both incoming and outgoing Battalions will be via RIVIERE & GROSVILLE. An officer from each Company, (except 'D' Company) will report relief complete at Battalion Headquarters.
TRENCH STORES.	All trench stores will be handed over, including sniperscopes, and lists signed by an Officer of both outgoing and incoming Battalions, sent to Headquarters as early as possible tomorrow morning.
REGIMENTAL STORES.	Periscopes, Verey Pistols, wire cutters, gloves, &c., in possession will be taken out by Companies and handed in to Q.M. Stores immediately on arrival at BAILLEULVAL. Any saws, hammers, sickels, &c., will be sent to dump by 9-0 am.
BILLET STORES.	Stores in billets at BAILLEULVAL will be left for the incoming Battalion. Lists need not be made, but care must be taken that they are left tidy.
OFFICERS SERVANTS & STORES.	Officers stores, &c., to be taken on Transport, will be at dump, BRETENCOURT, by 9-0 am. Two Officers servants per company may go out with these stores and accompany Transport to billets. Boxes for Mess Cart must be drawn from Q.M. and mess stores reduced to proper amounts as soon as possible after arrival at BAILLEULVAL.
REPORT ON WORK.	The usual report of work done during present tour will be required and will be sent in as soon as possible after relief.
SICK PARADE, DINNERS, &c.	O.C's.Cos. & Sections will arrange for dinners as early as possible after their arrival at BAILLEULVAL. Sick parade will be at 2-0 pm. Teas - 3.45 pm.
MOVE.	The Battalion will move by route march tomorrow night to WARLUZEL, via BAC-DU-SUD - Cross Roads 1/4 mile South of 2nd XX 'E' in SOLERNEAU - COUTURELLE, and take over billets vacated by 2nd Royal Scots Fusiliers.

1

BILLETING PARTY.
2nd Lieuts A.H.G.Cox & R.T.Skinner will proceed to take over billets at WARLUZEL and meet the billeting N.C.O's there at the Church.   2nd Lieut R.T.Skinner will report to Battalion H.Qrs. at 8.30 am.
A further party of 1 N.C.O. per Company and Section will parade at Orderly Room BAILLEULVAL at 3-0 pm tomorrow to proceed to WARLUZEL to help in billeting Battalion on arrival.

PARADE.
The Battalion will leave billets clean and tidy immediately after teas and proceed to parade ground, where they will parade in mass at 5.30 pm; Specialists Sections on right.   Markers 5.15 pm.
All Details - Pioneers, Sanitary men, &c., - must be on parade with their Companies.   (Officers servants may march in a formed body behind Officers Mess Cart.)
Transport will be drawn up ready to move by 5.30 pm on South side of BAILLEULMONT - BAILLEULVAL Road, facing North East, head of column clear of village.

MARCH DISCIPLINE.
The strictest march discipline must be maintained throughout and Officers will see that there is no straggling.
Lewis Gun handcarts and packponies will follow in rear of each Company.

CERTIFICATES.
Certificates that all billets are left clean will be handed in to by 4.30 pm.
The following will be handed in by O's.C.Cos. & Sections immediately after arrival at WARLUZEL:-
(1) Marching in state.
(2) Return of N.C.O's and men who have fallen out and not rejoined the Battalion on the march.
(3) Report that Cos. & Sections are in billets.

27-12-16.

Captain & Adjutant,
9th Sherwood Foresters.

S E C R E T.

OPERATION ORDERS BY LIEUTENANT COLONEL J.E.BLACKWALL, COMMANDING
       8th Sherwood Foresters.
       October 31st 1916.

MOVE.   The Battalion will move by route march tomorrow to NEUVILLETTE.

BILLETING PARTY.   2nd Lieut R.T.Skinner will complete the billeting tomorrow morning. 1 N.C.O. per Company and Section of all Headquarter Details will meet him at the cross roads on alarm post at 9.15 am.

STORES.   All blankets (rolled in bundles of 10 and properly labelled) and officers valises will be at Q.M. Stores by 9.15 am.

CERTIFICATES, &c.   Certificates that billets have been left thoroughly clean and Company Messes paid for will behanded in by 9.45 am. The usual returns and certificates will be required on completion of march.

PARADES.   8-0 am Sick Parade.   8.30 am Breakfasts.
Parade on Alarm Post facing south at 10.30 am in order, Scouts, Signallers, Bombers, 'D' 'C' 'B' 'A' Companies, Stretcher Bearers and Transport.   Markers - 10-0 am.

UNLOADING PARTY.   O.C. 'D' Coy. will detail party of 1 N.C.O. & 8 men to unload baggage. They will report to Q.M. immediately on arrival at NEUVILLETTE.

                Captain & Adjutant,
                8th Sherwood Foresters.

1/8th Sherwood Foresters

WAR DIARY
or
INTELLIGENCE SUMMARY.
(Erase heading not required.)

Army Form C. 2118.

1/8 Sherwood Foresters
Month of November 1916. Vol 21

Hour, Date, Place	Summary of Events and Information	Remarks and references to Appendices
Nov. 1916		
10.30 a.m. 1st	Left LE SOUICH marched to NEUVILLETTE.	Appendix I.
NEUVILLETTE 2nd	Usual firing practice at range & training.	
3rd		
9.0 a.m.	Left NEUVILLETTE marched to MAISON-PONTHIEU	" II.
MAISON-PONTHIEU 4th	in ST. RIQUIER Training Area.	
5th	Cleaned up, settled down to follow.	
6th to 21st	Church Parade.	
	General Training, including practice in open	
	warfare Attack.	
9.45 a.m. 22nd	Left MAISON-PONTHIEU marched to NEUVILLETTE	" III.
9.0 a.m. 23rd	Left BEAUCOURT marched to NEUVILLETTE	" IV.
24th NEUVILLETTE	Lital [?] in firing practice & training.	
9.15 a.m. 25th	Left NEUVILLETTE marched to HUMBERCOURT.	" V.
26th — 29th HUMBERCOURT	Training & wire cutting	
30th 11.45 a.m.	Took part in Divisional Cross-Country Run (2¾ miles)	
	finishing 6th out of 13 Batt[alio]ns	
	Casualties during month – Nil. [signed]	

Osmog. 8| Sherwood Foresters
Lieut. Colonel,

S E C R E T.

OPERATION ORDERS BY LIEUTENANT COLONEL J.E.BLACKWALL, COMMANDING
                    8th Sherwood Foresters,
                    November 2nd 1916.

MOVE.   The Battalion will move by route march tomorrow to MAISON
                PONTHIEU, via BARLEY - MEZEROLLES - BEAUVOIR-RIVIERE -
                BERNATRE.

BILLETING   The following billeting party will parade at 7-0 am at Orderly
PARTY   Room - 2/Lt C.H.Powell, 1 N.C.O. per company and 1 N.C.O.
                from Signal Section for Headquarter Details. Bicycles
                will be provided for this party by the Signal Section.
                This party will report to an Officer of the Brigade Staff at
                Mairie, MAISON PONTHIEU at 10-0 am.

STORES, &c.   All blankets (rolled in bundles of 10 and properly labelled)
                Officers valises and other stores will be sent to Q.M. Stores
                  by 6.15 am.

CERTIFICATES, &c. Certificates that billets have been left thoroughly
                clean and Company Messes paid for will be handed in to
                Orderly Room by 7.30 am. The usual returns and certificates
                will be required on completion of march.

PARADES.   6-0 am Sick Parade.   6.30 am Breakfasts.
                Battalion Parade in main street facing West at 8-0 am in
                order Scouts, Signallers, Bombers, 'A' 'B' 'C' 'D' & Stretcher
                Bearers.   Markers - 7.40 am.   Dinners on arrival about
                2-0 pm.

TRANSPORT.   Transport will move independently under orders of Captain
                H.Kirby.

                                        Captain & Adjutant,
                                        8th Sherwood Foresters.

S E C R E T.

OPERATION ORDERS BY LIEUTENANT COLONEL J.E.BLACKWALL, COMMANDING
8th Sherwood Foresters,
November 21st 1916.

MOVE. The Battalion will move by route march tomorrow to BEALCOURT via HEIRMONT and AUXI-LE-CHATEAU.

BILLETING PARTY. The following billeting party will parade at Orderly Room at 8.30 am:- Lieut R.Whitton, 2/Lt.R.T.Skinner and 1 N.C.O. per company and 1 from Signal Section for H.Q.Details. The Signalling Officer will provide all available bicycles for this party. The party will report to an Officer of the Brigade Staff at the Church BEALCOURT at 10-0 am.

STORES. All blankets (rolled in bundles of 10 and properly labelled) Officers valises, Company Mobilisation Boxes, wash bowls, picks and shovels, Drummers packs, properly labelled, and Other stores will be sent to Q.M. Stores by 8-0 am.

CERTIFICATES. Certificates that billets have been left clean and Company Messes paid for will be handed in to Orderly Room by 8.30 am. As soon as possible after completion of march the following will be required - Marching In State, Falling Out State, certificate that Companies, &c. are in billets and have sufficient accommodation (or otherwise).

PARADES. 7-0 am Sick Parade.   7.15 am Breakfasts.
Battalion parade in main street facing North in time to move off at 9-15 am, head of column at Brigade Headquarters in order Scouts, Signallers, Bombers, 'A' Drummers, 'D' 'C' 'B' Stretcher Bearers, Transport. Markers, 9-0 am.
Distances of 200 yards will be maintained on the march between Companies. Scouts Signallers & Bombers will march as one Company and Transport also as one Company. Dinners on arrival about 2-0 pm. Strictest march discipline must be maintained throughout. Orders in Divisional Memo recently issued being complied with.

PARTY FOR T.M.BATTERY. O.C. 'C' Company will detail a party of 1 Officer and 25 O.R. to assist the T.M. Battery on the march tomorrow. The party will report to the Battery at HEIRMONT at 10.30 am

Captain & Adjutant.
8th Sherwood Foresters

SECRET.

OPERATION ORDERS BY LIEUTENANT COLONEL J.E.CLACKWALL, COMMANDING
                                            8th Sherwood Foresters.
                                                November 22nd 1916.

MOVE. The Battalion will move by route march tomorrow to NEUVILLETTE, via BEAUVOIR RIVIERE – WAVANS – MEZEROLLES.

BILLETING EX PARTY. The following billeting party will parade at Orderly Room at 8-0 am – Lieut R.Whitton, 2/Lt R.T.Skinner and 1 N.C.O. per Company and 1 from Signal Section for H.Q. Details. The Signalling Officer will provide all available Bicycles for this party. The party will report to an Officer of the Brigade Staff at NEUVILLETTE CHURCH at 9.30 am.

STORES. All blankets (rolled in bundles of 10 and properly labelled) Officers valises and Company Mobilisation boxes, wash bowls, picks and shovels, Drummers packs (properly labelled) and other stores will be sent to Q.M. Stores by 8-0 am.

CERTIFICATES. Certificates that billets have been left clean and Company Messes paid for will be handed in to Orderly Room by 8.30 am also Marching Out States. As soon as possible after completion of march the following will be required:- Falling Out State and certificate that Companies, &c., are in billets and have sufficient accommodation (or otherwise).

PARADES. 7-0 am Sick Parade. 7.15 am Breakfasts.
Battalion Parade in Main street facing West, in time to move off at 9-0 am. Head of column 200 yards West of Battalion Headquarters, in order – Scouts, Signallers, Bombers, 'B' Drummers, 'A' 'D' 'C' Cos. Stretcher Bearers & Transport. Markers, 8.30 am. Dinners on arrival about 2-0 pm.
Strictest march discipline must be maintained throughout orders in Divisional Memo recently issued being complied with.

                                                        Captain & Adjutant,
                                                   8th Sherwood Foresters.

S E C R E T.

OPERATION ORDERS BY LIEUTENANT COLONEL J.E.BLACKWALL, COMMANDING
                                    8th Sherwood Foresters,
                                            November 24th 1916.

MOVE.   The Battalion will move by route march to HUMBERCOURT tomorrow,
                via IVERGNY & WARLUZEL.

BILLETING   The following billeting party will parade at Q.M'rs Stores at
PARTY.   8.30 am:- 1 N.C.O. per Company and 1 from Signal Section for
                H.Q. Details.   The Signalling Officers will provide cycles
                for this party.   They will report to 2/Lt C.H.Powell at
                HUMBERCOURT CHURCH at 10-0 am.

STORES.   All blankets (rolled in bundles of 10, properly tied and labelled
                Company Mobilisation boxes, wash bowls picks and shovels,
                Drummers packs (properly labelled) will be sent to Q.M. Stores
                by 7.30 am.   The Officers valises and packs of men unable
                to carry them (as certified by M.O.) will be at Q.M. Stores by
                8-0 am.   These packs must also be labelled.

CERTIFICATES. Certificates that billets have been left clean and Company
                Messes paid for, will be handed in to Orderly Room by 8.15 am
                also Marching Out states. As soon as possible after comple-
                tion of march following will be required:- Falling Out State
                and certificate that Companies, &c. are in billets and have

                sufficient accommodation (or otherwise).

PARADES.   6.45 am Sick Parade.
                7.15 am Breakfasts.
                9.10 am Battalion Parade on NEUVILLETTE - BOUQUEMAISON ROAD
                   head of column 100 yards West of junction of FREVENT -
                   DOULLENS & NEUVILLETTE - BOUQUEMAISON Roads. Order of
                   march - Scouts, Signallers, Bombers, 'D' 'B' Drummers, 'C'
                   'A' Stretcher Bearers & Transport. Markers at Q.M. Stores
                   at 8.30 am. Dinners on arrival about 1.30 pm.

                                                          Captain & Adjutant.
                                                          8th Sherwood Foresters.

1/1/8 Sherwood Foresters

WAR DIARY

INTELLIGENCE SUMMARY.

Army Form C. 2118.

1/8th Sherwood Foresters
for month of December 1916

Vol 22

Hour, Date, Place	Summary of Events and Information	Remarks and references to Appendices
December 1 – 5th HUMBERCOURT	Battalion in Corps Reserve at HUMBERCOURT. Training carried on as usual.	
December 6th HUMBERCOURT 8.30 AM	Battalion left HUMBERCOURT and went into Brigade Support in Sector Trenches taking over from 7th Sherwood Foresters A & D Coys being in Bell 6 at FONQUEVILLERS & C & B at SOUASTRE.	Appendix I
December 6th – 11th SOUASTRE & FONQUEVILLERS " 12th	Battalion in Brigade Support Distribution as above. Battalion took over LEFT SECTOR (ie × 2 sub-sectors) at FONQUEVILLERS from 7th Sherwood Foresters 6th Sherwood Foresters being on our Right and 138 Infantry Brigade on our Left.	Appendix II
" 12 – 18th FONQUEVILLERS " 18th 4.30 AM	Trenches very wet and muddy work chiefly connected in repairing & clearing the same, shewed considerable artillery & Trench Mortar activity. Relieved by 7th Sherwood Foresters & went back to SOUASTRE in Divisional Reserve.	

1/8 Sherwood Foresters

For month of December 1916   Army Form C. 2118.

Signed: R.H. Sherwood ??

WAR DIARY
or
INTELLIGENCE-SUMMARY.
(Erase heading not required.)

Instructions regarding War Diaries and Intelligence Summaries are contained in F.S. Regs., Part II. and the Staff Manual respectively. Title pages will be prepared in manuscript.

Hour, Date, Place	Summary of Events and Information	Remarks and references to Appendices
December 1916		
18-21 SOUASTRE	In rest Billets in SOUASTRE in Divisional Reserve. Training carried on, & working parties found	Appendix III
22nd SOUASTRE 2.30am	Left SOUASTRE & took over Left Sector at FONQUEVILLERS from 7th Sherwood Foresters, 6th Sherwoods being on right and 138 Infty Brigade on left.	Appendix IV
22-26 FONQUEVILLERS	Trenches very wet & muddy, work again consisting of clearing up and trying to keep enemy extremely quiet	
26 FONQUEVILLERS	Relieved by 7th Sherwood Foresters & went into Brigade Support. B & C Companies being at FONQUEVILLERS & A & D at SOUASTRE	Appendix V
26-29 SOUASTRE & FONQUEVILLERS	Battalion in Brigade Support. All men employed on working parties	
30 do	Left rest Billets and took over same south at FONQUEVILLERS from 7th Sherwood Foresters 6th Sherwoods being on our Right and 138 Infty Brigade on Left	
30-31 FONQUEVILLERS	Trenches again in very wet condition, same work	Appendix VI

1/8 Sherwood Foresters

WAR DIARY
or
INTELLIGENCE-SUMMARY.
(Erase heading not required.)

Army Form C. 2118.

December 1916 8th Sherwood Foresters

Hour, Date, Place	Summary of Events and Information	Remarks and references to Appendices
December 1916		
30-31 FONQUEVILLERS	carried on with. Enemy shelled intermittently and shewed some activity with Trench Mortars & Rifle Grenades. Casualties for month – 1 Officer Died of Wounds. 6 Other Ranks Wounded.	

J.E. Blackwall
Lieut. Colonel,
Comdg. 8| Sherwood Foresters.

1st January 1916

Appendix I   S E C R E T.

OPERATION ORDERS BY LIEUTENANT COLONEL J. E. BLACKWELL, COMMANDING
                                        5th Sherwood Foresters,
                                              December 5th 1916.

Reference Map   L E N S 11, 1/100,000

RELIEF.   THE Battalion will go in to support in "X" Sector trenches
                (now held by the 147th Infantry Brigade) tomorrow, 6th ins
                taking over from the 7th Sherwood Foresters.

DISTRIBUTION.   The distribution will be:-
                 'A' & 'D' Coys. with their Coy Signallers,)
                      Stretcher Bearers &c.   ) FONQUEVILLERS
                'B' & 'C' Cos   )
                Headquarters.   ) SOUASTRE.

MOVE.   Companies &c. will move off from present billets at the
                following times:-
                  'D' Company - 8.0 am   'C' Company - 9.15 am.
                  'A' Company - 8.15 am.   'B' Company - 9.30 am.
                  Headquarters - 9.45 am.   Transport - 10.0 am.
                Headquarter Details will parade on road running south near
                'C' Coy's billets in order - Scouts, Signallers, Drums,
                Bombers, Pioneers &c., and Stretcher Bearers.
                Cookers will move with their Companies.
                Drums will not play after reaching GAUDIEMPRE.

MOVEMENT.   Route will be via Ferme DE LA BREFFAYE - LA BELLEVUE - Cross
                roads just South of 'A' in SOLERNEAU - GAUDIEMPRE - ST AMAND
                East of GAUDIEMPRE movement will be by Platoons at 2 minute
                intervals; Transport will also split up.

GUIDES.   One Guide per Platoon will be provided by the 7th Battalion
                for 'A' & 'D' Cos. to meet platoons at SOUASTRE Cross roads
                at 1-0 pm and take them to FONCQUEVILLERS by the track North
                of the SOUASTRE - FONCQUEVILLERS Road. Arrangements as to
                taking up Lewis Guns will be made by Lewis Gun Offr. on
                arrival at SOUASTRE.

BILLETING   Lieut R.Whitton and Corpl A.B.North will travel on motor lor
PARTY.   ry leaving Q.M. Stores at 8-0 am and arrange billets for
                headquarters and 'B' & 'C' Cos in SOUASTRE. These 2 Cos.
                will billet in huts. Transport Lines and Q.M. Stores will
                be taken over from 4th West Riding Regt.

PARADES.   6.15 am Sick Parade.   6.45 am Breakfasts.
                Dinners on arrival at SOUASTRE.
                Dress for march tomorrow - fighting order, haversack
                carried on back with mess tin slung from fastening straps.

REGIMENTAL   The following stores will be handed in to Q.M. Stores
STORES.   tomorrow morning :- Picks, shovels, washing bowls,
                braziers, blankets (securely tied in bundles of 10 and
                labelled), Officers' valises, Company Mobilisation Boxes
                and all packs.   Stores from 'A' & 'D' Cos. will be
                handed in by 7.30 am and from remainder of Battalion
                by 9-0 am.

                                                    O V E R.

                    Companies and Specialist Sections will arrange to place their packs as far as possible in heaps by platoons and sections: places will be clearly marked at the stores where packs are to be piled.
                    'A' & 'D' Coy. will draw packs, leather waistcoats, &c. immediately on arrival at SOUASTRE.

TRENCH STORES. It is believed that there are no stores to be taken over in Support Battalion area. If however any are handed over by the outgoing Battalion they will be carefully checked and receipts given and lists sent to Orderly Room by 8-0 pm tomorrow. Nil returns to be rendered.

BILLETS. Billets must be left clean and tidy, all rubbish, tins, &c. being removed and burnt in incinerators and latrines properly filled in. Certificates that this has been done and Officers' Messes paid for will be handed in to Orderly Room before Companies, &c. move off. 2nd Lieut C.H.Powell will remain behind for three hours after the Battalion moves off to report to Town Major and investigate claims (if any).

FATIGUE PARTY. O.C. 'D' Company will detail a fatigue party of 1 N.C.O. and 20 men to report to Town Major, FONCQUEVILLERS at 3.30 pm tomorrow for duty in the village: this party will be at the disposal of the Town Major daily (if required) until further orders.

                                        Sd. W.C.C.WEETMAN.
                                              Captain & ADJUTANT.
5-12-16.   8th Sherwood Foresters.

Appendix II

OPERATION ORDERS BY LIEUT COLONEL J.E.BLACKWALL, COMMANDING
8th Sherwood Foresters.
December 11th 1916.

RELIEF	The Battalion will relieve the 7th Battalion Sherwood Foresters in LEFT SECTOR (i.e. "X.2.Sub-Sector") trenches tomorrow 12th inst
DISTRIBUTION.	The distribution will be as follows :-

SECTOR	COMPANY &c.
RIGHT (Right on GOMMECOURT ROAD)	'B' Company - 2 platoons in firing line and 2 in Support line and NOTTINGHAM STREET.
CENTRE	'C' Company - 2 platoons in front line, 1 in Support line near LINCOLN lane and 1 in dugouts near CALVAIRe ROAD.
LEFT (Left at BRAYELLE ROAD)	'D' COmpany - 3 platoons in front line, 1 in support in ROBINSON LANE with 1 Lewis Gun and team from support Company.
SUPPORT	'A' Company - (less 1 Lewis Gun and team) dugouts in SNIPERS SQUARE.

Battalion Scouts, Signallers and Bombers will be at Headquarter Billets: Lewis Gun Detachment in SNIPERS SQUARE. These sections will take over posts, stations, &c. from outgoing Battalion.

ORDER AND TIMES OF RELIEF.	Relief will take place in the following order :- 'D', 'A', Signallers, Scouts, Bombers, 'C', 'B' and Headquarter details. Lewis Gunners will relieve with their Companies. Movement will be by platoons (each Specialist section reckoned as 1 platoon), 'D' Company beginning at 8.30 am, 'A' Company at 8.40 am, the remainder beginning to leave SOUASTRE at 8.15 am with distances of 200 yards between platoons.
ROUTES.	From SOUASTRE the main road will be used as far as sentry at cross roads S.W. of 'F' in FONCQUEVILLERS (Map - LENS 11) from which point track running N.E. over the open will be used. Right Company will relieve via NOTTINGHAM STREET or GOMMECOURT ROAD. Centre via LINCOLN LANE and Left and Support via ROBERTS AVENUE.
BATTALION RUNNERS	Two Battalion Runners from each Company will report at H.Qrs at 10.0 am tomorrow.
COOKING.	No cooking will be done in the trenches, except in one or two cases where dugouts are suitable.
CARRYING PARTIES.	Parties for carrying R.E. Stores for all Companies and dry rations, water and meals for Centre and Left Companies will be found by the Company in Support, assisted when required by Battalion Bombers and Lewis Gun Detachment.

1.

over

REGIMENTAL STORES.	Os.C. 'B', 'C', & 'D' Cos. will each take to the trenches :- 2 Box Periscopes, 10 Vigilants, 3 1" Verey Pistols, 1 1½" Illuminating Pistol. These will be drawn from Q.M.Stores tonight by B and C Cos those for D Coy will be sent down to FONCQUEVILLERS by Transport Blankets at SOUASTRE will be handed in to Q.M.Stores by 7-0 am: those at FONCQUEVILLERS will be stacked at Battalion H.Qrs. and brought up by transport tomorrow night (all must be rolled in bundles of 10 and properly labelled). Officers' valises washing bowls, picks, shovels, &c. will be handed in to Q.M. Stores by 7-0 am. Valises at FONCQUEVILLERS will be stacked with blankets.
BILLET STORES.	Stores in billets at SOUASTRE will be handed over to 7th Battn. S.F., and at FONCQUEVILLERS to 5th S.F. and must be left tidily arranged: receipts to be obtained.
TRENCH STORES.	Lists of trench stores taken over, signed by representatives of both Battalions, to be handed in to Orderly Room by 10-0 am.
RETURNS and CERTIFICATES.	Following returns are due at Orderly Room tomorrow at times stated:- (1) RATION STRENGTH - showing details of strength by platoons with specialists attached, showing Companies which specialists belong and platoons to which their rations are to be sent, - 12-0 noon. (2) TRENCH GARRISON STATE - on usual proforma - 4-0 pm. (3) Report on VERMOREL SPRAYERS, GAS BLANKETS and APPARATUS - 9-0 pm. (4) Report on GENERAL SANITARY CONDITION - 9-0 pm. (5) Certificate that there is 1 PICK and 1 SHOVEL in every dugout - 4-0 pm. (6) Report as to accumulation (if any) of filled sandbags requiring to be emptied. 9-0 pm. Regtl. Sergt. Major will render these returns &c. for H.Qrs.
WATER DUTY MEN	The R.A.M.C. details attached will carry out their usual water duties at Transport lines, and FONCQUEVILLERS.
ARTILLERY SUPPORT.	Details will be issued separately.
BILLETS.	The usual billet certificates, including payment for Company Messes, will be rendered by 7-30 am tomorrow by Cos. &c. at SOUASTRE (Cos. at FONCQUEVILLERS - 10-0 am).
SICK PARADE.	Sick parade will be at 2-0 pm daily.
DRYING ROOM	The Scout Officer will arrange for the drying of clothing of N.C.Os. and men of Companies or sections after patrolling.
REPORTING RELIEF. GUMBOOTS.	"RELIEF COMPLETE" will be reported by "runner" to Bn. H.Q. All gum boots required will be drawn from the store near the Canteen and receipts given to the N.C.O. i/c. The Officer or N.C.O. i/c of each platoon or party drawing boots is responsible for returning the exact number to the stores.

Sd/ W.C.C. WEETMAN.
Captn and Adjt.
8th S.F.

Appendix III

OPERATION ORDERS BY LIEUTENANT COLONEL J.E.BLACKWALL, COMMANDING
8th Sherwood Foresters.
December 17th 1916.

RELIEF	The Battalion will be relieved tomorrow, 18th instant by the 7th Battalion Sherwood Foresters.
ORDER OF RELIEF.	Relief will take place in order:- Signallers, Scouts, Bombers, 'A' 'C' 'D' (with H.Q.Lewis Gun Detachment) and 'B' Cos, Headquarter details. Relief of 'A' Coy will begin at 7-0 am and of 'C' Coy about 9-30 am.
MOVEMENT.	Companies (moving by platoons) and sections will, on relief, proceed to take over billets vacated by the 7th S.F. at SOUASTRE, in Divisional Reserve. Movement will be via track in E.20 - E.13 - D.18 to BIENVILLERS - SOUASTRE ROAD.
BILLETS.	The T.O. will arrange for C.Q.M.Sergts. to take over billets and meet their Companies on arrival. Os. C. Sections will send 1 N.C.O. per section to take over Billets and meet their sections on arrival. They will proceed as one party.
BILLET STORES.	Stores in billets will be taken over in the usual way, and lists sent to Orderly Room tomorrow by 6-0 pm.
TRENCH STORES.	One Officer per Company will be detailed to check over with an Officer of the relieving Battalion, all trench stores, and will send down complete lists to Orderly Room (on attached forms) by 9-0 am tomorrow. This list will be marked at the end "Certified correct" and signed by both these Officers. It is realised that this time may be found to be very early, but every effort should be made to send the lists in as soon as possible.
REGIMENTAL STORES.	Periscopes, Verey pistols, Wire cutters, Gloves &c. in possession will be taken out by Companies and handed in to Orderly Room by 4-0 pm tomorrow.
OFFICERS' SERVANTS & STORES.	Officers' Stores &c. to be taken on Transport will be at Battalion Headquarters by 8-0 am. Two Officers' servants per Company may come out to Battn. Headquarters with these Stores and will march to billets as a formed party.
REPORT ON WORK.	Os.C.Cos. will render by 9-0 pm tomorrow, brief reports on work done during tour, under the usual headings (copy attached).
INDENTS.	Indents for material should be sent in as usual.

Sd/ W.C.C.WEETMAN,
Captain and Adjutant.
8th Sherwood Foresters.

17-12-16.

Appendix IV

OPERATION ORDERS BY LIEUT COLONEL J.B.BLACKWALL, COMMANDING
                                        8th Sherwood Foresters.
                                        21st December 1916.

RELIEF.   The Battalion will relieve the 7th Battalion Sherwood Foresters
                in LEFT SECTOR (i.e. "X.2. Sub-Sector") tomorrow, 22nd instant.

DISTRIBUTION.   The distribution will be as follows :-

SECTOR	COMPANY &c.
RIGHT (Right on GOMMECOURT ROAD)	'C' Company - 2 platoons in firing line and 2 in Support Line and NOTTINGHAM STREET.
CENTRE	'B' Company - 2 platoons in front line, 1 in Support line near LINCOLN LANE and 1 in dugouts near CALVAIRE ROAD
LEFT (Left at BRAYELLE ROAD)	'D' Company - 3 platoons in front line 1 in support in ROBINSON LANE with 1 Lewis Gun and team from Support Company.
SUPPORT.	'A' Company - (less 1 Lewis Gun and team) dugouts in SNIPERS SQUARE..

                Battalion Scouts, Signallers, and Bombers will be at Head-
                quarter billets: Lewis Gun Detachment in SNIPERS SQUARE.
                These Sections will take over posts, stations &c. from
                outgoing Battalion.

ORDER AND   Relief will take place in the following order :-
TIMES OF   Signallers, Scouts, Bombers, 'B' 'C' 'A' (less 1 Lewis Gun
RELIEF.   and team) and Headquarter details.   Lewis Gunners will
                relieve with their Companies.   Movement will be by platoons
                (each Specialist section being reckoned as 1 Platoon).
                Signallers will leave SOUASTRE at 8-30 am remainder following
                with distances of 200 yards between platoons.
                'D' Company and 1 Lewis Gun and team from 'A' Company will
                have dinners at SOUASTRE and will leave SOUASTRE at 2-0 pm,
                following same route and will relieve Company in Left Sector.
                They will have teas at FONCQUEVILLERS at 3-45 pm.

ROUTES.   From SOUASTRE the main SOUASTRE - BIENVILLERS ROAD will be
                used as far as track D.18 xxExExxxExEExxxFONCQUEVILLERS
                thence along track D.18 - E.13 - E.20 to FONCQUEVILLERS. Refce
                Map 57.D. N.E. Edition 3.a., which can be seen at Orderly Room
                tonight.   Right Company will relieve via NOTTINGHAM STREET
                or GOMMECOURT ROAD, Centre via LINCOLN LANE, and Left and
                Support via ROBERTS AVENUE.

BATTALION   1 from each Company in the line and 2 from the Company in
RUNNERS.   Support will report at Battalion Headquarters at 10-0 am
                tomorrow.

COOKING.   No cooking will be done in the trenches, except in one or
                two cases where dugouts are suitable.

CARRYING   Parties for carrying R.E.Stores for all Companies and dry
PARTIES.   rations, water and meals for Centre and Left Companies, will
                be found by the Company in support, assisted when required
                by Battalion Bombers and Lewis Gun Detachment.

                                                        OVER.

REGIMENTAL STORES.	Os.C. 'B' 'C' and 'D' Cos. will each take to trenches :- 2 Box Periscopes 10 Vigilants 8 1" Verey Pistols 1 1½" Illuminating Pistol. These will be drawn from Q.M. Stores tonight. Blankets at SOUASTRE will be handed in to Q.M. Stores by 7.15 am. Officers valises, washing bowls, picks, shovels, &c., will be handed in to Q.M. Stores by 7-0 am.
BILLET STORES.	Stores in billets at SOUASTRE will be handed over to 5th Bn. S.F. and must be left tidily arranged: receipts to be obtained.
TRENCH STORES.	Lists of Trench Stores taken over signed by representatives of both Battalions to be handed in to Battalion Orderly Room by 12 noon.
RETURNS & CERTIFICATES.	Following returns are due at Orderly Room tomorrow at times stated:- (1) RATION STATE. - Shewing details of strength by platoons with Specialists attached, shewing Companies to which Specialists belong and platoons to which their rations are to be sent - 12 noon: except by O.C. 'D' Company who will render this return to Orderly Room, SOUASTRE by 9-0am: also Trench Garrison State. (2) TRENCH GARRISON STATE - On usual proforma - 4.30 pm. (3) Report on VERMOREL SPRAYERS, GAS BLANKETS & APPARATUS - 9-0 pm. (4) Report on GENERAL SANITARY CONDITIONS - 9-0 pm. (5) Certificate that there is one pick and one shovel in every dugout - 4.30 pm. (6) Report as to accumulation (if any) of filled sandbags requiring to be emptied - 9-0 pm. Regimental Sergeant Major will render these returns, &c., for Headquarters.
WATER DUTY MEN.	The R.A.M.C. Details attached will carry out their usual water duties at Transport Lines and FONCQUEVILLERS.
SICK PARADE.	Sick parade will be at 2-0 pm daily.
BILLETS.	The usual billets billet certificates, including payment for Company Messes will be rendered by 7.30 am tomorrow by Companies at SOUASTRE.
DRYING ROOM.	The Scout Officer will arrange for the drying of clothing of N.C.O's and men of Companies and Sections after patrolling
REPORTING RELIEF.	"Relief Complete" will be reported by RUNNER to Battalion Headquarters.
GUMBOOTS.	All gumboots required will be drawn from the store near the Canteen and receipts given to the N.C.O. in charge. The Officer or N.C.O. in charge of each platoon or party drawing boots is responsible for returning the exact number to the store.
21-12-16.	Major, 8th Sherwood Foresters.

Appendix V

OPERATION ORDERS BY LIEUTENANT COLONEL J.E.BLACKWALL COMMANDING
8th Sherwood Foresters,
December 25th 1916.

RELIEF.	The Battalion will be relieved tomorrow, 26th inst by 7th Bn. Sherwood Foresters.
ORDER OF RELIEF.	Relief will take place in order:- Signallers, Scouts, Bombers, 'C' 'B' 'D', Headquarter Details, 'A' Company with Lewis Gun Detachment. Relief of 'C' Company will begin about 9.30 am. Relief of 'A' Company will begin about 4.30 pm.
MOVEMENT.	'B' & 'C' Cos. will, on relief, take over billets and Posts vacated by 7th S.F. at FONCQUEVILLERS. 'C' Company will find one platoon as garrison for PORT DICK. These two Companies will make arrangements to take over billets. The Bombing Officer and 13 O.R. detailed by him will remain at FONCQUEVILLERS and be attached to 'C' Company for rations. Signallers, Scouts, remainder of Bombers, 'D' & 'A' Companies, with H.Qrs. Lewis Gun Detachment, moving by platoons, will on relief proceed to take over billets and huts vacated by 7th S.F. at SOUASTRE. Movement will be via track E.20 - E.13 - D.18 to BIENVILLERS - SOUASTRE road, except 'A' Company who may use the SOUASTRE- FONCQUEVILLERS road.
BILLETS.	The R.Q.M.S. will arrange for C.Q.M.Sergts. to take over billets and huts at SOUASTRE and meet their Companies on arrival. O's.C.Sections will send on 1 N.C.O. per Section to take over billets and meet their Sections on arrival. They will proceed as one party.
BILLET STORES.	Stores in billets will be taken over in the usual way, and lists sent to Orderly Room by 6-0 pm.
TRENCH STORES.	One Officer per Company will be detailed to check over with an Officer of the 7th Battn., all trench stores, & C.Cos will send down to Orderly Room complete list (on proforma sent out) by 9-0 am tomorrow. A duplicate of this list will be marked at the end "Certified Correct" and signed by Officers of both Battalions.
REGIMENTAL STORES.	Periscopes, Verey Pistols, wire cutters, gloves, &c., in possession will be taken out by Companies 'A' & 'D' Cos. and handed in to Battalion Orderly Room by 10-0 am on 27th inst. 'B' & 'C' Cos. will retain these stores themselves.
OFFICERS SERVANTS & STORES.	Officers stores, &c., to be taken on Transport will be at Battn Headquarters by 8-0 am. Two Officers servants per Company may come out to Battalion Headquarters with these stores and will march to billets as a formed party.
REPORT ON WORK.	O's.C.Cos. will render by 9-0 pm tomorrow, brief reports on work done during tour, under the usual headings (copy attached)
INDENTS.	Indents for material should be sent in as usual.
REPORTS.	The usual Daily Reports will be sent in to Battalion H.Qrs. by Companies on relief by 11.30 am. O.C. 'A' Company will send his by runner.

(O V E R).

STRONG POST.   The garrison of FORT DICK will be relieved by 9-0 am
             O.C. "C" Company will withdraw 1 platoon from his
             Support platoons and will carry out this relief,
             reporting relief complete by runner to Orderly Room.

                                            J.R. Lane
                                            Major,
                                     8th Sherwood Foresters.

Blankets at SOUASTRE will be handed in to Q.M.Stores by 7.15 am, those at FONCQUEVILLERS will be stacked at Battn. Headquarters and brought up by transport tomorrow night (All must be rolled in bundles of 10 and properly labelled) Officers valises, washing bowls, picks, shovels &c. will be handed in to Q.M.Stores by 7.45 am.

BILLET STORES. Stores in Billets at SOUASTRE will be handed over to 5th S.F. and at FONCQUEVILLERS to 5th S.F., and must be left tidily arranged: receipts to be obtained.

TRENCH STORES. Lists of Trench Stores taken over and signed by representatives of both Battalions to be handed in to Battalion Orderly Room by 12.0 noon. O.C. 'D' Coy will hand this in by 7.0 pm.

RETURNS and CERTIFICATES. The following Returns are due at Orderly Room tomorrow at times stated :-
(1) RATION STATE - showing details of strength by platoons with Specialists attached, showing Companies to which Specialists belong and platoons to which their rations are to be sent - 12.0 noon, except by O.C. 'D' Coy who will render this return to Orderly Room, SOUASTRE, by 9.0 am; also Trench Garrison State..
(2) TRENCH GARRISON STATE - on usual proforma - 4.30 pm.
(3) REPORT on VERMOREL SPRAYERS, GAS BLANKETS and APPARATUS - 9.0 pm.
(4) REPORT on GENERAL SANITARY CONDITION - 9.0 pm.
(5) CERTIFICATE that there is 1 pick and 1 shovel in every dugout 4.30 pm.
(6) REPORT as to accumulation (~~brack~~ if any) of filled sandbags requiring to be emptied - 9.0 pm.
Regimental Sergeant Major will render these returns for H.Qrs.

WATER DUTY MEN. The R.A.M.C. Details attached will carry out their usual water duties at Transport lines and FONCQUEVILLERS.

SICK PARADE. Sick parade will be at 2 pm daily.

BILLETS. The usual billet Certificates, including payment for Coy. Messes will be rendered by 7.30 am tomorrow by Companies at SOUASTRE.

DRYING ROOM. 2/Lieut. J.B.White will arrange for the drying of clothing of N.C.Os. and men of Companies or Sections after patrolling.

REPORTING RELIEF. "Relief complete" will be reported by <u>runner</u> to Battalion H.Q

GUMBOOTS. All gumboots required will be drawn from the store near the Canteen and receipts given to the N.C.O. in charge. The Officer or N.C.O. in charge of each platoon or party drawing boots is responsible for returning the exact number to the store.

                          Sd. J.K.LANE, Major,
                     8th Sherwood Foresters.

Appendix VI

OPERATION ORDERS BY LIEUT COLONEL J.E.BLACKWALL, COMMANDING
8th Sherwood Foresters.
December 29th 1916.

RELIEF.   The Battalion will relieve the 7th Battalion Sherwood Foresters in the LEFT SECTOR (i.e. "X.2.Sub-Sector") trenches tomorrow 30th instant.

DISTRIBUTION. The distribution will be as follows :-

SECTOR	COMPANY &c.
RIGHT (Right on GOMMECOURT ROAD)	'C' Coy - 2 platoons in firing line and 2 in support line and NOTTINGHAM STREET.
CENTRE	'A' Coy - 1 platoon in front line 1 in support line near LINCOLN LANE and 2 in dugouts near CALVAIRE ROAD
LEFT (Left on at LA BRAYELLE ROAD)	'D' Coy - 3 platoons in front line 1 in support in ROBINSON LANE with 1 Lewis Gun and team from Support Coy
SUPPORT	'B' Coy - (less 1 Lewis Gun and team) dugouts in SNIPERS SQUARE

Battalion Scouts, Signallers and Bombers will be at Headquarter billets: Lewis Gun Detachment in SNIPERS SQUARE. These sections will take over posts, stations &c. from outgoing Battalion.

ORDER AND TIMES OF RELIEF.   Relief will take place in the following order :-
'C' 'B' (less 1 Lewis Gun and team) Signallers Scouts Bombers 'A' Headquarter details 'D'. Lewis Gunners will relieve with their Companies. Movement will be by platoons (each specialist section reckoned as 1 platoon) 'C' Coy beginning at 9.0 am 'B' 9.15 am; Signallers will leave SOUASTRE at 8.45 am, remainder following with distances of 200 yards between platoons. 'D' Coy will have dinners at SOUASTRE and will leave SOUASTRE at 2.0 pm following same route and will relieve Company in Left Sector. They will have teas at 3.45 pm at FONCQUEVILLERS where they will be joined by 1 Lewis Gun and team from 'B' Coy.

ROUTES.   From SOUASTRE the main SOUASTRE - BIENVILLERS ROAD will be used as far as Track D.18, thence along track D.18 - E.13 - E.20 to FONCQUEVILLERS. (Reference map 57.D. N.E. Edition 3.a. which can be seen at Orderly Room tonight.) Right Company will relieve via NOTTINGHAM STREET or GOMMECOURT ROAD, Centre via LINCOLN LANE, and Left and Support via ROBERTS AVENUE.

BATTALION RUNNERS.   1 from each Company in the line and 2 from the Company in Support will report at Battalion Headquarters at 10.0 am tomorrow

CARRYING PARTIES.   Parties for carrying R.E. Stores for all Companies, and dry rations, water and meals for Centre and Left Companies, will be found by the Company in Support, assisted where required by Battalion Bombers and Lewis Gun Detachment.

REGIMENTAL STORES.   Os.C. 'A' and 'D' Companies will each take to the trenches :-
    2 Box Periscopes   10 VIgilants
    3 1" Verey Pistols   1 1½" Illuminating Pistol
These will be drawn from the Q.M.Stores tonight,

O V E R.

1/1/8th Newton Forbes.

Army Form C. 2118.

WAR DIARY for the Month of January 1917.
—or—
INTELLIGENCE SUMMARY.
(Erase heading not required.)

Vol 23

Instructions regarding War Diaries and Intelligence Summaries are contained in F. S. Regs., Part II. and the Staff Manual respectively. Title pages will be prepared in manuscript.

Hour, Date, Place	Summary of Events and Information	Remarks and references to Appendices
1917 January		
1st – 3rd TRENCHES – FONCQUEVILLERS	In left sector – with 6th Kd/Scarro Forbes on Right + 138th Inf. Bde. on left. A certain amount of shelling. Quiet on the whole a fairly quiet time.	Appendix I.
12.0 noon. 3rd SOUASTRE	Relieved by 7th L.F. moved back to SOUASTRE in Divisional Reserve. Working parties + some training carried out.	
3rd – 7th SOUASTRE		
7th FONCQUEVILLERS TRENCHES	Relieved 7th L.F. in Trenches.	"II."
11.0 a.m. 7th – 11th TRENCHES	6th L.F. on Right + 139th Bde. on left. Considerable Artillery activity at times by both sides. Trenches very wet + deep in mud in many places.	
11th 11.0 a.m. SOUASTRE etc.	Relieved by 7th L.F. + moved to H.Qrs + 2 Cos. to SOUASTRE 2 Cos. to billets in FONCQUEVILLERS, in Brigade Reserve.	"III."
11th – 15th DITTO	Month occupied in Brigade working parties.	
11.0 a.m. 15th TRENCHES	Relieved 7th L.F. Distribution as above. Except for some Artillery activity + a quiet time.	"IV."
15th – 19th DITTO		follows

1/8 Sherwood Foresters

Army Form C. 2118.

WAR DIARY for the month of January 1917.

INTELLIGENCE SUMMARY.

(Erase heading not required.)

Instructions regarding War Diaries and Intelligence Summaries are contained in F. S. Regs., Part II. and the Staff Manual respectively. Title pages will be prepared in manuscript.

Hour, Date, Place	Summary of Events and Information	Remarks and references to Appendices
1917 January		
11.0 a.m. 19th SOUASTRE	Batt. relieved by 7th S.F. moved back to SOUASTRE in Divisional Reserve.	Appendix V.
19th – 23rd DITTO.	Some training carried out – working parties found – Hard frost.	" VI.
11.0 a.m. 23rd TRENCHES FONQUEVILLERS.	Relieved 7th S.F. Distribution as before.	
23rd – 27th DITTO.	Quiet front line – Very hard frost – snow.	
8.0 p.m. 27th SOUASTRE ye.	Relieved by 7th S.F. H.Qrs + 2 Cos. moved back to SOUASTRE, 2 Cos. at FONCQUEVILLERS in Brigade Reserve. Worked for Brigade working parties.	" VII.
27th – 31st DITTO.	Present strength of the Brigade.	
31st 8.0 p.m. TRENCHES FONCQUEVILLERS	Relieved 7th S.F. in left sector – Distribution as before.	" VIII.
	Casualties – Killed 3 O.R. wounded 9 O.R. (2 accidents).	

3rd February 1917.

Howe Major O.C.
8th Bn. SHERWOOD FORESTERS.

Appendix I

OPERATION ORDERS BY LIEUT COLONEL J.E.BLACKWALL, D.S.O., COMMANDING
8th Sherwood Foresters.
2nd January 1917.

RELIEF.	The Battalion will be relieved tomorrow, 3rd instant, by the 7th Battalion Sherwood Foresters.
ORDER OF RELIEF.	Relief will take place in the following order:- Signallers, Scouts, Bombers, "C", 3 platoons of "A" (2 at H.Qrs and 1 in Calvaire dugouts), "B" (with H.Q.Lewis Gun Detachment), Headquarter details and "D" Coy. Relief of "C" Company will begin about 9.30 am. Relief of "D" Coy and platoon in Support and forward posts of "A" Coy about 5.0 pm. O.C. "A" Company will detail an Officer to be at Battalion Headquarters at 9.0 am to meet an Officer of relieving Company of 7th S.F. to make necessary arrangements as to relief of Company.
MOVEMENT.	Companies (moving by platoons) and Sections will, on relief, proceed to take over billets vacated by 7th S.F. at SOUASTRE in Divisional Reserve. Movement will be via track in E.20 - E.13 - D.18, to Bienvillers - SOUASTRE Road, except "D" Company and remaining platoon of "A" Company who may use the FONCQUEVILLERS - SOUASTRE ROAD.
BILLETS.	The Q.M. will arrange for C.Q.M.Sergts to take over billets and meet their Companies on arrival. O's.C. Sections will send one N.C.O. per Section to take over billets and meet their Sections on arrival. They will proceed as one party.
BILLET STORES.	Stores in billets will be taken over in the usual way and lists sent in to Orderly Room by 6.0 pm tomorrow.
TRENCH STORES.	One Officer per Company will be detailed to check over with an Officer of the relieving Battalion all trench stores and will hand in complete lists to Orderly Room (on proforma sent out) immediately after relief. This list will be marked at the end "Certified correct" and signed by both these Officers.
REGIMENTAL STORES.	Periscopes, Verey Pistols, Wire Cutters, Gloves, &c. in possession will be taken out by Companies and handed in to Orderly Room by 4.0 pm tomorrow, except "D" and "A" Cos who will hand theirs in on arrival at SOUASTRE.
OFFICERS' SERVANTS & STORES.	Officers' Stores &c. to be taken on Transport will be at Battn Headquarters by 9.0 am. Two Officers' servants per Company may come out to Battalion Headquarters with these stores and will march to billets as a formed party.
REPORT ON WORK.	O's.C.Cos will render by 9.0 pm tomorrow brief reports on work done during tour under the usual headings.
INDENTS.	Indents for material should be sent in as usual.
REPORTS.	The usual daily reports will be sent in to Battalion H.Qrs by Companies on relief by 11.30 am. O.C. "D" Coy will send his by runner.

Sd/ J.K.LANE, Major,
8th Sherwood Foresters.

Jan. 2nd 1917.

Appendix II

OPERATION ORDERS BY LIEUT COLONEL J. R. BLACKWALL, D.S.O., COMMANDING
8th Sherwood Foresters.
January 6th 1917.

RELIEF   The Battalion will relieve the 7th Battalion Sherwood Foresters in LEFT SECTOR (i.e. "X.2.Sub-Sector") trenches tomorrow 7th instant.

DISTRIBUTION. The distribution will be as follows :-

SECTOR	COMPANY &c.
RIGHT (Right on GOMMECOURT ROAD)	'A' Company - 2 platoons in front line and 2 in Support line
CENTRE	'D' Company - 1 platoon in front line, 3 in Support Line and Dugouts near LINCOLN LANE or Battn. H.Qrs.
LEFT (Left at LA BRAYELLE ROAD)	'B' Company - 3 platoons in front line with 1 Lewis Gun and team from H.Q. Detachments, 1 in Support in ROBINSON LANE
SUPPORT	'C' Company - dugouts in SNIPERS SQUARE

Battalion Scouts, Signallers, Bombers, and 1 H.Q. L.G. Detachment will be at Headquarter billets: 1 gun and team of H.Q. Lewis Gun Detachment in SNIPERS SQUARE. These sections will take over posts, stations, &c. from outgoing Battalion. The H.Q. L.G. Detachment at Battalion Headquarters will consist of the new teams from 'A' and 'C' Companies who will report to Sergt. Sharrock tomorrow morning at 8.30 am.

ORDER & TIMES OF RELIEF   Relief will take place in the following order :- Signallers, 'A' 'D' 'B' 'C' Companies, Scouts, Bombers, H.Q. L.Gunners, and Headquarter details. Movement will be by platoons (each Specialist section reckoned as one platoon), Signallers beginning at 8.30 am, remainder following with distances of 200 yards between platoons.
'B' Company will have dinners at SOUASTRE and will leave SOUASTRE in time to have teas at 4.15 pm at FONCQUEVILLERS where they will be joined by 1 Lewis Gun and team from H.Q. Detachments. They will carry out relief immediately after teas.

ROUTES.   From SOUASTRE the main SOUASTRE - BIENVILLERS ROAD will be used as far as track D.18, thence along track D.18 - B.18 - E.20 to FONCQUEVILLERS. (Reference Map 57.D. N.E. Edition 3.a) Right Company will relieve via NOTTINGHAM STREET or GOMMECOURT ROAD, Centre via LINCOLN LANE, and Left and Support via ROBERTS AVENUE.

BATTALION RUNNERS.   One from each Company in the line and 2 from the Company in Support will report at Battalion Headquarters at 10.0 am tomorrow.

CARRYING PARTIES.   Parties for carrying R.E. Stores for all Companies, and dry rations, water, and meals for Centre and Left Companies, will be found by the Company in Support assisted when required by Battn Bombers and Lewis Gun Detachments.

O V E R.

REGIMENTAL STORES.	O.C. 'A' 'B' and 'D' Coys will each take to the trenches :-
	   1 Box Periscope 10 Vigilants
	   2 1" Verey Pistols 1 1½" Illuminating Pistol
	(O.C. 'C' Coy may draw 2 1" Verey Pistols tomorrow if he wishes to do so). These will be drawn from Q.M.Stores today.
	Blankets will be handed in to Q.M.Stores by 7.15 am. All must be rolled in bundles of 10 and properly labelled). Officers' valises, washing bowls, picks, shovels, &c. will be handed in to Q.M.Stores by 7.45 am.

BILLET STORES.	Stores in billets at SOUASTRE will be handed over to 5th S.F. and must be left tidily arranged: receipts to be obtained.
TRENCH STORES.	Lists of Trench Stores taken over and signed by representatives of both Battalions to be handed in to Battalion Orderly Room by 12.0 noon O.C. 'B' Coy. will hand in this by 7.0 pm.
RETURNS and CERTIFICATES.	Following returns are due at Orderly Room tomorrow at times stated (1) RATION STATE - Showing details of strength by platoons with Specialists attached, showing Companies to which Specialists belong and platoons to which their rations are to be sent - 12.0 noon, except by O.C. 'B' Coy who will render this return to Orderly Room SOUASTRE by 8.30 am, also TRENCH GARRISON STATE. (2) TRENCH GARRISON STATE - ON usual proforma - 4.0 pm (3) Report on VERMOREL SPRAYERS, GAS BLANKETS, and APPARATUS - 9.0 pm (4) Report on GENERAL SANITARY CONDITIONS - 9.0 pm. (5) CERTIFICATE that there is one pick and one shovel in every dugout - 4.0 pm. (6) REPORT as to accumulation (if any) of filled sandbags requiring to be emptied - 9.0 pm. Regimental Sergeant Major will render these returns &c. for Headquarters.
WATER DUTY MEN	The R.A.M.C. Details attached will carry out their usual water duties at Transport Lines and FONCQUEVILLERS.
SICK PARADE.	Sick parade will be at 2.0 pm daily.
BILLETS.	The usual Billet Certificate, including payment for Company Messes, will be rendered by 8.0 am tomorrow.
REPORTING RELIEF	"Relief complete" may be reported by Fullerphone.
DRYING ROOM.	Drying Room arrangements will be as before.

                            Sd/ W.C.C.WEETMAN,
                                 Capt. and Adjt.,
                        8th Sherwood Foresters.

Appendix III

OPERATION ORDERS BY MAJOR J.K.LANE, COMMANDING 8th SHERWOOD FORESTERS
10th January 1917.

RELIEF   The Battalion will be relieved tomorrow 11th instant by 7th Battn Sherwood Foresters.

ORDER OF RELIEF.   Relief will take place in order :- Signallers, Scouts, Bombers, 'A' 'C' 'D', Headquarter details, 'B' Company with one gun and team of H.Q. L.G. Detachment. Relief of 'A' Company will begin about 9.30 am, relief of 'B' Company will begin about 4.30 pm.

MOVEMENT   'A' and 'D' Companies will on relief take over billets and posts vacated by 7th S.F. at FONQUEVILLERS. One gun and team from H.Q. L.G. Detachment will be attached to 'D' Company. 'A' Coy. will find one platoon as garrison for FORT DICK, and will take over that post by 9.0 am. O's.C. 'A' and 'D' Companies will make arrangements to take over billets. The Bombing Officer and 14 other ranks detailed by him will remain at FONQUEVILLERS for work at the Crypt under Brigade Headquarters.
Signallers, Scouts, remainder of Bombers, 'B' and 'C' Companies with H.Q. L.G. Detachment (less 1 gun and team) and other H.Qr. Details, moving by platoons, will on relief proceed to take over billets and huts vacated by 7th S.F. at SOUASTRE. There must be no straggling: movement must be in formed bodies in all cases. Movement will be via track E.20 - E.13 - D.18 to BIENVILLERS - SOUASTRE ROAD, except 'B' Company who may use the SOUASTRE - FONQUEVILLERS ROAD.

BILLETS.   The Q.M. will arrange for C.Q.M. Sergts to take over billets and huts at SOUASTRE and meet their Companies on arrival. O's.C.Sections will send on one N.C.O. per Section to take over billets and meet their Sections on arrival. They will proceed as one party.

BILLET STORES.   Stores in billets will be taken over in the usual way, and lists sent to Orderly Room by 6.0 pm tomorrow.

TRENCH STORES.   One Officer per Company will check over all trench Stores, lists of which will be sent to Orderly Room (on proforma sent out) by 8.0 pm tonight. A duplicate of this list will be marked at the end "Certified correct" and signed by Officers of both Battalions, after the stores have been checked by Officers of incoming Battalion tomorrow.

REGIMENTAL STORES.   Periscopes, Verey Pistols, Wire cutters, Gloves &c. in possession will be taken out by 'B' and 'C' Companies and handed in to Battalion Orderly Room by 10.0 am on 12th instant. 'A' and 'D' Companies will retain these stores themselves.

OFFICERS' SERVANTS & STORES   Officers stores &c. to be taken on Transport will be at Battn. Headquarters by 8.0 am.
Two Officers servants per company may come out to Battn. H.Qrs with these stores and will march to billets as a formed party.

REPORT ON WORK   O's.C.Companies will render by 9.0 pm tomorrow, brief reports on work done during tour under usual headings.

INDENTS.   Indents for material should be sent in as usual tomorrow morning

O V E R.

REPORTS   The usual Daily Reports will be called for tomorrow by runners
          at 8.30 am.   If anything of importance happens between then
          and time of relief it should be notified to Orderly Room by
          Fullerphone or runner.

                                                    Captn. & Adjutant,
                                                 8th Sherwood Foresters.

Appendix IV

OPERATION ORDERS BY MAJOR J.K.LANE, COMMANDING 8th SHERWOOD FORESTERS.
14th January 1917.

RELIEF — The Battalion will relieve the 7th Battalion Sherwood Foresters in LEFT SECTOR (i.e. "Y.2.Sub-Sector") trenches tomorrow 15th instant.

DISTRIBUTION. The distribution will be as follows :-

SECTOR	COMPANY &c.
RIGHT (Right on GOMMECOURT ROAD)	'D' Company – 2 platoons in firing line and 2 in Support line and NOTTINGHAM STREET
CENTRE	'C' Company – 1 platoon in front line 1 in Support line near LINCOLN LANE, and 2 in LINCOLN LANE dugouts or Battn. H.Qrs.
LEFT (Left at LA BRAYELLE ROAD)	'B' Company – 3 platoons in front line (with one Lewis Gun and team from H.Q. Detachments), and one in Support line in ~~LINCOLN~~ ROBINSON LANE.
SUPPORT	'A' Company – with one Lewis Gun and team of H.Q. Detachment – dugouts in SNIPERS SQUARE

Battalion Scouts, Signallers, Bombers, and 1 H.Q. L.G. Det. will be at H.Q. billets : These sections will take over posts, stations, &c. from outgoing Battalion.

ORDER & TIMES OF RELIEF — Relief will take place in the following order :- 'D' 'A', Signallers, 'C' Coy, Scouts, Bombers, H.Q. details. Movement will be by platoons (each Specialist Section reckoned as one platoon), 'D' Company beginning at 9.0 am, 'A' Coy at 9.15 am; Signallers will leave SOUASTRE at 8.30 am, remainder following with distances of 200 yards between platoons. 'B' Coy will have dinners at SOUASTRE and will leave there in time to have teas at FONQUEVILLERS at 4.15 pm, where they will be joined by 1 Lewis Gun and Team from H.Q. Detachment. They will carry out relief immediately after tea.

ROUTES. — From SOUASTRE the main SOUASTRE – BIENVILLERS ROAD will be used as far as Track D.19, thence along track D.18 – E.13 – E.20 to FONQUEVILLERS. (Reference map 57.D. N.E. Edition 3 a). RIGHT Company will relieve via NOTTINGHAM STREET or GOMMECOURT ROAD, CENTRE via LINCOLN LANE, and LEFT and SUPPORT via ROBERTS AVENUE.

BATTALION RUNNERS. — One from each Company in the line and 2 from the Company in Support will report at Battalion H.Qrs at 10.0 am tomorrow.

CARRYING PARTIES. — Parties for carrying R.E.Stores for all Companies, water and meals for Centre and Left Companies, and dry rations the Company in Support, assisted when required by Battn. Bombers and H.Q. L.G. Detachment.

REGIMENTAL STORES. — O's. C. 'B' and 'C' Companies will each take to the trenches :-
    1 Box Periscope   10 Vigilants
    3 1" Verey Pistols   1 1½" Illuminating Pistol
These will be drawn from Q.M.Stores tonight. O.C. 'A' Coy will return the 1½" Pistol in possession to Battn. H.Qrs tomorrow.

Blankets at SOUASTRE will be handed in to Q.M. Stores by 7.15 am those at FONQUEVILLERS will be stacked at Battn. H.Qrs by 8.0 am and brought up by transport tomorrow night (all must be rolled in bundles of 10 and properly labelled). Officers' Valises, washing bowls, picks, shovels, &c. will be handed in to Q.M. Stores by 7.45 am.

BILLET STORES — Stores in billets at SOUASTRE and FONQUEVILLERS will be handed over to 5th S.F. and must be left tidily arranged: receipts to be obtained.

TRENCH STORES — Lists of Trench Stores taken over and signed by representatives of both Battalions to be handed in to O.Room by 12.0 noon tomorrow. O.C. 'B' Coy will hand this in by 7.0 pm.

RETURNS & CERTIFICATES — The following returns are due at O.Room tomorrow at times stated :-
(1) RATION STATE - showing details of strength by platoons with Specialists attached, showing Cos. to which Specialists belong and platoons to which their rations are to be sent - 12.0 noon except by O.C. 'B' Coy. who will render this return to O.Room SOUASTRE by 8.30 am; also Trench Garrison State.
(2) TRENCH GARRISON STATE - on usual proforma - 4.0 pm.
(3) REPORT on VERMOREL SPRAYERS, GAS BLANKERS, and apparatus - 9.0 pm.
(4) REPORT on GENERAL SANITARY CONDITIONS - 9.0 pm.
(5) CERTIFICATE that there is one pick and one shovel in every dugout - 4.0 pm.
(6) REPORT as to accumulation (if any) of filled sandbags requiring to be emptied - 9.0 pm.
R.S.M. will render these returns &c. for H.Qrs.

WATER DUTY MEN — The R.A.M.C. details attached will carry out their usual water duties at Transport Lines and FONQUEVILLERS.

SICK PARADE. Sick parade will be at 2.0 pm daily.

BILLETS — The usual billet Certificates, including payment for Company Messes, will be rendered by 7.30 pm tomorrow by Companies at SOUASTRE; Companies at FONQUEVILLERS will also render Certificates to O.Room by 9.30 am that their billets and dugouts were left clean.

DRYING ROOM. Drying arrangements will be as before.

REPORTING RELIEF. "Relief complete" may be reported by Fullerphone.

GUMBOOTS. Gumboots will be drawn from Brigade or Battn. Stores under the same arrangements as for last time.

OFFICERS' MESS DIXIES. Officers' Mess Dixies &c. to be taken from SOUASTRE must be at Battn. H.Qrs by 8.0 am.

PACKS. The packs of N.C.O's. and men of Centre and Left Companies will be left at Battn. H.Qrs. FONQUEVILLERS stacked by platoons under arrangements of R.S.M.

Sd/ W.C.C. WEEKMAN,
Captn. and Adjutant,
8th Sherwood Foresters.

Appendix V

OPERATION ORDERS BY MAJOR J.K.LANE, COMMANDING 8th SHERWOOD FORESTERS.
18th January 1917.

RELIEF	The Battalion will be relieved tomorrow 19th instant by the 7th Battalion Sherwood Foresters.
ORDER OF RELIEF	Relief will take place in the following order :- Signallers, Scouts, Bombers, 'D', 3 platoons of 'C', 'A' (with one H.Q. Lewis Gun team), Headquarter Lewis Gun Detachment, and headquarter details, and 'B' Coy. Relief of 'D' Coy will begin about 9.30 am; Relief of 'B' Coy and forward posts of 'C' Coy about pm.
MOVEMENT	Companies (moving by platoons) and Sections, will, on relief, proceed to take over billets vacated by 7th S.F. in Divisional Reserve. Movement will be via track in E.20 & E.13 - B.18 to BIENVILLERS - SOUASTRE ROAD, except 'B' Coy and remaining platoon of 'C' Coy who may use the FONQUEVILLERS - SOUASTRE ROAD. There must be no straggling: all parties however small must move off in formed bodies.
BILLETS	The Q.M. will arrange for C.Q.M.Sergts. to take over billets and meet their Companies on arrival. O's.C. Sections will send one N.C.O. per Section to take over billets and meet their Section on arrival. They will proceed as one party.
BILLET STORES	Stores in billets will be taken over in the usual way and lists sent to Orderly Room by 6.0 pm tomorrow.
TRENCH STORES	One Officer per Company will check over all Trench Stores and will hand in complete lists to Orderly Room (on proforma sent out) by 8.0 pm tonight. A duplicate of this list will be marked at the end "Certified correct" and signed by Officers of both Battalions after Stores have been checked by Officers of relieving Battalion tomorrow.
REGIMENTAL STORES	Periscopes, Verey Pistols, Wire cutters, Gloves, &c. in possession will be taken out by Companies and handed in to Orderly Room by 4.0 pm tomorrow, except 'B' and 'C' Companies who will hand theirs in on arrival at SOUASTRE.
OFFICERS' SERVANTS & STORES.	Officers' Stores &c. to be taken on Transport will be at Battn. Headquarters by 8.30 am. Two Officers' Servants per Company may come out to Battn. H.Qrs. with these Stores and will march to billets as a formed party.
REPORT ON WORK.	O's.C.Companies will render by 9.0 pm tomorrow brief reports on work done during tour under the usual headings.
INDENTS.	Indents for material should be sent in as usual tomorrow morning
REPORTS	The usual daily reports will be called for by runners tomorrow at 8.30 am. If anything of importance should happen between then and time of relief it should be notified to Orderly Room by runner or Fullerphone.

Sd/ W.C.C.WEETMAN,
Captn. and Adjutant,
8th Sherwood Foresters.

18th January 1917.

Appendix VI.

OPERATION ORDERS BY MAJOR J.K.LANE, COMMANDING 8th SHERWOOD FORESTERS.
22nd January 1917.

RELIEF   The Battalion will relieve the 7th Battalion Sherwood Foresters in LEFT SECTOR (i.e. "X.2. Sub-Sector") trenches tomorrow 23rd inst.

DISTRIBUTION. The distribution will be as follows :-

SECTOR	COMPANY &c.
RIGHT (Right on GOMMECOURT ROAD)	'B' Company - 2 platoons in firing line and 2 in support line
CENTRE	'C' Company - 1 platoon in front line, 3 in support Incaldanas, and dugouts in LINCOLN LANE, CALVAIRE ROAD or Battn. H.Qrs.
LEFT (Left on LA BRAYELLE ROAD)	'A' Company - 3 platoons in front line with 1 Lewis Gun and team from H.Q.Detachments, 1 in Support in ROBINSON LANE
SUPPORT	'D' Company - dugouts in SNIPERS SQUARE

Battalion Scouts, Signallers, Bombers, and 1 H.Q. L.G.Detachment will be at Headquarters billets : 1 Gun and team from H.Q. L.G. Detachment in SNIPERS SQUARE. These Sections will take over posts stations &c. from outgoing Battalion.

ORDER & TIMES OF RELIEF   Relief will take place in the following order :- Signallers, 'B', 'C', and 'D' Cos. Scouts, Bombers, H.Q.Lewis Gunners, and Headquarter details. Movement will be by platoons (Each Specialist Section reckoned as one platoon), Signallers beginning at 8.30 am, remainder following with distances of 200 yards between platoons. 'A' Company will have dinners at SOUASTRE and will leave SOUASTRE in time to have teas at 4.15 pm at FONQUEVILLERS, where they will be joined by 1 Lewis Gun and team from H.Q.Detach. They will carry out relief immediately after teas.

ROUTES.   From SOUASTRE the main SOUASTRE - BIENVILLERS ROAD will be used as far as track D.18, thence along track D.19- E.19 - E.20 to FONQUEVILLERS (Reference Map 57.D. N.E. Edition 3.a). Right Coy will relieve via NOTTINGHAM STREET or GOMMECOURT ROAD, Centre via LINCOLN LANE, and Left and Support via ROBERTS AVENUE.

BATTALION RUNNERS   One from each Company in the line and 2 from the Company in Support will report to Battalion Headquarters at 10.0 am tomorrow.

CARRYING PARTIES.   Parties for carrying R.E.Stores for all Companies, and dry rations, water, and meals for Centre and Left Companies, will be found by the Company in Support assisted when required by Battalion Bombers and Lewis Gun Detachments.

REGIMENTAL STORES   O's.C. 'A' 'B' and 'C' Cos. will each take to the trenches 10 Vigilants 3 1" Verey Pistols 1 1½" Illuminating Pistol (O.C. 'D' Coy. may draw 2 1" Verey Pistols if he wishes to do so) These will be drawn from Q.M.Stores today. Os.C. 'A' 'B' and 'C' Coys. will also draw 1 Box Periscope from Store at FONQUEVILLERS and return to same place at end of tour.

Blankets will be handed in to Q.M.Stores by 7.15 am. (all must be rolled in bundles of 10 and properly labelled). Officers' valises, washing bowls, picks, shovels, &c. will be handed in to Q.M.Stores by 7.45 am.

BILLET STORES — Stores in billets at SOUASTRE will be handed over to 5th S.F. and must be left tidily arranged : receipts to be obtained.

TRENCH STORES — Lists of Trench Stores taken over and signed by representatives of both Battalions will be handed in to Battn. OR. by 12.0 noon tomorrow. O.C. 'A' Coy will hand in his by 7.0 pm.

RETURNS & CERTIFICATES — The following returns are due at Orderly Room tomorrow at times stated :-
(1) RATION STRENGTH - showing details of strength by platoons with Specialists attached, showing Companies to which Specialists belong and platoons to which their rations are to be sent - 12.0 noon, except by O.C. 'A' Coy. who will render this return to O.Room SOUASTRE by 8.0 am, also TRENCH GARRISON STATE.
(2) TRENCH GARRISON STATE - on usual proforma - 4.0 pm
(3) Report on VERMOREL SPRAYERS, GAS BLANKETS, and apparatus - 9.0 pm
(4) Report on GENERAL SANITARY CONDITIONS - 9.0 pm
(5) Certificate that there is one pick and one shovel in every dugout - 4.0 pm.
(6) Report as to accumulation (if any) of filled sandbags requiring to be emptied. - 9.0 pm.
Pioneer Sergeant will render these returns &c. for Headquarters.

WATER DUTY MEN — The R.A.M.C. details attached will carry out their usual water duties at Transport lines and FONQUEVILLERS.

SICK PARADE. Sick parade will be at 2.0 pm daily.

BILLETS. The usual billet certificate, including payment for company Messes will be rendered by 8.0 am tomorrow.

REPORTING RELIEF "Relief complete" may be reported by Fullerphone.

DRYING ROOM Drying Room arrangements will be as before.

GUMBOOTS Gumboots will be drawn from Brigade and Battalion Store under the same arrangements as for last time.

OFFICERS' MESS DIXIES Officers' Mess dixies &c. to be taken must be at Battn. H.Qrs by 8.0 am.

PACKS. The Packs of N.C.O's. and men of Centre and Left Companies will be left at Battn. H.Qrs FONQUEVILLERS stacked by platoons under arrangements of Pioneer Sergeant.

Sd/ W.C.C. WEETMAN,
Captn. and Adjt,
8th SHERWOOD FORESTERS.

Appendix VII
SECRET.

OPERATION ORDERS BY MAJOR J.K.LANE, COMMANDING
8th Sherwood Foresters,
January 26th 1917.

RELIEF. The Battalion will be relieved tomorrow, 27th inst, by the 7th Battalion Sherwood Foresters.

ORDER OF RELIEF. Relief will take place in order:-
Signallers, Scouts, Bombers, 'B' 'C' 'D' 'A' Cos., H.Qrs. Details, except as mentioned below for FORT DICK relief will begin about 6-0 pm and will be completed before 9-0 pm.

MOVEMENT. 'B' & 'C' Cos. will, on relief, take over billets and posts vacated by 7th S.F. at FONCQUEVILLERS. 1 gun and team from H.Qrs L.G. detachment will be attached to 'C' Coy. 'B' Company will find one platoon under an Officer as garrison for FORT DICK, and will take over that Post by 11.30 am. O's.C. 'B' & 'C' Cos. will make arrangements to take over billets. The Bombing Officer and 20 O.R. detailed by him will remain at FONCQUEVILLERS for work at the CRYPT under Brigade Headquarters.
Signallers, Scouts, remainder of Bombers, 'A' & 'D' Cos. with H.Qr L.G. detachment (less one gun and team) and other H.Qrs., Details, moving by platoons at not less than 200 yards distance will, on relief, proceed to take over billets and huts vacated by 7th S.Foresters at SOUASTRE. There must be no straggling: movement must be in formed bodies in all cases. Movement will be via DOWN STREET joining the FONCQUEVILLERS - SOUASTRE ROAD just West of Sentry Box. A plan shewing this route may be seen at Orderly Room.

BILLETS. The Q.M. will arrange for C.Q.M.Sergts. to take over billets and huts at SOUASTRE and meet their Companies on arrival. O's.C. Sections will send on one N.C.O. per Section to take over billets and meet their Sections on arrival. They will proceed as one party.

BILLET STORES. Stores in billets will be taken over in the usual way and lists sent to Orderly Room by 12 noon on the 28th inst.

TRENCH STORES. One Officer per Company will check over all trench stores, lists of which will be sent to Orderly Room (on proforma sent out) by 12 noon tomorrow. A duplicate of this list will be marked at the end "Certified Correct" and signed by officers of both Battalions, after the stores have been checked by incoming Battalion tomorrow.

REGIMENTAL STORES. Periscopes, Verey Pistols, wire cutters, gloves, &c., in possession will be taken out by 'A' & 'D' Cos. and handed in to Orderly Room by 10-0 am on the 26th inst; 'B' & 'C' Cos. will retain these stores.

OFFICERS SERVANTS & STORES. Officers stores, &c., to be taken on Transport will be at Battn. Headquarters by 5.30 pm.
Two Officers servants per Company may come out to Battalion Headquarters with these stores and will march to billets as a formed party.

REPORT ON WORK. O's.C.Cos. will render by 4-0 pm on the 28th inst, brief reports on work done during tour under usual headings.

REPORTS.   Reports tomorrow will be called for or sent in in the usual way. Anything of importance happening after the afternoon report should be sent by FULLERPHONE or RUNNER.

STRONG POSTS, &c.   The attention of O's.C.Cos. is called to the memo issued on the 9th inst as to the garrisons of strong posts, straggler posts, &c., to be found by the Support Companies in FONCQUEVILLERs in case of attack.
The O's.C. these Companies will not leave their Companies during their tour of duty at FONCQUEVILLERS.

W.U.Weekman
Captain & Adjutant,
January 26th 1917.   8th Sherwood Foresters.

S E C R E T.

OPERATION ORDERS BY MAJOR J.K.LANE, COMMANDING 8th SHERWOOD FORESTERS.
January 31st 1917.

RELIEF The Battalion will relieve the 7th Battalion Sherwood Foresters in left Sector (less Right Company area) trenches today.

DISTRIBUTION. The distribution will be as follows :-

Sector	Company &c.
LINCOLN LANE	'A' Company - 1 platoon in front line, 3 in Support line and dugouts in LINCOLN LANE, CALVAIRE ROAD or Battalion H.Qrs.
LEFT (Left on LA BRAYELLE ROAD)	'D' Company - 3 platoons in front line with 1 Lewis Gun and team from H.Qrs. Detachments, 1 in Support in ROBINSON LANE.
SUPPORT	'B' Company - Dugouts in SNIPERS SQUARE

Battalion Scouts, Signallers, Bombers and 1 H.Qrs. Lewis Gun Det. will be at headquarter billets; 1 Gun and team from H.Qrs L.G. Det. in SNIPERS SQUARE. These sections will take over Posts, Stations, &c. from outgoing Battalion.

ORDER & TIMES OF RELIEF Relief will take place in the following order :-
'D' Company, Signallers, 'B', 'A', Scouts, Bombers, H.Qrs. L.Gunners and Headquarter details.
'B' Company will relieve independently during the day.
For Companies &c. proceeding from SOUASTRE movement will be by platoons (each Specialist section reckoned as one platoon), Signallers beginning at 4.30 pm, remainder following at distances of 200 yards between platoons.
'C' Company when relieved will proceed to take over billets at SOUASTRE to be arranged.

ROUTES. From SOUASTRE the main SOUASTRE - BIENVILLERS ROAD will be used as far as track D.18, thence along track D.18 - E.13 - E.20 to FONCQUEVILLERS (Refce. Map 57 D, N.E. Edition 3.a).
'A' Company will relieve via LINCOLN LANE and Left and Support via ROBERTS AVENUE.
'C' Company may proceed to SOUASTRE by the main FONCQUEVILLERS - SOUASTRE ROAD.

BATTALION RUNNERS. One from each Company in the line and two from the Company in Support will report at Battalion Headquarters at 8.0 pm tonight.

CARRYING PARTIES Parties for carrying R.E.Stores, dry rations, water and meals will be found by the Company in Support, assisted when required by Battalion Bombers and Lewis Gun Detachments.

REGIMENTAL STORES O's.C. 'A' and 'D' Cos. will each take to the trenches :-
10 Vigilants   3 1" Verey Pistols   1 1½" Illuminating Pistol
These will be drawn from Q.M.Stores today.
O.C. 'B' Coy will retain Stores in possession
O.C. 'C' Coy will return his to Q.M.Stores at SOUASTRE
Os.C. 'A' and 'D' Cos. will also draw 1 Box Periscope from Store at FONCQUEVILLERS and return to same place at end of tour.
Blankets will be handed into Q.M.Stores by 2.30 pm (all must be rolled in bundles of 10 and properly labelled.
Officers valises, washing bowls, picks, shovels, &c. will be handed in to Q.M.Stores by 3.30 pm.
Blankets at FONCQUEVILLERS will be stacked at Battn. H.Qrs by 4.0 pm.

OFFICERS MESS DIXIES	Officers Mess Dixies &c. to be taken must be at Battalion H.Qrs. by 4.0 pm.
BILLET STORES.	Stores in billets at SOUASTRE will be handed over to 5th S.F. and must be left tidily arranged: receipts to be obtained.
TRENCH STORES.	Lists of trench stores taken over and signed by representatives of both Battalions will be handed in to Battalion Orderly Room by 12 noon tomorrow. An Officer per Company will go up to trenches to take over by daylight.
RETURNS & CERTIFICATES	Following returns are due at Orderly Room as follows :- (1) RATION STRENGTH - showing details of strength by platoons with Specialists attached, showing Companies to which Specialists belong and platoons to which their rations are to be sent - 2.0 pm today (2) TRENCH GARRISON STATE - on usual proforma (3) REPORT on VERMOREL SPRAYERS, GAS BLANKETS, and APPARATUS (4) REPORT on GENERAL SANITARY CONDITIONS) 12 noon (5) CERTIFICATE that there is ONE PICK and ONE SHOVEL in every dugout) tomorrow. (6) REPORT as to ACCUMULATION (if any) of filled sandbags requiring to be emptied Pioneer Sergeant will render these returns for Headquarters.
WATER DUTY MEN	The R.A.M.C. Details attached will carry out their usual water duties at Transport Lines and FONCQUEVILLERS.
SICK PARADE.	Sick Parade will be at 2.0 pm daily.
BILLETS	The usual Billet Certificate including payment for Company Messes will be rendered by 4.0 pm today.
REPORTING RELIEF	"Relief complete" may be reported by Fullerphone.
DRYING ROOM.	Drying Room arrangements will be as before.
GUMBOOTS.	Gumboots will not be drawn until further orders.
PACKS.	The Packs of N.C.O's. and men of 'A' and 'D' Coys. will be left at Battalion Headquarters at FONCQUEVILLERS, stacked by platoons under arrangements of Pioneer Sergeant.

Sd/ H.C.C. WESTMAN,
Captain & Adjutant,
8th Sherwood Foresters.

Transport is expected to be up tonight by 6.0 pm.

January 31st 1917.

WAR DIARY / INTELLIGENCE SUMMARY

Army Form C. 2118

1/1/8 Sherwood Foresters
1/8 Notts & Derby
In trenches 1/8 Sqn of
February 1917

Hour, Date, Place	Summary of Events and Information	Remarks and references to Appendices
1917		
1st TRENCHES FONCQUEVILLERS	Quiet day. Enemy trench mortars + grenades very active. Received reft.	Appendix I.
2nd DITTO	Bn. just now relieved Northumb. Fus. right Coy. area Sq 4 Lincoln Regt. being taken over + then Bn HQrs at north end of FONCQUEVILLERS: new arrangements being completed at 3.55 pm. 138th Inf. Bde on left; 6th Sherwood Foresters on right.	
3rd DITTO	Quiet day.	II
4th 8.0pm SOUASTRE etc.	1st Sherwood Forts relieved Bn. Bn. HQr at night 2 Co. remained in Brigade support in FONCQUEVILLERS, 2/5th Lincoln Regt, 2 Co. in B.E.F. HQrs moving back to SOUASTRE. Regt. HQr on part office with R.E. etc. Working parties found for R.E. etc.	
5th - 7th DITTO	Working parties found for R.E. etc.	
8th FONCQUEVILLERS	The Bn. relieved 2nd S.S. in support trenches.	III
9.0pm TRENCHES	Co. 2/8 Lincoln Regt. attached for instruction.	
8th - 11 DITTO	Fine the day. Frost + days. Spent the 2 works doing on F.G.R. duty.	
12th 9.0pm SOUASTRE etc.	Casualties: Bn. now relieved by 2 S.F.F. + 2 Co. 2/8 London Regt. 2 Co. remained at FONCQUEVILLERS in Brigade support 1 Coy. in support to 6th in trenches. Moving back to SOUASTRE arriving 1.30 a.m. 13.2.17.	IV

Army Form C. 2118.

WAR DIARY
INTELLIGENCE SUMMARY.
(Erase heading not required.)

of .... of
February, 1917.

Instructions regarding War Diaries and Intelligence Summaries are contained in F.S. Regs., Part II. and the Staff Manual respectively. Title pages will be prepared in manuscript.

1917 Hour, Date, Place	Summary of Events and Information	Remarks and references to Appendices
13th 11.0/- SUKITRE	A.Coy. relieved F. Buller from Supporting 5th F.R.	
13th – 15th DITTO	Working parties found for T.M. Battery, R.E. &c. a little training carried out.	
16th 9.0/- TRENCHES FOUCQUEVILLERS	Batt. relieved 7 S.F.F. in left sub-sector. 2 Co. 2/11 London Regt. also in trenches for instruction. To follow... to Germans shelled us up to 5.30 am to follow nightly, many enemy sent over a number of fine shells & no bombs. From 5.30 to 6.0 in air... in various parts of the trenches. Many casualties, ng. Our Trench mortars & Artillery replied 2 casualties, ng.	Appendix V.
16th – 18th DITTO	Recd 4: bombers (Coy.pm) 24 Div— bombers. Considerable shell & T.M. activity on both sides.	VI.
19th 11.0/- PT. AMMO.	Batt. was relieved at night by 5 Leicesters, incident by 5 Leicesters. — T.M. activity on enemys part during day. Bodies at Pt. AMMO in reply.	
23rd 1.30/- IRESNY	Batt. ANNAND & S.G. ... marched via GOMIECOURT – COUTURELLE – WARLUZEL – ST. LEGER STREL at ICKESNY	VII.

1/8th Sherwood Foresters

WAR DIARY
INTELLIGENCE SUMMARY.

Army Form C. 2118.

1/8th month of February 1917.

Hour, Date, Place	Summary of Events and Information	Remarks and references to Appendices
1917.		
21st IVERGNY	Batt. spent day billeting, cleaning up equipment to.	Scott & Hundleby reported to 1st army to become experts in gas.
22nd "	Bath- moved to West End of Village. Spent day in cleaning up.	
23rd–24th "	Training in attack practice in LUCHEUX WOOD. Working in training.	
25th–26th "	Whole Bat'n digging practice trenches near LUCHEUX WOOD.	
27th "	Coy day cleaning up & ready to move.	
28th GREVAS	Having been urgently ordered to move to ST MENCOURT area. Orders were received to proceed to GREVAS, apparently an retirement in place and by withdrawal of enemy from FALLENBERG to his 2nd line. Marched via LUCHEUX, GOMMECOURT & POMMERA, arriving at GREVAS at 3.30 p.	Casualties for month:- Killed 5 other ranks (officers provisional) Wounded 35 " . (2 officers 2 "). Still provisional.

J.G. Blackwalle Lt.Col.
O.C. 1/8th Sherwood Foresters

1.3.17.

SECRET.

OPERATION ORDERS BY MAJOR J.K.LANE, COMMANDING 8th SHERWOOD FORESTERS,
1st February 1917.

EXTENSION OF FRONT The Battalion front will be extended Northwards tomorrow the 2nd instant to Trench 60 (inclusive), the new front to be taken over by 4.0 pm.

RELIEF Battalion Headquarters will take over those of 4th Battalion Lincoln Regiment, the present Battalion Headquarters being handed over to 6th Battalion Sherwood Foresters.
'C' Company with one H.Q. L.G. and Team will relieve the Right Company of the 4th Lincs.

ORDER & TIMES OF RELIEF Lewis Gunners, Observers (from the Scout Section) and gas personnel will carry out relief under arrangements of Os.C. Cos. and Sections concerned tomorrow morning. Guides for each team &c. will meet them at Headquarters 4th Lincs. at 9.55 am.
'C' Company will relieve in the afternoon by platoons at 10 minutes intervals, the first platoon reporting at new Battalion Headquarters at 1.55 pm: guides will meet them there.
Movement will be via SOUASTRE - BIENVILLERS ROAD - DOVER STREET, and CURZON STREET. H.Qrs Sections and Details will take over between 1.30 and 3.0 pm from corresponding sections &c. Scouts and bombers will be allotted dugouts &c. near Battalion H.Qrs by the Second in Command.

TRENCH STORES Trench Stores at Headquarters will be handed over with the exception of Food Containers and Dixie Carriers. Those taken over in new area will be carefully checked tomorrow morning and lists sent to Orderly Room by 2.0 pm.

REGIMENTAL STORES O.C. 'C' Coy will draw from Q.M.Stores any Regimental Stores required for trenches

BOUNDARY OF SECTOR On completion of this relief the Battalion and Brigade boundary on the North will be :- Trench 60 (inclusive) - junction of Ballyhooly Trench and Support Line - Gendarmerie (all inclusive) - thence a line through E.14.D.

ARTILLERY SUPPORT There will be a redistribution of supporting Artillery, details of which will be issued later. For the present the new Sector will be covered by B 252 (18pdr. Battery).

DRYING ROOM The Drying Room accommodation at the new Headquarters is very limited.

SICK PARADE The Medical Room will not be changed until after Sick Parade.

/Sd/ W.C.C.WEETMAN,
Captain and Adjutant,
8th Sherwood Foresters.

SECRET.

OPERATION ORDERS BY MAJOR J.K.LANE, COMMANDING 8TH SHERWOOD FORESTERS.
February 3rd 1917.

RELIEF The Battalion will be relieved tomorrow 4th instant by the 7th Battalion Sherwood Foresters and 'A' and 'B' Coys. 2/5th Battn. London Rifle Brigade.

ORDER OF RELIEF 8 Platoons of the 2/5th L.R.B. will relieve 2 platoons of 'B' Coy. and the following 6 platoons of the 3 Companies in the line during the afternoon :-
  'A' Coy - 2 platoons in support
  'D' " - 1 platoon in Centre Post and 1 in NEW CUT
  'C' " - 1 platoon in front line and 1 in support
This relief will begin about 4.0 pm. Os.C.Coys. will make the best arrangements possible for accommodating these platoons. The 7th Battalion S.F. will complete the relief in order :- Signallers, Scouts, Bombers, 'C', 'B', 'A' and 'D' Coys. and Headquarter details beginning about 6.0 pm.
The platoons of the 2/5th L.R.B. will merely occupy dugouts &c. and take over the duties of the platoons they relieve: the actual taking over of the general trench work, stores &c. will be carried out by the 7th S.F.

GUIDES. Os.C.Coys. will each detail 4 guides - (1 for each half platoon) for the 2/5th L.R.B. - to report at Battn. H.Qrs at 1.15 pm. These must all be intelligent men and know exactly to what points they are to take the incoming troops. They must also know the tracks from the SOUASTRE - BIENVILLERS ROAD to the cemetery and CURZON STREET. Instructions will be given them at H.Qrs.

MOVEMENT 'A' and 'D' Coys. will on relief take over billets and posts vacated by 5th Sherwood Foresters at FONCQUEVILLERS: 'D' Coy H.Q. will be at the Shrine: 1 platoon with 1 Lewis Gun of 'A' Coy will take over at the GENDARMERIE.
'D' Coy will find one platoon under an Officer as garrison for FORT DICK and will take over that post by 11.30 am.
Os.C. 'A' and 'D' Coys. will arrange for taking over billets &c. and for reconnoitring posts &c. to be occupied in case of attack.
2/Lieut. W.P.Duff and 20 other ranks detailed by Grenade Officer will remain at FONCQUEVILLERS for work at the Crypt under Bde Headquarters.
Other details and 'B' and 'C' Coys. will on relief proceed to take over billets and huts at SOUASTRE vacated by 5th S.F. in Brigade Reserve.
All movement must be in formed bodies: there must be no straggling.
During daylight parties will proceed by CURZON STREET or DOVER STREET to BIENVILLERS - SOUASTRE ROAD: after 6.0 pm by DOWN STR. to FONCQUEVILLERS - SOUASTRE ROAD joining road just WEST of Sentry Box.

BILLETS The Q.M. will arrange for billets as usual. One N.C.O. or Senior private will take over Sections billets.

BILLET STORES. Stores in billets will be taken over in the usual way and lists sent to Orderly Room by 12 noon on 5th instant.

TRENCH STORES The usual procedure will be adopted for trench stores; lists to reach Orderly Room by 12 noon tomorrow.

L.G. Officer will detail 1 Gun and Team from H.Q. L.G. Det. to be attached to 'A' Coy.

REGIMENTAL STORES	Periscopes, Verey pistols, wire cutters, gloves &c. in possession will be taken out by 'B' and 'C' Coys. and handed in to Orderly Room by 10.0 am on 5th instant. 'A' and 'D' Coys. will retain these stores.
OFFICERS' SERVANTS and STORES	Officers commanding Companies will be notified of the time at which Officers stores &c. to be taken on Transport are to be sent down. Two Officers servants per Company may come out to Battn. H.Q. with these stores and will march to billets as a formed part
REPORT ON WORK.	Os.C. Coys. will render by 4.0 pm on 5th instant brief reports on work done during tour under usual headings.
REPORTS	Reports tomorrow will be called for or sent in in the usual way. Anything of importance happening after the afternoon report should be sent by Fullerphone or runner.
STRONG POSTS &c.	The attention of Os.C.Cos. is called to the memo issued on the 9th January as to the garrisons of strong posts, straggler posts &c. to be found by the Support Companies in FONCQUEVILLERS in case of attack. Os.C. these Companies will not leave their Companies during their tour of duty at FONCQUEVILLERS.
GAS N.C.Os.	O.C. 'D' Coy will detail 1 Gas N.C.O. to report for orders at Town Majors Office each morning at 9.0 am.
REVOLVERS	Certificates as to unloading revolvers when leaving trenches to be sent in by 9.0 pm tomorrow.
L.G. AMMUNITION.	The L.G. Teams of 'A' and 'D' Coys. will draw ammunition from Lewis Gun Billet No. 54 (R.E.Dump) when coming out of trenches.
PACKS.	Os.C. Cos. will arrange for any men whose packs were left at Old Battalion H.Qrs to proceed there in small parties to draw them.

Sd/ W.C.C. WEETMAN,
Captain and Adjutant,
8th Sherwood Foresters

SECRET.

OPERATION ORDERS BY LIEUT. COLONEL J.E.BLACKWALL, COMMANDING
                                    8th SHERWOOD FORESTERS.
                                       7th February 1917.

RELIEF   Battalion will relieve the 7th Battalion Sherwood Foresters in
                LEFT SECTOR (X.2. Sub-Sector) trenches tomorrow :-

DISTRIBUTION   The distribution will be as follows :-
                  SECTOR   COMPANY &c.
                RIGHT (LINCOLN LANE)   ('B' Company - ¼ platoon in front line
) 3 in Support line and dugouts in
                                            (LINCOLN LANE and CALVAIRE ROAD.

                CENTRE (ROBERTS AVENUE)   ) 'D' Company - 3 platoons in front
                                            (line, 1 in Support

                LEFT   ) 'A' Company - 3 platoons in front
                                            (line, 1 in Support

                SUPPORT   ) 'C' Company - dugouts in SNIPERS
                                            (SQUARE

                Battalion Scouts, Signallers, Bombers, and H.Qrs. L.G.Detachment
                will be at Headquarter billets. These sections will take over
                posts, stations &c. from outgoing Battalion.

ORDER &
TIMES OF
RELIEF   Relief will take place in the following order :-
                'A', 'D', Signallers, 'B', 'C', Scouts, Bombers, H.Q. L.Gunners and
                Headquarter details.
                For Companies &c. proceeding from SOUASTRE movement will be by
                platoons (each Specialist Section reckoned as one platoon),
                Signallers beginning at 5.0 pm, remainder following at distances
                of 200 yards between platoons.
                The platoon of 'D' Company at FORT DICK will be relieved by 12
                noon. O.C. 'D' Coy will arrange for billets &c. for that
                ~~afterno~~ platoon for the afternoon.

ROUTES   From SOUASTRE the route will be SOUASTRE - BIENVILLERS ROAD, and
                DOVER STREET, 'B' Company entering FONCQUEVILLERS near the
                Cemetery and relieving via LINCOLN LANE.
                'C' Company will enter FONCQUEVILLERS by CURZON STREET, and relieve
                via ROBERTS AVENUE.

BATTALION   One runner from each Company will report at Battalion Headquarters
RUNNERS   at 6.0 pm tomorrow.

CARRYING   Parties for carrying R.E.Stores, water, dry rations, and meals will
PARTIES   be found by the Company in Support, assisted when required by HQ
                Details.

REGIMENTAL   O.C. 'B' Company will draw from Q.M.Stores and take to the trenches
STORES   10 Vigilants   3 1" Verey Pistols   1 1½" Illuminating Pistol
                OsC. 'A' and 'D' Cos. will retain stores in possession.

                OsC. 'A', 'B', and 'D' Cos. will also draw 1 Box Periscope from
                Store at FONCQUEVILLERS and return to same place at end of tour.
                O.C. 'C' Coy may draw 2 1" Verey pistols.
                Blankets will be handed in to Q.M.Stores by 3.0 pm (all must be
                rolled in bundles of 10 and properly labelled).
                Officers valises, washing bowls, picks, shovels, &c. will be
                handed in to Q.M.Stores by 3.30 pm.
                Blankets at FONCQUEVILLERS will be stacked near Cookers ready for
                Transport at 4.0 pm.

OFFICERS MESS DIXIES — Officers Mess Dixies, &c. to be taken must be at Battalion H.Qrs by 4.30 pm.

BILLET STORES — Stores in billets at SOUASTRE will be handed over to 7th S.B. and must be left tidily arranged: receipts to be obtained.

STORES — Lists of Trench Stores taken over and signed by representatives of both Battalions will be handed in to Battalion Orderly Room by 12 noon 9th instant. An Officer per Company will go up to trenches to take over by daylight.

RETURNS & CERTIFICATES — Returns in the usual form are due at Orderly Room at times mentioned :-

(1) RATION STATE — 2.0 pm tomorrow 8th inst
(2) TRENCH GARRISON STATE)
(3) Report on VERMOREL SPRAYERS, GAS BLANKETS and) 12 noon
    apparatus) on 9th inst.
(4) REPORT on General Sanitary Conditions)
(5) PICK & SHOVEL Certificate)
(6) Accumulation (if any) of filled sandbags)

Pioneer Sergeant will render these returns for H.Qrs

WATER DUTY MEN — The R.A.M.C. Details attached will carry out their usual water duties at Transport Lines and FONCQUEVILLERS: including the filling of tanks on motor lorry at COIGNEUX.

SICK PARADE will be at 2.0 pm daily

BILLETS — The usual billet certificates including payment for Company Messes will be rendered by 4.0 pm tomorrow.

DRYING ROOM — It is hoped to be able to make arrangements for a drying room. This will be notified later.

GUMBOOTS — Arrangements for drawing gumboots if the weather breaks have been issued by the 2nd i/c.

PACKS — Packs of N.C.Os and men of 'B' and 'D' Coa. will be left at Battn. trench H.Qrs, stacked by platoons, under arrangements of Pioneer Sergeant.

        sd/ W.C.C. WESTMAN,
           Captain and Adjutant.

NOTE — Transport is expected to be up tomorrow night by 6.0 pm.

February 7th 1917.

OPERATION ORDERS BY LIEUT COLONEL J.E.BLACKWALL, D.S.O., COMMANDING
8th Sherwood Foresters.
February 11th 1917.

RELIEF. The battalion will be relieved tomorrow the 12th instant by the 7th Battalion Sherwood Foresters and 'C' and 'D' Coy. 2/8th Battalion London Regiment.

ORDER OF RELIEF Companies will be relieved as follows :-
(1) 'A' Company by 'D' Coy. 2/8th London Regt.
(2) 'B' Company by 'C' Coy. 2/8th London Regt.
(3) 'C' and 'D' Coys. by 7th Battalion Sherwood Foresters.
Reliefs via CRAWLBOYS LANE and FRONT LINE of 'B' Coy. will take place as soon as possible after 5.30 pm; other changes in (1) and (2) will be carried out by daylight.
The platoon of 'C' Coy. 2/8th London Regt, in Left of 'D' Coy. front line will not proceed to 'B' Coy until relieved by 7th S.F.
The 7th S.F. will complete relief in order :- Signallers, Scouts, Bombers, 'C' and 'D' Coys, and H.Qr. Details, beginning about 6.0 pm.
Os.C. 'C' and 'D' Coys. 2/8th London Regt, will be responsible for their Company areas as soon as taken over.

MOVEMENT 'B' and 'C' Coys. will on relief take over billets and posts vacated by 7th S.F. at POMMIER: 'C' Coy. H.Qrs. will be at the SHRINE.
Os.C. 'B' and 'C' Coys. will make their own arrangements for taking over billets &c. and for reconnoitring posts &c. to be occupied in case of attack.
'C' Coy. will find One platoon under an Officer as Garrison for FORT DICK and will take over that post by 11.30 am.
On relief 'A' Coy. will proceed to THE BLUFF to act as Reserve Coy to "L.1. Sub-Sector" for 24 hours. They will be at the tactical disposal of 5th Battalion S.F., but will be used for Brigade Working Parties. O.C. 'A' Coy. will arrange to take over Stores &c. tomorrow morning and for guides &c. if necessary. This Company will proceed to billets at SOUASTRE on arrival of a Company of the 58th Division for instruction on the evening of 13th instant.
2/Lieut. W.I.Duff and 20 other ranks detailed by him will remain at POMMIER for work at the CRYPT under Brigade H.Qrs.
Other details and 'D' Coy. will on relief proceed to take over billets and huts at SOUASTRE vacated by 7th S.F. in Brigade Reserve.
All movement must be in formed bodies: there must be no straggling During daylight parties will proceed via CHURCH STREET or DOVER STREET to BIENVILLERS – SOUASTRE ROAD: after 6.0 pm via DOWN STREET to POMMIER – SOUASTRE ROAD joining Road just WEST of Sentry Box.

BILLETS. The Q.M. will arrange for billets as usual. One N.C.O. or senior Private per Section will take over Sections billets.

BILLET STORES. Stores in billets will be taken over in the usual way and lists sent to Orderly Room by 12 noon 13th instant.

TRENCH STORES The usual procedure will be adopted for Trench Stores; lists to reach Orderly Room by 12 noon tomorrow.

REGIMENTAL STORES	Periscopes, Verey pistols, Wire cutters, Gloves, &c. in possession will be handed over by 'A' and 'B' Coys. to relieving Companies of the London Regt: separate receipts to be obtained. The latter Companies will return these to Orderly Room COUASTRE after their relief on 13th instant. O.C. 'C' Coy. will retain his. O.C. 'D' Coy. will hand over his to O.C. 'B' Coy.
OFFICERS' SERVANTS & BOXES.	Os.C. Coys. will send down any Officers' Stores &c. to be taken on Transport by 8.30 pm.
REPORT ON WORK.	Os.C. Coys. will render by 4.0 pm on the 13th instant brief reports on work done during tour under usual headings.
REPORTS ✗	Reports tomorrow will be sent in or called for in the usual way. Anything of importance happening after the Afternoon Report should be sent by Fullerphone or Runner.
STRONG POSTS &c.	The attention of Os.C.Coys. is called to the Memo issued on the 9th of January as to the garrisons of Strong Posts, Straggler Posts, &c. to be found by the Support Companies in FONCQUEVILLERS in case of attack. The Os.C. these Companies will not leave their Companies during their tour of duty at FONCQUEVILLERS.
GAS N.C.O.	O.C. 'B' Coy. will detail one Gas N.C.O. to report for orders at the Town Major's Office each morning at 9.0 am whilst in Brigade Reserve.
REVOLVERS	Certificates as to unloading Revolvers when leaving trenches to be sent in by 9.0 pm tomorrow
PACKS	Os.C. Coys will arrange for any men whose packs were left at Battalion Headquarters to proceed there in small parties to draw them.
L.G. AMMUNITION	'A' Coy. will take over Lewis Gun Ammunition in the BLUFF and hand same over on relief. 'B' and 'C' Coys. will take over ammunition left by 7th S.F. in billets.

Captn and Adjutant,
8th S.F.

✗ Intents and programmes of work to be sent in as usual

OPERATION ORDERS BY LIEUT. COLONEL J.E.BLACKWALL, D.S.O., COMMANDING
8th SHERWOOD FORESTERS.
February 15th 1917.

RELIEF The Battalion will relieve the 7th Battalion Sherwood Foresters in LEFT SECTOR (X.2.Sub-Sector) trenches tomorrow.

DISTRIBUTION. At the time of relief there will be 2 Companies of 2/11th London Regt. in this Sub-Sector in addition to the 7th Battalion Sherwood Foresters; two Companies will therefore have to go into billets. Orders as to this will be issued tomorrow morning.

2 Companies The 2/11th London Regiment will go out on the 17th instant, and the distribution will then be as follows :-

SECTOR	COMPANY &c.
RIGHT (LINCOLN LANE)	'C' Company - 1 platoon in the front line, 3 in support line and dugouts in LINCOLN LANE and CALVAIRE ROAD
CENTRE (ROBERTS AVENUE)	'B' Company - 3 platoons in front line and 1 in Support
LEFT	'D' Company - 3 platoons in front line one in Support
SUPPORT	'A' Company - dugouts in SNIPERS SQUARE, with one Lewis Gun on LA BRAYELLE ROAD.

Battalion Scouts, Bombers, Signallers and H.Q. L.G. will be at H.Qr. billets. These Sections will take over posts, stations &c. from outgoing Battalion.

ORDER & Relief will take place in the following order :-
TIMES of 'B', 'C', Signallers, 'A', 'D' Scouts, Bombers, H.Qrs. L.Gunners
RELIEF and Headquarter details.
For Companies &c. proceeding from SOUASTRE movement will be by platoons (each Specialist Section reckoned as one platoon).
Signallers beginning at 5.30 pm, remainder following at distances of 200 yards between platoons.
The platoon of 'C' Coy at FORT DICK will be relieved by 12 noon.
O.C. 'C' Coy will arrange for billets &c. for that platoon for the afternoon.

ROUTES. From SOUASTRE the route will be SOUASTRE - BIENVILLERS ROAD and DOVER STREET.

BATTALION One runner from each Company will report at Battalion Headquarters
RUNNERS at 7.0 pm tomorrow

CARRYING Parties for carrying R.E. Stores, water, dry rations, and meals will
PARTIES be found by the Company in Support, assisted when required by Headquarter details.

REGIMENTAL Os.C. 'B' 'C' and 'D' Cos. will each draw from Q.M.Stores to make
STORES up to following strength per Company :-
10 Vigilants   3 1" Verey Pistols   1 1½" Illuminating pistol and 1 Box Periscope.
O.C. 'A' Coy may draw 2 1" Verey Pistols.
Blankets will be handed in to Q.M.Stores by 3.0 pm (all must be rolled in bundles of 10 and properly labelled).
Officers' valises, washing bowls, picks, shovels &c. will be handed in to Q.M. Stores by 3.30 pm.

Blankets at FONQUEVILLERS will be stacked near Cookers ready for Transport by 4.0 pm.

OFFICERS' MESS DIXIES
Officers Mess Dixies &c. to be taken must be at Battalion Headquarters by 4.30 pm.

BILLET STORES
Stores in billets at SOUASTRE will be handed over to 7th S.F. and must be left tidily arranged; receipts to be obtained.

STORES
Lists of trench stores taken over and signed by representatives of both Battalions will be handed in to Battalion Orderly Room by 12 noon on the 17th instant. One Officer per Company will go up to take over in daylight.

RETURNS & CERTIFICATES
Returns in the usual form are due at Orderly Room at times mentioned :-
(1) RATION STATE - 2-0 pm tomorrow 16th inst.)
(2) TRENCH GARRISON STATE)
(3) Report on VERMOREL SPRAYERS, GAS BLANKETS)
    and APPARATUS) 12 noon
(4) REPORT on GENERAL SANITARY CONDITIONS) on 17th inst.
(5) PICK AND SHOVEL CERTIFICATE)
(6) Accumulation (if any) of FILLED SANDBAGS)
Pioneer Sergeant will render these returns for Headquarters

WATER DUTY MEN
The R.A.M.C. Details attached will carry out their usual water duties at Transport Lines and FONCQUEVILLERS, including the filling of tanks on motor lorries at COIGNEUX,

SICK PARADE will be at 2.0 pm daily.

BILLETS
The usual billet certificates, including payment for Company Messes, will be rendered to Orderly Room by 4.0 pm tomorrow. Particular attention must be paid to the surroundings of billets being left clean, as well as the billets themselves. This applies to billets at both SOUASTRE and FONQUEVILLERS.

DRYING ROOM
Drying Room arrangements are the same as before.

GUMBOOTS
Arrangements for drawing gumboots if the weather breaks have been issued by the 2nd i/c.

PACKS
Packs of N.C.O's. and men of CENTRE and RIGHT Companies will be left at Battn./H.Qrs, stacked by platoons, under arrangements of PIONEER SERGEANT.

          sd/ W.C.C. WEETMAN,
             Captain and Adjutant,
               8th Sherwood Foresters.

NOTE - Transport is expected to be up tomorrow night by 6.30 pm.

February 15th 1917.

OPERATION ORDERS BY LIEUTENANT COLONEL J. H. BLACKWALL, D.S.O., COMMANDING
8th Sherwood Foresters,
February 18th 1917.

RELIEF The Battalion will be relieved tomorrow 19th instant, as follows :-
Left Company by one Company of 5th Lincoln Regt.
Centre and Right Companies by one Company of 4th Leicesters.
The latter Battalion will also take over SNIPERS SQUARE with a portion of their Reserve Company.
NOTE. (1) Battalion H.Qrs. of 4th Leicesters will take over the BRASSERIE from 5th S.F.
(2) The Brigade front will be taken over by 137th Infantry Brigade by 11.0 pm on 19th instant.

ORDER OF RELIEF Battalion Observers, L.G. and Gas personnel will be relieved between 2.0 and 4.0 pm. Companies will be relieved in order :- 'D', 'A', 'B', 'C', There will be no incoming troops to relieve Headquarter Details: Os.C. Headquarters Sections &c. will therefore, receive instructions later as to moving off.

GUIDES No guides will be required for 5th Lincolns.
For 4th Leicesters two Battalion Runners will meet one Officer and 4 N.C.O's. at the CEMETERY at 12.0 noon and conduct them to Battalion H.Qrs. and then to Right and Centre Companies to take over.
Two guides each from Right and Centre Companies will also report at Battalion Headquarters at 5.30 pm to conduct two platoons to each Company Sector. They will receive instructions at Battn. H.Qrs.

MOVEMENT Companies and Sections on relief will proceed via SOUASTRE to billets at ST. AMAND. During daylight parties will proceed to SOUASTRE via CURZON or DOVER STREET and BIENVILLERS - SOUASTRE ROAD: after 6.0 pm the FONQUEVILLERS - SOUASTRE ROAD or tracks may be used at the discretion of Os.C. Companies and Sections. Lewis Gunners and others relieved during daylight may proceed to billets at ST. AMAND immediately after relief.

BILLETS. The Q.M. will arrange to take over and allot billets: C.Q.M.Sgts and other guides to be found by Q.M. will conduct Cos. &c. to billets on arrival. Os.C. Cos. and Sections will report at H.Qrs after arrival the position of billets and Coy. H.Qrs. Billet distribution lists will be rendered by Os.C.Cos. and Sections as soon as possible after arrival at ST. AMAND. Transport and Q.M.Stores will remain for night 19/20th at SOUASTRE.

REPORTS Reports tomorrow will be sent in/or called for in the usual way.
Anything of importance happening after the Afternoon Report should be sent in by Fullerphone or Runner. Indents and programmes of work should be sent in as usual.

REVOLVERS Certificates as to the unloading of Revolvers when leaving trenches will be sent in by 10.0 pm tomorrow.

PACKS. Os.C. Cos. will arrange for any men whose packs were left at Battn, H.Qrs. to proceed there in small parties to draw them.

LEWIS GUN AMMUNITION. Lewis Gunners will bring out all remaining Lewis Gun Ammunition to H.Q. L.G. Dump.

TRENCH STORES	Trench stores will be handed over with the greatest care and will be tidily arranged in dumps &c. Lists will be sent in to Orderly Room as soon as possible after they have been checked and signed by Officers of both Battalions. The original will be kept by O.C. Coy. and duplicate sent to Battalion H.Qrs.
REGIMENTAL STORES	Such Regimental stores as are not required at night will be sent to Battalion H.Qrs. by 6.0 pm. Verey Pistols will be taken out by Companies and handed in to Orderly Room as ST. AMAND.

                                              Sd/ W.C.C. WELLEMAN,
                                                  Captain and Adjutant,
                                                  8th Sherwood Foresters.

18th February 1917.

OPERATION ORDERS BY LIEUT. COLONEL J.E. BLACKWALL, COMMANDING
8th SHERWOOD FORESTERS,
19th February 1917.

Reference map LENS 11 1/100,000

MOVE The Battalion will move by route march tomorrow (20th inst) to IVERGNY via GAUDIEMPRE – COUTURELLE – WARLUZEL – SUS-ST-LEGER.

BILLETING PARTY 2nd Lieut. C.H. Powell and one N.C.O. per Company will proceed to take over billets at IVERGNY reporting at Town Major's Office there at 9.30 am. They will parade at Orderly Room at 7.30 am: bicycles will be provided for the party by Signal Section.

PARADES Sick parade 6.0 am. Breakfasts 7.0 am. Dinners on arrival about 1.0 pm.
The Battalion will parade at 8.15 am on alarm post, positions of which will be notified later. Companies will move off at 200 yards distance, the first leaving at 8.20 am (Signallers, Scouts and Bombers will form the leading Company). Stretcher Bearers, Pioneers &c. will be with the rear Company. Transport will also count as one Company and will be drawn up facing NORTH with head near ST. AMAND CHURCH by 8.30 am.
A halt for 5 minutes will be made at 9.0 am. After crossing the ARRAS ROAD the leading Company will halt at a spot to be selected and the Battalion will close up.

STORES All blankets (rolled in bundles of 10 and properly labelled) and other stores will be sent to Q.M. Store at ST. AMAND (selected by Q.M.) by 6.30 am. Officers valises and packs of men unable to carry them by 7.0 am (packs must be labelled).

As certified by M.O.

CERTIFICATES. Certificates that billets have been left clean and Company Messes paid for will be handed in by 8.0 am, also marching out states (not parade states) by Os.C. Cos. Signallers, Scouts, Bombers, Transport and S.Bs., and on completion of march falling out states (Men who fell out and did not rejoin before march was completed) and Certificates that Cos. &c. are in billets.

MARCH DISCIPLINE &c. Particular attention must be paid throughout to march discipline and to uniformity of dress. Greatcoats will be carried in the pack and the leather jerkin &c. (folded according to pattern laid down) on top of the pack.
One Officers servant from each Mess may march in rear of Mess Cart.

[signature]

19th February 1917.
Captain and Adjutant,
8th Sherwood Foresters.

1/8th Newood Forster

WAR DIARY
INTELLIGENCE SUMMARY

for month of March 1917

Army Form C. 2118.

Hour, Date, Place	Summary of Events and Information	Remarks and references to Appendices
Feb. 1917		
1st 9.0 a.m. GRENAS	Marched from GRENAS to billets at ST. AMAND arriving about noon.	
2nd ST. AMAND	General routine work.	
3rd 3.30 a.m. DO.	Left ST. AMAND by platoons, beginning at 3.30 a.m. + marched to GOMMECOURT + took over trenches (recently evacuated by Enemy) from 5th Leicesters. Line taken over	
6.0 GOMMECOURT	was about GARDESTELLUNG — Pari-RIEGELSTELLUNG — Trenches N.E of GOMMECOURT Wood. Relief completed 10.0 a.m. Enemy continued withdrawal slightly during day + Bn. moved forward to keep touch. During afternoon 2 Cos. 5th Sherwood Foresters were sent up in support. About 6.0 p.m. Bn. held line 2nd GARDE STELLUNG — RIEGELSTELLUNG — E.29.A.5.5 — E.29.A.0.7. The 31st Division was on our Right + 7 K/Sherwood Foresters on Left.	
4th DO.	Enemy continued withdrawal more rapidly +Bn. H.Qrs. was moved forward 3 hrs. during day. THE "Z", PIGEON WOOD — RETTEMOY FARM were taken by us. Considerable opposition was met with about	

1/8th Sherwood Foresters

WAR DIARY
or
INTELLIGENCE SUMMARY.
(Erase heading not required.)

Army Form C. 2118.

for month of March, 1917.

Instructions regarding War Diaries and Intelligence Summaries are contained in F.S. Regs., Part II. and the Staff Manual respectively. Title pages will be prepared in manuscript.

Hour, Date, Place	Summary of Events and Information	Remarks and references to Appendices
4th Mch. 1917 GOMMECOURT.	PIGEON WOOD taken about 6.0.p. The enemy counter-attacked in force against C. Coy. in trench in front of 1/4 BRAYELLE FARM, forcing them to withdraw to trench in rear of farm. A hand line was essentially consolidated from RETTEMOY FARM – BRAYELLE GRABEN – LA BRAYELLE FARM – N.E. corner of THE 'Z'.	
5th Do.	Several bombing encounters near PIGEON WOOD during day. At 8.0 p. 5th Sherwood Foresters took over line. RETTEMOY FARM – BRAYELLE GRABEN.	
6th Do. 9.0 p.m.	Considerable shelling of our line during day. Relieved by 6th Sherwood Foresters. A. & B. Cos. moved to hutts in FONCQUEVILLERS, Hdqrs., C. & D. Cos. to dugouts in GOMMECOURT.	
7th Do.	At 6.0 p.m. A. & B. Cos. moved up to dugouts in RIEGEL STELLUNG.	
8th – 9th Do.	Clearing dugouts, salving material &c.	

MW

1/8 Sherwood Foresters

Army Form C. 2118.

WAR DIARY for month of INTELLIGENCE SUMMARY. March 1917.

(Erase heading not required.)

Hour, Date, Place Mch 1917	Summary of Events and Information	Remarks and references to Appendices
9.0 p.m. 10th GOMMECOURT	Relieved 6th Sherwood Foresters in left sector, in front of PIGEON WOOD. Trenches very bad, deep in mud.	
11th Do.	Quiet day. At night C. Coy. cut 2 gaps in wire east side of BURG GRABEN in front of enemy trench on W.N.W. of KITE COPSE.	
12th Do.	Preparations made for demonstration against HEDGE TRENCH.	APPENDIX - I.
13th 1.0 a.m Do.	To our right 5th Sherwood Foresters attempted French RETTEMOY GRABEN, but did not succeed.	
1.10 "	Strong parties from K.C & D Coys. made demonstration along Communication trenches towards HEDGE TRENCH.	
7.0 "	Capt. A. Hadley sent forward a patrol under 2 Lt. A. Michie which tried to establish KITE COPSE. During afternoon 2/Lt E. Hopkinson with a party tried to push through BURG GRABEN, but was met by strong opposition; he withdrew his party without casualties after inflicting reversal on enemy.	
7.0 p.m.	Enemy in some numbers attacked in force opposite KITE COPSE, but were driven off said line with heavy losses.	

W.W.

1/8th Newton Porter

WAR DIARY
INTELLIGENCE SUMMARY
(Erase heading not required.)

Army Form C. 2118.

of month of March 1917.

Hour, Date, Place Feb. 1917	Summary of Events and Information	Remarks and references to Appendices
14th 6.0 p GOMMECOURT.	Relieved by 6th Cheshires. Bn. moved back & stayed in billets in GOMMECOURT.	
15th Do.	Rearrangement of billets: Bn. concentrated in dugouts West of GIMMECOURT WOOD	
16th Do.	Salvage work & cleaning dugouts.	
17th 6.0 p Do.	Relieved by 4th Lincolns. marched back to billets at SOUASTRE 9.0 pm. Snowing. Successful ENTERTS & BUCQUOY.	
18th & 19th SOUASTRE	Cleaning, bathing &c.	
20th 10.30 am Do.	Left SOUASTRE marched to huts near BAYENCOURT	
21st nr BAYENCOURT.	Training, Batt drill &c.	
22nd 10.30 am	Left BAYENCOURT marched across country to COURCELLES-AU-BOIS.	
23rd 1.0 pm	Left COURCELLES marched to CONTAY by Bn of 4 pm.	
24th 11.45 am	Left CONTAY marched to BERTANGLES by 4 pm.	

98th Siege Battery

WAR DIARY
INTELLIGENCE SUMMARY
(Erase heading not required.)

Army Form C. 2118.

Month of March 1917.

Hour, Date, Place	Summary of Events and Information	Remarks and References to Appendices
Mch. 1917		
25th BERTANGLES	Left BERTANGLES at 2.15 p.m. marched toward road (AMIENS—DOULLENS). Entrained there at 5.0 p.m. Proceeded via AMIENS & REVELLES.	Appendix I.
26th & 27th REVELLES	Cleaning up.	
28th Do.	Entrained at BACOUEL Station at 3.0 p.m.	
29th WESTREHEM	Detrained at BERGUETTE Stn. at 10.0 a.m. & marched billets at WESTREHEM by 3.0 p.m. The Batty. by this move left 5th Army & joined 1st Army.	
30th Do.	Cleaning up & resting in new billets. Some training carried out.	
31st Do.	Inf. C. Jacob (Lt. Col. Commander Lt. Col.) met all Officers.	
	Casualties. Killed – Lt. A. Ahearn. Sick officers – 5 O.R. Wounded – 4 O.R. 25 O.R.	

H. Blackmore
Lt. Col. R.A.
Commanding
98th Siege Battery

OPERATION ORDERS BY LIEUT COLONEL J.E.BLACKWALL, D.S.O., COMMANDING
8th Sherwood Foresters.
12th March 1917.

Reference Map 57 D N.E..

1. The 5th Sherwood Foresters will tonight attack and consolidate RETTEMOY GRABEN F.25.a.22.72 (junction with LANDSTURM GRABEN) inclusive to F.25.d.12.90.

2. As soon as our artillery opens fire (Zero minus 5) the 8th Sherwood Foresters will bomb first second and third German lines BURG GRABEN and BRAYELLE GRABEN in order to ascertain enemys strength and dispositions.

3. Our Artillery and T.M's will barrage line E.24.d.1.7 - BURG - KITE COPSE.

4. On our artillery opening fire bombing parties will start as follows :- (a) From 'D' Coy bombing party of 1 N.C.O. and 8 men along old German first line covered by 3 riflemen with fixed bayonets on the top, each side the trench and in rear of party. Each rifleman to carry 6 bombs.
    (b) From 'D' Coy Similar parties to move up old second line trench.
    NOTE Neither (a) nor (b) will any case go beyond the HANNESCAMPS - ESSARTS ROAD
    (c) From 'C' Coy Similar parties to move up old third line trench. These will not proceed beyond HEDGE TRENCH.
    NOTE Os.C. 'C' and 'D' Cos. will arrange for recognizing parties in case they have occasion to meet in C.T. connecting second and third lines.
    (d) From 'C' Coy Similar parties to move up BURG GRABEN.
    (e) From 'A' Coy Similar parties to move along BRAYELLE GRABEN.
    NOTE Parties (d) and (e) will only advance within safety distance of barrage which will be intermittent and continue to time depending on circumstances.
    All parties will return to our front line and report by 11.0 pm.

5. Special reports will be rendered by Os.C. 'C' and 'D' Cos. as to possibility of occupying and holding the line E.24.a.2.5 - E.24.c.80.95 - E.24.c.35.70.

6. Bombs may be drawn as follows :- No. 5's from PIGEON DUMP (E.29.b.40.65) No. 5's and 23's from ROAD DUMP (E.29.b.85.25)

7. Dressing Station will be in dugout entrance in PIGEON TRENCH next to 'B' Coy's. H.Qrs.

8. 'B' Coy will carry rations and water forward to all Company H.Qrs also R.E.Stores to suitable points for consolidation of PIGEON TRENCH line. Work on this line to be completed by morning "stand-to" on the 13th instant.

9. Zero will be 10.0 pm.
10. Acknowledge.

Sd/ W.C.C.WEETMAN,
Capt. & Adjt,
Issued at 1.0 pm.
8th Sherwood Foresters.

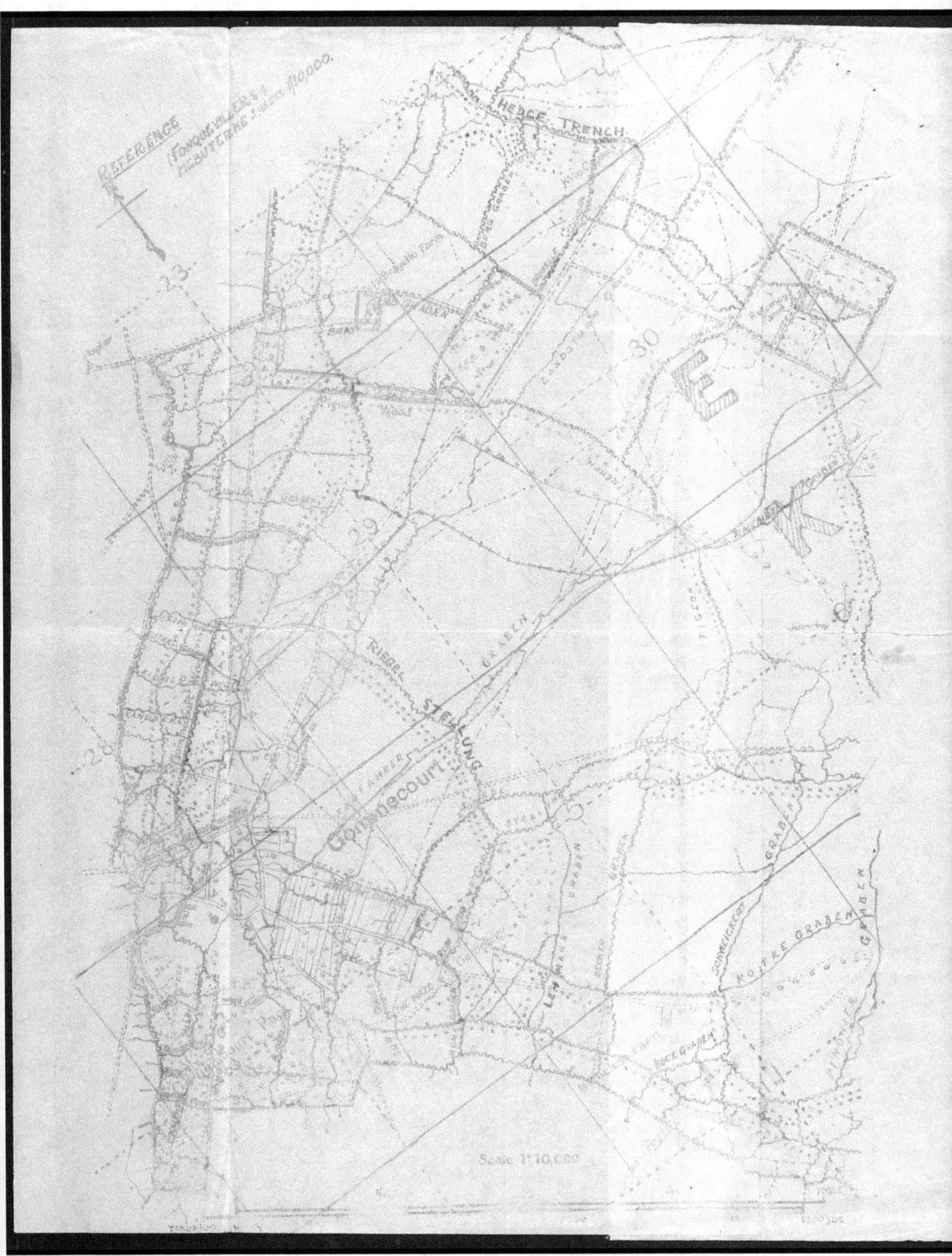

Army Form C. 2118.

WAR DIARY 1/8th Bn Sherwood Foresters for the month of April 1917

or

INTELLIGENCE SUMMARY.

(Erase heading not required.)

Instructions regarding War Diaries and Intelligence Summaries are contained in F. S. Regs., Part II. and the Staff Manual respectively. Title pages will be prepared in manuscript.

page 1   Vol 26   9.26

Place	Date	Hour	Summary of Events and Information	Remarks and references to Appendices
WESTREHEM	April 1 to April 12		The Bn was in rest billets. During this period training was carried out in the attack (Pln. Coy, & Bn), short route marches, outposts & advance guard schemes, musketry (especially description and recognition of targets) and range firing. Advantage was taken of the time to re-equip and clothe the men where necessary. All ranks derived great benefit from the rest.	
"	April 9		A Divisional Parade took place. The Bn. formed part of the advance guard of a Division following up an imaginary enemy. During the march a R.P.G. landed just by the 11 R.F.A. Commander.	
VENDIN LEZ BETHUNE	April 13		The Bn. marched to VENDIN LEZ BETHUNE and spent the night there.	
HOUCHIN	" 14		The Bn. marched to HOUCHIN where they were under Canvas, sharing a camp with the 7th Sherwood Foresters. During this time training was continued on similar lines to WESTREHEM. The Lewis Gunners fired on a 30 yds range.	
LIEVIN	" 15 to 17			
"	" 18		The Bn. marched from HOUCHIN to LIEVIN and took over Support Bn billets from 13 K.R.R. Middlesex Regt, 73rd Infantry Brigade, 24th Division.	
"	" 19		The Bn. took over the left Bn sector of the Brigade line in CITE de RAUMONT from 7th Bn. Sr. Hants Regt. Ref. LENS 36c S.W.1, eastern 3A./1000 from ABSENT TRENCH	

1/8th Bn Beaumont Forestno

WAR DIARY for the month of April 17.
or
INTELLIGENCE SUMMARY.

Army Form C. 2118.

page 2.

Place	Date	Hour	Summary of Events and Information	Remarks and references to Appendices
LIEVIN	Apl.19		M24c to MAIN ROAD from QUARRIES to LENS M30a. Relief was completed by about without casualties. A Coy were in front line in rows of houses in CITÉ de RAUMONT B Coy in Support, 2 Platoons in BOIS de RAUMONT and 2 Platoons in CITÉ des BURGAUX and C & D Coys in reserve in trenches near Bn H.Q. at M 28 to 70.10.	LENS 36C 1/10000
"	20	2-45am to 10am	9h front line was held as follows. One Platoon in CITÉ de RAUMONT with right post in at 200 yd s/meno SOUTH of ABBOLOM TRENCH, one Platoon in the double row of houses next North of MAIN ROAD and one Platoon EAST and one Platoon WEST of the THROUGH STREET.	
"	"	8.15pm	Patrols were sent out to establish posts in MAIN ROW, but operations were held up by one heavy artillery firing that posts were established about 11 pm at MAIN CROSS ROADS and in MAIN ROW at M30a 79. Ounces fire was dl with 8 T.M. Shrapnel to stop RIGHT flank in houses S.E of MAIN ROW. Enemy made attempt to rush post in	
"	"	11.30pm	MAIN ROW at M30a 79 but was driven back. A more determined attack was	
"	"	21 1-45am	made from direction of HILL 65, but was driven off by L.G. fire. One enemy was 1 killed and one wounded, the latter being brought in.	
"	"	"	Detailed report attached.	Appendix I
"	"	22	Detailed report attached (2) Copy of Operation Orders of 22nd April attached. (4.) Bn.	APPENDIX II (2) & (4)

Army Form C. 2118.

1/8th Bn. Sherwood Foresters WAR DIARY for the month of April 1917. page 3

INTELLIGENCE SUMMARY.

Instructions regarding War Diaries and Intelligence Summaries are contained in F. S. Regs., Part II. and the Staff Manual respectively. Title pages will be prepared in manuscript.

(Erase heading not required.)

Place	Date	Hour	Summary of Events and Information	Remarks and references to Appendices
LIEVIN	Ap.23		Retaliated after attack	APPENDIX III (a) & (b)
	23		Bn was relieved in the line by the 7th Sherwood Foresters & went into Brigade Support at RED MILL (Ref.M27d.70.80.) Relief was completed without casualties	
	25		Bn moved nearer to line into M16.6 in LIEVIN, remaining in Support (Ref.M22d.65.30)	
	26		Bn remained in Support & furnishing parties under the R.E. was found daily	
	30		for carrying R.E. materials & wiring the Reserve Line. The enemy shelled the Coy areas & some men were injured by gas shells.	
	30		The Bn was relieved by the 5th South Staffords and moved into Divisional Reserve at MOUBUEFFLES FARM near AIX NOULETTE. Relief was complete by 7.p.m. & was completed without casualties	APPENDIX II
			Returns of April. Strength Officers 36 and Other Ranks —. Strength 1st April Off. 36. O.R. 908. 30th April Off. 31. O.R. 748 Total killed O.R. 5. Wounded O.R. 66 including 7 men missing Off. 3. O.R. 70. Decorations awarded. 2/Lieut E. Hobkinson — Military Cross 30567. L/Sjt. W. Teare — Military Medal	

J. H. Blackwall Lieut. Colonel Comdg. 1/8 Sherwood Foresters

2nd May 1917.

APPENDIX 1.

DETAILED REPORT OF OPERATIONS from 12 noon 20th to 12 noon 21st April 1917 by Lieut Colonel J.E.BLACKWALL, D.S.O.

In conjunction with the 6th Battn. S.F. on our right we succeeded in pushing forward in CITE de RIAUMONT up to a line from M.30.a.10.50 along the MAIN ROW in a N.E. direction to cross roads at M.30.a.70.90. The 6th Bn. have established standing patrols in the two small houses S.W. of the MAIN ROAD. Operations of my Company commenced shortly before 8.0 pm. Patrols were sent out from No. 1 BIG ROW NORTH towards the cross roads. Patrols reported "all clear" and L.G. was immediately pushed up covered by Bombers. On reaching a position slightly in advance of 2 BIG ROW NORTH scattered parties of the enemy were seen in the neighbourhood of the MAIN CROSS ROADS to the N. and S. of it and coming towards us. Some of these men appeared to be without equipment. Bombs were thrown and L.G. fired and the enemy at once retired to cross roads. Our party continued to advance and parties of the enemy were again seen on the cross roads moving about as if picking up wounded. Our bombers eventually succeeded in occupying the houses right up to the CROSS ROADS about 9.30 pm, and patrols were at once pushed out towards the Platoon on the left. These men met with much opposition as far as M.30.a.70.90. Meanwhile the patrols of the platoon on the left had advanced towards the CROSS ROADS at M.29.a.70.90. In moving up an enemy M.G. was located and one of the team shot. His body was found later. The enemy was seen in small parties to the SOUTH. The patrol of this platoon not knowing how far the right platoon had advanced sent back information and before a stronger party was sent up the platoon on right had made good the corner and had established connection with the right. Patrols advanced in a N.W. direction along the MAIN ROW and No. 2 BIG ROW NORTH/but found no sign of the enemy. The advance on the left was delayed by our heavies dropping shells into the houses. A post was established near the EMBANKMENT to the N.W. of No. 2 BIG ROW NORTH but it was not considered advisable to push a patrol further down the main road. In the early hours of the morning the enemy made 2 counter attacks against M.30.a.70.90. The first by a small party and the second by a large one. These were driven off by our L.G., the enemy leaving one severely wounded man in our hands in the first attack and one or more men were evidently wounded in the second. We had no casualties in these operations. The enemy shelled CITE de RIAUMONT in the neighbourhood of ABSOLOM TRENCH both morning and evening of 20th April with 4.2s and 5.9s. also between 9.30 and 10.30 am 21st April they shelled the Chateau at M.29.b.60.70.

(Sgd) J.E.BLACKWALL,
Lieut Colonel
Commanding 8th Sherwood Foresters.

21/4/17.

APPENDIX II (a)

DAILY SITUATION REPORT by Lieut. Colonel J.E.BLACKWALL, D.S.O. from 12 noon April 21st to 12 noon 22nd April 1917.

At 8.30 pm we held MAIN ROW with posts of 2 men at EAST end - quite detatched - (the remainder of the section being in No. 2 BIG ROW NORTH) - one section at M.30.a.70.90 and one at MAIN CROSS ROADS. As the left supporting party was moving up a party of enemy estimated at 50 strong was seen to come up on the SOUTH side of MAIN ROAD evidently getting into houses. M.G. rifle and bomb fire was directed from different quarters to this post which had no protection and was withdrawn to EAST end of No. 2 BIG ROW NORTH. About 9.45 pm heavy M.G. fire was directed from vicinity of houses on S.E. of MAIN ROAD towards our centre post M.30.a.70.90. Enemy heavy artillery opened fire on neighbourhood of MAIN CROSS ROADS. Our 18pdrs. opened barrage on the EAST side of village causing us several casualties. Enemy was observed coming along SUNKEN ROAD towards our left post at 2nd BIG ROW NORTH. This attack was driven back; enemy losing one man who lies in road. An attack from the left on our post at M.30.a.70.90 also failed, but no enemy casualties were observed. Meanwhile our posts at MAIN CROSS ROADS had had 3 killed and about 10 wounded, the remainder being withdrawn to No. 2 BIG ROW NORTH - one wounded Sergeant and one man remaining behind. Two platoons of 6th S.F were believed to be in front. Enemy barrage gradually crept NORTH on WESTERN ROAD of Village. As soon as this was ascertained an Officer was sent with L.G. and Bombers to occupy main Cross Roads and post was reoccupied. No attack was made on this point although expected from nature of enemy barrage, but it is believed was given up as two platoons of 6th S.F. xxx were in fron t.

When this situation was clear and 6th S.F. had returned leaving posts out at WEST end of 2nd ROW SOUTH, patrols pushed forward towards EAST end of MAIN ROW. Small detatched parties of enemy fired from SOUTH side but gradually these withdrew and posts were established on both sides of the road about 20 yards from SUNKEN ROAD at EAST end. This post is untenable by day and in addition is continually being hit by our heavies firing on HILL 65. It was withdrawn at dawn,

(Sgd) J.E.BLACKWALL,
Lieut Colonel,
Commanding LEMBERG.

22/4/17.

APPENDIX II
(6) ffs

OPERATION ORDERS BY LIEUT COLONEL J.K.BLACKWALL, D.S.O., COMMANDING
8th Sherwood Foresters.
22nd April 1917.

1. On April 23rd the 8th Bn. Sherwood Foresters will attack HILL 65. The objective being ADVANCE, N.19.c.05.20 to M.24.d.9.7. The 6th Bn. Sherwood Foresters at the same time are attacking FOSSE 3 and sending clearing parties up ADMIRAL TRENCHES to meet clearing parties from 8th Bn. S.F.
137th Brigade on left are sending patrols to ABODE trench and will occupy them if not held by enemy. The 8th Bn. S.F. will endeavour to get in touch with these patrols from ADVANCE trench. The two houses on LENS ROAD at N.19.c.2.5 will be held by a post by 8th Bn. S.F. and blocks will be established in ADJACENT ABODE and ADULT trenches.
'C' Company will attack HILL 65 at Zero and occupy and consolidate ADVANCE trench and the two houses on LENS ROAD.
At 10.0 pm 'C' Company will relieve 'A' Company in the houses in CITE DE RIAUMONT occupying cellars &c. on each side of the LENS MAIN ROAD and the street North of it. 'D' Coy will relieve the remainder of 'A' Coy and occupy the cellars of the houses North of 'C' Coy with two platoons two platoons being in Support at the Chateau.
Coy Headquarters of 'C' & 'D' Cos. for assembly position will be at M.24.c.4.2. At Zero time 'C' Coy will be formed up for attack WEST of HILL 65 on a two platoon front in two lines on a 250 yards frontage and will follow the barrage up to ADVANCE TRENCH. One remaining platoon will clear ADMIRAL trenches and get in touch with 6th S.F. The remaining platoon will clear the houses and trenches on HILL 65. These two last platoons will occupy the trenches and houses on HILL 65 in support of the two leading platoons. As soon as the position of assembly of 'C' Coy is vacated it will be occupied by 'D' Coy with headquarters as before.
One platoon of 'D' Coy will mop up the line of the HOLLOW ROAD between HILL 65 and the CITE DE RIAUMONT.
The platoon of 'B' Coy now quartered at the Chateau and one platoon of 'B' Coy now quartered at CITE DES BUREAUX will occupy ABSALOM TRENCH from West wall of Chateau Garden to M.23.c.7.3.

2. Water for boiling will be drawn from Chateau and tea will be made in Mess tins by 'D' Coy only in cellars during night of 22/23rd April, care being taken to show no lights. All ranks will take tomorrow's rations with them and will be dependent on them and waterbottles until circumstances permit of a re-issue of rations.

3. Every N.C.O. and man of 'C' and 'D' Cos. will carry two No. 5 Grenades and two sandbags. Each platoon of 'C' and 'D' Cos. will carry two picks and 6 shovels also all wire cutters and breakers. O.C. 'C' Coy will take with his two leading platoons 12 ground flares which will be called for by contact aeroplane at 7.0 am.

4. At Zero minus eight, a bombardment by heavy artillery will commence ceasing at Zero minus 7 hours, recommencing at Zero minus 6½ hours and continuing until Zero. At Zero the 24th Divl Artillery will open on the line M.30.b.35.52. - M.24.d.21.20. - M.24.d.75.45 and remaining on this for 5 minutes then lifting at rate of 50 yards per minute to the trench line N.19.c.28.28. N.19.c.02.22. - M.24.d.90.68. - M.24.b.9.4. Five minutes after this line is reached the barrage will lift off this line to line N.19.c.28.28 - N.19.a.20.48 and remain there until ordered to cease fire.

The 138th M.G.Coy will fire on ADJACENT TRENCH from Zero to Zero plus 20 minutes. From Zero plus 20 to Zero plus 60 minutes they will barrage trenches in N.25.a. and the road N. 19.d. OO.75. From Zero minus 5 minutes to Zero plus 5 minutes NORTH side of HILL 65, from Zero plus 5 minutes to Zero plus 60 N.19.a. to N.19.c.

The 137th M.G.Coy have arranged to fire as under :-
One gun ABSALOM TRENCH - enfilade from Zero to Zero plus 3 M.24.d.2.2 and houses to EAST, - two guns M.17.d.85.00 traverse from Zero to Zero plus 5 minutes M.24.d.5.4 to 8.5 and from Zero plus 5 to Zero plus 12 minutes enfilade ADVANCE TRENCH - Two guns M.17.c.85.50 - enfilade from Zero to Zero plus 12 minutes ADVANCE TRENCH.

Two Stokes guns will be at disposal of O.C. 'C' Coy and will report at his Assembly H.Qrs at 10.0 pm. with 50 rounds of ammunition. A carrying party of 1 N.C.O. and 10 men will be detailed by O.C. 'D' Coy to report at 'C' Cos. Assembly H.Q. at Zero minus one hour to carry forward ammunition as required by O.C. 'C' Coy.

5. Brigade Signals are arranging to connect Forward Battn. H.Q. with Bde H.Q. by telephone and visual. The Signal Officer will connect by visual from HILL 65 to M.34.d.5.0 and Forward Battn. H.Q. and if possible from ADVANCE TRENCH.

6. Forward Bn. H.Q. from 11.0 pm tonight will be at the CHATEAU M.23.d.5.7.

7. Watches will synchronised at Forward Bn. H.Q. at 12 midnight and 2.0 am 22/23rd April 1917.

8. 'C' and 'D' Cos. will each leave behind at billets One Sergt and one Signaller per Coy and one N.C.O. and One Lewis Gunner per Platoon.
The 2nd in Command, Lewis Gun Officer, Orderly Room Staff, Scouts, (less 6 men), Police and Pioneers will remain at Battalion H.Q.

9. The Battn. Dressing Station will be at the CHATEAU M.23.d.5.7

10. Zero time will be 4.45 am 23rd April 1917.

Sd/ R. WHITTON,
Lieut. and A/Adjt.,
8th Sherwood Foresters.

8.0
Time 8/8 pm.

REPORT OF OPERATIONS.   23rd April 1917.

My leading Company formed up for attack at Zero time along the line of the Railway Embankment WEST of HILL 65. Three minutes after Zero enemy sent up red flares and his artillery put a strong and accurate barrage on Eastern edge of Village, CITE de RIAUMONT. A machine gun opened fire from a house on HILL 65 and another from a point further SOUTH. Our barrage was accurate. Two platoons followed the barrage to the most Westerly houses on HILL 65, one platoon started clearing ADMIRAL TRENCHES to the SOUTH. The two leading platoons were held up up M.G. fire, the third platoon began fetching Germans out of dugouts who were inclined to surrender. A platoon of the Support Company started mopping the HOLLOW ROAD WEST of HILL 65. The enemy then appeared in considerable numbers from the houses and trenches on HILL 65, the trenches SOUTH of the hill and dugouts on the Railway Embankment and surrounded the leading Coy, most of whom extricated themselves and withdrew to their original positions in the houses. 3 Officers and about 20 other ranks were left either killed or missing. The O.C. the Support Coy sent forward two sections to occupy positions not occupied by leading Company. Two platoons of the Support Company were sent forward from the Chateau to the small cottages south of ABSOLOM TRENCH. At 6.45 am he reported "post established at Cross roads on 2nd BIG ROW". Further support not required. Consider position in hand". Several good gaps were cut in the enemy wire by our own artillery and some of their trenches were considerably damaged. Cellars and dugouts however appear to be in a good state of repair and provide safe accomodation for strong garrison throughout a heavy bombardment. A post is held in 2nd BIG ROW NORTH, in the house next to the EAST end; a patrol visits MAIN CROSS ROADS. The remainder of MAIN ROW is untenable during bombardments by our heavy artillery, either by ourselves or the enemy the houses being demolished.

Our snipers occupy a post in the EAST straight through STREET between 2 BIG ROW NORTH and MAIN ROW, also in ABSOLOM TRENCH at Railway and have accounted for 7 of the enemy during the morning. From 10 to 10.30 am the enemy heavily bombarded our rows of houses with heavy artillery. Winged bombs are being fired continuously at 2 BIG ROW NORTH. Otherwise the situation is quiet. 6 enemy planes are patrolling, one of them very low, over ABSOLOM TRENCH.

A third Company is holding the frontage BOIS de RIAUMONT with one platoon, one platoon at CITE des BUREAUX, two platoons in ABSOLOM TRENCH. The last suffered 7 casualties during the night. The remaining Company is in reserve at the River LINE

Battalion H.Qrs. are at the CHATEAU M.23.d.5.7.

Patrols from 6th South Staffs. on left report ABODE TRENCHES strongly held with Machine guns. The gun of 137th M.G.Coy is "standing-to" in ABSOLOM TRENCH ready to deal with any movement observed on the NORTH side of HILL 65.

I am in touch on my right with the 6th Sherwood Foresters, who occupy first SMALL ROW SOUTH.

My total casualties have been 4 Officers and estimated 50 other ranks.

(Sgd) J.E.BLACKWALL, Lieut Colonel,
O.C., 8th Bn. The Sherwood Foresters.

APPENDIX VII

REPORT ON MOPPING UP PLATOON. 23/4/17.

The Mopping Up Platoon moved off when the barrage started. My O.C. Coy orders to them were to clear any existing dugouts in the SUNKEN ROAD and hold themselves ready to Support attacking Coy whereever needed. After satisfying themselves re SUNKEN ROAD they saw the attacking Company coming back followed by many Germans on the left. These they opened fire on on the flank with rifles, killing several. The Lewis Gun could not be used as attacking Coy prevented traversing fire. The attacking Coy came through them and entered the houses. The mopping up platoon stood fast until all attacking Company had passed them, and then the enemy at once returned to his trenches. The platoon then withdrew to Company H.Q. During this time they kept inside the enemy barrage and only had two casualties,

(Sgd) J.E. BLACKWALL, Lieut Colonel,
Commanding LEMBERG.

Appendix I

OPERATION ORDERS BY LIEUT COLONEL J.E.BLACKWALL, D.S.O., COMMANDING
                                    8th Sherwood Foresters.
                                    27th March 1917.

1. The Battalion will entrain at BACOUEL as follows :-
   'A' 'C' and 'D' Cos. Headquarter Details and Transport on Train
   No. 6 at 11-0 am tomorrow; 'B' Coy. on Train No. 7 at 3-0 pm
   tomorrow.
   Detraining Station will be BERGUETTE or ST. HILAIRE.

2. Captain E.M.Hacking and 2nd Lieut. C.H.Powell will act as
   Entraining and Detraining Officers and will report to R.T.O. at
   Station 4 hours before No. 6 train is due to start, with full
   details as to strength &c.   Captain E.M.Hacking will travel on
   No. 6 Train, 2nd Lieut. C.H.Powell on No. 7.

3. The Billeting Party will travel on No. 1 Train leaving at 3-0 pm
   today.   They will parade under Lieut. Whitton at Orderly Room
   at 12.30 pm.   The Quartermaster has arranged rations for
   tomorrow for this party.   These will be drawn at once from Q.M.
   Stores by Headquarter Billeting N.C.O.

4. A Loading Party of 1 Officer and 50 Other Ranks from 'B' Coy.
   also the Transport Sergeant will report to R.T.O. as early as
   possible this morning and remain at his disposal until their
   departure on No. 7 Train tomorrow.

5. Transport will move off under Transport Officer tomorrow morning
   in time to report at the Station 3 hours before departure of train
   'A' 'C' and 'D' Cos. and H.Q. Details will parade on Alarm Post
   in column of route at 8.30 am tomorrow in order Scouts, Sigs,
   'D' 'C' 'A' S.Bs. &c.
   'B' Company will move independently so as to be at the Station
   one hour before their train leaves.

6. Rations for tomorrow will be carried on the man.   Rations for the
   29th instant will be on Supply Wagons and will be issued at a time
   and place to be notified, except for parties mentioned in para 4
   who will draw them at the Station under arrangements to be made
   by Q.M.   Rations for the 29th will also be issued to the
   remainder of 'B' Coy at the Station before leaving.
   All Waterbottles must be filled.

7. All blankets, valises, Mess dixies and other stores will be
   sent to Q.M.Stores by 7.30 am tomorrow.

8. Billets must be left clean and usual Certificates sent in before
   the Battalion parades.

9. As Trains are not running to time it is possible that the above
   times may be slightly altered.

                                        Captain and Adjutant,
                                        8th Sherwood Foresters.

18th Bn. The Sherwood Foresters.

Army Form C. 2118.

WAR DIARY
or
INTELLIGENCE SUMMARY.
(Erase heading not required.)

Hour, Date, Place	Summary of Events and Information	Remarks and references to Appendices
1917		
May 1-5 MARQUEFFLES FARM.	The Battalion was in Divisional Reserve at MARQUEFFLES FARM. During this period advantage was taken of excellent ground to practice the attack in formations by Platoons, Companies and Battalion. Musketry, Lewis Gun firing & ceremonial drill were also practised.	Appendix 1. Copy Operation Orders 5/5/17
6/7 LOOS	The Battalion proceeded to the trenches and relieved the 5th Lincolnshire Regt in the left sector of Left Brigade front near LOOS. H.Q. near HARTS CRATER at M.6.A.80.10 (LENS 36c S.W. 1/10000) Relief was carried out without casualties. This was practically a return to the old French war zone. There was considerable enemy shelling and mortaring but no attack took place on either side. The Line was held as an outpost line by a series of posts. 3 Companies were in the front line and one in support, but on the 9th May they were changed and the front line was held by 2 Companies with one Platoon back from another Company, 1 Company in support & one Platoon in support and one Company in Reserve. The enemy shewed considerable activity with Rifle	
" 8 "		
" 9 "		Appendix 2. Copy Operation Orders 9/5/17
" 10 "		

1/8th Bn. The Sherwood Foresters.

Army Form C. 2118.

WAR DIARY
or
INTELLIGENCE SUMMARY.
(Erase heading not required.)

for the month of MAY, 1917

Instructions regarding War Diaries and Intelligence Summaries are contained in F.S. Regs., Part II. and the Staff Manual respectively. Title pages will be prepared in manuscript.

Hour, Date, Place	Summary of Events and Information	Remarks and references to Appendices
1917 May 11	Grenades and Priests Bombs. The Battalion had about 25 Casualties during this period occasioned by Trench Mortar & Shell fire. The Butts of Rifle and Bolts before were defaced and Surplus and wire put out in front of Posts.	
12	On the 12th May enemy shelled heavy bombardment Gas Shells inflicting 14 Casualties none of which were fatal	
12/13	The Battalion was relieved by the 7th Sherwood Foresters and went into Brigade Support H.Q. ELVASTON CASTLE (Ref	Appendix 3 Copy Situation Orders 11.5.17
13 to 19	During this period 1 Company was in support to and under the orders of the 7th Sherwood Foresters. The Battalion was employed in cleaning and repairing the line & before and carrying Trench Mortar Ammunition, both Heavy 2" & Stokes. 100 men per day worked under the Australian Tunnelling Company carrying each & every load from Dug outs	
19/19	The Battalion was relieved by 6th N Staffs and went into Divisional Reserve at NOEUX LES MINES Relief was	Appendix 4 Copy Operation Orders 17. 5. 17

3.

Army Form C. 2118.

11th Bn Sherwood Foresters

WAR DIARY
or
INTELLIGENCE SUMMARY.

for month of MAY, 1917.

(Erase heading not required.)

Instructions regarding War Diaries and Intelligence Summaries are contained in F.S. Regs., Part II. and the Staff Manual respectively. Title pages will be prepared in manuscript.

Hour, Date, Place	Summary of Events and Information	Remarks and references to Appendices
1917 May 18-19	completed without casualties	
" 19-25	During this period the Battalion practiced the attack and gained further firing on Range. Opportunity was taken to have all mens clothing disinfected at FOSSEUX.	
" 25/26	TRESH. The Battalion proceeded to the Trenches and relieved 5th Lincolns SHIRE Regt in left sector Right Brigade Front at LIEVIN H.Q. M 22 B 20.15 (Ref LENS 36 c S.W. 1/10.000). The line was held as an outpost line by a series of posts with a Main Reserve Line about 500 yards in rear. Two Companies plus one Platoon were in the front line, 1 Company and 2 Platoons in support and one Company in reserve. There was considerable Trench Mortar activity by the enemy on the Outpost Line. Our Artillery was active during the Tour.	Appendix 5. COPY Operation Orders 25.5.17
" 26	At about 9 a.m. at M 18 D 10.60 but was driven off by L.G. and Rifle fire inflicting casualties. He again attempted this on the early morning of the 27th & was again driven off.	
" 29/31	On the night of the 29.9."30." after a heavy Barrage the enemy attempted to raid our Trench at the Junction	

(9-29-6) W 3332—1107 100,000 10/15 H W V Forms/C. 2118/10

1/8th Bn. The Sherwood Foresters.

WAR DIARY

INTELLIGENCE SUMMARY

for month of MAY 1917

(Erase heading not required.)

Instructions regarding War Diaries and Intelligence Summaries are contained in F.S. Regs., Part II. and the Staff Manual respectively. Title pages will be prepared in manuscript.

Army Form C. 2118.

Hour, Date, Place	Summary of Events and Information	Remarks and references to Appendices
1917 MAY 29.30	of CROCODILE TRENCH & RAILWAY CUTTING and also hostile GARRISON kept this post. After sharp hand to hand fighting the enemy driven off and our posts reestablished. The original line was however lost. 3 Killed 2 missing & 7 wounded. The enemy shelled Back and Ailing this piece with H "2" 5'9" occasional gas shells. A large quantity of gas was put out in front of main between then trenches were empirised and our put-out in front of BUFFAT LINE. The dispositions were allied with night of the 30/31 & 3 Companies were placed in the Belfast line funding their own details	
30/31		
31/5/17 1/6/17	The Battalion was relieved by the 7th/8th Bn Sherwood Foresters and went into Brigade Support. H.Q. M 22. D 72. 20 1 Coy (A) was in Buffat and under the orders of the 5th Battalion Sherwood Foresters	Appendix 6. Copy Operation Orders 30.5.17

Army Form C. 2118.

18th Bn. The Sherwood Foresters

WAR DIARY
for month of MAY, 1917

INTELLIGENCE SUMMARY.

(Erase heading not required.)

Instructions regarding War Diaries and Intelligence Summaries are contained in F. S. Regs., Part II. and the Staff Manual respectively. Title pages will be prepared in manuscript.

Place	Date	Hour	Summary of Events and Information	Remarks and references to Appendices
	1917 MAY		Strength at beginning of month 777 " " " end of month 755 Casualties. Officers 1 wounded remaining at duty " O. Ranks. Killed 8 " " Died of wounds 1 " " Wounded 47 " " Wounded remaining at duty 4 " " Missing 2	

J. H. Rowe, Major
for Lieut. Colonel,
Commdg. 81 Sherwood Foresters.

APPENDIX. I.

OPERATION ORDERS BY LIEUT COLONEL J.E.BLACKWALL, D.S.O., COMMANDING
8th Sherwood Foresters.
5th May 1917.

RELIEF   The Battalion will relieve the 8th Battalion Lincolnshire Regt.
             In the LEFT SUB-SECTOR trenches on the night of the 6th/7th May,
             relief to be completed by 4.0 am.   "Relief complete" to be
             reported to Orderly Room as soon as possible.

DISTRIBUTION The section of trenches to be taken over by the Companies will
             be as reconnoitred by Company Commanders today, i.e. 'B' Company,
             Right,   'D' Company, Centre,   'C' Company, Left,   'A' Company,
             Support.

ORDER &   The Battalion will march as such as far as BULLY GRENAY, in order :-
TIMES OF   'B' 'D' 'C' 'A' Scouts, Signallers, Headquarter Details.
RELIEF   All movement EAST of BULLY GRENAY will be by platoons at 200 yards
             interval.
             The Battalion will move off from Billets at 7.30 pm.
             Route - via AIX NOULETTE, BULLY GRENAY, and MAROC.
             Os.C. Cos. will arrange to get to the line sufficiently early
             tomorrow evening so that they can visit their posts before daylight.
             Battalion parade in column of route on road facing WEST with head
             of column at farm at 7.20 pm.   Markers at Orderly Room at 7.10
             pm.

GUIDES.   Guides for this Battalion (one for each platoon and one for H.Qrs)
             will be at CROSS ROADS G.34.d.6.6 (Reference map Sheet 36 N.W. 3
             Scale 1/10,000) at 9.30 pm.

RATIONS &c. Rations for the 7th of May, Lewis Guns, Signal equipment &c. will
             be carried forward from MAROC.   They will be dumped at the
             British Cemetery, MAROC.   Company Q.M. Sergts. will be in charge
             of rations, equipment &c. to be carried forward and will be
             responsible that there is no delay in distribution as the Battn.
             must be clear of BULLY GRENAY Railway Bridge by 10.0 pm. to allow
             the 7th Bn. Sherwood Foresters to pass through.   Os.C. Cos and
             Sections will make all necessary arrangements for carrying up their
             own rations, Lewis Guns &c.
             Water bottles must be filled before leaving billets.

REGIMENTAL   Cos. will each draw from Q.M.Stores :-
STORES.   10 Vigilants   1 Box Periscope
                 3 1" Verey Pistols   1 1½" Verey Pistol.
             Blankets (rolled in bundles of 10 and properly tied and labelled)
             will be handed in to Q.M.Stores by 9.30 am.
             Packs will not be taken up to the trenches but will be handed in
             to Q.M.Stores by 9.30 am. properly labelled with Regimental No.
             Rank, Name and Company.
             Spare Signal equipment, Pioneers' Tools not required, and all
             other stores held by Cos. will be at Q.M.Stores by 9.45 am.
             Bicycles (with the exception of one being used by Cycle Orderly)
             to be returned to stores at FOSSE 10 tomorrow morning.
             Officers valises and Mess Boxes to be stacked outside Orderly Room
             at by 6.0 pm.

RUNNERS   Two Runners per Company will report at H.Qrs. on arrival.

STORES	Lists of Trench Stores taken over will be handed in to Battalion Orderly Room by 12 noon on the 7th.
RETURNS	Os. C. Cos. will send in to Orderly Room as soon as possible after relief the usual Trench Garrison and Ration States.
WATER SUPPLY.	Water will be brought up in petrol tins in limbers as far as ration dump. The 5th Lincolns will hand over to the Battn. 100 petrol tins - 60 at their Transport Lines and 40 at Battalion H.Q.
DRESS	Overcoats and Waterproof sheets will be taken to the trenches tomorrow. A man will be sent round tomorrow morning to shew correct method of carrying them.
LEWIS GUNS	O.C. "C" Coy will draw one Lewis Gun from "A" Company. All Lewis Guns will be taken to Q.M. Stores by 9.30 am.

R. Whitton
Lieut. and A/Adjutant,
8th Sherwood Foresters.

Operation Orders by Lieut. Col. J.E. Blackwall D.S.O.
Commanding 8th Bn. Sherwood Foresters.
May 9th/1917.

APPENDIX II

1. O.C. "C" Coy. will take over part of the front line now held by "B" Coy including the posts held by
   1. Bombers   2. L.G.   3. Rifle Bombers.

2. O.C. "A" Coy will relieve "B" Coy and that part of "D" Coy not relieved by "C" Coy.

3. "A" Coy H.Q. will be at present "B" Coy H.Q.

4. Three platoons of "B" Coy will be in support to "A" Coy. They will be under command of O.C. "A" Coy and will be available for finding patrols. "B" Coy H.Q. and two platoons will be at present "D" Coy H.Q.
   One platoon will be at H.Q. "A" Coy (old "B" Coy H.Q.)

5. One platoon "B" Coy will be in support to "C" Coy at "C" Coy H.Q. and will be under command of O.C. "C" Coy, and available for finding patrols.

6. "D" Coy will be the Support Coy. O.C. "D" Coy will take over from O.C. "A" Coy. "D" Coy will carry R.E. Stores, rations & water.

7. Arrangements are being made for one Coy of the 9th Battn. to work on the strengthening of the line of defence which will be N.1.c. 55.35. - 55-50 - 2.8 - N.1.a. 0.2. - 00-35 - 27.48 - 23.70.

8. Dispositions
   O.C. "A" Coy may replace the sentry post in NOVEL north of NETLEY with a L.G. Post.
   NETLEY - NOVEL junction with a bombing post and rifle grenade section. Bombers south of NETLEY with a sentry post.
   Rifle bombers North of NERO with a sentry post.
   NERO - NOVEL junction garrison with a bombing post and rifle bombers section with a sentry post to watch the railway.
   O.C. A Coy will have 4 L.Gs. three of which can replace

the three of B.Coy.

O.C. C Coy may hold junction N.1.a.23.70. with a bombing post, and rifle bombers section.

East side of quadrilateral with two L.Gs. and South side with one L.G.

Junction N.1.a.27.48. with a bombing post and rifle bombers section.

NOVEL with a L.G. and sentry post

9. Patrols will be employed to find exact location of enemy posts and best means of approach for possible future raiding purposes.

  The Left Coy will patrol, between the left flank and the Division on the left.

10. Arrangements are being made for a medium T.M. to be put in a position on the right of the Battn frontage.

11. O.C. Coys. will arrange that 'A' & 'C' Coys have 4 L.Gs. each, 'B' & 'D' Coys 3 each.

12. O.C. 'A' & 'C' Coys will start relieving 'B' & 'D' Coys as soon as they consider it dark enough tonight. When relieved O.C. 'B' Coy will tell off carrying parties to carry rations

(Sd) R WHITTON.

Lieut & A/Adjt.
8th Sherwood Foresters.

APPENDIX III.

Operation Orders by Lieut Colonel J.E. Blackwall D.S.O.
Commanding 8th Bn. Sherwood Foresters
May 11th 1917

Relief The Battn. will be relieved by the 7th S.F. on the night of 12th/13th May 1917.

Order & Times of Relief. Relief will be in the following order:—
"D" "A" "C" "B" and H.Q. Details. Relieving Coys are due at times as follows:—
"A" Coy relief at 10.30
"C" Coy relief at 10.50
"B" Coy relief at 11.10.
"D" Coys relief will march straight to Coy H.Q. from MARTYRS ALLEY. All movement will be by platoons. Relief complete to be reported to present Bttn. H.Q.
O.C. "D" Coy after relief will be under the orders of O.C. 7th S.F. both for tactical purposes and work and will report relief complete to him.

Guides One guide per platoon will be at Bttn. H.Q. at 10.15 No guides will be required from "D" Coy. Each relieving platoon will supply a guide to take relieved platoon to new quarters in Support.
2 guides are being provided to take H.Q. details to new Bn. H.Q.

Rations Rations and water will be fetched from new Bttn. Dump immediately Coys arrive at new quarters.
A guide will be provided who will meet Coys at present Battn. H.Q. on way out.
No movement to be by daylight.
305669 Sgt. Egglestone and 2 Pioneers will be at new Battn H.Q by 10 pm. to unload, & take charge of rations &c.

Stores. One Officer per Coy. of 7th S.F. will reconnoitre trenches tonight and will take over & sign for all Trench Stores before dark on 12th inst.
Stores lists to be left at present Bn HQ on way out. All Regimental Stores to be brought out.
All empty petrol tins will be sent to present Bn. H.Q. by 10 pm.
Lewis Guns and ammunition will be carried out by Coys.

Returns.	Ration States will be sent in to O. Room by 2 pm on 13th inst.

Alarm Posts	In case of attack Coys will assemble in trenches as follows :-
	    "A" Coy at M.5.d.2.8.
	    "B" Coy at M.5.d.5.1.
	    "C" Coy at M.5.c.55.45.
	where grenades will be issued to Bombers. These Coys will be in Brigade Reserve.

Working Party.	O.C. "B" Coy will detail one N.C.O. and 10 men to report to guide at Left Battn. H.Q at 3 pm on 13th May to work under Heavy Trench Mortar Battery.

(Sd.) R. WHITTON
Lieut + A/Adjt.
8th Sherwood Foresters.

APPENDIX IV

Operation Orders by Lieut Colonel J.E. Blackwall D.S.O.
Commanding 8th Battn Sherwood Foresters.
May 17th/1917.

Relief. The Battn will be relieved on the night of the 18th/19th May 1917 by the 6th North Staffords, and will take over billets at BRAQUEMONT.

Order and Times of Relief. Relief will be in following order:—
"D" Coy will be relieved by "A" Coy 6th N Staffs
"B" - - - - - - "D" - - - -
"C" - - - - - - "C" - - - -
"A" - - - - - - "B" - - - -

Platoons on relief will march out. All movement this side of BULLY GRENAY will be by platoons, where Coys will make their own arrangements for finding their way to BRAQUEMONT.

Guides. O.C. Coys will detail 1 guide per platoon and L.G. Officer 1 for H.Q. Details to be at CROSS ROADS G.34.d.3.4. at 9.45 p.m. where the 5th Lines guides will be on arrival.
The L.G. Officer will detail two Scouts to parade at Orderly Room at 10 a.m. to proceed to SAINS-EN-GOHELLE. and report to Capt J.W. Turner to make arrangements for billets for H.Q. Details. All C.Q.M.S's will make all Coy arrangements.

Stores. All Regimental Stores will be brought out and handed into Orderly Room by 12 noon the 19th May 1917. All trench Stores, aeroplane photographs, and maps giving any special information will be handed over. Lewis Guns and ammunition will be brought to Battn H.Q. on relief where limbers will take them to new billets. Lists of trench Stores handed over duly signed, to be handed in to O. Room by 12 noon 19th.

Returns. Lists of trench Stores to be handed over will be sent to O.R. by 2 p.m. tomorrow.
Return that all men are in billets, and Falling out certificate to be handed in immediately after arrival. Billet certificates to be sent in by 6 p.m. 19th.

(Sd) R. WHITTON.
Lieut & A/Adjt.
8th Bn. Sherwood Foresters.

APPENDIX V.

Operation Orders by Lt. Col. J.E. Blackwall, commanding 8th Sherwood Foresters
D.S.O.   25th May 1917.

Relief The Battalion will relieve the 5th Lincolns in the left sector of the right Brigade front on the night of 25th/26th, relief to be completed by 4.0 am. "Relief complete" to be reported to Orderly Room.

Distribution. One Officer per Coy and one NCO per platoon will reconnoitre trenches today and will report at 5th Lincs H.Q. at 8.0 pm. Arrangements to be made by Coy.
Batln and Coy Gas NCOs will report at the same place at 7.30 and will report at O Room at 4.30 pm. where instructions will be given them.
B Coy will be on the left, A Coy on the right (each with one platoon of D Coy), remaining 2 platoons of D Coy in Support, C Coy in Reserve.
A Coy will relieve A Coy 5th Lincs, B Coy will relieve D Coy 5th Lincs
D   "   "   D   "   "   C   "   "   C   "   "

Order and Times of Relief The Battalion will move off by Coys at times as under:-
B Coy and one platoon of D Coy - 6.45 pm. A Coy and one platoon of D Coy - 6.55 pm, 2 platoons of D 7.5 pm. C Coy 7.10 pm. H.Q. Details - 7.20 pm.
All movement EAST of BULLY GRENAY will be by platoons at 200 yards interval. A Guide will be at main cross roads BULLY GRENAY to show Coys the route to be taken.

Guides Guides for this Battalion (one per platoon and one for H.Q.) will be at M.21.c.60.10 at 9.30 pm.

Rations &c. Rations for tomorrow will be carried on the man. Rations will be sent up to the trenches cooked.
Lewis Guns & ammunition, Signal equipment & Medical Stores will be handed in to QM Stores at 2.0 pm. and will be taken up to the new Batln Dump.
Water bottles must be filled before leaving billets. No water will be sent up as there is a water supply for each Coy.

Regimental Stores Coys will each draw from QM Stores:- 10 Vigilants 1 Box Periscope. 3 1" Verey Pistols, 1½" Verey Pistol Spare Signal equipment, Pioneers tools not required and all other stores held by Coys will be at QM Stores at 2.0 pm. Bicycles to be returned to QM Stores at FOSSE 10.
Mess boxes to be at Batln HQ at 6.0 pm. These will be sent up to new Batln Dump.

Trench Stores. Lists of Trench Stores taken over will be handed in to Orderly Room by 12 noon tomorrow.

Runners 2 runners per Coy will report at Batln H.Q. on arrival.

Returns Os C Cos & Sections will send in to Orderly Room as soon as possible after relief Trench Garrison & Ration States.

Dress Overcoats and waterproof sheets will be taken to the trenches and will be carried in the manner previously laid down.

R Whitton
Lieut & a/Adjt
8th Sherwood Foresters.

APPENDIX VI.

Operation Orders by Lieut Col. J.C. Blackwall D.S.O. commanding
8th Bn. Sherwood Foresters.
May 30/1917

Relief The Battn. will be relieved on the night May 31st/1st June by the 7 Bn. Sherwood Foresters, and will return to billets in LIEVIN as BRIGADE SUPPORT (H.Qrs. M.22.d.75.20.) Relief to be completed by 2. a.m. Relief Complete to be reported to Orderly Room.

Order and Times of Relief The Right Coy will be at "A" Coys H.Q. at 10.30 pm. where O.C. "A" Coy. will have one guide per platoon.
The centre Coy will be at House where track leaves ROAD. (M.17.d.04.62.) at 10.30 pm. where one guide per platoon from B. Coy will meet platoons
The Left Coy will be at HOUSE where ROAD crosses COWDEN TRENCH. (M.17.b.60.30.) at 11 pm. One guide per platoon from "D" Coy. will be there to meet platoons.
The Support Coy. will relieve "C" Coy in support who will then garrison posts in Brigade Reserve line vacated by 7th Battn. The remainder of the Coy will proceed to billets.
On relief Coys. will proceed to the following billets.
   "A" Coy to dugouts at M.23.c.1.3.
   "B" Coy to cellars at LIEVIN POST OFFICE (M.28.b.35.65)
   "D" Coy to do at M.28 central.
   "C" Coy to dugouts under TOWER near CHURCH.
   H.Q. details will take over billets of 7th Battn H.Q.
The Scouts will be relieved at 7 pm. and will report at SUPPORT BATTN H.Q. They will be shewn Coy billets and will arrange to meet Coys at CROSS ROADS near SUPPORT BATTN H.Q. to guide Coys to billets.

Parties On arrival at billets Coys will send Ration parties to Support Bn. H.Q.

Reconnoitring Party O.C. C. Coys of the 7th Battn. will visit Coy commanders in line about 3 am on 31st May.

Support In case of hostile attack "D" Coy will be at disposal of O.C. 5th Bn. Sherwood Foresters.

Stores All Regtl. Stores will be brought out of trenches. All Trench Stores, aeroplane Photographs and maps giving any special information will be handed over. Lists of Trench Stores to be handed over, to be sent to O.R. by 12 noon tomorrow. Lists of Stores handed over duly signed and receipted to be handed in to O. Room. by 12 noon 1st June.

(Sd) C.H. Powell 2nd Lieut A/Adjt
8th Sherwood Foresters.

10. Bn. SHERWOOD FORESTERS.

WAR DIARY or INTELLIGENCE SUMMARY.

Army Form C. 2118.

Place	Date	Hour	Summary of Events and Information	Remarks and references to Appendices
LIÉVIN.	Night 30/May/June		The Batln was relieved by the 7th Batln Sherwood Foresters in the LIÉVIN left subsector and returned to Bde Support in LIÉVIN, where it remained until June 6th. During this period digging & carrying parties were found nightly for work & Bde & Dn & remedies & protective wiring.	
	June 6.		The Batln relieved the 7th Batln Sherwood Foresters in the LIÉVIN left subsector. Relief was completed without casualties.	Appendix 1. O.O.
	7		On night 7/8 June advanced posts were established in front of outpost line at M15d 80.10 - M15d 65.60. when they remained until night 8/9 June to prevent left flank of raid by 138 Bde a reinforce on	
	9		HILL 65. 2 Lieut A.M. Nichie and 36 other ranks raided an enemy post in front of ALARM Trackow N.13c.30.05. The objective was reached without casualties & the party found post vacated.	App. 2. O.O.
MARQUEFFLES FARM.	10.		On night 10/11 June the Batln was relieved by the 1st Leicestershire Regt and returned to billets as 16th Divisional Reserve at MARQUEFFLES FARM. Relief completed without casualties.	App. 3. O.O.
	11		During 11th June there was left at the FARM on this date, at which the Batln obtained first aid for transport turnout.	
LOOS.	15		The Batln relieved the 5th South Staffordshire Regt in LOOS support in LEFT subsector of the LOOS sector. Working parties were found nightly for the 7 Batln S.F. in the Outpost Line the 6th Division on the left & extended to their right so as to include the Crucifix in LOOS. Relief completed without casualties.	App. 4. O.O.

8th Bn. SHERWOOD FORESTERS.

WAR DIARY for month of JUNE 1917.
or
INTELLIGENCE SUMMARY.

Army Form C. 2118.

Instructions regarding War Diaries and Intelligence Summaries are contained in F. S. Regs., Part II. and the Staff Manual respectively. Title pages will be prepared in manuscript.

Place	Date	Hour	Summary of Events and Information	Remarks and references to Appendices
CALONNE	June 20		Left Lievin on night 18th June. The Batln vacated the above Support Billets & moved to CALONNE without casualties.	
LIÉVIN	21		On the night 21/22 June the Batln relieved the 5th Batln Leicestershire Regt. in the LIÉVIN Right Subsector, and occupied outpost line through CITÉ DE RIAUMONT, and therefore established the previous day, at FOSSE 3 and SLAG HEAP. about 11.30 and 20.50. by the 128th Inf Bde. The Batln was came under orders of 138th Inf Bde.	Appendix 5.000
	22		All four Coys were in the line and a Coy of the 5th Leicesters was in support. On the night 22/23 June the 137 Inf Bde relieved the 138 Inf Bde in the Bde Sector but the Batln was not relieved and came under orders of the 137 Inf Bde. The enemy was very active with shell, trench howitzer and about 50 casualties resulted from this town.	Appendix 6.000
CALONNE	23		The Batln was relieved by the 5th & 6th Batlns of South Staffordshire Regt. and returned to billets at CALONNE. Several casualties occurred during relief on the issue of enemy shelling & gas mortar. The 5th S.Staffs Regt relieved 3 Coys on right, the 6th S.Staff the left Coy in CITÉ DE RIAUMONT. There were the Batln frontages for the attack on HILL 65 by the 137 Inf Bde. On arrival at CALONNE the Batln came under orders of 139 Inf Bde. two carrying parties were found for 139 Bde to CITÉ DE RIAUMONT. HILL 65 was attacked and occupied by the 137 Bde on 24th inst.	Appendix 7
LIÉVIN	25		On night of 25/26 June the Batln came under orders of 137 Inf Bde moved to Brigade Reserve at	

Army Form C. 2118.

9th Bn. SHERWOOD FORESTERS.

WAR DIARY for month of June 1917.

or

INTELLIGENCE SUMMARY.

(Erase heading not required.)

Instructions regarding War Diaries and Intelligence Summaries are contained in F.S. Regs., Part II. and the Staff Manual respectively. Title pages will be prepared in manuscript.

Place	Date	Hour	Summary of Events and Information	Remarks and references to Appendices
MARRC.	June 7		LIÉVIN. HQS RED MILL CHATEAU M27d 75·75 Working parties found at night for carrying & dumping under 137 Inf. Bde.	
	29		On night 27/28 June the Batln moved into Divisional Reserve at MAROC. The Batln came under orders of 137 Inf.Bde. The 137 & 138 Inf.Bdes. attacked & consolidated the line N.19.c. 5·55 – N.13.b.6·12 Boundary between Brigades LENS – LIÉVIN RD. The 7th Batln carried out operations N of Rd. At the same time 6th Battn Sherwood Foresters carried a dummy attack opposite about N.7a.95·47 and a dummy raid bombardment was carried out successfully from Rwly in N.1a – N.1d – N.1c.02.	
CITÉ ST PIERRE.	June 30		On night 30th June/1st July, the Batln moved from MAROC to CITÉ ST PIERRE area. A&B Coys were placed under orders of 6th Battn Sherwood Foresters. (A Coy in LEFT Coy centre in outpost line and D in support). C Coy was placed under orders of 5th Battn Sherwood Foresters were in support in COWDEN TRENCH at M.9.c.50.10. B Coy was attached to the 2nd Battn Sherwood Foresters in support in CROOK. REDOUBT. Battn HQS moved to 6th Battn HQS in CITÉ ST PIERRE. M.11.d.55·45. These dispositions were for the Divisional attack on W. of LENS. ("ALOOF TRENCH and CITÉ DU MOULIN.) Two Battns of 6th Division were attached viz the 2nd Battn Sherwood Foresters and 9th Norfolk Battn. MAP REF. LENS. 36c. S.W. 1/10,000. Casualties during the month. Officers 1 wounded. Other Ranks. 15 Killed. 8 died of wounds. 49 wounded.	

M. Laws Major
Commanding 9th Sherwood Foresters

Appendix 1

"Operation Orders" by Lieut Colonel J.E.Blackwall D.S.O.
Commanding 8th Bn. Sherwood Foresters

June 6th/1917

Relief. The Battn. will relieve the 7 Bn. Sherw. For. tonight on the L 2 sub-sector. Bn. H.Q. M.22.b.15.10.
Relief complete to be reported to O.Room.

Distribution. Coys will be distributed as follows :—
"C" Coy Right Sector   "B" Coy Centre Sector.
"D" Coy Left Sector   "A" Coy Support.

Order & Times of Relief. Coys will move independently as follows :—
"C" Coy by platoons up the LENS – LIÉVIN ROAD, leading platoon to be at right Coy H.Q. at 10-30 pm.
"D" Coy by platoons up the LIÉVIN – CITÉ ST PIERRE ROAD the leading platoon to be at Left Coy H.Q. at 11 pm.
"B" Coy by platoons up the LIÉVIN – ST PIERRE ROAD and TRACK, leading platoon to be at centre Coy H.Q. at 11.pm.
"A" Coy by platoons into Support Coy billets at 10-30 pm. (billets in cellars – M.22.b.96.90. to M.17.c.20.07)
One guide per platoon will be at each front Coy H.Q.

Posts – Reserve Line. The posts on Bde Reserve line N. of LENS – LIÉVIN ROAD to be relieved by the 17th Bn. by 8 pm.
Posts S. of above named road will be withdrawn.

Conference The C.O. will see Coy Commanders at H.Q. Mess at 2-30 pm.

Stores A list of Trench Stores taken over will be handed in to O.Room by 12 noon tomorrow.
All Stores will be left as billet stores, to be taken over by 138th Bde. A list should be taken of such stores left, which should be sent in to O.R. by 3 pm.

Returns. O.C. Coys will send in to O.R. as soon as possible after relief the usual Trench Garrison & Ration States.
Ration states will be rendered daily to H.Q. by 8 pm. for the assistance of the Q.O.M.

Chasthowit
2nd Lieut & A/R A1.

Appendix 2

Operation Orders by Lieut Colonel J.K. Blackwell D.S.O.
commanding 8th Bn. Sherwood Foresters.

June 9th/1917

Raid. O.C. "A" Coy will send a party to raid a German Post in front of ALARM TRENCH at 1 am tomorrow morning.

Stokes Guns will not co-operate and Ammonal Tubes will not be used. Artillery support is being arranged between 12-45 pm & 1-45 pm 10th inst.

The two Stokes Mortars at M.18.d.3.4. and M.18.d.3.9. will fire their ammunition early in the evening and be withdrawn. The covering parties for these, must be out as soon as possible after dusk.

The Stokes Mortar Ammunition in CROCODILE will be carried back to T.M. A.Drs. O.C. "A" Coy will detail a party for this.

Wiring Party. A wiring party of 150 men will be found by the 7th Battn. tonight. 5 parties of 10 men will work between FOSSE 9 and RIGHT POST of LEFT COY. The covering parties for these will be found by "B" & "D" Coys. They must be in position as soon as it is sufficiently dark to prevent hostile observation. 100 Men will continue belt of wire northwards from the front of the CENTRE COY in front of the Defence Line.

Countersign The countersign from Stand To tonight will be OXO.

Relief The Battn. will be relieved tomorrow night & go into billets at MARQUEFFLES FARM.

Chas Howell
2nd Lieut & A/Adjt.
8TH SHERWOOD FORESTERS

Appendix. 3

Operations Orders by Lieut Colonel J.C. Blackwall D.S.O.
commanding 8th Bn. Sherwood Foresters.
June 10th/1917

Relief. The Battn. will be relieved tonight by the 4th Leicestershire Regt and will return to billets at MARQUEFFLES FARM. Relief Complete to be reported to Orderly Room, LIÉVIN.

Route. Movement as far as AIX-NOULETTE will be by platoons along Track D. This track is being reconnoitred by Scouts, and 1 per Coy will be detailed to show platoons the route as they pass Battn H.Q. From AIX-NOULETTE movement will be by Coys.

Guides. O.C. "C" Coy will have 1 guide per platoon at Right Coy H.Q. at 11 pm.
H.Q. details will send 1 guide, "B" & "D" Coys. will send 1 guide per platoon, and "A" Coy 1 guide for Coy to Battn. H.Q. at 11.0 pm.

Lewis Guns. Lewis Guns & ammunition will be brought to Battn H.Q. on the way out, from where they will be taken by Transport.

Stores. Artillery Boards, Petrol Tins, Wire Cutters & Gloves, and other Stores will be sent down to Battn H.Q. by 10 pm. All Trench Stores, aeroplane Photos, & maps giving any special information will be handed over.
Lists of Trench Stores to be handed over to be sent to O. Room by 4 pm.
Lists of Stores handed over and duly signed & receipted to be handed in to O. Room by 12 noon June 11th.

C. Ham Powell Lieut & Adjt
8th Battn Sherwood Foresters.

Appendix 4

Operation Orders by Lieut Colonel J E Blackwall. DSO, commanding.
8th Sherwood Foresters.
14th June 1917.

Relief. The Battalion will relieve the 5th South Staffords in the left support of the Left Brigade front tomorrow night 15th inst. Relief to be completed by 9.30 pm. Relief complete to be reported to Orderly Room. B and D Co will send their relief complete report to Brigade Hqrs at BULLY GRENAY for transmission to Batn Hqrs.

Distribution. A Coy will relieve the Coy in QUEEN STREET and C Coy the Coy in OLD GERMAN FRONT LINE. B and D Co will relieve the 2 Co in BULLY GRENAY. O.C. B and D Co will arrange to find out where the billets are now in GRENAY are, and will make all arrangements as to time of relief. Relief will be by daylight. No guides will be provided for these Co.

Order & Times of Relief. A Coy will move off at 5.45 pm. C Coy at 5.30 pm. HQ Details at 5.45 pm. All movement East of BULLY GRENAY will be by platoons at 200 yds interval.

Guides. One Guide per platoon for A & C Co and one for HQ Details will be at cross roads at NORTH EAST end of MAROC (M.7.b.2.6) at 7.30 pm. Movement from MAROC will be by PICCADILLY TRENCH.

Rations TC. Rations for the 16th inst will be carried on the man. Rations will be sent up to the trenches cooked. B & D Coys will take their cookers to BULLY GRENAY. Lewis Guns (with spare part bag attached to each box) and ammunition, Signal equipment and Medical Stores will be handed to QM Stores by 12 noon and will be taken up to a point in BULLY GRENAY and MAROC. Sergt KING and one Lewis Gunner from B and D Co will meet Cpl Enber at cross roads BULLY GRENAY at 6.30 pm. Sergt King will unload B and D Co Lewis Guns and will then meet another Limber at the N/E end of MAROC at 7.0 pm and unload A and C Co Guns and take charge of same until arrival of Co. Sergt King will arrange time for party to start. Waterbottles must be filled before leaving billets. Only a few tins of water will be sent up as there is a water supply for each Coy. O.Cs B and D Co will each draw from L/Cpl Pritlett and give a receipt and take to BULLY GRENAY one bicycle. L/Cpl Pritlett will also arrange to take one bicycle for HQ use.

Regimental Stores. Co will each draw from QM Stores – 10 Vigilants, 1 Box Phosphor, 3 Very Pistols and 8 th Illuminating Pistol. Spare Signal equipment, Pioneers tools not required, and all other stores held by Co will be at QM Lines by 10.0 am. Bicycles with the exception of the 3 to be taken to the trenches will be returned to Stores at FOSSE 10. Mess boxes to be at Q Room by 6.0 pm. Each Coy will send one servant to look after their boxes. These will be taken to the same place as the Lewis Guns.

Trench Stores. Lists of Trench Stores taken over will be handed in to O Room by 9.0 am the morning after relief.

Runners. Two runners per Coy will report at Battn HQ on arrival.

Returns. O.C. Co and Sections will send in to O Room as soon as possible after relief Trench Inventory Stats and Ration State.

Dress. Overcoats and waterproof sheets will be taken to the trenches and will be carried in the manner previously laid down. Packs will be stored at QM Stores by Cos at 10.0 am. Officers valises to be at QM Stores by 5.0 pm.

Billets. Billets must be left scrupulously clean and tidy.

R Whitton
Lieut and Adjutant
8th Sherwood Foresters.

Appendix 5

Operation Orders by Lieut. Colonel J.E.Blackwall, D.S.O., Comdg.,
8th Bn. The Sherwood Foresters, 18th June, 1917.

Move. The Battalion will move out of the present quarters tonight and proceed to billets at CALONNE. Movement will be Cavalry Track, through MAROC to GRENAY BRIDGE, where one guide per platoon and one for H.Qrs. will conduct platoons to new quarters at CALONNE.

Order and Times. Cos. will move out in the following order:- "C", "A", "B", "D", and H.Qrs. First Compy. will start to move out at 10-30 p.m. All movement by platoons at 2 minute intervals. Move to be completed by 2-0 a.m.

Lewis Guns. Lewis Guns and ammunition to be at Battalion H.Q. by 9-0 p.m. All petrol tins and Mess Boxes by 9-30 p.m.
Lewis Gun teams will fetch their guns and ammunition from Dump at CALONNE immediately on arrival.

Trench Stores. A list of Trench Stores in the Compy. Sectors will be handed in to Orderly Room by 9-0 p.m.

Cleanliness. As the Battn. is not being relieved by another Battalion O's. C. Cos. are responsible that all dugouts and trenches occupied by men of their Cos. are left clean and in order for the benefit of those coming in later.

Regimental Stores. All regimental stores will be taken out by Companies.

Return. Companies will report men in billets as soon as possible after arrival.

Lieut. & Adjutant.,
8th Sherwood Foresters.

Appendix 6

Operation Orders by Lieut. Colonel J.E. Blackwall, D.S.O., Comdg.,
8th Bn. The Sherwood Foresters, June, 21st., 1917.

Relief.	The Battn. will relieve the 5th Battn. Leicestershire Regt. in the right subsector of the Right Brigade tonight. Relief complete will be reported to Orderly Room. Battn. H.Q., will be at M.29.d.1.5.
Distribution.	"A" Compy. will relieve "A" Coy. 5th Leicesters. "B" Compy. do. "D" Compy. Do. "C" Compy. Do. "C" Compy. Do. "D" Compy. Do. "B" Compy. Do. in the Sectors reconnoitred by O's. C. Cos. this afternoon.
Order and times of relief.	Companies will move off in the following order:- "C", "B", "A" and H.Q. Details. "D" Compy. will move independently and will arrange their own time of departure. "C" Coy. will commence to move at 10-0 p.m. to arrive at QUARRY DUMP at 11-0 p.m. All movement to be by platoons at 2½ minutes interval. One guide per platoon for "A", "B" & "C" Cos. and one for H.Q. Details will be at the CHATEAU M.23.d.55.65 at 11-0 p.m.
Rations. &c.	Rations will be sent to QUARRY DUMP. One Compy. 5th Leicester Regt. will be available to carry rations. All rations will be sent up cooked. No. cooking can be done in trenches, other than on "Tommy's Cookers." Lewis Gun Ammunition will be collected from present Battn. H.Q. by transport and taken to QUARRY DUMP, where it will be collected by Cos. & taken up to trenches on arrival. Lewis Gunners will carry up their guns and spare parts from CALONNE. Signal equipment and medical stores will be sent in to Battn. H.Q. by 8-30 p.m. and will be taken to QUARRY DUMP.
Mess Boxes.	Mess Boxes will be at Battn. H.Q. by 9-0 p.m. Each Compy. will detail one servant to go with Mess Cart.
Trench Stores.	Lists of Trench Stores taken over will be handed in to O.Room by 9-0 a.m. tomorrow.
Returns.	O's. C. Cos. & Sections will render to O.Room as soon as possible Trench Garrison State and Rations State.
Dump.	The N.C.O. i/c Police and the 5 Police will be billeted at QUARRY DUMP and will take charge of all Battn. Stores and take over from 5th Leicesters at present there. The N.C.O i/c Police will take over One Copper, and 4 Thermos Containers from 5th Leicesters. Police to arrange to make tea for Companies.
Billets.	S.B's. and H.Q. Details will be billeted in a house opposite H.Q. in ASSIGN TRENCH, at M.29.d.1.5. Billets must be left scrupulously clean and tidy.

R.W.Litton

Lieut. & Adjt.,
8th Bn. The Sherwood Foresters.

Appendix 7.

Operation Orders by Lieut. Colonel J.E.Blackwall, D.S.O.,
Comdg. 8th Bn. The Sherwood Foresters, 23rd. June, 1917.

    The Battalion will be relieved tonight and on relief will proceed to billets at CALONNE.
    "D" Compy. will be relieved by one Compy. of 6th South Staffords. Four guides to be at CHATEAU at 10-30 p.m. or at a time which has been arranged by O's. C. Cos. concerned. O.C. "D" Compy. will hand over 15 empty petrol tins.
    "A", "B" and "C" Cos. will be relieved by 2 Cos. of 5th South Staffords. "A" Compy. will detail 3 guides and "B" Compy. 2 guides for "B" Compy. 5th South Staffs. "B" Compy. will detail 2 guides and "C" Compy. will detail 2 guides for "C" Compy. of 5th South Staffs.
    One guide will be sent for H.Q. Details from Battn. H.Q.
    All these guides will be at QUARRY DUMP at 10-30 p.m.
    All movement will be by platoons at 2½ minute intervals.
    The Pioneer Sergt. will hand over 40 full petrol tins of water to Companies as they come in.
    Lewis Gun ammunition of "A", "B" & "C" Cos. will be left at QUARRY DUMP on the way out and will be taken by transport from there to CALONNE.
    "D" Compy. Lewis Gun ammunition will be left at M.28.a.90.60 and O.C. "D" Compy. will leave one N.C.O. in charge of this ammunition. This N.C.O. will proceed to CALONNE with the Transport.
    Lewis Guns will be carried to new quarters by Companies.
    All empty petrol tins will be brought out by Cos. and handed in at Quarry Dump. Mess boxes will be sent down to QUARRY DUMP by 10-0 p.m. Signal equipment and medical stores and all stores will be brought out by Cos. on relief and handed in at QUARRY DUMP. Lists of trench stores handed over duly signed will be handed in on arrival in new quarters.
    Relief complete to be reported to present Bn. H.Q.

R.Whitton
Lieut. & Adjt.,
8th Bn. Sherwood Foresters.

WAR DIARY of 1/8th Bn Sherwood Foresters for July 1917

Army Form C. 2118.

INTELLIGENCE SUMMARY

Place	Date	Hour	Summary of Events and Information	Remarks and references to Appendices
CITE ST PIERRE	30/1st July	4.30 July 1	On night of June 30th/July 1st the Bn. moved from MAROC to CITE ST PIERRE. A & D Coys were attached to the 6th Bn Sherwood Foresters and C Coy to the 5th Bn Sherwood Foresters and helped to hold the line while that Bde attacked. The 46th Div. made an attack on the front opposite LENS on this date. B Coy was in billets close to Bn. H.Q. CITE ST PIERRE. In the afternoon this Company was attached to 2nd Bn Sherwood Foresters & moved into close support in the ST PIERRE Sub-sector in to C & D Coys. The other 2 Coys remaining attached Pots were taken over in close support to the 2nd & 5th Bns. Sherwood Foresters.	APPENDIX I
	2 3/4		B Coy rejoined the Bn & went into cellars near BHQ in support. The Bn. was relieved by the 27th Canadian Bn. & hung abouts on Sartcomo right by 23rd Canadian Bn. During period in this subsector altough many raids were attempted only 2 Officers & 2 men were wounded. Relief was completed without casualties. the Bn marched to GRENAY SQUARE where they entrained & went to KEU for CHELERS in CORPS reserve.	
	4/23		The Bn remained at CHELERS during this period. The time was spent in training and at musketry, special attention being paid to musketry 2 days Rifle meeting who he let at ROCOURT RANGE and the Bn that may would carried off 2 silver bugles and several cups as well.	

9.29

Page 2.

WAR DIARY of 1/8th Bn. Sherwood Foresters
INTELLIGENCE SUMMARY for July 1917
Army Form C. 2118.
(Erase heading not required.)

Place	Date	Hour	Summary of Events and Information	Remarks and references to Appendices
CHELERS	July 4/23		1. Inter-Company Rafooluting & rapid firing (teams) B. Coy. 2. Lewis Gun Competition B. Coy. 3. Knock-out Competition - Officers Lieut-Col J.E. Blackwall D.S.O., Capt A. Bedford, 2/Lieut G. H. de C. Martelli and Cpl Tomlinson	
	17		2nd Brigade was formed in G.O.C's A.B.	
	23		The Brigade was inspected by Major Gen W. Thwaites G.O.C. 46th Div.	
			The Bn. marched to VERQUIN and were billeted there	
	24/25		The Bn. took over the left Bn. area of the line of the ST ELIE sub-sector from 1st Leicestershire Regt, 71st Bde. 6th Div. Relief was completed without casualties. 2 Coys 7th Sherwood Foresters were attached in support	APPENDIX I
	24/30		During this period the Bn. occupied the line no events of any moment occurred. At times there was considerable enemy trench mortar activity but very little shelling	
	30/31		The Bn. was relieved by the 7th Bn. Sherwood Foresters and went into Brigade Support at PHILOSOPHE. 2 Corps were attached to 75th Sherwood Foresters in support	APPENDIX II
PHILOSOPHE			Strength on first day of month - 645. Strength on last day of month - 654. Casualties for month - Officers - Wounded 2. Other Ranks - Killed 4. Wounded 14. Wounded at Duty - 2. T.E. Blackwall Lieut-Col Commanding 1/8th Sherwood Foresters	

APPENDIX I

OPERATION ORDERS by MAJOR J.K. LANE Commanding 8th.Battn. Sherwood Foresters
July 3rd.1917

The Battn. will be relieved by the 27th. Canadian Battn. tonight.
All arrangements will be made by Os.C.Coys. concerned.
On relief Coys. will proceed to BULLY GRENAY where busses will be ready to take them to CHELERS.

Lewis guns and ammunition will be taken out by Coys. and will be dumped at M1 7.a.25.85. where a party will load them on limbers. Mess Boxes will be at Battn. H.Q. by 10.30pm. Medical and Signalling Stores, and all other stores to be carried on transport will be taken out and left at same place. Relief Complete to be reported to Bn.H.Q. Tea will be provided for men at BULLY GRENAY.

1/10000 Maps will be handed over.
Lists of Trench Stores duly signed will be handed in on arrival at new quarters.

R Whitton

(Sd.)R.WHITTON
Lieut. & Adjutant
8th Bn. Sherwood Foresters.

APPENDIX II

OPERATION ORDERS BY LIEUT COLONEL J.E.BLACKWALL, D.S.O., COMMANDING
8th Sherwood Foresters.
23rd July 1917.

RELIEF The Battalion will relieve the 1st Leicesters in the SUB LEFT SUBSECTOR on the night 24/25th.

DISTRIBUTION The distribution of Companies will be as follows :-
Front line 'B' Coy - Right 'C' Coy - Centre 'D' Coy Left
Support 'A' Coy.

ORDER and TIMES OF RELIEF Companies will parade at times as under :-
'D' Coy 7.0 pm   'C' Coy 7.20 pm   'B' Coy 7.40 pm.
'A' Coy 8.0 pm   H.Q. Details 8.20 pm.
The route will be via VERQUIGNEULS - LABOURSE - and SAILLY LABOURSE - NOYELLES. Companies will call at Transport lines at LABOURSE to leave packs. Clean underclothing will be put on in the morning and dirty clothing will be placed on top of the pack and taken out and left at Transport lines. Dress - fighting order with greatcoats.
All movement on the main BETHUNE - NOYELLES ROAD and beyond will be by platoons at 250 yards interval.

GUIDES Guides will be at Brigade H.Q. at G.13.d.30.65 (PHILOSOPHE) at 9.45 pm.

LEWIS GUNS &c. Lewis Guns and Artillery Boards will be taken to MANSION HOUSE DUMP in VERMELLES by Transport and will be collected there by Companies as they pass. Sergt. Sharrock and one L.G. N.C.O. per Company will go with Transport. Sergt. Sharrock will notify these N.C.Os. time of parade.

RATIONS. Details as to rations will be issued tomorrow. All meat will be sent up cooked. No fires are allowed in trenches or tunnels. Tommys Cookers will be taken up. Indents can be sent to Orderly Room for refills. Company Messes must use Primus Stoves or Tommys Cookers.

REGIMENTAL STORES. Regimental Stores will be drawn by Cos. and taken up to the trenches. Details re Signalling and Medical Stores will be issued in the morning

GAS N.C.Os & RUNNERS H.Q. and Company Gas N.C.Os and 6 Battalion Runners will parade at Orderly Room at 11.30 am and report to Bde H.Q. PHILOSOPHE. Their packs and dirty clothes will be left at Transport lines at LABOURSE. One days rations will be taken.

Relief complete will be reported to Battn. H.Q. as soon as possible by telephone. Code word - BLACKPOOL.

DUTIES Officer of the day tomorrow   2nd Lieut. R.K.Russell
Company for duty   'B' Company
Battalion Orderly Sergt.   Sergt. W.Harrison.

PARADES. Breakfast 8.0 am   Sick parade 9.30 am.   Dinners 1.0 pm.

R Whitton

Lieut. and Adjutant,
8th Sherwood Foresters.

APPENDIX III

Operation Orders by Lieut Col J.S. Blackwall
D.S.O. Comdg 8th Sherwood Foresters
29 July 1917

Relief The Battn. will be relieved in the line by the 7th Bn Sherwood Foresters tomorrow night 30 inst.

Order of Relief &c Relief will be in the following order :-
"B" Coy 7th S.F. will relieve B Coy at 10.0 P.M.
"C"   "   C Coy at 10.15 P.M.
"D"   "   D Coy at 10.30 P.M.
"A"   "   A Coy at 10.45 P.M.

On relief A & C Cos will take over dugouts and trenches occupied by C & D Cos 7th Sherwood Foresters. B & D Cos will proceed to PHILOSOPHE and take over billets of A & B 7th Sherwood Foresters. A Coy will only be relieved by Compy H.Q. Details as the platoons will be attached to Cos. in the line.

A & C Cos will come under the orders of the O.C. 7th Sherwood Foresters as soon as relieved.

Relief complete will be reported to O Room present Battn. H.Q. personally

Billeting Party A & C Cos will each send an N.C.O to take over dugouts and O.P.s. by 7.0 P.M

2nd Lieut C.N. Powell and one N.C.O from B & D Cos + one Signaller from H.Q will report to H.Q. 7th Sherwood Foresters in PHILOSOPHE at 5.0 P.M. Their N.C.O.s will report at H.Q at 4 P.M.

Stores Duties &c The 7th Sherwood Foresters will send up about 5-0 P.M their R.S.M., Orderly N.C.O, Scout Corpl & Pm N.C.O.s to take over Stores, duties & etc

Receipted Stores List will be handed in to O Room before relief, if possible.

The Senior cook will be responsible that the Tea Containers are handed over clean.

Cookers The Transport Officer will arrange for B & D Cos cookers to be sent to PHILOSOPHE

L. Gun ammunition Regt Stores &c B & D Cos will carry Lewis Gun ammunition to EXETER CASTLE DUMP, where it will be loaded on trucks, under the supervision of Sergt. Sherrock. O.C. B & D Cos will each detail one L.G. N.C.O to remain in charge of the ammunition until loaded on one of the Battn. limbers.

Lewis Guns will be carried out. Mess Boxes, Signallers Equipment & Medical Stores will be sent to the dump by 10-0 P.M to be loaded on Trucks.

The Transport Officer will send a limber to MANSION HOUSE DUMP by 3 A.M to bring ammunition and other Regimental Stores to PHILOSOPHE

Periscopes, Very Pistols and all other Regimental Stores will be carried out by Cos & retained by them.

Work Report — A work report made up to 5-0 p.m. tomorrow giving progress since the last report was sent in, will be handed in to O Room by 6-0 p.m tomorrow

R W Litton
Lieut & Adjt.
8th Sherwood Foresters

WAR DIARY of 1/8th Bn. Sherwood Foresters

Army Form C. 2118.

INTELLIGENCE SUMMARY.

for August 1917.

Vol 30

Mrs Chapman

Place	Date 1917	Hour	Summary of Events and Information	Remarks and references to Appendices
PHILOSOPHE	Aug 1	11.05	The Bn. was in support to the 7th Bn. Sherwood Foresters in the left sub-sector of the ST. ELIE A.C. B & D Coys were in trenches in PHILOSOPHE and A & C Coys in the trenches in close support to and under the orders of the 7th Sherwood Foresters. During this period B & D Coys practised a raid on ground was similar to the enemy line lay B & D Coys under the command	APPENDIX 1
	4	11.30pm	A raid was made on the enemy line by B & D Coys under the command of Capt. H.R. SIMONET. Operation orders attached. B. Coy reached the enemy trenches and a few men got into the 2nd line but were recalled as D. Coy were unable to advance owing to heavy M.G. fire from the flanks. All damage arrangements were excellent and both Coys got back to our lines with very few casualties. PHILOSOPHE was heavily shelled by enemy for 4 hours with 5.9 shells. The Bn. moved into the open country behind the village and suffered no casualties.	
ST ELIE Left Sub Sector	5/6		The Bn. relieved the 7th Bn. Sherwood Foresters in the left sub-sector of SAINT ELIE. During this period the Bn. held the trenches and nothing of any importance occurred. The enemy was rather active with T.M's but we had very few casualties.	
	6 h 10			
NOYELLES	10/11		The Bn was relieved by the 7th Bn. Sherwood Foresters and went into support of the 7th Bn. Sherwood Foresters at NOYELLES and B & D in close support in trenches under orders of 7th Bn Sherwood Foresters	30

WAR DIARY of 1/8th Bn. Sherwood Foresters for August 1917

INTELLIGENCE SUMMARY

(Erase heading not required.)

Army Form C. 2118.

Place	Date 1917	Hour	Summary of Events and Information	Remarks and references to Appendices
FOUQUIERES	Aug 14		The Bn. was relieved by the 5th Leicesters Regt. and went into Divisional Reserve at FOUQUIERES. B & D Coys remaining in trenches.	
VERQUIN	16	16.00	Bn. moved to VERQUIN where they were joined by B & D Coys. During this period training has been carried out on various subjects in the neighbourhood & consisted of musketry and attack practices. Regimental sports were held in conjunction with 139 Bde M.G. Coy.	APPENDIX II
CAMBRIN	26		The Bn. relieved the 23rd Bn. Royal Fusiliers in the CAMBRIN Left Sub-sector, all four Coys being in the line. A Coy in left of the 5thBn Sherwood Foresters went under the orders of the B.Bn. in support 1 Coy of 5th Bn Sherwood Foresters from support took over the Coy front on our left from K.O.B.L.I., 2 Lieut.	
	29		The 4 Coys were redistributed & took over the whole front line, the Coy of the 5 th Bn. Sherwood Foresters returning to support.	
	30	26/30	This was a very quiet sector & nothing of importance occurred. 2 Lieut D. TANNER and 1 N.C.O. & 2 men went out on patrol to examine the enemy wire, the 2 men returned but unfortunately the officer & N.CO. are missing.	
	30		Casualties for month Officers Missing 1. O.R.s Killed 1, Wounded 22, Missing 2. Accidentally wounded 5. Strength at end of month. V. Oakshott Lieut Col. Commanding 1/8th Sherwood Foresters O. 33 O.R.s 648.	

APPENDIX I

Operation Orders by Lieut. Colonel P.E. BLACKWALL D.S.O.
Commanding 9th Bn Sherwood Foresters.
3rd August 1917

1. On the night of 5th/6th August 1917 'B' & 'D' Coys under the command of Capt. H.K. SIMONET will raid enemy's trenches in the area G.5.d.11.30. — G.5.c.98.54. — G.5.c.62.20 — G.5.c.98.11 — G.5.d.11.30.

2. The attack will be carried out under a shrapnel barrage which will be lifted as follows :—

   From zero to zero plus 5 mins
   G.5.d.40.42. — G.5.c.99.05. — G.5.c.40.23

   From Zero plus 5 mins to Zero plus 6 mins
   G.5.d.40.42
   G.5.d.08.25
   G.5.c.61.48
   G.5.c.40.23.

   From Zero plus 6 mins to Zero plus 11 mins
   G.5.d.40.42 — G.5.d.20.58 — G.5.c.94.48 — G.5.c.61.48 — G.5.c.40.23.

   From Zero plus 11 mins to Zero plus 60 mins.
   G.5.d.40.42. — G.5.d.00.74 — G.5.c.61.48. — G.5.c.40.23.

   4.5" Howitzers will bombard the following points from Zero to Zero plus 60 mins. :—

   Trench Junction   G.5.d.80.48
   — ditto —   G.5.d.87.79.
   O.P. at   G.5.b.97.21.
   Dump at   G.5.b.20.72.
   Trench Junction   G.5.d.05.90.
   Trench   G.5.d.28.81. — 15.87.
   Craters   G.5.c.21.61.
   Trench Mortar   G.5.a.55.61.

   Medium Trench Mortars will bombard hostile Trench Mortars, G.12.a.26.78., G.11.b.98.68., G.12.a.82.30. from Zero to Zero plus 60 mins.
   Heavy Artillery will carry out counter battery work

3. 139th Bde M.G. Coy. with eight guns will barrage from Zero to Zero plus 60 mins :—
   (i) DUMP G.5.a and b. (ii) FOSSE ALLEY in G.5.b. and G.5.a. and
   (iii) CRATERS. G.5.c. 10.40. and G.N.d. 90.45.
   One gun and team will be at disposal of O.C. Raid, and will cover the left flank from a position in "No Man's Land"

4. 139th T.M. Battery will co-operate as follows :-
   (a) From Zero to Zero plus 60 mins. one gun each on :-
       1 Crater G.5.c.05.36.   3 Trench angle G.5.c.2.29.
       3 Trench 50 yards E. and W. of G.5.c.30.34.
       4 Trenches round G.5.c.25.75. 5 Trenches round G.5.d.25.85.
   (b) One gun bombard trench junction G.5.d.0.3. from Zero to
       Zero plus 5 mins. and trench junction G.5.d.33.40. from
       Zero plus 5 mins to Zero plus 60 mins.
   (c) Two guns will make a demonstration against the crossroads from Zero
       to Zero plus 18 mins. Rate of fire. Zero to Zero plus 20 mins.
       Rapid. Zero plus 20 mins to Zero plus 60 mins. Slow.

5. Nine sappers, 1st S. Field Coy. R.E. with 7 × 20 lb., and 20 × 1lb mobile charges
   are at the disposal of O.C. Raid.

6. 99th Inf. Bde. are co-operating by Trench Mortar and M.G. demonstration on
   the area G.5.c.05.48 to 03.80 - G.5.d.60.82.

7. The object of the raid will be to :- 1 Cause enemy casualties. 2 Take
   Prisoners. 3 Secure Identifications. 4 Demolish 3 trench Mortar
   suspected emplacements. 5 Destroy tunnel and dugout entrances.
   6. Lower enemy's moral, and raise our own.

8. Gaps have been cut in the enemy wire by Artillery, and are being kept open
   by M.G. fire. Gaps in the enemy's front line wire will be examined by
   Scouts, and gaps cut in our own wire on the night 3rd/4th August
   Directly after dark, on the night of 4/5th Aug. Scouts will lay two tapes
   from gaps in our wire to those in the enemy's wire.

9. Two S.B.'s, to act as dressers, will accompany the party as far as the
   enemy front line. A Regt. Dresser Post will be established in our front
   line opposite. O.C. Raid will arrange for a parapet party to carry
   wounded or escort prisoners across "No Man's Land". Men told off
   to escort prisoners will report to an Officer detailed by O.C. Raid
   at Regt. Aid Post on O.R.O. tape.

10. Four L. Gs. will be taken with 4 carriers of ammunition each.
    Rifle men will wear one cotton bandolier instead of equipment.
    Steel helmets will be worn. All Ranks will carry 2 Mills bombs,
    one in each side pocket of the jacket. Smoke helmets will be worn
    at the back under the jacket, the satchels slings being tied round
    the waist. All bayonets will be blackened. Sappers and
    Scouts will not carry rifles or equipment. All means of identification
    will be left in billets. A dagger with thong and hook only will
    be carried in right breast pocket.

11. A Power Buzzer, arranged for by Bde. will be established in the enemy's lines
    to communicate with Batn. Forward H.Q.

12. Watches synchronised, will be issued at forward Batn. H.Q. at 9.45 p.m.

13. The party will begin to withdraw at Zero plus 45 mins. The recall
    signal will be three Thermite Bombs fired by 4" Stokes Mortar
    from DROMORE TRENCH. A searchlight will be situated at
    VICTORIA STATION, and will be turned on at Zero plus 30 mins
    to give direction. The party will be checked in O.C.'s
    between BULLOCK BISET and Regtl. Aid Post. Squad leaders
    will stay and report in detail. The remainder will return
    independently to FUSILIER PT.

14. Batn. Forward H.Q. will be at left Coy. H.Q. dugout in HIGHLAND TRENCH.

15. ZERO will be 11.30 pm.

(Sgd) R.C. Whitton Lt./Adjt.
8th Bn. SHERWOOD FORESTERS.

WAR DIARY of 1/8th Bn. The Sherwood Foresters

INTELLIGENCE SUMMARY for Sept. 1917.

Army Form C. 2118.

Place	Date	Hour	Summary of Events and Information	Remarks and references to Appendices
ANNEQUIN	Sept 1		The Bn. was in Brigade support with H.Q. in ANNEQUIN. 2 Coys in support to 7th Sherwood Foresters on the left and 2 coys in support of 5th Sherwood Foresters on the right in trenches in CAMBRIN sector.	Miss Brown ①
CAMBRIN SECTOR	2		The Bn. relieved the 7th Sherwood Foresters in CAMBRIN left sub-sector. Relief was completed without casualties.	
	8		1 Coy of the 7th Sherwood Foresters relieved "C" Coy in the line, the latter going to ANNEQUIN to train for a raid.	
	11		The raid was planned to be carried out by "C" Coy and half of "A" Coy, under the command of Capt H de Mar[telli?] When the raiding party were forming up in No Mans Land, the enemy opened an intense bombardment on the party. Box respirators were put on, but it was almost impossible to advance with them on in the dark. On seeing this Capt Martelli, un-[masked?] the party. He total casualties incurred were Away. [?] Wounded killed 2. O.R. Died of wounds 1. O.R. Wounded 1. O.R. 30. O.R.	APPENDIX 1.
	12		C Coy returned to the Coy of 7th Sherwood Foresters in the line. During the night this Coy was heavily bombarded with heavy T.M's. 9 casualties were caused.	
BEUVRY ?	13		The Bn. was relieved by the 7th Sherwood Foresters and went into Div Res [...]	

WAR DIARY of 1/8th Bn. Sherwood Foresters for Sept 1917

INTELLIGENCE SUMMARY
Army Form C. 2118.

Place	Date	Hour	Summary of Events and Information	Remarks and references to Appendices
FOUQUIERES	Sept 13 to 20		Recce at FOUQUIERES. During this period training was carried out in ceremonial, company fighting & "bivouacking" of Brigade.	
MAZINGARBE HILL 70	20		Bn. moved into MAZINGARBE	
	21		The Bn. relieved 1 Coy of the 9th Norfolk Regt & 2 coys of the 1st Leicestershire Regt in support behind HILL 70	
	22		The Bn. relieved the 9th Suffolk Regt on Hill 70. Left inf. sector. No casualties occurred during relief. 3 Coys were in the line and 1 Coy in close support.	
	26		½ Coy of Centre Coy in the line was withdrawn into close support	
	26/27		This period consisted of shelling, trench mortars. The trenches were very little shelled, but at times the Left Coy experienced some trouble from heavy enemy TM's	
	28		The Bn. was relieved by the 7th Sherwood Foresters & moved into Brigade support in Ginchy. 2 Coys being in support to 5th Sherwood Foresters on right & 6th Sherwood Foresters on left. The Bn. remained in support	
	28 & 30		Strength 1st Sept 32 off. 643 O.R. " " 30th " 33 off. 684 O.R. Total casualties during month Killed, died of wounds 6 O.R. Wounded 1 off. 50 O.R. Missing, believed killed 5 O.R.	

K.P. Shortwell Lieut. Col.
Commanding 1/8th Bn. The Sherwood Foresters.
Rea

APPENDIX II

"Operation" Orders by Lieut Colonel J.E. Blackwall. DSO commanding
8th Sherwood Foresters
25th August 1917.

The Battalion will relieve the 23rd Bn. Royal Fusiliers in the Left Sub-Sector of the Right Brigade front of the 2nd Division, tomorrow 26th inst, relief to be complete by 5-0 p.m. "Relief complete" will be reported to Battalion H.Q. by phone Code word "BOULOGNE"

Coys will take over the line from left to right as under: A, B, C, D.

Coys will move off at 8-minute intervals commencing at 9.0 a.m. in the following order:- A, C, B, D, H.Q. details. All movement EAST of the Divl. Canteen in SAILLY LABOURSE will be by platoons at 2½ minute intervals.

Guides will meet A and B Coys at the Bomb Stores at CAMBRIN CHURCH at 11.0 a.m. and C & D Coys at ANNEQUIN CHURCH at the same time. Guides for H.Q. details will be at ANNEQUIN CHURCH at 11.0 a.m.

One Officer per Coy, each Coy Sergt. Major, Pioneer Sergt. Bomb Sergt, Signalling Sergt, Sniping Corpl. 1 Gas NCO per Coy and H.Q. Gas NCO and 2 H.Q. runners will meet guides at ANNEQUIN CHURCH at 8.45 a.m. This party will parade at O.Room at 7.0 a.m. All Stores are to be checked and signed for as soon as possible before the Battalion arrives and the receipted lists sent in to O.Room at once. All Stores, secret plans, aeroplane photos, Defence Schemes &c. will be taken over and receipted lists sent in to O.Room by 9.0 am following morning.

The following men will be detailed by Cos:- C Coy 1 NCO and 2 men for duty at CAMBRIN Bomb Store, D Coy 2 men for duty at CAMBRIN Gum Boot Store. These parties will parade at O.Room at 8.0 a.m. tomorrow for instructions and will report at the H.Q. 99th Inf. Bde DEUVRY at 12.0 noon tomorrow where guides will be provided for them. Rations for the 27th inst must be taken. Afterwards they will be rationed by 99th Bde

O.C. A & B Coys will each detail 2 men to parade at O.Room at 8.0 a.m. tomorrow to proceed to ANNEQUIN CHURCH where they will be met by a guide. These men are for duty at BRAY KEEP and CHURCH WEST KEEP.

All Lewis Guns and ammunition and Signalling equipment will be sent in to Transport lines by 6.0 p.m. tonight. The H.Q. L.G. N.C.O. and one Signaller will take charge of these. Lewis Guns &c. of A & B Coys will be taken to CAMBRIN CHURCH Bomb Store and those of C & D Coys to BRAY'S KEEP by 11.0 a.m. in each case, where they will be picked up and carried forward by Coys. 4 Lewis Gunners per Coy will march with the limbers also one Signaller. The H.Q. L.G. N.C.O. will be in charge of this party and will notify them what time the limbers will leave.

Rations for tomorrow will be carried on the man. Rations will be cooked in the trenches. One cook per Coy will go up to the trenches. Water is in tanks in the trenches and petrol tins are not required. The Cook Corpl will send up dixies with the L.G. limbers and the 4 cooks will go with these limbers to take charge of same.

Packs will be sent in to Q.M. Stores by 7.0 a.m. tomorrow and stacked by Coys & Sections.

Picks shovels and other regimental Stores will be sent in at the same time.

Officers valises to be at Transport lines by 8.15 a.m.

Mess boxes, Medical Stores &c. to be taken to the trenches to be stacked outside Batn H.Q. by 8.30 a.m.

2 runners per Coy will be sent to H.Q. immediately after relief. Garrison & ration states will be sent to Orderly Room by 9 p.m.

R.W. Litton.
Captain and Adjt.
8th Sherwood Foresters.

Army Form C. 2118.

WAR DIARY
or
INTELLIGENCE SUMMARY.

(Erase heading not required.)

Place	Date	Hour	Summary of Events and Information	Remarks and references to Appendices
HILL 70 24th				

APPENDIX I.

WAR DIARY of 1/8th Bn. Sherwood Foresters Army Form C. 2118.
or
INTELLIGENCE SUMMARY. for November 1917

Place	Date	Hour	Summary of Events and Information	Remarks and references to Appendices
	1917			
HILL 70 Left	Nov 1		The Bn. was in the line in the left sub-sector of the Bde front. No event of importance occurred. There was a considerable amount of enemy shelling and T.M. activity, but no damage was done.	
	1-3		The Bn. was relieved by the 1/7th Bn Sherwood Foresters and went into Bde. reserve in MAZINGARBE. During this period training was carried out, consisting	
MAZINGARBE	3	9.33	of Pltn. & Coy. in attack, musketry & PT & BF	Miss Harris
	3-9		The Bn. relieved the 1/7th Bn. Sherwood Foresters in the left sub-sect. This period	
HILL 70 Left	9		consisted of ordinary trench warfare, the enemy being quiet except for	
	9-15		occasional shelling & T.M. activity	
			The Bn. was relieved by the 15th Lancashire Regt & went into Bde. support	APPENDIX I
PHILOSOPHE	15		at PHILOSOPHE in the ST ELIE sect. BHQ and 2 Coys being in PHILOSOPHE	
			& 2 Coys in the huts O.10, one in support to 7th Sherwood Foresters on the left &	
	18		one to 5th Sherwood Foresters on the right.	
			The army & the Corps changing over	
ST ELIE G/A	22		The Bn. relieved the 1/7th Bn. Sherwood Foresters in the line in the left sub-sect	APPENDIX II
	22-28		of the Bde. sector. Very little other than sniping by enemy of any kind occurred. Bn. patrols	

WAR DIARY of 1/8th Bn. Sherwood Foresters
for November 1917.

Army Form C. 2118.

INTELLIGENCE SUMMARY.
(Erase heading not required.)

Place	Date	Hour	Summary of Events and Information	Remarks and references to Appendices
	1917			
ST. ELIE Left	Nov 22		was very active & on several occasions entered the enemy lines without encountering any of the enemy.	
VERQUIN	28		The Bn. was relieved by the 7th Bn. Sherwood Foresters & went into Div. Reserve at VERQUIN, where training was carried out & the Bn. was refitted with clothing.	
	28/30		Strength 1st Nov Off. 36 OR's 671	
			" 32 " 658	
			Casualties during month. Off. wounded 3 OR's killed 2 wounded 6 died of wounds 1 wounded at duty 2 missing 1	
			Honours. M/Lieuty Cross. 2/Lieut A.C. Fairbrother.	

J.C. Blackwell Lieut Col.
Commdg. 1/8th Sherwood Foresters.

APPENDIX I SECRET   No 12

Operation Orders by Lieut Col: J.E. Blackwall
Commanding 1/8th Bn Sherwood Foresters.
            Nov 14th 1917.

The Battn will be relieved by the 1/5th
Battn Leicestershire Regt. in the line
on the night of the 15th/16th November
1917, and on relief will go into
Support in the ST. ELIE Sector and
take over from 4th S.F.
        Relief complete to be reported
by BAB Code.
        Coys will be relieved as under:-
    "A" Coy by "A" Coy 5th Leicesters
    "B" Coy by "B" Coy   -do-
    "C" Coy by "D" Coy   -do-
    "D" Coy by "C" Coy   -do-
In Support in ST. ELIE sector —
    "A" Coy will be in CURLY CRESCENT
    "C" Coy   do   CHAPEL ALLEY
    B & D Coys + H.Q. will go into
    billets in PHILOSOPHE.
O.C. Coys will detail 2 guides
per Coy to report at Bn HQ at
3 pm. 15th Nov for instructions
to guide relieving platoons
    O.C. "D" Coy will detail one
Officer to be in charge of this
party.
    The R.S.M. will arrange for one guide
for H.Q. details

All defence schemes, air photos, tracings, trench stores and Gun Books, Food Containers, Petrol Tins, and Yukon Packs, will be handed over. Receipted Lists to be in O. Room by 12 noon 15th Nov. All Gun Books to be returned to store by 10 am tomorrow.

O.C. Coys will each detail 1 N.C.O. to take over stores etc in Support.
O.C. "B" Coy will detail one Officer for H.Q. and "B" & "D" Coys, and O.C. "A" & "C" Coys. one each.

This party will parade at O. Room at 12 noon tomorrow. Receipted Lists of Trench Stores to be in O. Room as soon as possible after relief.

"A" & "C" Coys will hand over all Lewis Gun ammunition and tins to the relieving Coys, and will carry guns, and spare part bags, to CURLY CRESCENT and CHAPEL ALLEY.

They will take over ammunition in these places as arranged by L.G.O.

"B" & "D" Coys will dump L.G. and ammunition etc at TOSH ALLEY on relief. Two Lewis Gunners from each of these Coys, will report to Sgt King at TOSH ALLEY at 6pm for loading.

Transport Officer will arrange for one large truck to be at TOSH ALLEY.

Mess boxes, Signalling, Medical, Pioneer and all other stores, to be carried on transport, to be at O.G.1 by 6pm or Tosh Alley by 6.30pm.

Two Servants from "A & C" Coys and one from B & HQ. details will accompany the trucks.

T.O. will make arrangements for trucks and Limbers.

Regtl. Stores, will be carried out by Coys.

Coys will report arrival in new quarters by phone or runner.

R Whitton
Capt Adjt
1/8th Bn Sherwood Foresters.

Copies to:-
172 1. Commanding Officer.
     2. Second in Command.
     3. O.C. A Company.
     4. O.C. B   "
     5. O.C. C   "
     6. O.C. D   "
     7. O.C. 1/5th Bn Leicesters.
     8. O.C. 1/7 Sher: Foresters.
     9. T.O & Q.M.
    10. R.S.M.
    11.⎫ War Diary.
    12.⎭

APPENDIX II   (COPY)

Operation Orders by Major E. McLingall.
Commanding 1/8th Bn. Sherwood Foresters.

Nov. 21st. 1917

The Battn will relieve the 7th Bn. Sherwood Foresters, in the Left Sub Sector of the ST ELIE Sector on the afternoon of 22nd Nov. 1917.

Coys will relieve as follows:-

"A" Coy. 8th S.F. will relieve "D" Coy 7th S.F. RIGHT.
"B"   - do -   "C"   - do - in RESERVE
"C"   - do -   "B"   - do - on LEFT.
"D"   - do -   "A"   - do - in SUPPORT.

Coys will move off in the following order:-

B Coy will move off at 3-45 pm.
D -   -   -   - 3-55 pm.
C -   -   -   - 4- 0 pm.
A -   -   -   - 4-10 pm.
H.Q. Details   -   4-20 pm

All movement will be by Platoons at 5 min intervals. Advance Parties of 1 Officer per Coy. 1 N.C.O. per Platoon Coy Gas NCOs. C.S.Ms, will report at respective Coy H.Qrs re by 2-30pm. to take over Stores &c. Receipted lists of Stores to be sent in to O.Room by 6pm. The Pioneer Sgt, Bomb Sgt, H.Q. Gas N.C.O. and 2 runners will compose the H.Q Party.

If Coys require Guides, they will send runners with their advance parties to act as guides.

Rations will be sent up by train. Cpl Bateman and 1 Cook per Coy will go to the trenches.

The Reserve Coy will carry all meals from the Cookhouse.

A & C Coy will pick up Lewis Guns and ammunition at MANSION HOUSE DUMP. Transport Officer will arrange for 2 limbers to be at PHILOSOPHE by 2-30pm and also for a truck to be at MANSION HOUSE DUMP, to bring up to Battn H.Q. the reserve Lewis Gun Ammunition. One Lewis Gunner each from 'A' & 'C' Coy, will report at O.Room at 2-30pm to accompany limbers.

Sketches, and map references of dispositions, Ration and Garrison States will be sent in to O.Room by 11-0 am the morning after relief. Daily Reports to be sent in as usual.

"Relief Complete" to be reported to O.Room by 'phone.
Code Word - "DAILY MAIL".
Runners will be sent to H.Q as usual.
Blankets rolled in bundles of 10, to be at Stores by 10 am

Officers rations by 2 pm.

Spare Equipment, Pioneers tools, Medical and other Stores to be sent to the trenches by transport, to be at Stores by 3.0. pm. Mess Boxes 3pm.

Care is to be taken that all Billets &c, are left clean and tidy.

(sgd) R.WHITTON. Capt & Adjt.
11th Bn Sherwood Foresters.

Army Form C. 2118.

Instructions regarding War Diaries and Intelligence Summaries are contained in F. S. Regs., Part II. and the Staff Manual respectively. Title pages will be prepared in manuscript.

WAR DIARY of 1/8th Bn. The Sherwood Foresters
INTELLIGENCE SUMMARY. for December 1917.
(Erase heading not required.)

Vol 34

Place	Date	Hour	Summary of Events and Information	Remarks and references to Appendices
	1917			
YERQUIN	Dec 1		The Bn. was in Divisional Reserve at VERQUIN. During this period training was	
	1-4		carried out, consisting of physical training & bayonet fighting, ceremonial drill and route marching.	
ST ELIE (Left)	4		The Bn. relieved the 7th Sherwood Foresters in the Left Sub-sector of the Bde front. Relief	
	4-10		was completed without casualties. This period consisted of ordinary trench warfare. Enemy Trench Mortars were active.	
PHILOSOPHE	10		The Bn. was relieved by the 7th Sherwood Foresters & moved into Bde support. 4 S and	
	10-16		2 Coys being in PHILOSOPHE and 2 Coys in support to the right. Right Bn. of the Bde Front. 1 Coy Lewis Guns changed over with 2 Coys at PHILOSOPHE after 3 days. A successful raid was carried out by 5th Sherwood Foresters on the Right flank which the 2 Coys in Close Support found 120 men to hold the line while the raid was in progress.	
ST ELIE (Left)	16		The Bn. relieved the 7th Sherwood Foresters. Relief being completed without casualties.	
	16-22		The period consisted of ordinary trench warfare & was very quiet with the exception of a little French Mortars.	
VERQUIN	22		The Bn. was relieved by 7th Sherwood Foresters. Moved into Divisional Reserve	
	22-28		at VERQUIN. During this time a little training was carried on west of the	Rev.

T2134. Wt. W708-776. 500000. 4/15. Sir J. C. & S.

WAR DIARY of 1/8th Bn The Sherwood Foresters

Army Form C. 2118.

INTELLIGENCE SUMMARY

for December 1917

(Erase heading not required.)

Instructions regarding War Diaries and Intelligence Summaries are contained in F.S. Regs., Part II. and the Staff Manual respectively. Title pages will be prepared in manuscript.

Place	Date	Hour	Summary of Events and Information	Remarks and references to Appendices
	1917			
VERDUN	Dec 22-28		Whole time was taken up in preparation for an inspection by the Army Commander at a shorts notice on Dec 26th. This inspection was cancelled at the last moment. Xmas dinners were given to all Coys.	
ST ELIE (A4)	28		1/8th Bn relieved the 7th Sherwood Foresters in the left sub sector. No casualties on relief. This period was very quiet with the exception of some hostile Trench Mortar activity.	
	28-31		Strength 1st Dec Off. 33 O.R. 652.	
			31st Dec " 38 " 746.	
			Casualties. Killed O.R. 2. Died of wounds O.R. 2 Wounded O.R. 3.	
			Honours and Awards.	
			Mentioned in Despatches Hon. Lieut & Capt. H. Torrance and No. 6164 C.S.M.	
			(Temp R.S.M.) W. Mountney.	
				Rm.

Awalking
Major
O.C. 1/8th Bn The Sherwood Foresters.

8th Sherwood Foresters

WAR DIARY
INTELLIGENCE SUMMARY for month of Jan. 1918

Army Form C. 2118.

Place	Date	Hour	Summary of Events and Information	Remarks and references to Appendices
Trenches St Elie Left	1918 Jan 1–3		On the night of 2/1/18 the Bn successfully repulsed a hostile raid. A detailed account is contained in copy report by Major A Hacking – appendix 1. Two unwounded prisoners were taken by us, being men of the 6th & 10th Bavarian Infantry & one dead German was brought in. In recognition of his masterly leadership this was subsequently the subject of the situation on this occasion, Captain H.K. Vermont has been awarded the Military Cross. Awards have also been made to L/Sgt Martin, L/Sgt Turner & the wildwrite for their gallantry & good work on the same occasion.	Nil. Copy report by Major A Hacking
	3		Bn. in Brigade support, with Coys at Philosophe & then in close support in Lindley Trench & Chapel Alley. The Bn supplied working parties for front-line Battalions & carried out short periods of training.	
	6			2.
	9			3.
Trenches St Elie Left	10 to 17		Coys changed over at end of three days. Ten enemy sniping movement. Special front repairs had to be carried out owing to weather conditions.	1st N

8th Sherwood Foresters

WAR DIARY

INTELLIGENCE SUMMARY
(Erase heading not required.)

Army Form C. 2118.

for the month of January 1916

Instructions regarding War Diaries and Intelligence Summaries are contained in F. S. Regs., Part II. and the Staff Manual respectively. Title pages will be prepared in manuscript.

Place	Date	Hour	Summary of Events and Information	Remarks and references to Appendices
Verquin	15/16 January 1916		In Divisional Reserve. Bathing & physical training & lectures in War Camps.	
	21		Relieved by the 11th Manchesters & moved to Burbure into Corps Reserve. Operation orders attached - appendix 2.	Appendix 2 Operation Orders
Burbure	21b.		Reorganisation of Platoons. Prepared training immediately under Corps + Divisional schemes	
	28			
	29		Draft of 6 Officers & 131 OR posted to the Bn from the 1/7 Sherwood Foresters on latter unit being disbanded	
	30		A detachment of 460 Officers & OR proceeded by motor lorries to Hazingarbe for digging training in rear localities	Appendix III
	31		A draft of 5 Officers & 85 OR posted to the Bn from the 2/8 Sherwood Foresters on latter unit being disbanded	
			Strength of Bn on 1st Jan — 41 Officers 31 Jan — 30 Officers	
			Awards during month of January [illegible]	
			Casualties: Officers Killed Wounded Missing — 1 Officer wounded	
			OR ditto — 8 wounded (including 1st July)	

Sd. Lt Col Sherwood Foresters

/C O P Y./

Appendix I

To, Headquarters,
    139 Brigade.

Refce. Sheet QUARRIES (2) 1/10,000.

Report on enemy raid 2/1/18.

At 3-30 p.m. a message was received from O.C. 6th Sherwood Foresters that an obvious gap had been cut in enemy wire at G.12.c.45.95 and asking for co-operation in the event of a raid on BRESLAU.

My Right Company Commander took steps to cover the HAIRPIN - BRESLAU front with L.G. fire from HAIRPIN, and secret post behind. Similar arrangements were made by Support Company Commander from STUDIO II. Special precautions were necessary, in view of a fighting patrol known to be going out from LOOK OUT. Trench Mortar co-operation was arranged and all Companies were warned to be particularly alert.

The patrol of 6th S.F. was heard at 7-30 p.m. and O.C. my Right Company sent a patrol to BRESLAU, which returned with the information that the patrol was back.

At 5-0 p.m. enemy working party was heard at about G.5.C. 05.15. My Left Company Commander at once sent a patrol to treat it exactly. This patrol returned at 7-30 p.m. with the information that a large digging party were at work at about G.5.c.80.45. Our 18 prs. were turned on to this target, and was said to have made very good shooting. The existence of this party did not suggest trouble on my left front.

At 9-20 p.m. heavy Trench Mortar and 77 min. barrage was opened on right of BRESLAU. This gradually extended north. There was also a barrage put down on the Battalion on my left. By 9-30 p.m. the barrage covered the whole of my front, being particularly heavy on HAIRPIN.

At 9-24 S.O.S. LANCER was received from Right Battn. Group, and Companies being at once informed out 18 pr. barrage which was opened at once extended beyond the right of my front and is described as being "magnificent". Lewis Gun fire was at once opened between BRESLAU and HAIRPIN and between HAIRPIN and BORDER as previously arranged. My Right Company Comdr. did not consider it necessary to sen"Attack QUARRIES" under the circumstances.

Between 9-35 and 9-45 various enemy groups approached the right and left posts of HAIRPIN - STUDIO II - and RAT CREEK, and 77 min. barrage lifted to O.B.1. The groups appeared to consist of from 8-12 men. All groups seemed quite confused and our men had no difficulty in driving them off with bomb and rifle and L.G. fire. The parties on being challenged replied "FREUND" in one case and "SECHSISCH" (6th) in another.

Smoke bombs fell in HAIRPIN which made some men think there was gas. Bombs fell in RAT CREEK causing some casualties.

Two of the enemy were seen approaching a post south of HAIRPIN and the men threw bombs behind the enemy, and rushed out and captured them.

Patrols were sent out from HAIRPIN - STUDIO II and RAT CREEK when barrage died down at about 10-0 p.m. One dead German was found about 40 yards from STUDIO II. No further trace could be found of any of the enemy, but the ground is extremely difficult and broken.

The casualties were:- 1 Officer and 7 O.R. wounded - none serious.

The enemy evidently intended to surround HAIRPIN, so far as their left was concerned

Page 2.

It must have been disorganised from the start.   On both flanks those that got through must have completely lost direction.

Our men were ready for the raid and anxious for it.

Recommendations will follow, but I should like to call attention in this report to the preliminary arrangements made by Capt. H.K.SIMONET, who also exercised a very wise judgment in deciding not to send "S.O.S." or "ATTACK QUARRIES"   He controlled the situation throughout in a most admirable manner.

Our Stokes Mortars fired 150 rounds on the arranged lines during the raid.   Machine gun co-operation was also prompt and most effective.

          (Signed) A.HACKING, Major,
            O.C.,8th Sherwood Foresters.

3-1-18.

Appendix V

OPERATION ORDERS BY MAJOR E.M.G INGELL, Commanding 8th Sherwood Foresters.
20th January 1918.

RELIEF. The 8th Sherwood Foresters will be relieved by the 11th Manchester Regiment on the 21st instant and on relief will take over billets in BURBURE vacated by 5th Dorset Regt. The route will be by HESDIGNEUL - BRUAY - and MARLES-LES-MINES.

STORES. Blankets and leather jerkins labelled and rolled in bundles of 10, Lewis Guns and ammunition and packs and rifles of the drums to be at Q.M.Stores by 8.45 am. Officers valises to be at Stores by 9.0 am. Coy Mess boxes (less utensils required for dinner) to be at Q.M.Stores by 9.0 am.

CERTIFICATES. Marching-out states and the usual Billet Certificates to be sent in to O.Room by 10.0 am. Usual Falling-out states and billet returns to be handed in on arrival.

CLAIMS. 2nd Lieut. Russell will remain behind for 3 hours after the Battalion moves out and will see the Maire to settle any claims A Bicycle will be provided for him.

PARADES. Sick parade 7.30 am Breakfasts 8.0 am Dinners 12 noon. The Battalion will form up in the following order :- Signallers, Drums, 'A' 'B' 'C' 'D' Cos. in column of route, head of column at cross roads near 'B' Coy's Mess facing S.W. ready to move off at 1.0 pm. Dress - full marching order with steel helmets under the supporting straps of pack. No parcels or sandbags are to be carried. The transport will move independently in one body via BETHUNE and CHOCQUES.

The C.O. will inspect billets at 11.30 am and if fine all kits must be outside billets by 11.15 am.

(sgd) J.B.White

Lieut and A/Adjt.,
8th Sherwood Foresters.

Appendix III

Operation Orders by Lieut. Colonel J.E.Blackwall, D.S.O.
Commanding 8th Bn. The Sherwood Foresters. 30th January, 18.

The Battalion Staff, 12 Officers and 400 Other Ranks, proceeding to MAZINGARBE and PHILOSOPHE to-day, will parade on Battalion Alarm Post at 1-30 p.m., in Order _ "A" "C" "B" and "D" Cos. Dress - Full marching order; steel helmets and leather jerkins to be worn.

"A" and "C" Cos. will proceed to MAZINGARBE by lorry, and "B" and "D" Cos. to PHILOSOPHE by lorry. The cookers of "B" and "C" Cos. will accompany the Transport.

One N.C.O. and 6 men of "D" Compy. will be detailed from those staying behind to load blankets, Officers valises, mess boxes &c.

All ranks staying behind (less Transport and Stores) will parade with all their kit, blankets &c. outside Orderly Room at 2-30 p.m. today.

Cos. will report "all in" to Orderly Room at MAZINGARBE.

(Sgd.) J.B.WHITE, Lieut. & A/Adjt.,
8th Bn. The Sherwood Foresters.

WAR DIARY of 8th Bn. The Sherwood Foresters Army Form C. 2118.
or
INTELLIGENCE SUMMARY. for February 1918

(Erase heading not required)

Place	Date 1918	Hour	Summary of Events and Information	Remarks and references to Appendices
MAZINGARBE	Feb 1		The Bn was divided HQ and 450 O.R. being at MAZINGARBE working on tunnels & wire in two defended localities, the remainder being in BURBURE where training was carried out.	
BURBURE	7		training was carried out.	
	7		The party left MAZINGARBE and the whole Bn was in I Corps Reserve at BURBURE	
LAIRES	9		The Bn moved to LAIRES HQ & 2 Coys being in billets at LAIRES and 2 Coys at LIVOSSART. On 12th the Bn marched past the G.O.C. Division	
ENQUIN	13		Bn moved to ENQUIN	
	13 & 28		The period was occupied in training, particular attention being paid to musketry. All Coys commenced firing the Divisional Musketry Course and considerable progress was made. Trench to trench attack and open warfare attacks were also practised. An A.R.A. Competition was also carried out won by No 15 Platoon of D Coy. 1st this pltn was beaten in the Bde Competition	
			Strength 1st Feb 1918 Off. 53 O.R. 987	
			" 28th " " 47 " 983	
			Casualties during month — Nil —	

The Bridgwe Major
Commd'g 8th Sherwood Foresters

WAR DIARY or INTELLIGENCE SUMMARY

Army Form C. 2118.

1/8th Bn. The Liverpool Regt. for March 1918

Place	Date	Hour	Summary of Events and Information	Remarks and references to Appendices
ENQUIN	March 1 to 5		9th Bn was in G.H.Q. Reserve & carried out training, practised attacks, fing. Reference Map.	
WESTRE HEM BETHUNE	5 6 to 14		9th Bn moved with I Corps Reserve 9th Bn moved to BETHUNE & was in 1st H.Q. as the advance Parry the pursuing forces coming up time can't button but was ordered back.	BETHUNE Map Continued
ANNEQUIN	14		9th Bn relieved the 5th Inniskilling Regt in ANNEQUIN Sector of SAILLY LABOURSE Front	
	16		16th was transferred from SAILLY LABOURSE to ANNEQUIN FOSSE	
CAMBRIN	20		9th Bn was relieved by 11th N.F.Bn. Relieved practice in the ANNEQUIN locality returned to the CAMBRIN SECTOR of the BLACK WATCH	Reference Map
	21/22		Bn. carried at night HUYBARD Reserve area until sent to caves etc. was caused that I hand the Coma cling and quiet the night	APPENDIX E
BEUVRY	24		9th Bn was relieved by 11th R.S. Fusiliers transition. H.Q. & 2 Coys going to BEUVRY & 2 Coys remaining in temporary CAMBRIN in support of 11th R.S.F. that Bn went up 1st Bn as a perilous line in front of CAMBRIN in close support to the occupy in that Bn my company returned in truth 11th S.Coys returned to BEUVRY	
	25			
SALOMNE	27		9th Bn relieved the 11th R.S. Fusiliers in reserve at SALOMNE & and ST EMILE Line. 9th Bn proceeded from BEUVRY marching the 2 coys in Close support at BEUVRY	Ref map LEN.S 36.SW1 Huno
ST EMILE	28		9th Bn relieved the 7th Canadian Infantry for in the right sub sector	

Army Form C. 2118.

WAR DIARY of 8th Bn. The Sherwood Foresters for March 1918.

INTELLIGENCE SUMMARY.

(Erase heading not required.)

Instructions regarding War Diaries and Intelligence Summaries are contained in F.S. Regs., Part II. and the Staff Manual respectively. Title pages will be prepared in manuscript.

Place	Date 1918	Hour	Summary of Events and Information	Remarks and references to Appendices
ST. EMILE	March 28 to 31		At ST EMILE sector. During this period nothing of any importance occurred, the enemy being quiet. The Bn. was relieved by 1/6 Sherwood Foresters & went into Bde. reserve in ST. PIERRE	
ST. PIERRE	31		Strength 1st March - Off. 47. O.R. 983 " 31st " " 43 " 9.6 Casualties during month Off. wounded 2 (1/8th marked) (also from our O.P.) O.R. Killed 3. Died of wounds 1. Missing 26. Wounded 20 RR R. Osburn Lieut/Col. O.C. 8th Sherwood Foresters	

APPENDIX I

8th Sherwood Foresters.
Report on Raid carried out by the enemy on Night 21/22nd. MARCH, 1918.

At about 12-30 a.m. the enemy opened an intense bombardment on the whole Brigade front; this bombardment was in considerable depth and extended back as far as the VILLAGE LINE. Almost immediately telephonic communication to the two flank Companies was nonexistent.

At 12.44 a.m. the ATTACK message was received by the Battalion from the Right Company by Power Buzzer. The next news that was received was that the enemy were in our front trenches on the Right - this came via the Support Company.

It would appear that he came across in three parties, one between our Right Post and the left of the 138th Infantry Brigade, one approximately where DUNDEE WALK meets the front line and one North of entrance to MUNSTER TUNNEL.

The total strength of the Raiding Party is estimated at about 250.

The centre of the locality was apparently attacked in rear.

It would appear that a stiff struggle took place and that most of our men were wounded before being taken prisoners in view of the many pools of blood found in our front line trench during reconnaissance this morning.

One of the parties evidently worked Southwards, probably along the old disused Trenches East of the Railway and succeeded in capturing a Machine Gun in the RESERVE LINE - some of this same party it would appear then turned Westwards and took the Lewis Gun Post in DUNDEE WALK in rear; none of the enemy reached the RESERVE LINE in my Sector.

Apparently some of the enemy reached a point about half way between the front and Reserve Line as he was seen near a 3" T.M. emplacement at A.27.d.65.55. and we know he took a Lewis Gun Post which is situated at A.27.d.80.25.

With reference to the latter 5 empty Lewis Gun Drums have been found in the Post and it appears that the team fired these before being taken by surprise from the rear.

The statement that a Platoon was out wiring proves incorrect. The facts are that a Platoon had been wiring but was also doing its own carrying and had just been back for more material when the bombardment commenced, they therefore immediately resorted to their "Stand to" positions.

The enemy left behind many bombs and a few rifles - he did not attempt to blow up any dugouts or tunnel entrances with mobile charges, but contented himself by throwing bombs.

The Officer on duty in the front line was wounded near the front line entrance to MUNSTER TUNNEL early on in the bombardment; other Officers made frequent attempts to get out of the front line tunnel entrance but were bombed back.

Eventually a party succeeded in forcing an exit and took one of the enemy wounded.

The total casualties were:-

	Officers.	O.Ranks.
KILLED.		3
MISSING.		26.
WOUNDED.	1	10.

Page. 2.

    1 wounded and 1 unwounded German were left in our hands, the former has since died - both belonged to 263rd. Regt.

    In conclusion I should like to add, that after careful consideration of all the available information I am of opinion that the garrisons of the front line Posts were attacked on all sides, the enemy having succeeded in getting behind them and thus overwhelming them and that they put up a good fight before being actually taken prisoners.

    The bombardment was very heavy expecially on the front line, C.T's and Battalion Headquarters, and during the earlier stages of it no doubt a good deal of front line wire was cut.

    In anticipation of a Raid, positions had been dug out 50 yards behind the Right flank Posts behind RAILWAY CRATERS and Left flank Post behind junction of LEWIS ALLEY and Front line trench, as I considered, that while it was necessary to have Posts in these areas they were extremely isolated and liable to be cut off, and that if they were about 50 yards in rear of the front line they would escape the main part of the enemy barrage and would still be able to cover the area for which they were responsible.

    They did not in any way uncover the Company's flanks or those of contiguous Companies.

    An Observation Post was left at junction of DUNDEE Walk and front line; hourly patrols between this Post and left Post of the Brigade on our Right were carried out alternately.

    My Right Company Commander warned the Company Commander of the Left Company of the Brigade on my Right of the new emergency positions of these Posts on the 17th inst. and arranged to have patrols between the Companies hourly.

R.W. Currin Lieut Col
Major, O.C.,
8th Bn. The Sherwood Foresters.

22-3-18.

139th Brigade.

46th Division.

1/8th BATTALION

SHERWOOD FORESTERS

APRIL 1918.

Army Form C. 2118.

WAR DIARY 1/8 Bn Sherwood Foresters
or
INTELLIGENCE SUMMARY.
(Erase heading not required.)

For week ending 7 APRIL 1918

Vol 38

Instructions regarding War Diaries and Intelligence Summaries are contained in F. S. Regs., Part II. and the Staff Manual respectively. Title pages will be prepared in manuscript.

Place	Date	Hour	Summary of Events and Information	Remarks and references to Appendices
CITE ST PIERRE	APRIL 1	10 PM	Relieved by the 6th Bn Sherwood Foresters and went into Brigade support. Here the battalion provided carrying and working parties to the Battalions in the line	
TRENCHES IN LEFT SUB SECTOR	APRIL 3rd		Relieved the 5th Sherwood Foresters in the left sub sector. Three coys in the front line and one in support. Heavy hostile Trench mortars were active against our front and parties of men were continually repairing trenches damaged by their fire	
"	April 5	2 AM	In retaliation to a projector of our gas the enemy put a heavy barrage of French Mortars and artillery onto our trenches	
CITE ST PIERRE	April 9		Relieved by the 6th Bn Sherwood Foresters and went into Brigade support. Here the usual carrying parties were provided. Hostile artillery was more active than when the battalion was here last	
NEOUX LES MINES	April 11	5:00 AM	Relieved by the 116 Bn Canadian Infantry and marched to NEOUX LES MINES	
		8 AM	Arrived at NEOUX LES MINES. Here the battalion had breakfast and dinners	
		2:30 PM	Received orders to march to VAUDRICOURT where in the locality the Division was going into Army Reserve.	
VAUDRICOURT	April 11	4 PM	Arrived at VAUDRICOURT. Here the battalion received orders to carry out training, firing etc	
	April 12		Training was carried out in the vicinity of billets close order drill musketry, P.T. B.T. and Lectures were given by officers	
	April 13		The battalion fired on range No 5 each man fired 5 rounds application. coys not firing practised open warfare schemes	
	April 14		as for the 12th	
	April 16 17		Training in vicinity of billets and on the range where the battalion practised open warfare as a battalion	

Army Form C. 2118.

Page 2

WAR DIARY of 8th Stewart Frontier
or
INTELLIGENCE SUMMARY. for month ending APRIL 1916

(Erase heading not required)

Instructions regarding War Diaries and Intelligence Summaries are contained in F.S. Regs., Part II. and the Staff Manual respectively. Title pages will be prepared in manuscript.

Place	Date	Hour	Summary of Events and Information	Remarks and references to Appendices
SAILLY LABOURSE	April 18	2.30 AM	Battalion received orders to man the SAILLY LABOURSE LOCALITY Battalion fell in and marched off	
		4.30 PM	Took up position in the locality A Coy on the right B and D centre and C on the left	
		11.30 AM	In the day to the beavily resched casualties were sustained owing to the heavy shelling of the roads and villages preparatory to the enemy attacking GIVENCHY for which the battery had to man the locality. The enemy shelling ceased at 11 PM and everything remained afterwards	
	April 19		Remained in the locality	
VAUDRICOURT	April 20	2 PM	Received orders to move back to the vicinity of BETHUNE	
	21			
	22		Training was carried out in the vicinity of BETHUNE	
VAUDRICOURT	23	6 PM	Received orders to move to BETHUNE	
BETHUNE	23	8.30 PM	Billeted in Infantry barracks and officers evacuated here which battalion could easily be marched up	
BETHUNE	24	8 PM	Left for the trenches	
FRONT SECTOR Right Battalion	24	11 PM	Relieved 2 Bn Royal Scots & coys in front line A & D and Bn B & C coys in support B and C	
			The front was fairly quiet but the whole time was used endeavouring to put the trenches in a decent state by putting up wire and erecting shelters	
TRENCHES	28		Relieved by the 11th division and went into divisional reserve. The whole Brigade billeted in the locality	
	29			
	30		Training and tuning up the ranks was carried out, many fatigues of mapping	

Strength end of month
45 Officers 966 OR

Strength beginning of month
42 Officers 913 OR

Casualties
Officers   OR
1 Officer wounded   6 killed in action
at duty   1 died of wounds
                         40 wounded
1 Officer wounded   7 wounded and duty
at duty   self inflicted

signed R. Blackwell
Lieut Col
Commanding 8th Bn
Royal Innisk(illing) Fus.

2/Lt G.G.27 Capt A Cobb Comdy 8th Bn RIFus

WAR DIARY of 8th Bn. 1/o Sherwood Foresters
for May 1918.
INTELLIGENCE SUMMARY.
(Erase heading not required.)

Army Form C. 2118.

p. 29

Hour, Date, Place	Summary of Events and Information	Remarks and references to Appendices
1918 May 1 FOUQUIERES	The Bn. was in Divisional Reserve. Between 26am the Bn. stood to as an attack was expected on Corps front.	Map Ref. BETHUNS contoured sheet 1/40000
2 LE QUESNOY	The Bn. relieved the 1/6th North Staffs in Bde Reserve in GORRE Section.	
4 GORRE RIGHT	The Bn. relieved the 1/6th Sherwood Foresters in the right Sector. 2 Coys in the line, 1 in support, 1 in reserve. A tunnel was dug in front of the organized strongpoints which had previously been the front line. Enemy artillery was quiet but his aircraft was very active over the Sector.	
8 LE QUESNOY	The Bn. was relieved by the 1/5th Sherwood Foresters & went into Bde. reserve.	
10 VAUDRICOURT	The Bn. was relieved by the 1/5th Leicestershire Regt & went into Div. Reserve in VAUDRICOURT WOOD. On the way up the Bn. stood to in BETHUNS locally as an attack was expected while barrage the Bn. was at Bourecq in Res. to Brigade.	
12 ESSARS	The Bn. relieved the 1/5th S. Staffs in the right subsector. 2 Coys front in the line, 2 in support. The enemy was quiet & a tunnel was dug on canal (Rue de Bois)	

Army Form C. 2118.

WAR DIARY of 2/8th Bn Sherwood Foresters
INTELLIGENCE SUMMARY. for May 1918.

(Erase heading not required.)

Place	Date 1918	Hour	Summary of Events and Information	Remarks and references to Appendices
ESSARS	May/18		The Bn. was relieved by 1/5th Sherwood Foresters went into Bde Reserve in ESSARS	
"	20		The Bn. LEHINIEL took was continued in finch or camel front. The Bn. relieved the 1/6th Sherwood Foresters in left sub sector. 2 coys in front line, 1 in support, 1 in reserve. The enemy being quiet, continuous trench was dug. Shelters made for the men.	
VERQUIN	25		The Bn. was relieved by 1/5th S. Staffs went into Div Reserve in VERQUIN	
	28		The Brigade was inspected & medals presented by the G.O.C. 46th Div at QUISMAY	
GORRE	30		The Bn. relieved the 1/5th Lancashire Regt in the right sub-sector, chief duty completed without casualties. The Bn. was quiet.	

Strength 1st May Off. 39 O.R. 843
" 31st "   " 37   " 902

Casualties during month 8/Rs wounded 5. O.R. killed 13 wounded 13
Mentions & Awards. Legion d'Honneur (Chevalier) Lieut Col J.E. Blackwall DSO.
Croix de Guerre 306039 Sgt. A. Cobb.

Mentioned in Despatches Capt. & A/Maj R. Whitton
Lieut C.G. Inchman
305058 R.Q.M.S. J.A. Pritchard
305284 Sgt. R. Harvey

J.W. Campbell
J.W. Campbell Major
O.C. 2/8 Sherwood Foresters

WAR DIARY of 8th Bn Sherwood Foresters for month ending June 30, 1918.

INTELLIGENCE SUMMARY

Army Form C. 2118.

Instructions regarding War Diaries and Intelligence Summaries are contained in F.S. Regs., Part II. and the Staff Manual respectively. Title pages will be prepared in manuscript.

(Erase heading not required.)

Place	Date	Hour	Summary of Events and Information	Remarks and references to Appendices
LINE, GORRE RIGHT SUBSECTION	1/6/18		How the Battalion was holding the line with B and C Coys in the front line and A support and D reserve. The S.S. Barrier was in the right of the Battalion area. The 6 Sherwoods on the left. The enemy were fairly quiet. Snipers & M.G.s giving trouble on all fronts and disturbing the exit. Work was during the past and mending the wires etc.	
"	2/6/18		orders were received that the battalion would be relieved by the 5 Sherwoods and that the Bn. would go into Brigade support.	
LEQUESNOY	3/6/18		relieved by 5 Sherwoods and billeted LEQUESNOY and GORRE A and B Coys during the night of the 13th. C and D on the morning of 14th.	
L. QUESNOY	12 noon		were relieved by the 5 Bn Suffolks Regt and went into Divisional reserve.	
VAUDRICOURT	3 AM		Battalion arrived at destination and went all transported in the wood adjoining VAUDRICOURT VILLAGE. Here the usual inspections and Brigade test places.	
VAUDRICOURT	13/6/18	9pm	took marching orders and proceeded to the line	
LINE ESSARS left subsect.	14/6/18		relieved the 1/6 Bn Hawich Regt on the left subsector A and D Coys front line and C and B support and reserve. Patrolling ... activity in this front. Tied attempting raid for 2nd night. Enemy were very quiet on the left flank by the river the S.S. Runlets and ... the 5 Sherwoods. Chief work was mending the wire and and working on the front line.	
ESSARS	15/6/18		relieved by the 6 Bn Sherwood Foresters and went into Brigade support around ESSARS village. The 1st was for the front line but also improved its own position plants	

WAR DIARY 1/8th Bn Sherwood Foresters

Army Form C. 2118.

Instructions regarding War Diaries and Intelligence Summaries are contained in F.S. Regs., Part II. and the Staff Manual respectively. Title pages will be prepared in manuscript.

INTELLIGENCE SUMMARY
(Erase heading not required.)

for month ending June 30 1918

Place	Hour, Date	Summary of Events and Information	Remarks and references to Appendices
ESSARS	22/6/18	Orders were received that Bn would be relieved by the 6th Bn S. Staffords	
ESSARS	23/6/18 11.30pm	Relieved by 6th S. Staffs and went back into divisional reserve	
VAUDRICOURT	23/6/18 3 AM	Arrived at resting area. During the time the men were all sleeping or bathing or employed cleaning parades and equipment	
VAUDRICOURT	27/6/18 2.30pm	Left Vaudricourt for the line	
GORRE A/B Subsector	28/6/18 1 PM	Relieved the 8th Bn Lancashire Regt. Bruat. E Coy front line and A and D in reserve and support. During the night our raid whilst patrolling we were met with a burst of enemy machine gun and rifle fire. It was noticed by the patrols that the enemy were seldom in his own front line it was continued advisable not to carry on with the practice and insufficient quantity of wire were put out on the Bn front and the wire well installed	
GORRE A/B Subsector	30/6/18	Casualties for month: Officers: Nil O. Ranks — Killed 2 Wounded 22 Wounded at duty 6 Self inflicted wound 1 Accidental wounds 1	Strength Beginning of month officers 37 OR 902 End of month " 39 " 902 Honours awarded: Captain A Andrews the Military Cross Gazette 3.6.18 328930 Sergeant T Taylor att 139 I.y Bde the Meritorious Service Medal 20.6.18 R S Currin Lt Col Condg 8 Sherwood Foresters

WAR DIARY of 6th Bn Sherwood Foresters

Page 1
Army Form C. 2118.

INTELLIGENCE SUMMARY
For month ending July 1918.

(Erase heading not required.)

Hour, Date, Place			Summary of Events and Information	Remarks and references to Appendices
	LIVE-GORRE Left Sector	1/7/18 11PM	This was the battalions last day in the sector before going back to rest.	
	GORRE	2/7/18 2AM	Relieved by the 6th Bn North Staffordshire Regiment and went into Div reserve.	
	VERQUIN	2/7/18	Arrived in Div reserve. Most of the time being spent in cleaning up and inspections etc.	
	VERQUIN	3/7/18	Received orders to take over the trenches from 5th Leicestershire Regt.	
	ESSARS	5/7/18 11PM	Relieves the Leicesters in Bde support. Two Coys were in the line and two in the defences which the Bn held. A great amount of A framing and wiring being done.	
	ESSARS	9/7/18	Received orders to relieve the battalion holding the front line in the right subsector.	
	RIGHTSUB-SECTOR	10/7/18	Relieves the 5th Bn Sherwood Foresters. A and D Coys going into the front line and C and B in support. The enemy were fairly quiet here. Bn HQ at LE HAMEL received a little attention from enemy shells. The work was concentrated on wiring the reserve line and wiring front line posts. A good deal of night and also day patrolling was done, and several enemy posts were located.	
	RIGHTSUB-SECTOR	15/7/18	Relieved by 6th North Staffs and went back into Div reserve	
	VAUDRICOURT WOOD HESDIGNEUL	16/7/18 17/7/18	Arrives in Div reserve and the whole battalion went into bivouacs amidst the wood. Here the usual routine was carried out. Cleaning up etc. Bn had a sports day whole battalion being present. Sports started at 4 PM and finished at about 7.30 PM	
	VAUDRICOURT	20/7/18	139 Bde Sports at which several men in the battalion won events	

Army Form C. 2118.

G.1362

WAR DIARY of 6" Sherwood Foresters
or
INTELLIGENCE SUMMARY.

Page 2 — 1st entry
July 1916

(Erase heading not required.)

Instructions regarding War Diaries and Intelligence Summaries are contained in F. S. Regs., Part II. and the Staff Manual respectively. Title pages will be prepared in manuscript.

Place	Date	Hour	Summary of Events and Information	Remarks and references to Appendices
VAUDRICOURT	21/7/18		Received orders to relieve the 6th Bn. North Staffs	
ESSARS. RICHT.	22/7/18	a.m. 7.45	Relieves the 6 N.Staffs B and C Coys going into the front line and A and D in support. Enemy daylight patrol estimated at twelve strong attacked a forward post of C Coy the L/Cpl Coy from the rear and captured 1 NCO and ten men. He sent out fighting patrols after but nothing could be seen.	
"	23/7/18	3.30 A.M.	Enemy put down rather a heavy barrage on the Bn. front for about 15 minutes. No infantry action took place. Remainder of the tour was rather quiet. The battalion H.Q.nrs LE HAMEL still suffered daily from enemy shell fire. Chief work was relieving LIVERPOOL LINE during first line getting come.	
"	29/7/18		Relieved by 5th Sherwood Foresters	
ESSARS. TOLN Support.	29/7/18 31/7/18		Bn. held trenches around ESSARS and found working parties for the rest of the Bde. an exhausting night. On LIVERPOOL LINE on night side another Coy working under left battalion. Remainder improved their own positions. The weather being fine the work was awarded most satisfactory	

CASUALTIES
Officers = Nil   Other Ranks
Killed Nil   Wounded (at duty) 4.
Wounded 19   Wound (self inflicted) 2.
Missing 3

HONOURS & AWARDS
Nil.

Strength beginning of month officers 39 OR 883
Strength end of month officers 41 OR 953

W.Crnn Lt Col Comdg 6 Sherwood Foresters

WAR DIARY of 8th Battalion Sherwood Foresters

INTELLIGENCE SUMMARY for month ending August 31/1918

Army Form C. 2118.

(Erase heading not required.)

Instructions regarding War Diaries and Intelligence Summaries are contained in F.S. Regs., Part II. and the Staff Manual respectively. Title pages will be prepared in manuscript.

Place	Date	Hour	Summary of Events and Information	Remarks and references to Appendices
ESSARS (BOESUPPORT)	1/8/18		Here the Battalion was in Bde support. Employed in taking up strong pts. to the battalion on the front line and working on our defences on the NEWCASTLE LINE which was the trench situated N.E. of ETRIPES.	
ESSARS	2/8/18	11.30 pm	Relieved by the 1st Bn. South Staffordshire Regt. and proceeded to rest billets.	
VAUDRICOURT	3/8/18 4/8/18 5/8/18	3 am	Arrived in rest billets which were hutments on the west schematic close to the village. Here the time was spent in training, firing a range small tactical schemes etc.	
VAUDRICOURT to CUIRRE	6/8/18		Proceed to the line. Relieved the 1/6 Bn South Staffordshire Regt in Bde support. The enemy were fairly quiet in this sector.	
CUIRRE			2 Bn. Leicester Regt. That enemy planes frequently troubled our positions at night. During this time the enemy at GORRE BRIDGE was shelled up by our troops. Chief work was improved our own defences.	
GORRE NIGHT (BridgeHead)	13/8/18		Believes the 1st Sherwood Foresters in the night front line. A and D Coy in the front line, C Coy in support, B Coy in reserve. While here we were informed by higher authorities and by our own listening posts that the enemy were carrying out extensive demolitions behind their lines which pointed to a withdrawal on his part. Patrolling was carried out extensively by us in this sector with a view to keeping the enemy under observation.	CP 42
ESSARS	13/8/18	1 am	Bayon received orders to move across to the Left Bde sector and relieve the 6 Bn N. Staffs in the night relieving of that sector, after being relieved at GORRE by the 1/5 Leicester Regt.	
	14/8/18		In this sector (ESSARS) A and D will the front line and B and C in close support. Received orders that the enemy were withdrawing from his positions. Our front coys (A and D) immediately sent out strong patrols in order to keep track the rest of the coy going after them in small mobs. By evening a line was held and being considerably the N.E. side of the village of LE TOURET. Our advance in all of nearly a thousand yards.	
		7 pm		

Army Form C. 2118.

WAR DIARY of 8/9th Shwood Foresters.
or
INTELLIGENCE SUMMARY for Month ending August 31/16

(Erase heading not required.)

Instructions regarding War Diaries and Intelligence Summaries are contained in F. S. Regs., Part II. and the Staff Manual respectively. Title pages will be prepared in manuscript.

Place	Date	Hour	Summary of Events and Information	Remarks and references to Appendices
ESSARS	1/8/16		Relieved by 6' Bn. N. Staffs and proceeded to Rest billets.	
VERQUIN	2/8/16		Arrived at Annotnales. A and D Coys and B H.Q. in VERQUIN. B and C Coys in VAUDRICOURT WOOD.	
FOUQUERIES	12/8/16		H and D moved to this village also Bn H.Q.	
ESSARS			B and C moved here. An alteration in disposition was made in the ESSARS SECTOR with the result that there his Coys had to move.	
FOUQUERIES			A and D Coys carried out training forming in usual etc.	
FURRI	25/8/16		Bn relieved the 4th Lincoln Regt in Bde support and B and C Coys coming from ESSARS begin the Bn for this purpose. The enemy had retired some distance in this sector which had settled the disposition somewhat since we held this sector. The last Coun. Work was uncalculated in improving defences. While here the outpost Bn. opposite the enemy withdrawing still further.	
"	31/8/16			

Casualties for month
Officers
Wounded ....1. Wounded (acc.) 3
Wounded (acc.) 1. Gas (4 wounds) 3
Other Ranks
Killed 7
Wounded 76
Missing .... —
Wounded (acc. only) 8

Strength
Beginning of month   30 officers   915 O.R.
End of month   40 officers   897 O.R.

Honours and awards
Nil

[signature]
Lt Col Comdg 8/9 Sherwood Foresters

Army Form C. 2118.

WAR DIARY
or
INTELLIGENCE SUMMARY.

(Erase heading not required.)

of the 8th Bn. Sherwood Foresters

for the Month of Sept. 1916

Sheet 1

Instructions regarding War Diaries and Intelligence Summaries are contained in F.S. Regs., Part II. and the Staff Manual respectively. Title pages will be prepared in manuscript.

Place	Date	Hour	Summary of Events and Information	Remarks and references to Appendices
Trenches RICHEBOURG ST VAAST	1st Sept		The Battn. were in Brigade Support in TUNING FORK BREASTWORKS. Relieved about 10 p.m. by 4th Bn. Lincoln Regiment. Brigade front reorganised. REF MAP - LE TOURET 1/20,000	
"	2nd Sept		The Battn. relieved 6th Sherwoods on the outpost line B by night from C. Coy - centre, a/c A Coy. left front, will D Coy in support. All movements were carried out by sections on the relief was commenced at 6.30 p.m. Ref Map. RICHEBOURG 1/10,000	
"	3rd Sept		C. Coy relieved HEN'S POST, WINDY CORNER, & EDWARD'S POST taking an armament with B. Coy occupied DOG'S POST without opposition. REF MAP RICHEBOURG 1/10,000	
"	4th Sept		In cooperation with the 138th Brigade the 139th Brigade occupied the Old British Line.	See APPENDIX I
		5 A.M.	Barrage opened in front of ANSTATH, ORCHARD, ALBERT, EDWARDS' DOG's and the empaced caused the enemy By C Coys of the Battn pushed forward every slowly and occupied Old British Line from S.5.c.80.50. - Six losses without any serious opposition.	
	5th Sept	12.30 P.M.	About mid day the enemy scored a direct hit on Battn. Head Quarters at LANSDOWNE POST wounding the whole of Battn. Headquarters officers with the exception of Capt A. ANDREWS the Medical Officer. Lt.-Col. A. ANDREWS M.C. assumed command of the Battn.	
		6.0 P.M.	The Battn. were relieved in the RICHEBOURG SECTOR by the 9th Battn.	9.43

Army Form C. 2118.

Sheet II

WAR DIARY
or
INTELLIGENCE SUMMARY of the 8th Batt. Cheshire Regiment
(Erase heading not required) For the month ending Sept 30th 1918

Instructions regarding War Diaries and Intelligence Summaries are contained in F.S. Regs., Part II and the Staff Manual respectively. Title pages will be prepared in manuscript.

Place	Date	Hour	Summary of Events and Information	Remarks and references to Appendices
RICHEBOURG ST VAAST	Sept 5th to 6th Sept	6.0 A.M	CHESHIRE Regiment. 19th Division, and in relief reliived to BEUVRY. This was carried out without casualties.	
"	Sept 7th		The Battalion at BEUVRY on the left. Railway proceeding to FERFAY from which place they marched to AUCHEL Battn TRAINING in the attack was carried out in this area	
AUCHEL	Sept 8th		Lieut Col J. Finlay Dinkart D.S.O. 2nd Manchester Regt joined the Battn and took over command from Major Andrew M.C.	
"	11th + 12th Sept		The Battn marched from AUCHEL to CALONNE RICOUART when it entrained for an unknown destination	See APPENDIX 1.
CORBIE	12th Sept		Detrainment eventually took place at CORBIE when the Battn arrived in the afternoon, and later marched from there to LA HOUSSOYE	
LA HOUSSOYE	13th to 18th Sept		Journey by Battn carried out in this area.	
"	18th Sept	9 p.m	At the end on night 18/19th the Batt marched from LAHOUSSOYE to FRANVILLERS to BONNAY where it embussed for an unknown destination. Transport followed by road under BRIGADE arrangements.	
POEUILLY	19th Sept	About 4 A.M	About 4 A.M debussing was accomplished about 1 mile west of POEUILLY. Heavy Bivouac shelters were erected + the Batt bivouaced in this.	

A 3534 Wt.W4973/M687. 750,000 8/16 D.D. & L. Ltd. Forms/C.2118/13.

Army Form C. 2118.

Sheet III

WAR DIARY
or
INTELLIGENCE SUMMARY of the 6th Batln Sherwoods
Forester for the month of Sept 1916
(Erase heading not required.)

Instructions regarding War Diaries and Intelligence Summaries are contained in F. S. Regs., Part II. and the Staff Manual respectively. Title pages will be prepared in manuscript.

Place	Date	Hour	Summary of Events and Information	Remarks and references to Appendices
BELLENGLISE	Sept 20th to 23rd		On the afternoon of the 19th the Battn relieved the 2nd Batn Royal Irish Regiment in Brigade Reserve in the line W. of BELLENGLISE. Battn H.Q. Ecole Quarry. The relief was carried out without casualties.	
	23rd Sept		On night of 23rd Batln Head Quarters was transferred to Quarry 700 yds S.S.W. of TUMULUS in conjunction with the 6th Batn Sherwood Foresters. Battn 1.P.M. Brigade order left in execution with the 6th & 6th Sherwoods to carry out a minor operation to capture enemy trenches E. of PONTRUET and the village. The Battn were to relieve the 6th Sherwoods in captured positions. Owing to the objective not being taken the relief was cancelled.	See APPENDIX 3.
	Sept 24th	11 a.m.	At this hour orders were received for the Battn to relieve the 6th Sherwood Foresters on the right subsector. Battn Head quarters in Brescia on Hill 1000 yds S. of PONTRU. Relief was completed without casualties. We had a number of wounded during stay in the sector.	
	Sept 26th		On the night of the 26th the Battn was relieved by 1st Batn Royal Highlanders and after relief returned to Bivouacs about 1 mile S. of VENDELLES on the VENDELLES - DIHECOURT ROAD.	See APPENDIX 4.
	Sept 27th & 28th		On the night of the 27th the Battn marched to assembly trenches about 500 yards S.W. of SOMERVILLE WOOD and remained there the following day.	

10H

Sheet IV.

Army Form C. 2118.

WAR DIARY
or
INTELLIGENCE SUMMARY.
(Erase heading not required.)

of the 8th Batln. Sherwood Foresters for the month of Sept 1916.

Instructions regarding War Diaries and Intelligence Summaries are contained in F.S. Regs., Part II. and the Staff Manual respectively. Title pages will be prepared in manuscript.

Place	Date	Hour	Summary of Events and Information	Remarks and references to Appendices
BELLENGLISE	29th Sept		At 3 A.M. the Batln. moved up to forming up position in ASCENSION VALLEY for the attack which formed part of a major operation against the HINDENBURG LINE at BELLENGLISE, E. of the ST QUENTIN CANAL. The operation was entirely successful the Batln. gaining all its objectives and taking 300 prisoners. Total casualties 12- killed, wounded & missing 112. Batln. to further objective, in the other units passed through B. Gn. on Ridge on CANAL in beyond Augoyelle Ravine with BELLENGLISE, MONDIDES ROAD, BELLENCLIF. Batln in trenches 700 M. E. of BELLENEUSE.	See APPENDICES 5, 6, & 7.
	30th			

Casualties during Month.

	Officer	O.R's
Killed	1	19
Wounded	7	104
Wounded at Duty	—	10
Missing	—	—
Died of Wounds	1	2

Strength at Beginning of Month.
Officers 42
O.R's 892.

Strength at End of Month.
Officers 40
O.R's 752.

Honours & Awards.

91299 Pte. G. Stanford - Military Medal.
(VIII Corps R.O. No 1905 of 12.9.18)

H Hallam 2nd Lt. A/Adjt
for O/C. 8th Battn. Sherwood Foresters

APPENDIX I.   No 38.

SECRET   Pg.1   Sept 4th 1918.

Ref. Map. RICHEBOURG 1/10,000.

The Battn. co-operating with 138th Inf Bde. on the RIGHT will attack on the morning of Sept 4th 1918. Objectives will be from S.9.b.60.60 along FACTORY TRENCH to FACTORY KEEP at S.9.d.60.10 inclusive.

"B" Coy. will carry out the attack and will jump off from a line running S.9.b.00.60 to DOGS POST, ORCHARD POST, Brigade Boundary at S.14.b.60.50.

On objective being gained strong patrols of both "B" & "C" Coys will be pushed forward taking advantage of the confusion of the enemy to the old BRITISH FRONT LINE from S.5.c.80.60. S.10.b.80.10 to S.10.c.30.00 where they will be reinforced by the whole of "A" Coy in the centre of the line.

This line will be the OUTPOST LINE and consolidated. A contact aeroplane will call for ground flares at 8.0 a.m. from these out post troops.

At ZERO hour the artillery will barrage 200ft east of the line HAYSTACK, ORCHARD, ALBERT, DOGS, & EDWARDS POSTS, where it will remain for 4 minutes. On moving forward it will travel at the rate of 100 yds in 2 minutes to the final objective (OLD BRITISH FRONT LINE) where it will rest for 10 minutes. It will then move forward to the old GERMAN FRONTLINE in S.5.a. S.11.b. and S.10.d.

The closest liason must be kept with flanks, especially in the cases of the Patrols who push in the OLD BRITISH FRONT LINE.

On the first objective being taken "D" Coy will move forward and establish platoon post at HEN and EDWARD TRENCH in S.9.b with Head Quarters at WINDY CORNER. Bn. H.Q. will also move at this time to WINDY

APPENDIX T Pg2

CORNER. The R.A.P. will be established at this place at the same time.

ZERO HOUR. 5.15. a.m.

Prisoners will be sent back to H.Q. of 6th S.F. 2 men to every 20. An N.C.O. to take charge if party exceeds 30. Watches will be synchronised at B.H.Q at 3.0. a.m.

Sg. C. H. Powell.
Lieut & Adjt.
8th. Bn. Sherwood Foresters.

APPENDIX 2

8th. Bn. Sherwood Foresters.   Order No. 42.
                                10th September, 1918.

1. The Battalion less "C" Company and 1 Cooker and Team will entrain from CALONNE RICOUART by No. 18 train, starting at 5.15.a.m. 12th September.   All Transport and Riding horses to be at the Station 3½ hours before departure of train(i.e. 11.45.p.m. 11th Sept)

2. BILLETING PARTY - 2ndLieut. H.HALLAM and 1 N.C.O. from each Coy and 1 from H.Qrs. will proceed by No. 1 Train leaving CALONNE RICOUART at 6.32.p.m. 11th September to billet for the Battn.   This party to parade at Orderly Room at 4.0.p.m. 11th inst Haversack Rations will be carried.

3. LOADING PARTY. - Letter "C" Company will act as loading party and will report to Lieut. LYTLE M.C.(Brigade Entraining Officer) at CALONNE RICOUART STATION at 5.0.p.m. 11th Sept. The Company Cooker will accompany this party. They will load Nos. 1, 4, 7, 10, 15, 16, and 18 trains. Half the Company will work, the other half resting. Billets being arranged by the Brigade Entraining Officer. Coys will move off at 1.45.p.m. The Company with Cooker and Team will remain at the Station and will travel by train No. 18 on 12th Sept, starting at 12.45.p.m.

4. ENTRAINING PARTY - 2ndLieut. C.P.C.BRAMISH and 1 N.C.O from "A" "B" & "D" Coys and 1 from H.Qrs. will report to the R.T.O at 1.0.a.m. on 12th inst (½ hour before arrival of Unit) and will assist him with the entrainment and forming up of the Battalion.   This party must have in possession a State shewing number of men, horses, vehicles and cycles. Particulars from Orderly Room where they will parade at 12 midnight 11th inst.

5. MOVE - The Battalion less Letter "C" Company parade on ALARM POST in close column of Coys in order - "A" "B" "D". H.Qr.Details at 12.30 on 12th inst and will march to the station. (usual distances between Coys) Transport will parade independently under T.O's Orders.   On arrival at the station all Coys will close up as detailed in TRAIN ORDERS.

6. DRESS - For all parties - F.M.O.

7. RETURN - All Coys and sections will send in to Orderly Room by 10.0.a.m. 11th inst. exact entraining State shewing number of Officers, Men, vehicles and bicycles proceeding with the Batln.

8. RATIONS - Haversack rations for 12th inst will be carried on the men.   Q.M. will arrange for the following days rations to be placed on Cookers.
"C" Company's unexpended rations for 11th and those for 12th inst to be carried.   Rations for 13th to be placed on the cooker.

9. MEALS - Hot suppers will be served to the men at 9.45.p.m. Arrangements to be made by O's C. Coys.

(P.T.O)

APPENDIX II

Page 2

10. ST ORES - All Officers' Valises and Orderly Room stores to be dumped at the Quartermaster's Stores by 7.30 p.m. 11th inst. Mess boxes by 9.0 p.m.

11. WAR D-CARDS.- Water Carts will be filled.

12. TRAIN ORDERS - See Attached.

Champion(?)
Lieut & A/Adjt.
8th Bn. Sherwood Foresters.

Copies issued to :-
    No. 1. O.C. 'A' Coy.
        2. O.C. 'B' Coy.
        3. O.C. 'C' Coy.
        4. O.C. 'D' Coy.
        5. Q.M.
        6. M.O.
        7. Details.
        8. H.Q. Mess.
        9. War Diary.
       10. Signalling Officer.
       11. L.G.O. & M.G.O.
       12. File.

APPENDIX II

8TH. BATTN. SHERWOOD FORESTERS.

TRAIN ORDERS.

1. On arrival at the station the Battalion will form up as close as possible in column of route in the Goods Yard, and will turn to the left and remain in fours. No men will leave their Coy. positions.

2. ENTRAINING - Nobody will en train until one "G" has been sounded by the Bugler. Platoon Commanders will ensure that their men are under control and that they entrain in an orderly manner.

3. HALTS - Whenever halts are made on the journey, the Police will at once picquet at entrances if at stations, to allow no men to wander about.

4. DETRAINING - On arrival at the destination the following to be adhered to :-
   On the sound of one 'G' the R.S.M. & Right Markers only will alight from the train. On the 'Advance' being sounded all ranks will alight and fall in on their markers quickly and silently.
   The Battalion will form up in mass in close column of Coys.

5. The following orders applicable to all ranks travelling by train are published for information and compliance.
   (a) No man is to travel on the top of, or on the steps of a vehicle.
   (b) No Officer or man is to be allowed to travel on the engine or in the compartment or brakevan set apart for the railway Staff.
   (c) No man is allowed to leave the train at any but authorised stopping places, and only then on the order being given by the O.C. Train.
   (d) No beer, wines or spirits to be allowed on the train.
   (e) Any man left behind at a station will report at once to the R.T.O.
   (f) When the train is moving all carriage doors must be kept closed.
   (g) The Iron Ration is on no account to be touched.
   (h) Under no circumstances are rations(drawn by troops for subsistence during the journey) to be destroyed, Thrown away, or given away.
   (i) All station refreshment rooms and buffets are out of bounds to all ranks.
   (j) Bottles, and other articles are not to be thrown out of the windows; any rubbish should be put under the seats.
   (k) No braziers or fires whatever are allowed in or hanging from vehicles occupied by troops.
   (l) No British Officer, Soldier or civilian is allowed to join the train without the authority in writing of the R.T.O.
   (m) In trucks carrying horses, the door on the right when facing in the direction the train is moving, must always be kept closed.

These orders are to be brought to the notice of all ranks before proceeding by train.

Lieut & A/Adjt.
8th Bn. Sherwood Foresters.

WARNING ORDER   No 1   APPENDIX 3.

23rd Sept. 1918

MAP GRICOURT. 1/10,000.

INFORMATION.

1. The 46th Division co-operating with the 1st Division in an attack tomorrow 24th inst.

GENERAL PLAN

2. At ZERO 2 Coys of the 5th Leicester Regt. are attacking on both sides of FOURGANS TRENCH, the farthest objective being H.10.b.40.20.
At the same time 2 Coys. are attacking PONTRUET VILLAGE advancing in four waves from the point of assembly with their right on the PONTRUET – ST HELENE ROAD. When the leading wave has reached approx. M.10.a.7.5. the 2 Coys will face W. and at a given time will rush through the village to PALARIE and PONTRUET TRENCHES and the BLOCKHOUSE at M.9.b.2.3.

The 6th Battn. SHERWOOD FORESTERS will co-operate by occupying FOURMI TRENCH from M.3.c.8.6 to M.3.d.7.7. advancing at ZERO hour abreast with the 5th LEICESTER REGT. and keeping in close touch with the barrage. Prior to ZERO most parts of the Battn. will be in FOURMI TRENCH south of the sunken road running through M.3.c. & d.

RELIEF.

3. The Battn. will 2/Z plan 1 night relieve the 5th LEICESTER Regt as far north as the Inter Brigade Boundary.

GUIDES.

4. O/C. 6th SHERWOOD FORESTERS will arrange for guides for 8th SHERWOOD FORS. to direct men as far as junction of FOURMI TRENCH and Sunken Road at M.3.c.8.6. These guides will meet Coys at M.1.d.9.1. From the former ref M.3.c.8.6

APPENDIX Pg 2

GUIDES
4. (cont.) 1 guide per Coy H.Qrs. and 1 guide per platoon from 5th LEICESTERS REGT. will meet the Battn. to guide to positions.

DRESS
5. Fighting Order will be worn with greatcoat rolled round HAVERSACKS and tools, grenades, ground flares &c. will be carried on the man.

RATIONS
6. Haversack Rations for 26th inst will be carried on the man.

DUMPS
7. A Brigade Emergency Dump will be established tonight at Quarry M.2.d.7.4 for the use of the Battn. if required after relieving the 5th LEICESTER REGT.

  40 Boxes S.A.A.
  50 " No. 23 with R.v.C.
  30 " No. 23 without R.v.C.
  50 " No. 36.
  3 " No. 27.
  2 " V.P.A.

SYNCHRONISM
8. Watches will be synchronised by O/C. Coys at 8.0 p.m. tonight.

DISPOSITIONS
9. Advanced Bde. H.Qrs. will open at COOKER QUARRY R.11.c.8.9. at 4.30 a.m. 24th Sept.
Advanced B.H.Q. will open at 11.0 p.m. tonight at M.7.b.5.7.
Advanced B.H.Q. 5th LEICESTERS REGT will be at M.1.b.9.7.

R.A.P.
10. Regtl. Aid Post will open at 9.0 p.m. at M.7.b.5.7.

ZERO
11. Zero Hour will be at 5.0 a.m. 24th Sept 1918.

        Sd. C.W. Powell
Copies - 1 to 4 Coys.   Lieut & Adjt.
  5. C.O.   8th Sherwood Foresters.
  6. T.O. & A.M.
  7. File. H.Q. details.

VERY SECRET.

APPENDIX 4
Copy No. ..

BELENGLISE OPERATION.
1/8th Bn. Sherwood Foresters. INSTRUCTION No. 1.

Reference Map OMMISSY 1/20,000.   27th September, 1918.

GENERAL.
1. (i)   At an hour and date to be notified later, the 46th Division, as part of a major operation, will cross the ST. QUENTIN CANAL between G.34.d.6.5. and G.22.b.6.0.; capture the HINDENBURG LINE and advance to a position shewn on the attached Map "A" (GREEN LINE).

   (ii)   The 137th Infantry Brigade will capture the first and second objectives (BROWN LINE) after which the 139th Infantry Brigade on the RIGHT, and the 138th Infantry Brigade on the LEFT, will pass through the final objectives (GREEN LINE).

  (iii)   On completion of the capture of the GREEN LINE, the 32nd. Division passes through to the RED LINE.

   (iv)   Objectives and Approximate times are shewn on Map "A" and Appendix "A" (attached).

    (v)   Tanks will co-operate with the 138th and 139th Infantry Brigades, passing through the gap made by the American Division, and joining the Brigades before the advance to the YELLOW LINE.

DETAIL.
2. (a) OBJECTIVE.
        Objectives are allotted as under:-

        YELLOW OBJECTIVE   - 8th Bn. Sherwood Foresters.
        DOTTED BLUE OBJECTIVE - 6th Bn. Sherwood Foresters.
        GREEN OBJECTIVE   - 5th Bn. Sherwood Foresters.

    (b) FORMING UP.
        On Y/Z night the 137th Infantry Brigade will be in the line; and the 138th and 139th Infantry Brigades in rear, each on a one Battalion front.

    (c) ADVANCE.
        The 137th Infantry Brigade advances at ZERO; the 138th and 139th Infantry Brigades will not advance until orders are received from Divisional Headquarters.

    (d) ADVANCE FROM BROWN LINE.
        The tanks should join the Brigade on this Line. The Infantry will assist them forward by every means in their power and smoke rifle grenades will be carried for this purpose. A proportion of the tanks allotted to this Brigade will be detailed to advance along the trenches immediately North of the CANAL where considerable opposition may be expected.

    (e) GUIDES.
        Companies guides will follow in rear of the 137th Infantry Brigade to direct their Battalion to the Canal crossings.

    (f) FLAGS.
        Battalion and Company Headquarters will be marked by flags.

APPENDIX 4

Page 2.

(g) "Z" DAY.
"Z" Day is not known, but all preparations must be made assuming that the attack commences on the morning of 29th September.

(h) ZERO HOUR.
Zero hour will be notified to all concerned on the afternoon of "Y" Day.

COMMUNICATIONS.

3. 1. All possible arrangements will be made so that once the advance has commenced communications may be maintained by visual signalling, mounted messengers, &c. The Battalion Signallers will establish posts at G.30.c. (120 contour).

2. Red flares, discs, and rifles placed three in a row and parallel to each other, muzzles towards the enemy, will be employed to indicate position of the most forward troops to our aeroplanes.
It is again to be impressed on all ranks how essential it is to use these means of communication when called for.

3. The following light signals will be employed:-
   (i) SUCCESS SIGNAL   - 32 grenade.
       "We have reached   White over White over White.
        objective".
   (ii) S.O.S.   - 32 grenade.
                                Red over Red over Red.

Each Company of the 137th Infantry Brigade will fire SUCCESS ROCKETS when they have gained their objectives. Companies of the 139th Inf. Bde. will do likewise when their objectives have been gained.

3. CAVALRY SIGNAL   White star turning to red
    "ADVANCED TROOPS OF   in a parachute (Used by Cavalry
    CAVALRY ARE HERE".   only).

LIAISON.   2nd. Lieut. R.F.PLANT, "C" Coy. will report to 137th Inf. Bde.
4.   Headquarters tonight. (mounted).
            2nd. Lieut. C.P.O. BRADISH, will report to 139th Inf. Bde. Headquarters tomorrow night at 7-0 p.m.
            2nd. Lieut. J.F.WINTER will report to 6th Bn. Sherwood Forstrs. tomorrow night at 7-0 p.m.

RATIONS.   On ZERO day men will carry their unexpended portion of their
5.   day's rations, one iron ration and their emergency ration.

OFFICERS   An Officers patrol of One Officer and Ten men under 2nd Lieut.
PATROL   A.N.DAVIS, will keep in touch with the 137th Inf. Bde. which will
6.   follow the rear Battalion.

Tanks SIGNALS.
7.   From TANKS
        "COME ON"
        "BROKEN DOWN.   Green and White.
        "COMING OUT"   Red and Yellow.
                                       Red, White and Blue.

        From INFANTRY.
        Helmet on rifle, in direction they want the tanks to go, or

smoke grenades fired in direction they want tanks to go.

8.   On the night 27/28th September, 1918, the 8th Bn. Sher. Fors. will go into trenches about R.6.a. (Battalion Headquarters will be at HUDSONS POST at R.6.a.6.6.1)

Order of march - "D", "C", "A" "B", Headquarters, No. 4 Section T.M.B.   Parade by Companies at 7-30 p.m.

On Y/Z night the Battalion will have moved into positions in ASCENSION VALLEY by Zero - 30 minutes.

At Zero, plus 10 minutes, the Battn. will be disposed in trenches on HELONE RIDGE.

Guides. One guide per platoon, and one for Battn. H.Qrs. will meet the Battn. tonight at TWIN CRATER to guide to positions.

Stores. Lewis Guns and Ammunition will be dumped by Companies outside Orderly Room by 6-30 p.m. Transport Officer will arrange limbers to take these to TWIN CRATER, where they will be dumped by Companies, and collected from this point.

P. C.W. Powell
Lieut. & Adjt.,
8th Bn. Sherwood Foresters.

27-9-18.

APPENDIX "A" TO ACCOMPANY 8th Bn. Sherwood Foresters
INSTRUCTION NO. 1.

Objective.	Barrage lifts off.	Pause.	Infantry again advance.	Pace of Barrage. per 100x.
BLUE.	0 plus 1 hr. 40 mins.	30 mins.	0 plus 2 hrs. 10 mins.	2 mins.
BROWN.	0 plus 2 hrs. 30 mins.	3 hrs.	0 plus 5 hrs. 30 mins.	4 mins.
Yellow.	0 plus 6 hrs. 10 mins.	30 mins.	0 plus 6 hrs. 40 mins.	4 mins.
DOTTED BLUE.	0 plus 7 hrs. 20 mins.	30 mins.	0 plus 7 hrs. 50 mins.	4 mins.
GREEN.	0 plus 8 hrs. 40 mins.			4 mins.

SECRET.

T9   APPENDIX. 5.

8th. Battn. Sherwood Foresters
Operation Orders. No.1.

Ref. Map - OMISSY 1/20,000.   28th Sept. 1918.

INFORMATION
1. The Germans are holding the line on our front very strongly.

INTENTION.
2. The 46th. Division will attack the Hindenburg LINE on 29th Sept. 1918 in conjunction with American Division attacking on our left, and will cross the ST. QUENTIN CANAL between G.34. d.6.5. and G.22.6.6.0.

OBJECTIVES.
3. The Objectives allotted to 139th Inf. Bde. are.
3rd Objective - YELLOW LINE from M.6.a.35.36 to H.36.b.10.40.
4th Objective - DOTTED BLUE LINE from H.1.b.10.90 to H.31.b.40.30.
5th Objective - GREEN LINE H.2.c.90.35 - H.22.b.45.35

DISTRIBUTION.
4. The 8th. Battn SHERWOOD FORESTERS will capture the 3rd Objective on the right from M.6.a.35.30 to G.36.b.10.00 on a front of 1200 +.
The Dividing Line between the 8th. Battn Sherwood Foresters and a Battn of the 138th. Inf. Bde. will be from G.29.c.45.65 to G.36.a.60.70. and G.3.b.10.60.

FORMING UP.
5. On Y/Z night the 8th Sherwood Foresters will be formed up in 2 lines.
"C" & "D" Coys in front line.
(C. on the right.)
"A" & B. Coys. to be in support
A. Coy. on the right on a line from G.35.a.30.40 to G.26.a.99.00.
Battn. H. Qrs. in rear of "A" & B. Coy, + No 4 Section 139th T.M.B.

APPENDIX 5. Pg. 2.

FORMING UP
5 (Cont.) All troops will be formed in these positions by ZERO – 30 mins.

METHOD OF ADVANCE.
6. The 8th Battn. SHERWOOD FORESTERS will advance at ZERO and at ZERO plus 10 mins. The Battn. will enter the trenches from G.33.b.10.20 to G.27.c.90.80 and from G.33.b.60.10 to G.27.d. 50.99. No further advance will take place until orders are received from DIVISIONAL HEADQUARTERS.

The Battn. will start with 3 Platoons of each Coy in line of sections in file, with 1 Platoon in Support, maintaining a distance of 250x between front line and support.

DIVIDING LINE.
7. The Dividing Line between the Right & Left Coys when the Battn. has crossed the ST. QUENTIN CANAL will be from G.34.b.99.60. G.36.c.20.16. to M.31.c.40.10. Platoons will then advance on a 200ft front.

LIASON
8. 2nd Lieut R.F. PLANT will report to H.Qrs. 137 Inf. Bde. at ZERO – 60 mins.

2nd Lieut C.P.O. BRADISH will report to H.Qrs 139th Inf. Bde. at ZERO minus 30 mins.

2nd Lieut J.F. WINTER will report to O/C 6th SHERWOOD FORESTERS at ZERO minus 30 minutes.

OFFICERS PATROL.
9. An officers patrol under 2nd Lieut A.N. DAVIS will keep in touch with RIGHT BATTn. of the 137th Inf. Bde.

Company Scouts of all Coys. will follow in rear of 137th Inf. Bde. to direct the Battn. to CANAL CROSSINGS.

APPENDIX
MEDICAL ARRANGEMENTS. Pg 3

10. Regimental Aid Post will be established near Batt'n. H. Qrs. at G.26d.9.7.

REPORTS.
11. will be sent to Batt'n. H. Qrs. at G.26d.

POSITION OF HEADQUARTERS.
12.
137. Inf. Bde.   G.21.c.15.65.
138. Inf. Bde.   G.25d.4.5.
139. Inf. Bde.   G.31.d.7.8.

WATCHES.
13. Watches will be synchronised by the Signalling Officer at 6.0 p.m. on 28th inst. and at 4.0 a.m. on 29th inst.

ZERO.
14. ZERO hour will be notified later.

Issued at.

No 1. Copy.   139 Inf. Bde.
   2.   "   137 Inf. Bde.
   3.   "   6th Sherwood Foresters.
   4.   "   6th Sherwood Foresters.
   5.   "   O/C A Coy.
   6.   "   O/C B. Coy.
   7.   "   O/C C. Coy.
   8.   "   O/C D. Coy.
   9.   "   War Diary.
  10.   "   C.O.

Sd. C.H. Powell
Lieut & Adjt
8th Sherwood Foresters.

APPENDIX 6

VERY SECRET

8th Sherwood Foresters.

BELENGLISE OPERATION.

28-9-18.

Instruction No 2.

Ref. Map. OMISSY. 1/20000.

ACTION OF 1st DIVISION.

1. A Detachment of the 1st Division is advancing at ZERO in touch with 46th Division rt. & forming a defensive flank from the rt. of the original starting point to the CANAL and at about G.24.b.5.0.

CONTACT AEROPLANES.

2. Contact aeroplanes will be marked with a black rectangular board hanging from the edge of the plane. Flares will be called for at:-

ZERO plus 3 hours.
ZERO " 5 "
ZERO " 7 " 30 mins.
ZERO " 9 "

TANKS.

3. Tanks working with the 46th Division will carry a 46th Division flag - RED over GREEN.

HOPPING UP

4. "A" Coy. will detail 4 sections to report to "D" Coy.

"B" Coy will detail 6 sections to report to "C" Coy after the Battn. has formed up for mopping up.

It is of vital importance that the main weight of the attacking troops do not get left behind the barrage.

WATER

5. It will be necessary for Medical Officers of Units to test any sources of water within the forward area before they are to be used by our troops for fear of poisoning or pollution. Strict orders are to be issued that no water supply

APPENDIX 6 P2

WATER
5 (cont.) within the enemy's lines is to be used for drinking until it has been passed by a Medical Officer.

AMMUNITION.
6. Ammunition will be worked on a DUMP principle. A forward dump is being formed at G.27.c.0.5 containing S.A.A. clip & Bundle packed, Lewis Gun Magazines, and all bombs and lights. If ammunition is required by any unit an Orderly should be sent to DUMP at ADV. BDE. H Qrs. or G.31.d.7.8.

MEDICAL
7. The chief line of evacuation for wounded will be along the BELENGLISE – VADENCOURT ROAD. Any Bearer Post, Aid Post, or A.D.S. should be used irrespective of the DIVISION to which they belong.

Sd. C.H. Powell.
Lieut and Adjt.
8th. Sherwood Foresters.

P.4

APPENDIX. 7

Report on the BELLENGLISE OPERATION.

The Batt. having received orders to co-operate in a Major operation on the HINDENBURG LINE was duly formed up in accordance with the general plan on the western slopes of ASCENSION VALLEY.

The formation adopted was that of a Double Coy frontage of Sections in file on a frontage of about 600 yards. A certain amount of hostile Gas & H.E. shelling was encountered, and as a dense fog had accumulated it made formation & direction difficult.

The right Front Coy had received orders to assist the 137th Inf. Bde. in the mopping up of enemy trenches W. of the CANAL. On completion of this task they were to reform in old GERMAN FRONT line, and wait for the arrival of the other Coys. before pushing forward.

At Zero + 15 the remaining 3 coys. of the Batt. moved forward in Artillery formation to NIB & QUILL TRENCHES on HELENE RIDGE, the original jumping off points of the leading troops. Owing to the density of the fog direction could not be maintained by compass Bearings.

On arrival in these Trenches further orders were awaited before advancing as laid down in the general plan.

At 10:20 a.m. orders were received for the Batt. to go forward across the CANAL to the BROWN LINE (the jumping off trench for the Batt.) assisting the 137th Inf. Bde. if necessary in reaching their line. Accordingly the Coys. advanced in Artillery formation crossed the Canal by the remaining BRIDGES. On arrival in the village of BELLENGLISE Coy. Commanders found considerable resistance owing to remaining snipers & machine gun nests. They proceeded to mop up the village before

APPENDIX 7
Pg 2

proceeding to the BROWN LINE which was the jumping off trench for the Battn.

The Right Coy. was temporarily held up by hostile opposition, but the weight of the Right Support Coy reinforcements overcame this and the village was eventually cleared and the Battn. formed up in BROWN LINE about 10 minutes after scheduled time.

It was found that the Tanks had not arrived to co-operate E of this point. Nevertheless Coys. then advanced in extended order from this position to the final objective of the Battn. Considerable hostile shelling was encountered in the village and the Eastern outskirts but objective was gained and consolidated about 12.15 p.m.

This line was held and the 6th Battn. Sherwood Foresters passed through to further Allotted Objectives.

Total prisoners taken about 300.
Total Casualties. Killed 1 off. 10 O.R's.
Wounded 1 off. 101 O.R's
& Missing

(Signed) J. Finlay Dempster D.S.O. Lieut Col.
Comdg. 8th Battn. Shw. Foresters.

30/9/18

WAR DIARY
or
INTELLIGENCE SUMMARY.

Army Form C. 2118.

8th Bn. Sherwood Foresters for the Month of October 1918.

Place	Date	Hour	Summary of Events and Information	Remarks and references to Appendices
	Oct 1st 1918		Battalion out of the line in trenches in SPRINGBOK VALLEY 1000" NE of Canal Crossing at BELLENGLISE. Reorganization carried out, refitting &c.	
	Oct 2nd		The Battalion proper there to form a defensive flank to the 32nd Division in the Neighbourhood of Swiss COTTAGE that THORIGNY 5000 Orders for the operation uncancelled and at 11.30 pm the Battalion left SPRINGBOK VALLEY to take part in a Major operation the following morning.	
	Oct 3rd		RV Sheet 62 B N.W. The 139th Brigade attacked RAMICOURT and MONTBREHAIN in the morning of Oct 3rd at 6.50 am. The 137th Bgde on the right and the Australians on the left.	Orders No 2 Vol A.3 Appendix No. 1

WAR DIARY or INTELLIGENCE SUMMARY

Army Form C. 2118.

2nd/9th Stewart Hoplrs [Highlanders?] 4th Month Sp. October 1916

Place	Date	Hour	Summary of Events and Information	Remarks and references to Appendices
	4th 5th		During the attack the prisoners captured by the Battalion amounted to nearly 1000 together with many machine guns.	
			Further two days the Battalion was at MARTINPUICH in Bivouacs for Rest & Reorganization. During this time Bn Reinforcements joined.	
	Oct 9		On the N9th D Sto Bn Orders were received for the 139th Bde Brigade to take over the SEDGEHART (map 62R NW) from from the 97th Bgde. which suffered heavily in the Capture of the village. The Bgt Summers took over the trenches held by the 11th Bgde consisting of 2 bns 5th H.L.I. and Royal Scots. The Battalion departure was	

WAR DIARY or INTELLIGENCE SUMMARY

Army Form C. 2118.

8th Sherwood Foresters
4th Month 9
October 1918

Place	Date	Hour	Summary of Events and Information	Remarks and references to Appendices
	Oct 7		C Coy on the Right, D Coy on the left, B Coy in close support. A Coy in Battalion Reserve. During the day the Bn. was on the Right of the British line the R of the Coy' establishing an International post with our Allies the FRENCH. The Battalion occupied this sector till the evening of the 7th when I was relieved by the Monmouth Pioneer Bn. The short tour was remarkable for the intense enemy artillery fire during the whole of the time.	
	Oct 8		Lt. Riddel the Battalion moved to LIERAUCOURT when the day was spent in Reorganizing & cleaning up.	
	Oct 9		On this day the Battalion again moved to LEVERGIES	

WAR DIARY or INTELLIGENCE SUMMARY.

Army Form C. 2118.

8th Sherwood Foresters   Battalion 9   October 1916

Place	Date	Hour	Summary of Events and Information	Remarks and references to Appendices
	9th/10th		Ret. THORIGNY (30M) when the night only was spent and when the 134th Brigade was (eventually) made to MERICOURT (Ref. ETAVES I/40000) when a man were gaven into Bivouac. The following day was also spent in when Cleaning up was carried out. Lt Col R.V. Turner D.S.O. Returned from England and took over Command.	
	11th			
	12th		9 men were again made on the afternoon 9 12th when the Battalion proceeded to TONCOURT FARM (Ref ETAVES) when several days were spent in Reorganisation, Refit,	
	13th			
	14th			
	15th		Baths and training	
	16th		On the evening 9 16th orders further was received that the 139th Bgde would take part in a major operation	Memorandum No 1, Appendices 2, 3, 4

WAR DIARY
or
INTELLIGENCE SUMMARY.

Army Form C. 2118.

2nd Sherwood Foresters
1st/7th Month 9
October 1916

Place	Date	Hour	Summary of Events and Information	Remarks and references to Appendices
	9.10.16		The attack on the REGNICOURT- ANDIGNY- LES FERMES ROAD	App 4
			The Battalion was Relieved on the 10th after line to 6th Bn. Sher and withdrew to the divisional reserve for three days rest and on the following day marched to Billets at FRESNOY-LE-GRAND	App 2
Bohain			These days were spent in cleaning up, Re-organisation and Training together with Football during the afternoon day. The Battalion received about 130 Reinforcements trained men to bring from home to bring the Battalion up to Preventive establishment.	
to Bohain			2nd Lieut Hughes who led his Platoon taken Service	
Bohain	22.9.16		In the day the Battalion again moved forward this time to BOHAIN where fourth Renown day 9th the month Trains were Composed at	

Army Form C. 2118.

WAR DIARY
or
INTELLIGENCE SUMMARY.

8th Stafford 4th Bn (?) forming 9 October 1918

(Erase heading not required.)

Instructions regarding War Diaries and Intelligence Summaries are contained in F.S. Regs, Part II. and the Staff Manual respectively. Title pages will be prepared in manuscript.

Place	Date	Hour	Summary of Events and Information	Remarks and references to Appendices

Strength.

Bayonet Strength   Officers   46   O/Ranks   752

2nd Q.M.S.   "   34   745

Casualties   Officers

Killed
2/Lt O.B.A. Burton
W.T Lt B.N. Ramsbur MC
2/Lt R.S. Pearse
Capt Q.S. Gray MC
2/Lt H.G. Inwin

Wounded
2/Lt R.N. Barker
2/Lt H.T.H. Saunders
L/Col T. Finlay-Dingwall DSO
Capt C.P. Ellan MC
R/Capt B. Harley MC
Lt H.M. Tryon
2/Lt John HySmith
Lt J.S. Whitley
Capt (R.c) E.L. Shute C.F.

Died of Wounds
2/Lt T.F. Mitchell

Casualties   Other Ranks
Killed 39   Wounded 171   Wounded at duty 5   Missing 6   Died of Wounds 11

WAR DIARY
or
INTELLIGENCE SUMMARY.

Army Form C. 2118.

(Erase heading not required.)

Of Sherwood Foresters both hurt 9 October 1916

Place	Date	Hour	Summary of Events and Information	Remarks and references to Appendices

Names (left column):
- 29758 Pte W.H. Tully
- 301451 " G. Tutt
- 305942 Sgt W. Udall
- 204711 L/Cpl F. Allen
- 305229 L/Cpl T. Nutt
- 47045 Pte G. Whitley
- 305144 " W. Woodhole
- 305230 Sgt G. Sexton
- 305845 L/Cpl C. Shuter
- 305853 Pte G.H. Smethurst
- 301792 " T. Thorne
- 307008 Pte C.W.P.
- 300529 " C. Middleman
- 4093 " G. Saddy
- 301647 Cpl S. Clerc
- 266238 " W. Foster
- 102640 Pte T. Tutler
- 301819 " H. Stapleton
- 305074 L/Cpl R. Henry
- 301401 Sgt T. Ingham
- 242227 Pte E. Eaux
- 305861 Sgt C. Yeomans
- 229996 L/Cpl G. Slater
- 305760 Cpl T. Hays

} M.M.

Names (right column):
- 305786 Pte F. Green
- 305422 " G.H. Martin
- 305307 " T.W. Starr
- 305924 L/Cpl F. Bailey
- 307605 Cpl W. Clark
- 305712 Sgt H. Wrightsworth
- 305026 L/Cpl L. Thorne — Bar to M.M.
- Capt. W.E. Newman — French Croix de Guerre
- 265734 Sgt T. Wilson — "
- 305864 Bandsman T. Eglin — D.S.M.

W. Robinson Major
for Lieut Colonel
Comdg. 1/8 Sherwood Foresters

APPENDIX

SECRET.

8th Bn. Sherwood Foresters. — Instructions No. 2.

2nd. October, 1918.

Reference Sheet 62B. N.W.

1. The 139th Infantry Brigade will capture RAMICOURT and MONTBREHAIN on the morning of 3rd October, 1918. The 137th Infantry Bde. will co-operate on the Right and an Australian Division on the Left.

2. 9 Tanks will co-operate with the 139th Infantry Brigade and will advance immediately behind the first wave.

3. (a) Objectives are allotted as under :-

   RED OBJECTIVE - 5th & 8th Sherwood Foresters.
   BLUE OBJECTIVE - 6th Sherwood Foresters.

   The 5th Sherwood Foresters on the Right.
   (b) Forming Up - On Y/Z Night the 8th Sherwood Foresters will be formed in 2 lines. H.9.c.8.9. to H.15.b.9.3.
   'A' & 'B' Companies in the Front Line,
   'C' & 'D' Companies in Support. 'A' Company on the Right.
   All Companies will be formed up and be in position by ZERO - 60 minutes.
   A distance of 150 yards will be maintained between first and second lines. Battalion frontage - 1,000 yards.

4. Dividing Line between the Right and Left Companies will be from H.15.b.9.3. to H.6.d.4.9.

5. The Support Companies will follow the 6th Sherwood Foresters to mop up MONTBREHAIN and will return to the RED LINE when completed.

6. 'A' & 'B' Companies will throw out a line of Outposts 300 yards in front before the Battalion form up on a line.

7. LIAISON - 2nd. Lieut. Plant will report to the Australian Battalion on Left.
   2nd. Lieut. Newton, 239th Brigade Headquarters at H.25.a.1.1.
   2nd. Lieut. Jacques to 5th Sherwood Foresters at H.15.b.9.3.

8. R.A.P. will be established at H.15.a.8.2.

9. Reports at H.15.a.8.2.

10. ZERO HOUR will be 6.5% a.m.

11. Trench Mortar Battery will join the Battalion Headquarters at 2.30.a.m. and will remain with B.H.Qrs.

12. Success Signals. - WHITE upon WHITE upon WHITE will be put up when the object is gained.

13. Aeroplane will call for Flares at ZERO plus 30.

Page 2)

14. Guides from 32nd Division at the rate of 6 per Battalion will be at S.W. entrance to JONCOURT, H.25.b.20.30.

15. Barrage opens at ZERO and stays on opening line for 6 minutes to enable troops to come up. Pace of Barrage from OPENING LINE to RED LINE will be 100 yards in 4 minutes.

A.B.Mms
Capt & Adjt.
8th Bn. Sherwood Foresters.

Appendix No 1

RAMICOURT.
Report on attack on MONTBREHAIN & (WIANCOURT)
3rd. Oct. 1918.

On 3rd. Oct. 1918 the 139th Inf. Bde. cooperated with an Australian Division on the left flank, & the 137th Inf. Bde. on the Right Flank, in a major operation against BEAUREVOIR, and MONTBREHAIN. The Battn. objective was a line facing N.E. on the W. outskirts of MONTBREHAIN, on a front of 1000 yards, the centre being about CROSS ROADS. W. of CEMETERY. The 6th. Battn. were to pass through the village to the E. outskirts & consolidate. Two Coys. in the Battn. in conjunction with the 5th. Sherwood Foresters were to mop up the village of MONTBREHAIN. The Battn. marched from SPRINGBOK VALLEY to the position of assembly facing N.E. on the E side of JONCOURT.

Formation was complete at 5.30 a.m. on a two company frontage, leading companies extended in two lines. Rear Coys. in lines of Platoons in sections in file. At Zero 6.50 a.m. the barrage opened 500 yards in front of assembly positions, remaining stationary for 10 minutes, to enable the Infantry to get close to the protective screen.

A creeping barrage was then maintained at the rate of 100 yards in 4 minutes, which was found to be rather slow.

The first organised resistance came from the direction of WIANCOURT, and the high ground S.E. of SWISS COTTAGE. A flank machine gun having been rushed & the garrison killed, a shallow trench thickly held was discovered. The garrison tried to escape but were killed or taken prisoners.

The village of WIANCOURT although in the Australian Division's area was next dealt with. The Australians were unable to advance, and the left company realizing this, diverted to the left to deal with the obstacle. Heavy Lewis Gun fire was brought to bear on the village, and after a stubborn resistance the enemy began to withdraw. The village was then rushed and mopped up, the garrison being killed or taken prisoners.

The capture of WIACOURT enabled the Australians to advance. The Battn then resumed its advance towards RAMICOURT & MONTBREHAIN, taking advantage of cover in SUNKEN ROAD to N. of RAMICOURT. Machine Gun nests were encountered in great strength in RAMICOURT, but these were eventually overcome mostly by outflanking and rushing the posts. Enemy guns from heights beyond MONTBREHAIN were observed to be firing with open sights. This caused many casualties and resulted in the Tanks cooperating & being mostly put out of action. Coys had by this time all become engaged and reorganised parties were formed to push on to MONTBREHAIN. On reaching the objective the Battn. commenced to consolidate.

The 6th Battn commenced to pass through to the E outskirts of the village, mopping up being carried out by parties of the 5th and 8th Battns.

Considerable resistance was encountered from house at CROSS ROADS W. of MONTBREHAIN CEMETERY. A large nest of Machine Guns were eventually in a fortified house and the adjoining orchard.

Several unsuccessful frontal attacks on the post had failed, but the garrison were outflanked with great dash, by a party of the right support company, 10 M.G's. & 60 prisoners being taken. These prisoners wore new RED CROSS amulets.

About 2.30 p.m. large parties of the enemy counter attacked forming up N.E. of the village, and passing round under cover to the S.E. attacking the QUARRIES.

Heavy pressure was brought to bear on the 6th Battn. Sherwood Foresters, and they were forced to fall back to the E. of RAMICOURT, along railway cutting. The Battn had to conform to this movement occupying railway and sunken road N.E. of RAMICOURT.

After dark the Battn was relieved by the 4th Leicester Regt. and returned to MAGNY LA FOSSE, arr.

J. Robinson Major for
8ID. BN. SHERWOOD FORESTERS

S E C R E T.   Copy. No.   11

              8th Bn. The Sherwood Foresters.   Movement Order No. 1.
                                                    16th October, 1918.

Ref. Map:- 62.b.N.E. 1/2M.606. Edn. 5A. (Local).

1. GENERAL.   At an hour and date to be notified later the 139th Infantry
              Brigade will attack, as part of a major operation, the BLUE
              LINE shown on Map "A".   This Map also shows:-
                 (a) "Jumping off line"   GREEN.
                 (b) Inter Brigade Boundary   YELLOW.
                     Divl. Boundaries.   BROWN.

              The RED LINE is that held by our troops at present.

2. DETAIL.   The 8th Bn. Sherwood Foresters will carry out the
              attack on the 139th Inf. Brigade front with two Companies of
              5th Sherwood Foresters detailed for a Special purpose (see
              para 4).

3. FORMATIONS.   The 8th Bn. Sherwood Foresters will attack on a three
              Company frontage, the 4th Company being in Battalion Reserve:
              this provides a Company frontage of about 600 yards.

4. SPECIAL PARTIES.   The 5th Sherwood Foresters will detail two
              Companies for special purpose as follows:-
              (a) One Company to follow in rear of the Right front Company
              of the 8th Sherwood Foresters.   On the protective barrage
              covering the BLUE LINE lifting, this Company of 5th Sherwood
              Foresters will move through, and with two platoons occupy
              the Trench running N. and S. in E.13.d;   This Trench will
              be occupied as far South as E.14.d.7.1; 2/3 of these troops
              on arrival will face West, care being taken that the approx.
              position of the 137th Inf. Brigade is previously explained
              to them, the remaining 1/3 will face East and be prepared to
              engage with fire any attempt on the part of the enemy to emerge
              for counter-attack, from the Northern EDGE of HENNECHIES WOOD.
                The third Platoon of this Company xxxxxxxxxxxxxxxxxxxxxx
              will on the protective barrage lifting, attack the small wood
              about E.14.c.2.7., and consolidate a position on the
              Southern edge or South of the wood itself, from where fire can
              be brought on to the Northern edge of the HENNECHIES WOOD.
              (b) One Company to follow in rear of the centre Company
              8th Sherwood Foresters.   This Company will have two tasks:-
                 (i) To move through the clearings in E.7.d., E.13.b., and
              E.8.c., and mop up any of the enemy in the elements of
              trenches there.
                (ii) To again move forward in close support of the
              8th Sherwood Foresters and assist in the mopping up
              of RENNICOURT.

              On completion of this latter task, this Company will be
              withdrawn to trench elements on high ground in E.7.d., and
              E.13.b., where it will take up fire positions.

5.   CONSOLIDATION.   In addition to the consolidation parties
              detailed in para 4 (a), the 8th Sherwood Foresters will on
              reaching the BLUE LINE consolidate it; strong points being
              formed at about E.13.b. 6.8. and RENNICOURT. R.E's. will be
              allotted to O.C. 8th Sherwood Foresters for this purpose.
              On the BLUE LINE protective barrage lifting, platoons will

Page 2.

be pushed forward well South of the BOHAIN - ARMIGNY les FERMES ROAD and posts will be established. Machine Guns will be allotted for the defence of the BLUE LINE.

6. BARRAGE. The attack will be carried out under a double barrage which works on the leap-frog system. The barrage will rest on the opening line for three minutes, and then advance at the rate of 100 yards in three minutes. On reaching a line approx. 700 yards South of the BOHAIN - ARMIGNY les FERMES ROAD the barrage will rest thirty minutes and then cease.
One round of Smoke shell will be fired at each lift
Smoke shell will be fired on the Northern Edge of the FORET D'ARMIGNY.

7. MACHINE GUNS. "A" Company, 46th Battn. M.G.Corps will work with the 139th Infantry Brigade, and is detailed for special work as under:-

(i) One Section (2/Lt. GREGORY) to move with the Company ("B" Company) of 8th Sherwood Foresters, detailed for the consolidation of RAMICOURT. This Section will move forward and occupy a position in Orchard on South side of BOHAIN - RAMICOURT ROAD.
(ii) One Section (2/Lt. LANE) to move forward with left Compy. ("C" Company) of 8th Sherwood Foresters and occupy position well forward on the left flank to protect high ground in E.8.a. and E.9.c.
(iii) One Section (Lt. HARRISON) to move forward with Reserve Company ("D" Company) of 8th Sherwood Foresters and occupy position in reserve also at E.14.b.

8. TRENCH MORTARS. (T.M.). One Section of Stokes Mortars (2 guns) will be attached to O.C 5th Sherwood Foresters to assist in the capture of RAMICOURT. As soon as this place is captured, this Section will move over to the right flank, and assist the Company of 5th Sherwood Foresters, detailed for the capture of the Trench Line in E.15.d. All Trench Mortar personnel exclusive of the two gun teams, will carry ammunition.

9. AEROPLANES. Aeroplanes will call for flares at ZERO plus One hour thirty minutes.

10. R.E. Half a Section of R.E. (465 Fd. Coy.) will be attached to the Right Company ("A" Company) 5th Sherwood Foresters, for the purpose of assisting the consolidation of a strong point at E.15.b.5.6. and another half section will be attached to the Centre Company ("B" Company) 8th Sherwood Foresters, to assist with the consolidation of strong point at RAMICOURT.

11. FLANKS. Touch with flanks on BLUE LINE must be established. A Liaison post with 4th Leicester Regt. will be established at house, E.9.c.7.4. as soon as the BLUE LINE is captured. A patrol will be sent to get in touch with 137th Inf. Brigade on the Right.

12. AMMUNITION. Transport Officer will arrange for pack mules, loaded with ammunition, to proceed to Advanced Battn. H.Qrs. on the final objective being taken. Ammunition will be dumped here and the mules returned.

Page. 3.

13. **PARADE.** The Battalion will parade at 10-0 p.m. in close column of Companies, in order - C, D, B, H.Qrs. & A Company. The R.E. attached will fall in with the Companies to which they are allotted. Movement by platoons at 100 yards interval. Dress – Fighting order. Leather jerkins to be worn.

14. **ROUTE.** Companies will move across country to the junction of the BOHAIN – St. QUENTIN ROAD with Railway (J.Z. a. 70.75, Sheet 62b.N.E.) and from there by marked track to D.17.c., and along road to D.11.d.25.85. At this point the Battalion will close up in the Quarry where a hot meal and tools, Lewis Guns &c. will be drawn.

15. **HEADQUARTERS.** Battn. H.Qrs. will be at D.6.c.50.40. and the R.A.P. at same place. On final objective being taken B.H.Q. and R.A.P. will move forward to approx. E.7.b.50.50.
O's. C. Cos. must mark their H.Qrs. with their flags as soon as they are settled, in order that runners may be able to find them without unnecessary trouble.

16. **TOOLS.** Pioneers and Police will parade under Provost Sergt. at 7-30 p.m. and proceed to Battn. Dump at D.11.d.25.85 for the purpose of sorting out tools, ammunition &c. into 4 Company dumps. Picks and shovels in the proportion of 1 pick to 4 shovels will be carried.

17. **WATER.** All water bottles will be filled before parade tonight.

18. **PRISONERS.** All prisoners to be sent to Bn. H.Q. and handed over to R.S.M. On no account must men be sent with prisoners further than Bn. H.Q.

17 **DUMP.** A Brigade Ammunition Dump is being formed at D.18.b.55.65.
18. **STORES &c.** Officers valises, mess kit and surplus medical and signalling stores will be dumped at Bn. H.Q. Mess, JONNECOURT FARM, at 8-0 p.m. Mens packs, and all tents and trench shelters will be stored in an out house of the Farm by 8-30 p.m.. A guard from the Battle D stalls will remain with these stores until they are fetched away by transport. T.O. will arrange to move these stores on receipt of orders from Bn. H.Q.

19. **SYNCHRONIZATION.** O's. C. Cos. will send one Officer to Bn. H.Q. at 21.00 hrs. to synchronise watches.

20. **LIAISON.** 2nd. Lieut. V. B NEWTON will report to Brigade H.Q. rs. to act as Liaison Officer.

XXX
XXXX

R B Umes
Capt & Adjt
2nd. Lieut. & A/Adjt.,
8th. Bn. The Sherwood Foresters.

Appendix 2

REPORT ON ATTACK ON REGNICOURT.
17th OCTOBER, 1918.

On the 17th October, 1918, the IX Corps an American Corps and the XIII Corps carried out an attack with the immediate object of enlarging the South Flank of the LE CATEAU Salient. In this attack the 46th Division were responsible for the Southern Pivot and carried out a successful attack which resulted in the outflanking of the large Forest of ANDIGNY on its North side, eventually forcing the enemy to withdraw from the Forest.

The 139th Infantry Brigade starting from the HOHAIN-VAUX-ANDIGNY ROAD were responsible for capturing the Village of REGNICOURT and the Line of the REGNICOURT-ANDIGNY-LES-FERMES ROAD, facing South.

The 8th Bn. Sherwood Foresters were the assaulting Battalion, with 2 Companies of the 5th Bn. Sherwood Foresters attached, the remaining 2 Companies being in Support. The 6th Bn. Sherwood Foresters were in Brigade Reserve.

The Attack commenced at 5.20. a.m. and was carried out under a creeping barrage moving at the rate of 100 yards in 3 minutes.

The Battalion was formed up on a tape on the BOHAIN-VAUX-ANDIGNY ROAD, the Left resting on VALLEE HAZARD FARM. 3 Companies were in line, 'A', 'B', 'C' from Right to Left; behind 'A' Company was ' ' Company, 5th Sherwood Foresters; behind 'B' Company, ' ' Company 5th Sherwood Foresters and behind 'A' Company was 'D' Company 8th Battn. Sherwood Foresters in Battalion Reserve.

The objective was distant 2,500 yards and consisted of REGNICOURT VILLAGE on a Ridge from the Centre of which the REGNICOURT SPUR ran out towards our lines.

The Smoke from the Artillery Barrage drifted in our direction and soon formed a fog, so thick that it was impossible to see five yards. In these circumstances, and in spite of the use of the Compass, it was not surprising that the attack was split in two by the REGNICOURT RIDGE and a gap left of nearly 500 yards.

The Left and Right of the attack progressed well and destroying the enemy opposition in their front, gained their objectives on both sides of the Village of REGNICOURT, capturing many Prisoners and Machine Guns in doing so.

As soon as the fog lifted the Right, Captain Gearey, 'B' Company, 'A' Company and also ' ' Company, 5th Battn. Sherwood Foresters came under a galling fire from the untouched SPUR and Village on their Left. In spite of heavy casualties and the loss of their Officers, these Companies held on to their gains with the greatest gallantry.

They were materially helped to do so by the action of Lieut-Colonel Pratt, Commanding 5th Bn. Sherwood Foresters, who, seeing the precarious condition of the Right Companies immediately sent forward another of his Companies to their aid.

(Over)

On the Left of REGNICOURT a similar position had been reached, only the Germans, not content with pouring Machine Gun Fire into the disconnected Left Wing, had pushed down the REGNICOURT SPUR and succeeded in surrounding a part of our assaulting troops. In these circumstances, a portion of 'B' Company under 2nd.Lieut. W.J.Winter withdrew slightly to form a flank, whilst 'C' Company, under 2nd.Lieut. C.G.Druce, continued to hold their objective although pressed on every side by the enemy.

In the meantime Lieut-Colonel. R.W.Currin, Commanding the 8th Bn. Sherwood Foresters, had collected a force of 150 men of all Battalions and placing these under the Command of Major. V.O.Robinson, it was agreed that a fresh attack should be made on the REGNICOURT SPUR, at the same time the re-enforced Right Wing was to attack towards the centre of the objective, REGNICOURT VILLAGE.

These two attacks were successful by 9.45.a.m., the centre of the objective was gained and touch obtained with the two disconnected flanks.

From the start of the operation about 290 men and 34 Machine Guns were captured, whilst a large force retreating from REGNICOURT and considering themselves surrounded, surrendered to the troops occupying the line on our Right, 137th Infantry Brigade.

At 11.0.a.m. the enemy were seen forming up for a Counter attack, 1,500 yards away on our Right front. Our guns were opened on them with the result that they made a half hearted attempt to move forward, only one man reaching our lines, who was captured.

The Successful troops in digging in came under fire from Field Guns over open sights and distant Machine Gun fire, but about 12.noon, the enemy in the forest realised that they were in danger of being surrounded by the success of the attack of the 138th Infantry Brigade on our Left and commenced to withdraw.

8th Bn. Sherwood Foresters pushed out Patrols in to the forest and found it evacuated as far as the bottle neck 2,000 yards South East of REGNICOURT. Patrols gained touch with the 126th French Division, 1,000 yards West of MENNEVRET, and by nightfall the 46th Division was occupying the line from the French, through the Wood to PETIT ANDIGNY FARM to ANDIGNY LES FERMES.

The 8th Bn. Sherwood Foresters were relieved by the 6th Bn. Sherwood Foresters the same night and went back in to Brigade Reserve near REGNICOURT.

V.O.Robinson Major   Lieut Colonel
                        Major.
22nd October, '18. O.C., 8th Bn. Sherwood Foresters.

Army Form C. 2118.

WAR DIARY or INTELLIGENCE SUMMARY.
(Erase heading not required.)

WAR DIARY of the 8th Batn. SHERWOOD FORESTERS for the month of NOVEMBER 1918.

Instructions regarding War Diaries and Intelligence Summaries are contained in F.S. Regs., Part II. and the Staff Manual respectively. Title pages will be prepared in manuscript.

Place	Date	Hour	Summary of Events and Information	Remarks and references to Appendices
BOHAIN	Nov 1st		The Battn. were in billets in the BOHAIN AREA. The intensive training was carried on for the day.	
	Nov 2nd		During the morning the Coy. Commanders were carried on. Followed by football games in the afternoon.	
ESCAUFOURT	Nov 3rd Sun	2 p.m	The Battn. moved to a new area in the locality of ESCAUFOURT starting from BOHAIN about 2 p.m. In column of route, in following order A. & B. Coys. Donand, C. & D. Coys. Not long after the Battn. were billeted in the village of ESCAUFOURT for the night.	
ST SOUPLET	Nov 4th	6 A.M	The advance was continued towards the SAMBRE CANAL on the western of CATILLON about 6 A.M. A two hour halt was made at ST SOUPLET after which the Battn. marched into CATILLON. Here the troops were billeted in the village where a number of German Civilians.	
CATILLON				
MENIERES	Nov 5th	7 A.M	The Battn. paraded at 7 AM & proceed to the SAMBRE CANAL BY BRIGADE CATILLON on Paris road up a position on the NE side of the canal in RESERVE from where two attacks were continued and the Battn. headed on during to MENIERES. Here the night was spent in billets in the village.	
PRICHES CARTIGNIES	Nov 6th		On the 6th of Nov. the 8th Sherwoods again moved forward in Bugnie, Cie. support to a Jon. attack by the 8th N.F. CRESSE, ABL 5th Battn. Sherwoods attacking took the objective for the day. They were "PRICHES" CARTIGNIES during the march forward the Battn. passed thro. the village of PRICHES	

A.092 W. W12839/M1293. 750,000. 1/19. D. D. & L. Ltd. Forms/C.2118/14.

Army Form C. 2118.

WAR DIARY
of the 8th Batn.
SHERWOOD FORESTERS
or
INTELLIGENCE SUMMARY.
(Erase heading not required.)

for the month of November 1918.

Instructions regarding War Diaries and Intelligence Summaries are contained in F. S. Regs., Part II. and the Staff Manual respectively. Title pages will be prepared in manuscript.

Place	Date	Hour	Summary of Events and Information	Remarks and references to Appendices
PRICHES to CARTIGNY	Nov. 6th		CARTIGNY ROAD: A Coy. acting as the advance guard. PRICHES was outflanked by the attacking troops at 10/30 A.M. and A Coy. pushed through the village which was occupied by enemy troops and continued advance and supported Batt. through Bermies and established on the further side of village with advance guard companies in front of village. Majors of the Batt. were issued a fight side and left to further the advance along the outskirts of CARTIGNY. In afternoon B C & D Coys. entered the Batn. marched into CARTIGNY which was being heavily shelled. Outposts were the troops billetted for the night.	
CARTIGNY	Nov. 7th 8th & 9th		For the next three days the 8M Batn. remained in billets in CARTIGNY. Here the work of reorganisation was carried on.	
BOULOGNE SUR HERPE	Nov. 10th & 11th	1/30 pm	SHEET 57A. BALLA. 10.0.05. The Batn. moved forward to BOULOGNE SUR HERPE coming up the Battn. at 1/30 P.M. Here they found an excellent village BOULOGNE having been for the night in the village. The troops were a little enemies there was carried to render the Employment	
BOULOGNE SUR HERPE	Nov. 12th		Major General G. F. BOYD. C.M.G., D.S.O., D.C.M. Commanding 46th Division brought the advance for yesterday immediate reasons at 11 A.M. he the afternoon a parade said with troops between & N.C.O's assembly on a view for the N.C.O's.	N.M.
BOULOGNE SUR HERPE	Nov. 13th		The day was spent in organisation and company training.	

WAR DIARY or INTELLIGENCE SUMMARY

Army Form C. 2118.

of the 6th Battn. SHERWOOD FORESTERS for the month of NOVEMBER 1918.

Place	Date	Hour	Summary of Events and Information	Remarks and references to Appendices
LANDRECIES	Nov 11th		On this date the 139th Brigade moved back from the BOULOGNE - CARTIGNY - LANDRECIES. This Battn. moved off at 12 noon, by the following route CARTIGNY - PRICHES - PETIT TAYN - GRAND TAYN and reached LANDRECIES about 6 p.m. where 39th Brigade was billeted. During the first two days of our stay in the Town the Battn. encamped the work of clearing it. On the 13th of the month Major Eckitts D.S.O. who had been Acting C.O. of the 2nd Battn. E.F. FOXD. E.N.C. D.S.O. P.S.C. left us with our congratulations and F. Major Semple, E.F.FOXD. from the Division to command the Battn. During this period the companies carried out immediate requirements.	
LANDRECIES	Nov 15th to Nov 30th		The remaining days of the month were spent on the Battlefields. The work was carried on by all ranks from 4 hours each morning. The remaining part of each day was allotted for the supervision of all company officers, sports were arranged by all companies. Running, Association and Battn. football matches being played. On the evenings of the various Sunday afternoons and evening were arranged at the Church for the unity of the regiment. One trouble of the men from the unsophistication that remained on the supervision of the General officer of the Brigade, a great service was rendered to the Corps. The Corps & Band assisted us to the Soldiers Concerts where held on Nov 17th & 28th in the theatre. On the 27th of November the first batch of miners were sent away for the English. In order to fit themselves for civil work in the manner of These wholesome names of the anyone worked on the Bath were viewed of the 6th Division in February 1918.	

Army Form C. 2118.

WAR DIARY of the 8th Battn. SHERWOOD FORESTERS
or INTELLIGENCE SUMMARY for the month of NOVEMBER 1918.

(Erase heading not required.)

Place	Date	Hour	Summary of Events and Information	Remarks and references to Appendices
	NOVEMBER 1918.		Casualties NIL.	
			Strength at beginning of month :- Officers 34, O.R.s 745	
			Strength at End of month :- 45, 767	
			Honours & Awards.	
			306026 L/Cpl. L. THOMAS. Awarded Military Medal.	2nd Lt. S. BRADWELL D.C.M. awarded M.C.
			306091 Sgt. J. STINSON. " Military Medal.	2nd Lt. J. HOWARD SMITH awarded M.C.
			241127 Pte. E. CROW. " " "	Lt (A/Capt) G. THOMAS " M.C.
			305607 Sgt. C. VANN. " " "	Lt (A/Capt) J.B. WHITE " M.C.
			241990 L/Cpl. S. SLATER. " " "	2nd Lt. J. BLOOR. M.M. " M.C.
			305986 Cpl. J. WRIGHT. " " "	305007. C.S.M. J.F. RAWDING. " D.C.M.
			306411 Pte. G.H. WESLEY. " " "	(deceased)
			306307 Pte. J.W. STARR. " " "	305067 Sgt. J. PEACH " D.C.M.
			300964 L/Cpl. F. BAXTER " " "	56728. Cpl. S. GADSBY " M.M.
			307005 Cpl. W. CLARKE. " " "	14207 Pte. (Cpl) E. MOSGRUE " M.M.
			305112 Sgt. H. WRIGGLESWORTH 2nd Bar to Military Medal	
			306028 L/Cpl. L. THOMAS. M.M. " Military Medal.	Lieut Colonel R.W. CURRIN D.S.O.
			305151 Sgt. C. SHARROCK " " "	(1st YORKS & LANCS. ATT. 6th SHERWOODS.)
			307026 Sgt. W.H. MARTIN " " "	awarded Bar to D.S.O.
			308189 Sgt. A. SHEPPERSON " " "	Major V.O. ROBINSON M.C.
			207519 Cpl. It. WINSON " " "	(4th SHERWOODS att. 8th SHERWOODS)
			265017 L/Cpl. J.V. ROE " " "	awarded 2nd Bar to M.C.
			245151 Pte. F. LOOMBES " " "	
			2014 Pte. A.Z. DRAPER " " "	2nd Lt. W.T. WINTER awarded M.C.
			307060 Pte. T. TURPIN " " "	Capt. A.B. MINERS. " M.C.
			305344 Pte. J. KERS. " " "	2nd Lt. F.L. HARRAP awarded M.C.
			94454 Pte. W.C. VIPOND. " " "	2nd Lt. T.F. MITCHELL " M.C.
			106838 Pte. C. HOUGHTON " " "	(deceased)
			305231 Pte. H. NICHOLSON " " "	2nd Lt F.L. MITCHELL 6th Manchester attached 6th Sherwoods
			305929 Pte. H. SMITH " " "	
			15177 Pte. H. BERRESFORD " " "	
			Acting Lieut Colonel J. FINLAY DEMPSTER D.S.O. Bar to D.S.O.	

Army Form C. 2118.

WAR DIARY of the 8th Battn. SHERWOOD FORESTERS
INTELLIGENCE SUMMARY for the month of November 1918.
(Erase heading not required.)

Place	Date	Hour	Summary of Events and Information	Remarks and references to Appendices
			Honours & Awards (continued)	
			Capt. St. G. M. L. HOMAN. R.A.M.C attached 6" Sherwood Foresters awarded M.C.	
			Rev. D.E. STURT. A.C.D " " M.C.	
			2nd.Lt. E.G. BRUCE awarded M.C.	
			Lieut F.J. WARNER " M.C.	
			2nd Lt. T.R. SHACKLETON " M.C.	
			305179 C.S.M. F. ATTENBOROUGH " Bar to D.C.M.	
			305192 C.S.M. E. CLAXTON " D.C.M.	
			306651 Cpl. A. COBB " D.C.M.	
			301412 C.S.M. G.H. WESLEY " D.C.M.	
			306040 Cpl. R. FRANCIS " D.C.M.	
			204842 Pte. A. JACKSON " Military Medal.	

B Henman
Lieut Colonel.
O.C. 6th Battalion
Sherwood Foresters.

Army Form C. 2118.

WAR DIARY of 8th Batt. Sherwood Foresters.

INTELLIGENCE SUMMARY.
(Erase heading not required.)

for the month of December 1918

48 / 46

Place	Date	Hour	Summary of Events and Information	Remarks and references to Appendices
LANDRECIES	1/12/18 to 31/12/18		During the whole of the month of December the 8th Battn. Sherwood Foresters remained in billets in LANDRECIES. During this period the Battn. was engaged in clearing the area of war material, and taking in shellholes & trenches. Each Batln. in the Bde. were allotted two days on which to carry out training under Batln. arrangements. Almost every afternoon was devoted to sport of some description — Corps & Bde. Football Competitions were played off, while annual cross country runs were held. On Dec. 1st H.M. The King, accompanied by H.R.H. the Prince of Wales paid a visit to the town. They motored about 2.30 p.m. and whilst she while they passed through the town, the troops who lined the streets gave them a hearty reception. The following Sunday Dec 8th the Batln. received a visit from the Duke of Portland who with a Recruiting	J.46

WAR DIARY of the 8th Battn. Sherwood Foresters

INTELLIGENCE SUMMARY
(Erase heading not required.)

for the month of December 1918.

Army Form C. 2118.

Place	Date	Hour	Summary of Events and Information	Remarks and references to Appendices
	1/12/18 to		Lt Col. G.S. Folgambe, & Col. H Mellish, the Bishop of Southwell & Major F.I. Baines the Duke inspected the Bath at 2 p.m. and then presented medals to officers & men of the Bath. During the month the work of demobilization was carried	
	3/12/18		On and by the end of the month over 130 employment had been dispatched to England. For work in the mines. Similarly the Education & Instructional Course Scheme progressed rapidly and by Dec 31st over 80 NCOs & men had attended practical & technical courses of instruction. Lastly the Christmas festivities were a great success owing to the late arrival of Yorkshire the dinner had to be held on Boxing Day. Each company held a separate dinner in their several rooms followed by the usual concert. Then for the next three nights the Batt. Concert Party	

LANDRECIES

Army Form C. 2118.

WAR DIARY of the 8th Batn. Sherwood Foresters. Page 3

INTELLIGENCE SUMMARY. for the month of December 1918.

(Erase heading not required)

Instructions regarding War Diaries and Intelligence Summaries are contained in F. S. Regs., Part II. and the Staff Manual respectively. Title pages will be prepared in manuscript.

Place	Date	Hour	Summary of Events and Information	Remarks and references to Appendices
	1/12/18 to		gave three splendid performances in the theatre. The last day of the month brought to a close a year which had brought many honours and much honour to this Batn.	
LANDRECIES	31/12/18		HONOURS & AWARDS. (killed in action) Capt. (A/Lt.Col.) B.W. VANN M.C. (att. 6th Sherwood Foresters.) VICTORIA CROSS. Lt. Col. R.W. CURRIN D.S.O. (att 8th Sherwoods from 1st Batt. York & Lancs.) Bar to D.S.O. Major V. ROBINSON M.C. (att 8th Sherwoods from 6th Sherwood Foresters) 2nd Bar to M.C. 2nd Lt. W.I. WINTER awarded M.C. Capt. & Adjt. A.B. MINERS att. 8th Sherwoods from A.S.C. awarded M.C. 2nd Lt. F.E. HARRAP awarded M.C. 2nd Lt. F. MITCHELL (deceased) awarded M.C. Capt. & Q.M. L. HOMAN (R.A.M.C. attached) awarded M.C. Capt. Rev. D.E. STURT. (Chaplain) awarded M.C. A/Capt. E.G. BRUCE awarded M.C. A/Capt. E.W. WARNER " " M.C. 2nd Lt. S.E. SHACKLETON " " M.C. 306319 C.S.M. F. ATTENBOROUGH. D.C.M. awarded Bar to D.C.M. 305193 L/Sgt. C. CLAXTON M.M. " " D.C.M. 300060 Cpl. R. FRANKIS " " " D.C.M. 306422 Pte. G.H. WESLEY M.M. " " Bar to M.M. 305956 Pte. F. GREEN M.M. " " Bar to M.M. CASUALTIES. Officers NIL O.R.	MENTIONED IN DESPATCHES. Lt.Col. A. HACKING M.C. (attached to 5th Sherwoods) Lt.Col. C.J. HUSKINSON T.C. Lt. C.H.S. STEPHENSON Capt.& A/Lt.Col. B.W. VANN V.C.M.C. (deceased) W/S/194 L/Cpl. W. BEECH. Strength at beginning of Month Off 49 O.R. 754 " " " " End " 49 684 V.O.Robinson Major C.O. 8th Bn. SHERWOOD FORESTERS.

SECRET.   No. 7003/28.

D.A.A.G.(1).,
    War Diaries.
    - - - - - - - - -

    The attached War Diary (one sheet) of 8th. Bn. Sherwood
Foresters, for the month of Jany. 1919, received without
covering memo., is forwarded for disposal.

G.H.Q.,
3rd. Echelon.   N J Filgate
5.2.1919.   Major.
DD.   Officer i/c No. 4 Infantry Section.

WAR DIARY

INTELLIGENCE SUMMARY

8th Bn Stewart Tonside Army Form C. 2118.

Month of January 1919

Place	Date	Hour	Summary of Events and Information	Remarks and references to Appendices
LANDRELIES	Jan 1st		The Bn. later known to New Area	9/SC 47
	Jan 3rd		Battalion Move to New Area PRISCHES and Scotts area & Butts	
PRISCHES	Jan 1st		Bading of Battn. Area continued sections, every Saturday with short Rout march. Football, Torchplane	SJ. 47
	Jan 31st		Inter Coy. and half Coy Football and Torchplane etc Karnal	
			Honors & Awards:	
			W. Shanly. Carne. M.C. (dressed)	
			Cecil W. Stoker. bim Mentioned	
			W/Sgt W. Been Mentioned	
			Pte Nolan m.m	
			Capt J.B Rowley " (award)	
			Stoynas an Bagum g hands Officers 47 SR 622	
			." 41. OR 560	

WAR DIARY or INTELLIGENCE SUMMARY

Army Form C. 2118

WAR DIARY for month of February 1919 of 8th Batt. SHERWOOD FORESTERS

Vol 48

Place	Date	Hour	Summary of Events and Information	Remarks and references to Appendices
PRICHES	1/2/19 to 18/2/19		The Batt. remained in billets in PRICHES until Feb 19th. During the period clearing the area and registered training was continued. The Batt. Concert Party gave two successful shows almost every evening. The work of demobilization still continued & reduced the Batt. considerably. On Feb 19th the Batt. marched to a new area in BETHENCOURT by the following route PRICHES, MEZIERES, CATILLION, BAZUEL, LE CATEAU INCHY, BEAUMONT, PETIT CAUDRY, BETHENCOURT.	
Ret. Sheet 57M 1/40000				
BETHENCOURT				
Ref. VALENCIENNES Sheet No.13 1/100,000			The night of Feb. 19th we slept in BAZUEL & the march to BETHENCOURT completed the following day. At BETHENCOURT reorganisation & training was carried out for the rest of the month.	

Strength at beginning of month: Offrs 41 O/Rs 319
" end " ": Offrs 37 O/Rs 317

A. Ambrose
O.C. 8th Batt
Sherwood Foresters
Major

WAR DIARY
or
INTELLIGENCE SUMMARY.

Army Form C. 2118.

War Diary of the 8th Battn. SHERWOOD FORESTERS for March 1919.

Wet & dry

Place	Date	Hour	Summary of Events and Information	Remarks and references to Appendices
			During the whole of the month of March 1919 the Battalion was in billets at BETHENCOURT. The work carried on consisted of clearing the area, securing spare dumps of ammunition & burying the Battn intelligence of all available men returned the Battn were at the end of the month only the Cadre. Men	Air little
			returned from the Base of Reinforcement were sent to March 28. all available strength to the Transport attached England, whilst on the 31st all went to the Cadre, including Major B Cramer's I.C. Battn and 2nd Lieut J.L. Short Batt'n & left for to Albion. Army Bollard	I 249
BETHENCOURT			Strength at beginning of March. Offrs. O.R.s	
Sheet 57 A			" " end of " " 21 197	

B. Cramer
Major O.C. 8th Sherwood Foresters

Army Form C. 2118.

WAR DIARY
or
INTELLIGENCE SUMMARY

War Diary of the 8th Battn. Sherwood Foresters
For the month of April 1919.

(Erase heading not required.)

Instructions regarding War Diaries and Intelligence Summaries are contained in F.S. Regs., Part II. and the Staff Manual respectively. Title pages will be prepared in manuscript.

Place	Date	Hour	Summary of Events and Information	Remarks and references to Appendices
BETHENCOURT Ref Sheet 61? 1/100,000			During the whole of the month of April the Battn. y remained at BETHENCOURT. Several parties of the Battn. were despatched to various points employed at PERONNE & VAUX. Thus the end of the month found the Battn. practically down to cadre strength, & other awaiting transport ... home.	N.L. 5.0 I. 3
	1/4/1919 to 30/4/1919		Strength at beginning of month. Offrs. O.R.'s 20. 196. " " end " " 9. 52.	

Signed 1st Lieut Colonel
OC. 8th Batth
Sherwood Foresters

Army Form C. 2118.

WAR DIARY of 8th Sherwood Foresters
INTELLIGENCE SUMMARY. month of May 1919.

Vol 51

Place	Date	Hour	Summary of Events and Information	Remarks and references to Appendices
BÉTHENCOURT (NORD)	31/5/19		During the month the Battalion was in billets at BETHENCOURT (NORD). Strengths at end of month was 9 officers and 52 ORs. This was decreased owing to demobilisation & a draft of 28 including P.O.W. Coy on command. The cadre establishment Battalion was considerably reduced owing to numerals were being posted to other units. At end of month 4 officers & 18 ORs.	

T. W. Curran Lt. Col.
O.C. 8th Sherwood Foresters.